The Office ^{6e}

Procedures and Technology

MARY ELLEN OLIVERIO
Lubin School of Business
Pace University
New York, New York

WILLIAM R. PASEWARK
Professor Emeritus
Texas Tech University
Office Management Consultant
Lubbock, Texas

BONNIE R. WHITE
Distinguished Professor
College of Education
Auburn University
Auburn, Alabama

DIANNE S. RANKIN
Rankin Consulting, LLC
Contributing Author

SOUTH-WESTERN
CENGAGE Learning

Australia • Brazil • Japan • Korea • Mexico • Singapore • Spain • United Kingdom • United States

The Office: Procedures and Technology, Sixth Edition

Mary Ellen Oliverio, William R. Pasewark, Bonnie R. White

Vice President of Editorial, Business: Jack W. Calhoun

Vice President, Editor-in-Chief: Karen Schmohe

Senior Developmental Editor: Dr. Inell Bolls

Consulting Editor: Dianne S. Rankin

Editorial Assistant: Anne Merrill

Marketing Manager: Kara Bombelli

Senior Marketing Communications Manager: Sarah Greber

Internal Designer, Production Management, and Composition: PreMediaGlobal

Media Editor: Mike Jackson

Rights Acquisition Director: Audrey Pettengill

Rights Acquisition Specialist, Text and Image: Amber Hosea

Manufacturing Planner: Charlene Taylor

Manufacturing Director: Denise Powers

Senior Art Director: Michelle Kunkler

Cover Designer: Lisa Langhoff

Cover Image: © Thomas Barwick/Getty Images; Adie Bush/Getty Images; Ali Mazraie Shadi/ Shutterstock

For product information and technology assistance, contact us at
Cengage Learning Customer & Sales Support, 1-800-354-9706
For permission to use material from this text or product,
submit all requests online at **www.cengage.com/permissions**
Further permissions questions can be emailed to
permissionrequest@cengage.com

Exam*View*® is a registered trademark of eInstruction Corp. Windows is a registered trademark of the Microsoft Corporation used herein under license.

© 2013 Cengage Learning. All Rights Reserved.

The Career Clusters icons are being used with the permission of the:

States' Career Clusters Initiative, 2012, www.careerclusters.org

Screenshots used with permission from Microsoft Corporation. © 2012 Microsoft Corporation. All rights reserved.

Library of Congress Control Number: 2012930928

ISBN-13: 978-1-111-57435-2

ISBN-10: 1-111-57435-9

South-Western
5191 Natorp Boulevard
Mason, OH 45040
USA

Cengage Learning products are represented in Canada by Nelson Education, Ltd.

For your course and learning solutions, visit **www.cengage.com/school**

Visit our company website at **www.cengage.com**

Printed in the United States of America
1 2 3 4 5 6 7 16 15 14 13 12

Brief Table of Contents

Sukiyaki/Shutterstock.com

Detailed Table of Contents

Sukiyaki/Shutterstock.com

v

Sukiyaki/Shutterstock.com

Sukiyaki/Shutterstock.com

Sukiyaki/Shutterstock.com

Sukiyaki/Shutterstock.com

Sukiyaki/Shutterstock.com

Sukiyaki/Shutterstock.com

Sukiyaki/Shutterstock.com

Sukiyaki/Shutterstock.com

Sukiyaki/Shutterstock.com

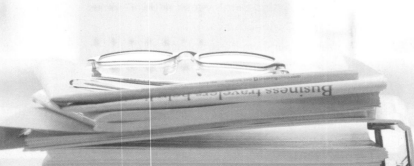

Sukiyaki/Shutterstock.com

Prepare for the **real business world** with the most **comprehensive** and **updated text** on the market – The Office

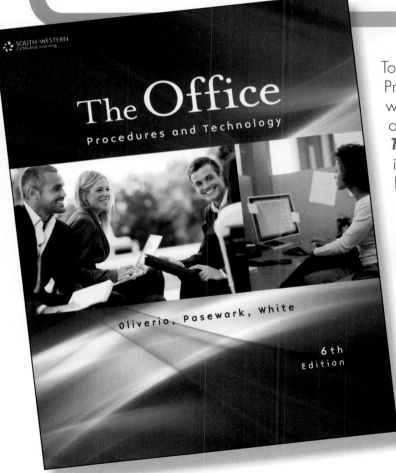

Today's workplace is constantly changing. Prepare yourself for the real business world with the most comprehensive and updated text on the market – *The Office: Procedures and Technology, 6th Edition*. Leading the market in office technology curriculum, *The Office* builds on core concepts for career success. This edition focuses on the changing workplace, building critical communication skills, polishing key financial skills, managing a work/life balance, and planning a career path. With new learning checkpoints to ensure you are understanding the material, this text provides the working skills you'll need to be a productive and successful employee, no matter what career path you choose.

Walkthrough of New and Key Features

Prepare for the real business world with these NEW FEATURES

Streamlined Organization and Design

NEW Checkpoints: Reorganized to better fit your learning needs, this edition includes chapters divided into lessons with checkpoints so you can stay on the right track. Reviews at the end of the chapter summarize key points and provide reinforcing activities.

Two NEW Chapters: Chapter 8 *Financial Reports and Procedures* and Chapter 14 *Ongoing Professional Development*.

---

vendor a seller of goods or services

a purchasing agent often makes telephone calls to place an order for materials or supplies. To answer questions that the vendor may ask, the employee needs to know the details about what is being ordered. The employee also needs to know when the item is needed, the cost of the item, and similar details.

CHECK POINT Why is it important for office workers to have current and accurate information?

Office Functions Are Varied

In some offices, every employee does a wide variety of tasks. In other offices, each employee's work is focused on a few tasks. Some common office tasks are shown in Figure 1-1.1 on page 5. Can you identify two activities that might be completed by a manager? Can you identify two that might be performed by an office assistant? Think of a particular career and identify two activities that might be performed by someone in that career.

Workers in many jobs handle office tasks. Some workers, however, devote full time to office tasks. For example, some employees in an Accounting Department process invoices, checks, and other documents related to customer accounts. of their time to these office tasks.

Ongoing Professional Development

CHAPTER **14**

14-1 Leadership Skills
14-2 Lifelong Learning

Professional development involves increasing skills or knowledge to succeed on the job. Developing leadership skills is an important aspect of professional development. Employees in many positions need leadership skills. As you study this chapter, you will learn about leadership roles, traits, styles, and strategies.

Lifelong learning is also an important aspect of professional development. As business products, services, and procedures change, you will need to learn new skills and knowledge to be an effective employee. In this chapter, you will learn about the need for ongoing learning as well as formal and informal learning environments.

483

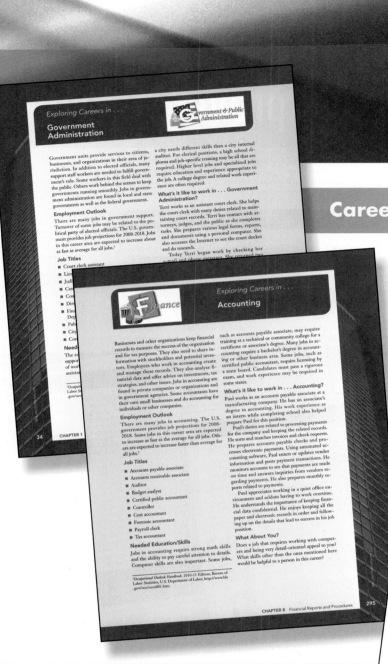

NEW Exploring Careers in...:

Through this feature, you will connect to information about careers in one of the 16 Career Clusters identified by the U.S. Department of Education. You will have a better understanding of the career options available.

Technology Focus

NEW Technology Connection: These

boxed features about technology in the workplace help describe many work and business situations. Each is followed by a critical-thinking question, which is provided to help you focus and survive in the real business world.

Real world content and proven activities

Key Features

Workplace Connections boxed features in each chapter describe work/business situations.

Focus on Business highlights business practices, procedures, or issues. It is followed by a critical-thinking question.

A virtual library might be a computer station that gives you access to many libraries from your school or home. Although the virtual library has no physical form, it allows you to gather information just as you would at a real physical library. The virtual office, therefore, is a setting that allows you to perform work activities as you would in a traditional office.

virtual office a setting that allows you to perform work activities as you would in a traditional office

✴ WORKPLACE CONNECTIONS ✴

Joe Park is a successful interior designer in St. Louis. Although Joe refers to his office as a portable office, it is really a virtual office. Joe visits clients to plan and discuss projects. In his bag, he carries a cell phone; a laptop computer with wireless access to fax, e-mail, and the Internet; and a portable copier/printer. Joe can provide plans for a room, cost estimates, and a contract right in the client's living room.

How does Joe's virtual office allow him to serve clients effectively?

Just as some office workers use virtual offices, some offices employ virtual assistants. A virtual assistant is a person who performs tasks normally handled by a secretary...

Focus on BUSINESS

E-commerce and Planning Strategies

...they want, as long as it's ...ker Henry Ford

...he way businesses oper- ...ew planning strategies. ...stablished, most manu- ...business models. The ...uction or customized ...ese business models ...ed for many years. ...volution, mass pro- ...er costs by making ...exactly the same. ...Henry Ford were ...ot able to choose ...s can today. The ...ers in the form of

...d model, a prod- ...ustomer's needs ...might be de- ...bride's wishes. ...en expensive

to make. Few people could afford customized products of good quality.

With the advent of e-commerce, many companies sell directly to customers via the Internet. E-commerce has made a third business model, mass customization, more widely used. In this model, many products are made to meet specific customers' needs. Customers enter their product order on the company's website. For example, a youth group leader orders 15 shirts printed with the youth group's name and logo. Although the company makes thousands of products each year, each one can be customized for a particular customer.

Companies can now offer the best of both worlds—customized products at reasonable prices. This business model requires creative strategies for planning and budgeting. Customers may have several choices when ordering products. Companies who use this business model often rely on market research to help them create forecasts for future sales and supply needs.

Have you ordered a customized product from a retail store or using the Internet? Were you pleased with the product? Describe your experience.

Focus on BUSINESS

Employee Empowerment

"Our employees are empowered. We couldn't function in this fast-paced world without every employee

others were waiting to know where they should go. Melissa realized that a problem existed due to lack of information and clear communications.

Melissa had not been told that she would need to guide individuals to the right room. When she realized this task would be a routine part of her job, however, she began to think about how she could resolve the problem. Melissa knew that conference rooms were reserved and that those assistants making arrangements submitted the details of the meeting via e-mail. She called the office that handled room assignments and asked: "Could you add my name to your list for a copy of your confirmation for a room? I will be able to direct visitors to the right room with this information." The staff member was cooperative and responded: "Melissa, that is no problem at all. We'll also keep you informed of changes in plans." In addition, Melissa decided to post a schedule for the day inside the entrance so visitors could check the time and location of the day's meetings.

Melissa remembered her orientation to the company and how she and other new employees were informed of the functions of each department of the company. She realized how that information was now helping her as she thought of better ways to handle her assignments. She enjoyed being empowered!

What could be an advantage to the company when employees are empowered? What could be an advantage for the employee?

empowerment being able

⊘DECA WinningEdge

Accounting Applications Event

In this competitive event, you will be judged on your skills and knowledge of accounting applications. You will collect and organize data, develop reports, and analyze data to make business decisions.

The event includes a written test and two role-playing situations. Finalists in the events will have a third role-playing situation. No reference materials are allowed. You may make notes to use during the role-play while when you read the role-play description and prepare for the event.

Performance Indicators Evaluated

Participants will demonstrate skills related to the finance career cluster and accounting pathway. Sample indicators include showing an understanding of:

- Tools, strategies, and systems used to maintain, monitor, control, and plan the use of financial resources
- Ways to maintain cash controls and track cash flow
- Performing accounts payable and account receivable functions
- Tracking inventory and the value of current assets
- Completing payroll procedures
- Using cost accounting methods
- Applying internal controls and conducting audits

The following indicators are in addition to the accounting specific lists above.

- Communication (writing, speaking, reading, or listening)
- Analyzing data to form conclusions and recommendations
- Critical thinking and problem solving
- Setting priorities and managing time

For more detailed information about this event, go to the DECA website.[‡]

http://www.deca.org

Think Critically

1. Why do you think communication is evaluated in this event for accounting?
2. Do you think a test or a role-playing event gives a better indication of accounting skills? Why?

[‡]DECA, "High School Competitive Events Guidelines" (DECA, 2011), http://www.deca.org/competitions/highschool.

WinningEdge activities describe competitive events available in student organizations – DECA, FBLA, and BPA. This feature includes performance indicators that highlight skills and knowledge you need to be successful in the event. Related questions stimulate thinking about the event topic.

prepare you for Real World Business

Integrated Skill Sets

- **End-of-lesson activities** include many of the twenty-first-century skills needed in today's office.

- **Making Academic Connections** exercises review math and English skills.

- **Integrated computer applications** are covered, offering practice with computer skills you'll use every day.

End-of-Chapter Reinforcement

- Enhanced end-of-chapter activities help to review, apply, and extend **chapter outcomes**.

- Every chapter includes a **concise summary** for a quick review of chapter concepts.

- **End-of-chapter activities** help build important skills, such as presentation, research, teamwork, and word processing. All activities are task-oriented, enabling you to apply knowledge and skills learned to solve problems.

Digital Options

- An **eBook** provides a digital version of the text.

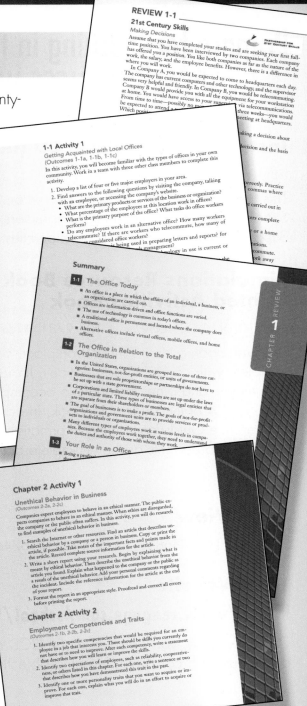

Technology options

Prepare for teaching in the REAL BUSINESS WORLD with these resources!

Instructor's Resource CD (IRCD)

ISBN 10: 1111574707   13: 9781111574703

This instructor resource includes PowerPoint® Slides, Lesson Plans, Data Files, Instructors Manual, Supplemental Activities, and Solution Files.

Simulations Resource Book – Printed Activities Book

ISBN 10: 1111574669   13: 9781111574666

This workbook contains three workplace simulations, complete with company descriptions, instructions, documents, and other materials to accompany Parts 2, 3, and 4 of the student textbook. In addition, a Reference Guide containing information that will be helpful to students as they complete activities is included.

ExamView

ISBN 10: 1111574685   13: 9781111574680

Text Website

http://www.cengage.com/school/theoffice

On the website, you'll find all of the IRCD materials, as well as flash cards and learning objectives per chapter.

PHOTO CREDIT: Digital Vision/Punchstock

The Office in a Changing Business World

PART
ONE

CHAPTER 1
The Office Environment

CHAPTER 2
Office Competencies

CHAPTER 3
Managing Information to Enhance Productivity

Vadym Andrushchenko/Shutterstock.com

Millions of Americans spend much of each workday in offices. Many changes in technology have occurred during the last decade. These changes have created a widespread need for knowledge and skills that are commonly referred to as office competencies. Whatever their fields or careers, workers share a need to know how to perform efficiently and effectively in offices. The Office in a Changing Business World introduces you to the office as a workplace. Competencies needed to complete office tasks are introduced. Ways to manage information using technology and information systems are also discussed.

Dmitriy Shironosov/Shutterstock.com

The Office Environment

1-1 The Office Today

1-2 The Office in Relation to the Total Organization

1-3 Your Role in an Office

Alistair Berg/Digital Vision/Jupiter Images

Wire_man/Shutterstock.com

Many workers in many different types of jobs perform office tasks. Examples include the recruiter in a Human Resources Department, the technician in a chemical laboratory, the buyer in a department store, and the auditor in a public accounting firm. All these workers perform a range of office tasks during a typical workweek. All office workers, regardless of their duties, must understand how office functions relate to their work. They must also know how their work relates to the total organization.

In Chapter 1, you will learn about various types of offices and office workers. You will gain an understanding of typical goals and structures of businesses, not-for-profit entities, and government units. You will also learn about your role in an office.

1-1 The Office Today

OUTCOMES

1-1a Describe the purpose of an office and office activities.
1-1b Explain how technology influences office practices.
1-1c Describe alternative offices.

Purpose of an Office

The term *office* is used in a variety of ways. An office is a place in which the affairs of an individual, a business, or an organization are carried out. For example, you may have heard a lawyer say, "I will be out of the office during the afternoon." A teacher might say, "Come by my office." The office is a place of work for many types of workers. Accountants, marketing managers, systems analysts, human resource directors, as well as secretaries, records clerks, administrative assistants, and many others work in offices. Although each of these employees has varying duties, all of them must know about many office practices.

This textbook focuses on the many workers who need to understand office practices and use office skills. Regardless of what you plan for your life's work, you will benefit from studying the topics in this book and from the skills you will develop.

KEY TERMS

office p. 3
information p. 4
vendor p. 4
World Wide Web p. 6
intranet p. 6
telecommuting p. 7
Internet p. 7
virtual office p. 7
hoteling p. 8
freelancer p. 8

office a place in which the affairs of an individual, a business, or an organization are carried out

✳ WORKPLACE CONNECTIONS ✳

Gloria Diaz is an internal auditor for an international bank. The company's headquarters are in Philadelphia. Her work requires traveling to branches throughout the United States. She also visits cities such as Paris, Milan, and Tokyo. She must write many reports to share her conclusions and recommendations. Gloria composes her reports at her laptop computer. She usually completes the reports with no help from office support staff.

What other tasks might Gloria complete using her laptop computer?

This executive prepares reports using her laptop computer.

Mike Harrington/Jupiter Images

Offices Are Information Driven

Information consists of data or facts that have been organized into a meaningful form. Information is at the core of all office activities. Office workers use information in many ways. Some illustrations include:

- A manager writes the policy for sales returns.
- A stockbroker accesses a database for the current price of a company's stock.
- A sales clerk enters the details of a customer's order at a computer.
- A customer service associate responds by telephone to questions about installing electronic equipment.

Workers need to understand thoroughly the business or organization in which they are employed. Each task is related to the organization's purposes and goals. Current and accurate information is needed to complete the tasks. For example, a purchasing agent often makes telephone calls to place an order for materials or supplies. To answer questions that the may ask, the employee needs to know the details about what is being ordered. The employee also needs to know when the item is needed, the cost of the item, and similar details.

CHECK POINT   Why is it important for office workers to have current and accurate information?

Office Functions Are Varied

In some offices, every employee does a wide variety of tasks. In other offices, each employee's work is focused on a few tasks. Some common office tasks are shown in Figure 1-1.1 on page 5. Can you identify two activities that might be completed by a manager? Can you identify two that might be performed by an office assistant? Think of a particular career and identify two activities that might be performed by someone in that career.

Workers in many jobs handle office tasks. Some workers, however, devote full time to office tasks. For example, some employees in an Accounting Department process invoices, checks, and other documents related to customer accounts. They devote all of their time to these office tasks.

Some workers devote their full time to office tasks.

PM Images/Riser/Getty Images

Figure 1-1.1 **Key Office Activities**

KEY OFFICE ACTIVITIES
1. Creating/Analyzing Information
• Composing memorandums, letters, and reports • Organizing, summarizing, and interpreting data • Creating presentations • Making decisions and recommendations based on information studied
2. Searching for Information
• Accessing databases, the Internet, and company intranets • Requesting information from persons within the company • Requesting information from persons outside the company • Using reference manuals and books
3. Processing Information
• Editing and proofreading • Keyboarding • Opening and reviewing incoming communications • Entering data in databases • Photocopying • Preparing outgoing communications • Preparing checks, orders, invoices • Preparing spreadsheets
4. Communicating Information
• Answering telephones • Greeting callers • Responding to persons within and outside the organization • Providing instruction to coworkers • Preparing and delivering presentations
5. Managing Information
• Maintaining calendars • Maintaining databases and files • Maintaining financial records

© Cengage Learning 2013

 CHECK POINT What are five broad areas into which information-related tasks might fall?

Technology in Modern Offices

The use of technology is common in today's offices. For example, an architect who designs buildings works at a computer. An executive uses the World Wide Web to find a schedule for travel to London. Sales people from several states communicate with the regional manager in Dallas using a company intranet.

Many companies use up-to-date technology in their offices to help employees be productive. Because the technology available is always changing, the way work is accomplished is also changing. Workers should expect their duties, as well as the way they work, to change from time to time. The need for high productivity and quality performance means that all workers must be willing to change work methods. Office workers must be skillful learners—on their own and in more formal training and educational settings.

Technology and procedures used in offices are changing. However, all companies do not apply change at the same rate or in the same way. Some companies monitor changes in technology. They introduce the newest equipment and software related to their work as quickly as possible. Such organizations see value in updating their operations. At the same time, other companies decide that no changes are needed.

Using current technology does not guarantee productivity. A company may use the latest ideas and equipment. However, its workers may not be as effective as those at a company that uses more traditional methods. For example, workers who want to complete work quickly and well may be able to do so even without new equipment. They may be more productive than indifferent workers who use the latest equipment. As author Trish Smith comments, "It's up to us to decide how technology will bring us success in our lives and our careers. Remember that technology is a tool, like any other. How we use it—or how we let it use us—will be an important step toward that success."[1] Over time, however, new equipment and methods that aid workers tend to be used by most organizations.

Using current technology can make employees more productive.

STELIOS VARIAS/Reuters/Corbis

World Wide Web resources on the Internet that support hyperlinks, text, graphics, and multimedia

intranet a private computer network that looks and operates similar to web pages

---

 CHECK POINT What factors other than technology are likely to determine how productive office workers are?

---

[1]Trish Smith, "Five Common Myths about Technology and Productivity," The Security Catalyst (April 23, 2010), http://www.securitycatalyst.com/five-common-myths-about-technology-and-productivity/.

Alternative Offices

Where is the office? The office may be at headquarters, in a carrying bag, or at home. It may be a temporarily assigned workspace. No longer is the office always a particular space used for the same purpose day after day.

The typical office from earlier days is referred to as the traditional office. A traditional office is permanent and located where the company does business. In such an office, employees travel daily to a central location. They spend the working day at the same desk or in the same workspace and generally report directly to a supervisor or manager. Many businesses still use traditional offices. However, other types of work arrangements are being used more frequently.

The practice of working and communicating with others from a home office or other remote location is called telecommuting. A worker who telecommutes shares information with clients or coworkers using the Internet or an intranet. Equipment, such as a computer, telephone, and fax machine, makes talking and sharing data easy. These workers may work in virtual offices, mobile offices, or home offices.

Virtual Office

The term *virtual* refers to a representation of something—not something you can see or touch. For example, you are acquainted with your local library. It is in a building that contains shelves of books you can use to get information. A virtual library might be a computer station that gives you access to many libraries from your school or home. Although the virtual library has no physical form, it allows you to gather information just as you would at a real physical library. The virtual office, therefore, is a setting that allows you to perform work activities as you would in a traditional office.

> **telecommuting** the practice of working and communicating with others from a home office or other remote location
>
> **Internet** a public, world-wide computer network that spans the globe
>
> **virtual office** a setting that allows you to perform work activities as you would in a traditional office

✱ WORKPLACE CONNECTIONS ✱

Joe Park is a successful interior designer in St. Louis. Although Joe refers to his office as a portable office, it is really a virtual office. Joe visits clients to plan and discuss projects. In his bag, he carries a cell phone; a laptop computer with wireless access to fax, e-mail, and the Internet; and a portable copier/printer. Joe can provide plans for a room, cost estimates, and a contract right in the client's living room.

> How does Joe's virtual office allow him to serve clients effectively?

Just as some office workers use virtual offices, some offices employ virtual assistants. A virtual assistant is a worker who performs tasks normally handled by a secretary or administrative assistant. This growing field provides advantages to both the company and the virtual assistant. A virtual assistant can work from a home office. He or she can set the work schedule and work only as many hours per week as desired. Virtual assistants do not require on-site office space and are usually paid only for the hours they work. This means cost savings for the company, which can be especially important for small businesses.

CHECK POINT What is telecommuting?

Mobile Office

Mobile offices are very much like traditional offices, but they are temporary. Offices set up at construction sites and manned by office staff are one type of mobile office. Another type of mobile office is the nonterritorial workspace. Nonterritorial workspaces are available on an assignment basis. They are not assigned to anyone permanently. This type of workspace is often found in professional organizations. For example, an accounting firm or law firm may have many staff members who work away from the company a great deal of the time. Because such personnel do not need a permanent office, they can request an office on their arrival at the company offices.

hoteling using workspace that is assigned as needed

Using workspace that is assigned as needed is sometimes referred to as hoteling. The process is similar to that of a hotel assigning a room to a guest. Computer software makes assigning space prompt and effective. Employees who generally work from a home office, for example, may be assigned office space on those occasions when they do work at the company office.

Two architects review building plans in a mobile office.

Fuse/Jupiter Images

✓ **CHECK POINT** What does the term *nonterritorial workspace* mean? What is another name for this term?

Home Office

A space within a person's home that is used to perform office tasks is referred to as a home office. In many home offices, workers can communicate easily with others using e-mail, the Internet, an intranet, fax, and a telephone. People who work at home can also take part in teleconferences with persons at other locations.

freelancer an independent contractor who works for others for a project fee or hourly fee

Many people who work in home offices are self-employed. Such a person is often called a freelancer. Freelancers may occasionally meet with customers or clients in person. However, they may communicate primarily by e-mail, telephone, and mail.

REVIEW 1-1 _____

21st Century Skills

Making Decisions

Assume that you have completed your studies and are seeking your first full-time position. You have been interviewed by two companies. Each company has offered you a position. You like both companies as far as the nature of the work, the salary, and the employee benefits. However, there is a difference in where you will work.

In Company A, you would be expected to come to headquarters each day. The company has current computers and other technology, and the supervisor seems very helpful and friendly. In Company B, you would be telecommuting. Company B would provide you with all the equipment for your workstation at home. You would have access to your supervisor via telecommunications. From time to time—possibly no more than once in three weeks—you would be expected to attend a training session or a team meeting at headquarters. Which position would you accept?

1. Make a list of the factors you would consider in making a decision about which job to accept.

2. Write a brief paragraph in which you discuss your decision and the basis for it.

Making Academic Connections

Reinforcing English Skills

For written messages to be clear, commas must be used correctly. Practice your skill in using commas. Write each sentence and add commas where needed.

1. The affairs of an individual a business or an organization are carried out in an office.

2. Although the professions of workers may vary many workers complete some office tasks.

3. An alternative office may be a virtual office a mobile office or a home office.

4. Some office workers compose reports and others create presentations.

5. As a recent survey noted about a quarter of American workers telecommute.

6. For example an accounting firm may have employees who work away from the company much of the time.

7. Because the technology is always changing the way work is done is also changing.

8. Using current technology however does not guarantee that workers will be productive.

1-1 Activity 1

Getting Acquainted with Local Offices
(Outcomes 1-1a, 1-1b, 1-1c)

In this activity, you will become familiar with the types of offices in your own community. Work in a team with three other class members to complete this activity.

1. Develop a list of four or five major employers in your area.
2. Find answers to the following questions by visiting the company, talking with an employee, or accessing the company's website.
   - What are the primary products or services of the business or organization?
   - What percentage of the employees at this location work in offices?
   - What is the primary purpose of the office? What tasks do office workers perform?
   - Do any employees work in an alternative office? How many workers telecommute? If there are workers who telecommute, how many of them are considered office workers?
   - What technology is being used in preparing letters and reports? for telecommunications? for records management?
   - In general, determine whether the technology in use is current or somewhat out of date.
3. Prepare a written report of one to two pages in which you present the information you gathered.
4. Participate in a discussion that summarizes what offices are like in your community.

1-1 Activity 2

Qualifying as a Home Office (Outcome 1-1c)

In the United States, a person who works in a home office may be able to deduct costs related to the home office from federal income taxes. The home office and its use must meet certain requirements, however. You will learn about those requirements in this activity.

1. Open the file 1-1 Deduction from the data files. Read the excerpt from IRS *Publication 587, Business Use of Your Home.*
2. Kalina Aaron, a freelance writer, uses a portion of her den for a home office. The den is also used as a family gathering place for watching TV and playing games. Does this home office qualify for a business tax deduction? Why or why not?
3. *Publication 587* was published for use in preparing tax returns for a previous year. Have the regulations changed for the current year? Access the U.S. Internal Revenue Service website. Search the site using the term *home office* to find current regulations. Using the information you find, prepare a brief summary of the requirements a home office must meet to qualify for a business tax deduction.

OUTCOMES

1-2a Describe common types of businesses and other organizations.
1-2b Identify goals for different types of organizations.
1-2c Describe a common structure for personnel in an organization.

Types of Organizations

In the United States, organizations are grouped into one of three categories. They may be businesses, not-for-profit entities (but not government), or units of governments. The goals of these organizations vary, as well their methods of operation.

Businesses

Businesses are organizations that seek to make a **profit**. They may be organized in different ways. Some forms of businesses are required to secure approval from the states in which they are formed. All businesses must follow the laws and regulations governing business activity.

profit monetary gain, advantage

Sole Proprietorship

A business owned by one individual is a **sole proprietorship**. These businesses are also sometimes called single proprietorships. Sole proprietorships may be of any size, but many of them are small. Financial planners, caterers, and lawn care providers are examples of businesses that are often sole proprietorships. The owner may run the business, or a manager or other employees may handle the operations of the company. In this type of business, the owner receives all the profit from the business. The owner is also responsible for the debts of the business.

sole proprietorship a business owned by one individual

Lise Gagne/iStockphoto.com

Small businesses are often in the form of a sole proprietorship.

Partnership

A business that is not incorporated and has two or more owners is a **partnership**. Different types of partners may participate in a partnership. Some partners may provide funds for the business but not take part in running it. Other partners may actively lead and manage the business. All partners share in the profits of the business and are responsible for the debts of the business.

Partnerships may be of any size. Many are small, however. Restaurants, building contractors, and convenience stores are examples of businesses that are often organized as partnerships.

partnership a business that is not incorporated and has two or more owners

Corporation

A **corporation** is a business set up under the laws of a particular state. A charter must be secured from a state for a corporation. Owners have shares of ownership called stock. Owners are called stockholders or shareholders. The business may be privately or publicly owned. Shares of stock in a publicly owned corporation are typically traded on a stock exchange, such as the New York Stock Exchange. Publicly owned corporations are required to report information about the business to shareholders on a timely basis. Such reports become available to many others besides the stockholders.

A corporation is a legal entity, separate from its shareholders. Shareholders may receive a share of the profits of a corporation in the form of dividends. Shareholders are not responsible for the debts of a corporation. Most large companies and many small ones in the United States are corporations. Broadcast networks, software companies, and car makers are examples of corporations.

corporation a business organized under the laws of a state for which a charter is secured

Frances Roberts/Alamy

Stocks for many corporations are bought and sold on the New York Stock Exchange.

Limited Liability Company

A limited liability company (LLC) is another type of business. It must be registered and approved by a state government. However, forming an LLC is not as complicated as forming a corporation. An LLC may be formed by one or more members in various types of industries. An LLC is a legal unit, separate from its members. It provides personal liability protection to members of the company. For example, a member generally cannot be forced to use personal money to pay for debts of the company.

CHECK POINT What are four common types of business organizations?

Not-for-Profit Entities

Many organizations in the United States provide services without the intent of making profits. Some organizations sponsor programs for young people. Examples include 4-H clubs, Girl Scouts, Boy Scouts, and the Future Business Leaders of America. Other common not-for-profit groups include arts galleries, museums, libraries, hospitals, and private colleges. Many hospitals and schools, however, do operate as businesses and seek to be profitable.

Not-for-profit organizations receive funds from a variety of sources. Many depend on money received from individuals and groups. They may receive money from dues and fees paid by participants. Some funds may come from government agencies at the local, state, or federal level. Often, these groups operate in what is referred to as a businesslike manner. This means that resources are carefully budgeted as though the entity were a profit-making business.

✹ WORKPLACE CONNECTIONS ✹

Henry Serreno works as an office assistant to the director of a relatively new not-for-profit museum. Henry talks about his job in these words:

I never know what a day will be like. I handle many office tasks as I assist the director, the art assistant, and the manager of exhibits. I do some tasks every day, such as respond to e-mail messages, open and organize the mail, and handle phone calls. I have a personal computer, a photocopier, a fax machine, e-mail and Internet access, and a wide range of software programs that I use daily.

How might the type of organization affect an office worker's duties?

 CHECK POINT From what sources do not-for-profit entities receive funds?

Government Units

Government units at the local, state, and national levels play a critical role in society. These units are called by different names. They may be agencies, bureaus, departments, or boards. Each unit has specific duties related to services considered important for the citizens served. For example, the Department of Homeland Security's mission is to lead a unified national effort to secure the country and preserve freedoms. The department's mission and other information are available on its website as shown in Figure 1-2.1. Other examples of government units include:

- National — Department of the Treasury, Bureau of Labor Statistics
- State or Province — Department of Commerce, Occupational Safety & Health Division
- Local — Marriage License Bureau, Board of Education

Figure 1-2.1 **Homeland Security Website**

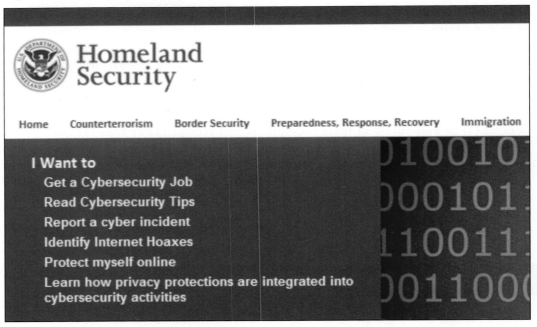

Source: U.S. Department of Homeland Security (2010), http://www.dhs.gov/files/cybersecurity.shtm.

 CHECK POINT Name three government units from your local area or state.

Goals of Organizations

Each of the three major types of organizations has different overall goals. Businesses seek to make a profit. On the other hand, not-for-profit entities and government units do not seek to earn profits. Their goals relate to the services they provide. The goals of the organization influence the work of the employees.

✳ WORKPLACE CONNECTIONS ✳

Many tasks that workers perform relate to helping to meet the profit goals of the business. Hans Welenz works in the Customer Service Department for a company that makes personal computers. The company sells computers nationwide, primarily to businesses. Hans's main task is to understand exactly a complaint or question from a customer. He then does research or talks with other employees to find an answer. Hans and other staff members try to answer all complaints or questions within 24 hours. Hans knows that his work helps the company keep satisfied customers.

How does Hans's work aid the company in meeting profit goals?

Businesses

You may have heard a comment such as, "It's the bottom line that counts." Prior to the comment, a discussion may have taken place about what a business should choose to do. Various strategies for increasing profits may have been discussed. In general, strategies that will provide the most profit are selected. This increases "the bottom line"—the amount of profit shown on the bottom line of the company's profit and loss statement. Profits allow a business to expand through investment in new facilities and new equipment. Profits also provide the means to make payments (called dividends) to shareholders in a corporation.

A profit and loss statement may also be called an income statement. An income statement shows profit or loss for a business for a certain period of time. It answers the question, "How successful was the business during the time period?" The income statement lists the amounts and sources of revenues, as well as expenses, and the income (profit) or loss of a business for the reporting period. A net income results if revenues are greater than expenses. A net loss results if expenses are greater than revenues. An income statement for Sweet Treats (a sole proprietorship) for the recently ended fiscal year is shown in Figure 1-2.2.

income statement a document that shows profit or loss for a business for a certain period of time

 CHECK POINT What information is included on an income statement?

Figure 1-2.2 **Income Statement**

SWEET TREATS
INCOME STATEMENT
For the Year Ended December 31, 20--

		% of Sales
Sales	$200,000	
Cost of Goods Sold	100,000	
Gross Profit on Sales	$100,000	50%
Operating Expenses		
Advertising Expenses	500	
Delivery Expense	1,000	
Office Supplies Expense	800	
Payroll Taxes Expense	4,500	
Salaries Expense	58,200	
Utilities Expense	3,500	
Miscellaneous Expense	500	
Total Operating Expense	69,000	
Net Income from Operations	$31,000	16%
Other Income and Expenses		
Interest Expense	2,000	
Net Income before Income Tax	$29,000	15%
Less Income Tax	8,200	
Net Income after Tax	$20,800	10%

© Cengage Learning 2013

Not-for-Profit and Governments

Not-for-profit organizations, as the title states, do not seek to make a profit. The chief goal of such organizations is to provide valuable services to those who can benefit from them. For example, museums provide interesting exhibits of various types of art. Social agencies provide food and cleaning services for the elderly. Many types of services are provided by other organizations.

Governments, like not-for-profit entities, do not seek to make a profit. These units are supported primarily by taxes. The overall goals of government are related to providing services that citizens desire or need. For example, the government maintains a federal highway system. This system ensures ease of travel throughout the country. Such a system is an aid to commerce and to the quality of life that citizens enjoy. Many workers in government are required to handle the tasks required to meet the needs of citizens.

 CHECK POINT What do non-profit organizations and governments have in common?

Structure of Organizations

Many different types of employees work at various levels in companies. Because they work together, they must know who is responsible for each activity. They must also know what authority each person has. Office workers, especially, find it helpful to understand the duties and authority of those with whom they work.

Knowing how a company is structured will give you a better understanding of how it operates. Many companies prepare a chart that shows positions in order of rank or authority. As you can imagine, the chart for a large company will have many pages. Figure 1-2.3 shows a partial organization chart for a small company. Note the levels of responsibility and the different titles.

Board of Directors

Many large corporations have boards of directors. Publicly owned corporations must have such boards. Owners elect members of the board of directors. The board sets the policies that guide senior managers in directing the company. Generally, some senior managers of the company are members of the board. The board has a number of committees that may meet more often than does the full board. Some members of boards of directors are not employees of the company. These directors are expected to provide guidance and to make decisions that will serve the best interests of the company. Such outside directors may receive a payment for their services. Generally, the full board of directors may meet no more than four to five times each year.

A not-for-profit entity may also have a board of directors (sometimes called a board of trustees). The board's duties are similar to those of a corporation's board. Members provide guidance regarding goals and operations.

Figure 1-2.3 **Organization Chart**

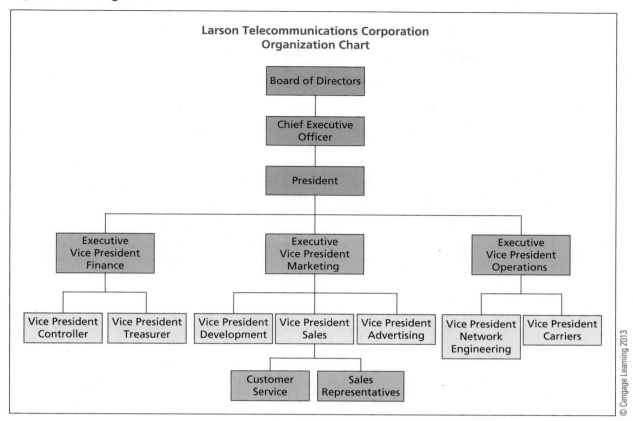

Larson Telecommunications Corporation
Organization Chart

CHECK POINT What is the function of a board of directors for a company or organization?

Management Employees

Persons who give direction in carrying out the policies of the board of directors are called senior managers or top management. The chief executive officer (CEO), the president, the chief operating officer (COO), and the chief financial officer (CFO) are generally included in this group. The CEO and president have overall responsibility for everything that happens in the company. In some companies, one person holds both of these positions.

Large companies are often subdivided into units. The units are organized in some manner that is appropriate for the work of the company. Often the units are called divisions or strategic business units. Divisions are usually managed by vice presidents.

Managers who direct the daily activities of a company are called middle management. Many companies have fewer middle managers than in the past. Increased use of computers has allowed companies to have fewer middle managers. In some companies, more work is done in teams with all members taking part in making decisions. This type of structure is sometimes referred to as a flatter organization.

In many companies, workers are given guidelines to follow. They are then allowed to make some decisions without review by managers. This concept is called employee empowerment.

> **✓ CHECK POINT** The daily activities of a company are directed by what level of management?

Department Employees

The nature of a company's activities determines the types of workers that are needed. Each type of employee has certain duties. Working together, they are expected to meet the goals of the company. In many companies, employees are organized in departments or teams that relate to the functions of the company. These functions may include finance and accounting, communications, sales and marketing, information technology, legal services, and human resources. Office workers can be found in all these areas.

Production workers are found in manufacturing companies. These workers make the products the company sells, such as cars, computers, or furniture. This type of company will also have workers in departments, such as research and development, inventory control, and shipping. Many companies sell or provide services rather than products. Employees, such as financial counselors, legal assistants, and real estate agents, who provide these services are needed in these companies.

Department employees may work in an office, a factory, or other areas.

Cultura/Jupiter Images

The size of a company influences the types of workers needed. In a small company, a single person may, as is commonly stated, wear many hats. For example, one manager may approve all expenses and sign all payments for goods and services. The manager may also be present to oversee the business on a daily basis. You can imagine that an office assistant in such a company would be likely to do tasks related to communications, records management, and purchasing. In a large company, one person probably would not have the range of duties and authority that is common in a small company.

As you have learned, employees in an organization work at various levels and in many different departments. With few exceptions, you will find office workers in all areas of an organization. Even in departments such as production, office workers are needed to process information.

> **✓ CHECK POINT** What are some functions around which departments in a company are typically organized?

Employee Empowerment

"Our employees are empowered. We couldn't function in this fast-paced world without every employee responding wisely to the changes that surround us. We rely on the common sense and wise judgment of every employee."

The president of a bank in a large North Carolina city who spoke these words is not alone in his belief in empowering all 300 of the bank's employees. He understands the value of empowerment, which is being able to make decisions or changes in what you do without having to get approval.

Empowerment requires that you understand your company. You learned earlier in Chapter 1 that workers need to understand thoroughly the business or organization in which they are employed. By understanding your organization, you will find every aspect of your job of greater interest. You will better understand what you are doing, and you will be able to use the privilege of empowerment successfully. Consider this example of employee empowerment:

Melissa works in a large consulting company that believes in employee empowerment. She is a new receptionist on the fourth floor, which serves as a center for meetings and conferences for employees and clients. Every day, three, four, or even more individuals would come to her desk asking: "Where is the meeting for _____?" She would have to get the name of the person responsible for the meeting, call that person's office, and get the needed information. In the meantime, others were waiting to know where they should go. Melissa realized that a problem existed due to lack of information and clear communications.

Melissa had not been told that she would need to guide individuals to the right room. When she realized this task would be a routine part of her job, however, she began to think about how she could resolve the problem. Melissa knew that conference rooms were reserved and that those assistants making arrangements submitted the details of the meeting via e-mail. She called the office that handled room assignments and asked: "Could you add my name to your list for a copy of your confirmation for a room? I will be able to direct visitors to the right room with this information." The staff member was cooperative and responded: "Melissa, that is no problem at all. We'll also keep you informed of changes in plans." In addition, Melissa decided to post a schedule for the day inside the entrance so visitors could check the time and location of the day's meetings.

Melissa remembered her orientation to the company and how she and other new employees were informed of the functions of each department of the company. She realized how that information was now helping her as she thought of better ways to handle her assignments. She enjoyed being *empowered!*

> What could be an advantage to the company when employees are empowered? What could be an advantage for the employee? **?**

empowerment being able to make decisions or changes without seeking approval

21st Century Skills

Interacting with Others

PARTNERSHIP FOR
21st CENTURY SKILLS

You were standing at a desk of a coworker when her telephone rang. This is what you heard her say:

> *Who do you want?*
>
> *A Mr. Ted Wells? Are you sure he works for this company?*
>
> *Gee, I really don't know who the executives are. I don't work for any of them. I work for the director of catering services.*
>
> *Oh, you work for Johnson Corporation. Well, you know how hard it is to know your own job, let alone know what is going on in the company.*
>
> *You say our operator gave you this extension? Possibly, the operator doesn't know much more about the company than I do.*
>
> *If I knew the extension for the president's office, I'd transfer you because I'd guess the president's secretary knows where everyone is—but, I don't know the number offhand. I could never find my directory on this messy desk . . . Let me transfer you back to the operator. Is that okay? I so wish I could be helpful.*
>
> *Just hold on. But, first where are you calling from? Why don't you call when you aren't busy, and we can have a chat? Do you have my number?*
>
> *It's 513-555-0192, extension 344.*
>
> *Hold on. Good luck in finding Mr. Wells. Goodbye.*

1. Describe the impression you think the caller has of your coworker's knowledge of the company and of her way of working.
2. Identify what you think the coworker said that reflects positive attitudes toward others.
3. If your coworker maintained an orderly desk, what would she have done as soon as it was clear that the caller had the wrong extension? What might she have said instead of the comments shown here?

Making Academic Connections

Reinforcing Math Skills

As you learned in this chapter, the goal of a business is to make a profit. To judge the extent to which the profit goal is being met, businesses analyze their sales on a regular basis. Open the Excel file 1-2 Sales Figures found in the data files. Use formulas to analyze the sales to answer the questions below.

1. For each year, what are the total yearly sales for U.S. and international sales?
2. For each year, what percent of the total yearly sales are U.S. sales? Round to an even percent.
3. For each year, what percent of the total yearly sales are international sales? Round to an even percent.
4. For U.S. sales for each year, what is the percentage of increase over 2007 sales?
5. For international sales for each year, what is the percentage increase over 2007 sales?
6. For total sales for each year, what is the percentage increase over 2007 sales?

1-2 Activity 1

Organization Types and Goals (Outcomes 1-2a and 1-2b)

Work with a classmate to research organizations in your area or state.

1. Identify one business and one not-for-profit organization or government unit in your local area or your state.
2. For the two organizations, do research to find answers to the following questions.
   - What is the name and address of the organization?
   - What type is the organization (business, not-for-profit, government unit)?
   - About how many employees does the organization have?
   - What goods or services does the organization provide?
   - What are the main goals of the organization?
3. Write a brief report to summarize your findings.

1-2 Activity 2

Organization Chart (Outcome 1-2c)

An organization chart is often used to show the structure of an organization. Prepare an organization chart showing the management team for the World Wide Sales and Service Division of a multinational company. Refer to Figure 1-2.3 for a sample chart.

1. Begin with the company name, GLOBAL MANUFACTURING, followed by the division name, centered at the top as the chart title.
2. Place Thomas McEwen's name and title, CEO, at the top of the chart.
3. Insert a block for Paul B. Kalis, Sr. Vice President, who is head of the division and reports to Thomas McEwen.
4. Insert blocks for the following vice presidents who report to Paul B. Kalis:
   Marco Ortiz, Vice President, Latin America
   Akira Komuro, Vice President, Asia, Pacific
   Rachel J. Kohnstamm, Vice President, Europe, Middle East, Africa
5. Insert a block for James E. Phelps, Assistant Vice President, Europe, who reports to Rachel J. Kohnstamm.
6. Insert blocks for Jean L. Lucent, Manager, France, and Howard A. Toole, Manager, Denmark, who report to James E. Phelps.

OUTCOMES

1-3a Discuss the behaviors and attitudes of an office professional.
1-3b Recognize the importance of having a customer focus.
1-3c Describe strategies for working effectively in teams.

professional someone who conforms to expected ethical and quality standards and behaviors

work ethic a value system that places importance on work or other purposeful activity

Office Professionals

Although your duties will vary depending on your job, certain attitudes and behaviors will be expected of you in your role as an office worker. You will be expected to act in a professional manner. A professional in any field is someone who conforms to expected ethical and quality standards and behaviors. Being a professional is important to your career success. The attitudes that mark a professional are related to your work ethic and your interactions with others.

Work Ethic

Professionals have a strong work ethic. Work ethic is a general term that combines a deep belief in the value of work in one's life and a willingness to meet the demands of work. Persons with a strong work ethic value both tangible and intangible rewards of work. Tangible rewards, such as pay and benefits, are important to most workers. Persons without a strong work ethic may not place much value on intangible rewards. For example, they may not enjoy doing work or take pride in a job well done. Persons with a strong work ethic tend to define job satisfaction differently from those without a strong work ethic.

Workers in the United States have long been credited with a strong work ethic. A positive attitude toward work, willingness to work overtime, and a desire to do quality work all reflect a strong work ethic.

✴ WORKPLACE CONNECTIONS ✴

Sam Wong is a manager in one of the finest jewelry stores in the United States. Managers are not salespersons. Yet, Sam is likely to be assisting customers through much of a very busy shopping day. Sam pays no attention to the typical end of his working day. He stays on the job through the closing time for the store. He realizes that, at a busy time, the most important task is assisting customers.

> Do you think Sam has a strong work ethic? Why or why not?

Cooperation

At the heart of a strong work ethic is cooperativeness. A cooperative worker is willing to participate in what needs to be done to achieve a goal. You may have heard someone say, "We would have missed our deadline if everyone hadn't chipped in and helped." This statement describes the cooperativeness of workers.

cooperative willing to agree or take part in what needs to be done to achieve a goal

Aldo Murillo/iStockphoto

Office workers must often cooperate to meet goals.

Professionals are cooperative and flexible. Many companies develop job descriptions for each job in the company. Given the changing nature of business, however, workers often need to perform tasks not included in their job descriptions. A positive attitude and a willingness to be helpful are critical at such a time.

Loyalty

Professionals are loyal to the company and to their workgroup or department. Being loyal means supporting the efforts of the company and workgroup. A loyal employee does not make unfavorable remarks about the company or workgroup outside the group. For example, several members of a department may have different ideas about plans for a new project. Each person may offer suggestions and criticisms of proposed plans. Once the manager or the group has made a decision about how to proceed, however, all members of the team are expected to do their best to make the plan successful.

Learning

Professionals are open to change. Work procedures can change often. Some changes may be needed to adapt to new technology. Other changes may be needed to produce new products or offer new services. As companies change, managers cannot always know what new skills each employee needs to learn. Companies expect workers to be independent learners. As an office professional, you are expected to show a willingness to learn and to improve your understanding or skills that relate to your job.

Strive to be aware of new technology and methods that relate to your field. Industry magazines and professional organizations are good sources of information. Tell your employer about opportunities for training that will improve your job performance. The company may be willing to pay the cost of such training for you and other workers.

CHECK POINT Are you more interested in the tangible or intangible rewards of work? Give examples of your choice.

Interacting with Coworkers

Even though much of your work may be done independently, at times you will need to interact with others. You may have common needs for information, tasks that overlap, or joint responsibility for some task. When a colleague from another department calls you, your response should be to want to provide the needed help. Professionals treat coworkers, managers, and customers with courtesy and respect. They are ethical in all their dealings with others.

Confidentiality

confidential *private or secret*

Professionals know how to treat confidential information. You will want to be sure you understand what aspects of your work are confidential. Revealing confidential data may cause harm to the company or its employees or customers. Information about plans of the business might seem routine. If the information reaches the company's competitors, however, the results could be disastrous.

In some cases, information is confidential only for a period of time. Later, when decisions are firm, information that was earlier restricted may be widely distributed.

✳ WORKPLACE CONNECTIONS ✳

Valeria works in the Human Resources Department of her company. In her position, she meets the candidates for key management positions. She reviews resumes and assists the director in making decisions. She knows which candidates are invited to headquarters for interviews. Valeria understands that all aspects of the recruiting process must be kept confidential. She never reveals any hiring details. The director is grateful for Valeria's attitude.

What are some other types of confidential information that Valeria might see as a worker in the Human Resources Department?

Sharing Information

Professionals share information in appropriate ways. Information is often shared informally in a company. The informal network by which employees share information is sometimes called the "grapevine." Some informal communication can be good. Employees are naturally interested in the plans and events that affect the company and its employees.

Unfortunately, rumors and gossip are also often spread by employees. Rumors are incomplete or false statements about people or situations. They may be harmful to the company or its employees. Think carefully about the information you share with others. Avoid discussing company plans or events that you do not know are correct or that may be confidential at the present time. Do not discuss personal issues or affairs of fellow employees.

Professionals share information with coworkers in appropriate ways.

Accepting Responsibility for Mistakes

People are not perfect; they make mistakes. You may have a firm goal to be sure that the facts you communicate to others are accurate and to use good judgment in making decisions. Even with your best efforts, however, you will still make mistakes.

When you make a mistake, accept responsibility for the error as soon as you realize it was made. Take steps to correct the error immediately so that coworkers will not make decisions or plans based on incorrect information. Explain what led to the error if you think doing so will help resolve the problem. Do not, however, subject your coworkers to a long list of excuses about why you made the mistake. If possible, offer a solution to whatever problem the mistake may have caused when you alert others to the mistake or problem. Learn from your mistakes whenever possible to help avoid making a similar error in the future. Never blame others for your mistakes.

 CHECK POINT Should you be courteous to a coworker who is being difficult or disagreeable? Why or why not?

Customer Focus

"We are here to serve customers" is a message that many companies send to employees. A customer is someone who buys or uses an organization's products or services. Having a customer focus is an important part of your role as an office worker in any field. Customer focus is paying attention to fulfilling the needs and wants of customers.

In many organizations, paying attention to both external and internal customers is very important for long-term success. As you learned earlier, a goal of most businesses is to make a profit. Meeting the needs and wants of customers helps companies achieve this goal. Companies that do not make a profit often fail or go out of business.

customer someone who buys or uses an organization's products or services

customer focus paying attention to fulfilling the needs and wants of customers

External and Internal Customers

External customers are people or organizations outside your company that buy or use your products or services. You may be in a job where you deal directly with external customers. Examples of such jobs are sales associates, cashiers, and teachers. Sales associates show products to customers or answer their questions. Cashiers assist customers in paying for purchases. You may not think of a teacher as having customers. However, students receive services from a teacher. The service is instruction in a certain skill or subject. So students are customers of a school or teacher.

Customers do not always pay for the goods or services received. For example, a public library may allow people to check out books, read periodicals, and use computers. There is typically no charge for these services for people who have a library card. People who use the services provided by the library are its customers. A community center may provide programs and activities for individuals at no charge. However, the satisfaction of the people who take part at the center is important to the organization.

In many companies, not all employees deal with external customers. However, almost everyone in a company deals with internal customers. Internal customers are people inside your organization who use products or services you provide. For example, suppose you have a problem with your computer. A computer technician may help you resolve the issue. In this case, you are an internal customer for the computer technician. Managers use data provided by the Accounting Department to make decisions. They are internal customers of the Accounting Department. Giving prompt, quality service to internal customers is important. Doing so helps the organization run smoothly and give good service to external customers.

 CHECK POINT   Why is giving good service to internal customers important?

TECHNOLOGY CONNECTION

Customer satisfaction is important to businesses. To learn about external customers' opinions, companies sometimes use online surveys. The surveys can be distributed in various ways. Customers may be given the option to complete a survey when they access the company's website. In other cases, customers receive an e-mail message asking them to take part in a survey. Surveys can also be made available through social networking sites, such as Facebook or Twitter.

Once the customer agrees to take the survey, it is typically shown in the user's browser. The survey may ask questions about the company's policies, such as about shipping or returns. It might also ask about one or more products the company offers. Customers may be given a coupon for money off a purchase or some other incentive to encourage them to complete the survey. The survey results can provide valuable information to help an organization improve its customer service.

Have you taken an online survey? If yes, was it easy to complete?

Customer Service Strategies

As an office professional, you may deal with only internal customers or also with external customers. You should strive to give good service to all your customers. The following strategies will help you achieve this goal.

- Show respect for customers. Give them your attention and listen to their needs or concerns.

- Show empathy when dealing with customers who are angry or concerned.

  empathy understanding or concern for someone's feelings or position

- Ask for customer input. When working with customers, there may be a problem to resolve or a challenge to meet. Ask the customer for suggestions on how to handle the issue.

- Build effective relationships with customers. Give your customers quality service on a regular basis. This builds goodwill that will be helpful if a problem occurs.

  goodwill a friendly or kindly attitude

- Accept responsibility for errors or mistakes you or your company makes. Apologize for the error and move on to identifying a solution.

- Give customers complete information when discussing an issue. Do not assume that they have all the information that you have.

- Follow up later to see that solutions or changes have been put in place and that the proposed solution was helpful.

- Keep a positive attitude, even in difficult situations. Be polite and courteous at all times.

CHECK POINT Which one strategy for providing effective customer service do you think is most important? Why?

Working Effectively in Teams

One common question asked of job applicants is: "How willing are you to participate in teamwork?" Interviewers are asking this question because today's business world is complex. Many of the tasks performed in any department require the skills and knowledge of several staff members. Part of your role in an office will be to work with others to identify what is to be done, how it is to be done, and who will accept responsibility for parts of the task.

Working as a team, employees bring varying experiences, observations, insights, and knowledge to tasks. This helps them determine what actions should be taken and to follow through with those actions. A team, thinking critically, can be far more successful than an individual working alone. For a team to be successful, its members must be reliable in carrying out their responsibilities, and they must be committed to the team and its goals. Commitment is shown in both a team member's attitude and actions.

You have probably had experience as a team member—possibly as a member of a sports team, in a science laboratory, or in an after-school club. You may enjoy teamwork, or you may think that you would rather work alone. If you have a positive view of teamwork, you will be a valuable employee. If you have a negative view of teamwork, reconsider your attitude.

Team members should communicate clearly and often about team goals and tasks.

Wavebreakmedia Ltd/Shutterstock.com

As an office professional, you will be expected to work in teams, and you will want to be successful in this aspect of your job. Consider these guidelines for working effectively in teams:

- Set clear goals for the team and create an action plan for achieving the goals.
- Define the tasks or duties of each team member in achieving team goals.
- Identify how success will be measured. How will the team know its goals have been accomplished?
- Identify obstacles to achieving the team's goals and discuss ways to overcome the obstacles.
- Communicate clearly and often with all team members and be open to all feedback and ideas. Schedule regular meetings or reports to track the progress toward achieving team goals.
- Discuss how differences will be resolved. Understand that all members of a team may not have the same level of authority.
- Build on the strengths of individual members. Encourage all members of the team to participate in making decisions and contributing ideas.
- Recognize the accomplishments of team members and the team as a whole.
- As an individual team member, develop your colleagues' trust by fulfilling your responsibilities. Act in a professional manner and show a positive attitude when discussing team activities.

 CHECK POINT Why is it important to define the tasks or duties of each member of a team?

REVIEW 1-3 _____

21st Century Skills

Interacting with Others

PARTNERSHIP FOR 21ST CENTURY SKILLS

The assistant curator at the County Historical Society, Delores, realized that she had given a staff member the wrong dates for an exhibition. When the staff member called, Delores was very busy completing a report and failed to check the calendar. She merely gave the dates as she recalled them. Later in the day, she realized that she gave the staff member the wrong dates. She called the staff member and confessed: "Marion, I gave you the wrong dates! I am sorry. I hope it isn't too late to give you the correct information."

1. What mistake did Delores make when interacting with a coworker?
2. Did Delores handle the situation effectively when she realized her error? What could she have done differently?

Making Academic Connections

Reinforcing English Skills

For written messages to be clear, words must be spelled correctly. For each sentence, write the correct spelling of all words that are spelled incorrectly.

1. The techncian in a chemical labaratory, the curater in a museumn, and the buyer in a department store all perform a range of office tasks during a typical workweek.
2. An officie is a place in which the affaires of an individual, a business, or an organizition are carried out.
3. All the employes must be knowledgable about many office practices.
4. A customer service assoiciate responds by telephone to questions about installing electranic equipement.
5. The mansger must write many reports to share her conclutions and recommendations.
6. Because the technolgy availible is always changing, the way work is ac-commplished is also changing.
7. You are probably acqauinted with your local libary, which contains shelfs of books you can use to find information.
8. Sole propreitorships may be of any size, but many off them are small.
9. A coperative worker is willing to particapate in what needs to be done to acheive a goal.
10. Many of the tasks preformed in any department require the skills and knowledge of several staff members.

1-3 Activity 1

Professional Standards and Organizations (Outcome 1-3a)

Many career areas have professional organizations for workers in that particular field. The organizations have set recommended standards for the work, ethics, or behavior of those working in the field. They may also offer training opportunities or articles to help workers learn new information related to their jobs.

1. Identify a career area that interests you.
2. Do research to learn about any professional organizations or associations related to this career. Write a short report that includes information such as the following:
   - The career area
   - The name of the professional organization or association
   - The website address of this professional organization or association
   - The type of information or services provided by this professional organization or association
   - A mission statement, code of ethics, or standards for workers in this field

1-3 Activity 2

Customer Focus (Outcome 1-3b)

1. Write a description of a situation where you (or a friend or family member) received excellent customer service. Give examples of why the experience was positive. Explain why you (or they) continue to do business with this company or organization.
2. Write a description of a situation in which you (or a friend or family member) received poor customer service. Give at least three suggestions for ways the situation could have been handled better.

Summary

1-1 The Office Today

- An office is a place in which the affairs of an individual, a business, or an organization are carried out.
- Offices are information driven and office functions are varied.
- The use of technology is common in today's offices.
- A traditional office is permanent and located where the company does business.
- Alternative offices include virtual offices, mobile offices, and home offices.

1-2 The Office in Relation to the Total Organization

- In the United States, organizations are grouped into one of three categories: businesses, not-for-profit entities, or units of governments.
- Businesses that are sole proprietorships or partnerships do not have to be set up with a state government.
- Corporations and limited liability companies are set up under the laws of a particular state. These types of businesses are legal entities that are separate from their shareholders or members.
- The goal of businesses is to make a profit. The goals of not-for-profit organizations and government units are to provide services or products to individuals or organizations.
- Many different types of employees work at various levels in companies. Because the employees work together, they need to understand the duties and authority of those with whom they work.

1-3 Your Role in an Office

- Being a professional is important to your career success. The attitudes that mark a professional are related to your work ethic and your interactions with others.
- Professionals have a strong work ethic, are cooperative, loyal, and open to change and continued learning.
- Professionals treat coworkers, managers, and customers with courtesy and respect. They are ethical in all their dealings with others.
- Customer focus is paying attention to fulfilling the needs and wants of customers. Having a customer focus is an important part of your role as an office worker.
- Part of your role in an office will be to work with others to identify what is to be done, how it is to be done, and who will accept responsibility for parts of the task.
- A team, thinking critically, can be far more successful than an individual working alone.

Wire_man/Shutterstock.com

Chapter 1 Activity 1

Customer Service
(Outcome 1-3b)

1. Go to the website of a major company that sells products to consumers.

2. Find and print the company's privacy policy. Does the company sell or share information about you with other companies?

3. Locate information about the company's policy regarding returns for items purchased by customers. Is the policy clear and easy to understand? Briefly summarize the policy.

4. What methods are provided for customers to contact the company? Is there an e-mail address for customers to use? If yes, what is the address? What is the customer support telephone number? Does the company provide a live chat feature?

5. Can you access information in the form of frequently asked questions? Is there a database of information that you can search to find answers to questions related to buying or using the company's products? Are these features easy to use?

6. What is your overall impression of the customer service provided by the company judging from the information you find on the website?

Chapter 1 Activity 2

Teamwork
(Outcome 1-3c)

You and two coworkers have been asked to create an article to be included in the online newsletter for your company. Use the information in this chapter and information you find on the Internet. (Work with two classmates to complete this activity.)

1. Create an article about teamwork and include the following:
   - A definition of teamwork
   - General principles for working effectively in teams
   - A quote regarding teamwork
   - One or two photos or other graphics that relate to teamwork
   - At least one game or activity that teaches or builds teamwork

2. Give the article an appropriate title and arrange it in an attractive format. Include source information for material that you quote or paraphrase. Proofread and correct all errors.

3. Save the document as a single file web page. View the article in a browser program. Make changes to the format, if needed, so the article is easy to read in the browser window.

Accounting Applications Event

In this competitive event, you will be judged on your skills and knowledge of accounting applications. You will collect and organize data, develop reports, and analyze data to make business decisions.

The event includes a written test and two role-playing situations. Finalists in the events will have a third role-playing situation. No reference materials are allowed. You may make notes to use during the role-play while when you read the role-play description and prepare for the event.

Performance Indicators Evaluated

Participants will demonstrate skills related to the finance career cluster and accounting pathway. Sample indicators include showing an understanding of:

- Tools, strategies, and systems used to maintain, monitor, control, and plan the use of financial resources
- Ways to maintain cash controls and track cash flow
- Performing accounts payable and account receivable functions
- Tracking inventory and the value of current assets
- Completing payroll procedures
- Using cost accounting methods
- Applying internal controls and conducting audits

The following indicators are in addition to the accounting specific lists above.

- Communication (writing, speaking, reading, or listening)
- Analyzing data to form conclusions and recommendations
- Critical thinking and problem solving
- Setting priorities and managing time

For more detailed information about this event, go to the DECA website.[2]

http://www.deca.org

Think Critically

1. Why do you think communication is evaluated in this event for accounting?
2. Do you think a test or a role-playing event gives a better indication of accounting skills? Why?

---

[2]DECA, "High School Competitive Events Guidelines" (DECA, 2011), http://www.deca.org/competitions/highschool.

Exploring Careers in . . .

Government Administration

Government & Public Administration

Government units provide services to citizens, businesses, and organizations in their area of jurisdiction. In addition to elected officials, many support staff workers are needed to fulfill government's role. Some workers in this field deal with the public. Others work behind the scenes to keep governments running smoothly. Jobs in government administration are found in local and state governments as well as the federal government.

Employment Outlook

There are many jobs in government support. Turnover of some jobs may be related to the political party of elected officials. The U.S. government provides job projections for 2008-2018. Jobs in this career area are expected to increase about as fast as average for all jobs.[3]

Job Titles

- Court clerk assistant
- License clerk
- Judicial assistant
- Case manager
- Court operations manager
- Director of water resources
- Financial manager for Public Works Department
- Public Housing Department assistant
- City internal auditor
- Congressional aide

Needed Education/Skills

The education and skills needed in government support jobs vary widely. They depend on the area of work to which the job relates. For example, an assistant in the Public Housing Department for a city needs different skills than a city internal auditor. For clerical positions, a high school diploma and job-specific training may be all that are required. Higher level jobs and specialized jobs require education and experience appropriate to the job. A college degree and related work experience are often required.

What's it like to work in . . . Government Administration?

Terri works as an assistant court clerk. She helps the court clerk with many duties related to maintaining court records. Terri has contact with attorneys, judges, and the public as she completes tasks. She prepares various legal forms, reports, and documents using a personal computer. She also accesses the Internet to see the court docket and do research.

Today Terri began work by checking her e-mail and phone messages. She returned two calls and answered four messages from people inquiring about court cases. She sorted the incoming mail and delivered it to the recipients. Later in the morning, Terri used spreadsheet software to prepare a monthly financial report for her department. Two people came into the office to pay fines. Terri collected the money and issued receipts. During the afternoon, Terri prepared several legal documents—three warrants, six subpoenas, and one summons. She organized several other documents and decided which ones should be scanned and sent to court staff or others. At the end of a busy day, Terri balanced the cash drawer and prepared a deposit to drop off at the bank.

What About You?

Does a job in government administration sound appealing to you? What type of job in this career area would you like best? Would you like working for a government unit rather than a business? Why or why not?

---

[3]*Occupational Outlook Handbook*, 2010-11 Edition, Bureau of Labor Statistics, U.S. Department of Labor, http://www.bls.gov/oco/oco20054.htm.

Office Competencies

2-1 Employment Outlook

2-2 Employment Competencies

Rocketclips, Inc./Shutterstock

As you learned in Chapter 1, office competencies are a requirement for many workers in performing their jobs. You will find the content of this textbook valuable in preparing for almost any job. You will develop skills and understandings that have application to all types of careers and will be useful preparation for work of any kind.

In this chapter, you will find a brief overview of job projections through 2018. You will be introduced to basic office competencies. These competencies are discussed in relation to basic skills and job opportunities. You will also learn about basic employment competencies. A discussion of how you can plan to develop these competencies follows.

Wire_man/Shutterstock.com

OUTCOMES

2-1a Explore the need for workers in the future.
2-1b Identify office competencies needed in chosen careers.

KEY TERMS

projections p. 36
word processing p. 39
desktop publishing p. 39
proficiency p. 40
data processing p. 41
information
    management p. 42

projections estimates or guesses about the future based on known data

National Overview of Employment

Much information is available about types of jobs in the United States. The U.S. Department of Labor monitors the total workforce. It provides information about the current employment situation. Also, the Department of Labor does research to predict the need for workers in the future. Such information is valuable to individuals as they plan for their future careers. Schools and universities, too, use such **projections** to plan courses that prepare students for jobs.

Job projections help schools prepare courses for students.

Sofos Design/Shutterstock

The U.S. Department of Labor provides *The Occupational Outlook Handbook* online. The *Handbook* discusses the major occupations in the country. From this book, you can learn about job prospects in a wide range of fields. The 2010–11 issue, which is current at the time of this writing, has projections to 2018. The edition for the current year will have projections for later years. The monthly magazine *Monthly Labor Review* is also available online. It updates projections and provides additional information about job opportunities.

In projecting jobs to 2018, the government's economists judged the rate of increase. The overall projected rate of increase in jobs is 10.12 percent. Management, business, and financial occupations are expected to increase by 10.57 percent from 2008 to 2018. Office and administrative support jobs are expected to increase by 7.64 percent during the same period. Note the percentage of change (growth rate) projected for other job groups in Figure 2-1.1.

Figure 2-1.1 **Employment Projections by Group**

EMPLOYMENT BY MAJOR OCCUPATIONAL GROUP 2008 AND PROJECTED 2018			
	Employment (Numbers in Thousands)		
Occupational Group	2008	2018	% Change
Total, all occupations	150,931.7	166,205.6	10.12
Management, business, and financial occupations	15,746.7	17,410.9	10.57
Professional and related occupations	31,053.5	36,280.0	16.83
Service occupations	29,575.9	33,645.1	13.76
Sales and related occupations	15,902.7	16,883.1	6.16
Office and administrative support occupations	24,100.6	25,942.7	7.64
Farming, fishing, and forestry occupations	1,035.4	1,026.3	−0.88
Construction and extraction occupations	7,810.3	8,828.8	13.04
Installation, maintenance, and repair occupations	5,798.0	6,238.2	7.59
Production occupations	10,083.0	9,733.9	−3.46
Transportation and material moving occupations	9,825.5	10,216.6	3.98

Source: Employment Projections Program, U.S. Department of Labor, U.S. Bureau of Labor Statistics, http://www.bls.gov/emp/ep_table_101.htm.

 CHECK POINT What kind of information is provided in *The Occupational Outlook Handbook*?

Workers Face Expanded Job Responsibilities

Office activity is increasing because of the growth of business in the global marketplace. A change has taken place, however, in who handles office tasks. Far more workers are doing office tasks than in the past. New technology is responsible for the shift. Many types of workers can handle office tasks because of the technology available. If no innovations in technology had occurred during the last 20 years, about six times as many office support employees as are now employed would be needed to handle the volume of activity.

Figure 2-1.2 on page 38 shows several occupations that are projected to grow in number of jobs from 2008 to 2018. Note that office competencies are needed in many of these occupations.

Tatagatta/Shutterstock

Jobs for personal financial advisors are expected to grow in the next few years.

Figure 2-1.2 Employment Growth Projections

PROJECTED GROWTH FOR SELECTED OCCUPATIONS 2008 AND PROJECTED 2018

Occupation	Employment (Numbers in thousands)		% Change
	2008	2018	
Biomedical engineers	16.0	27.6	72.02
Network systems and data communications analysts	292.0	447.8	53.36
Financial examiners	27.0	38.1	41.16
Physician assistants	74.8	103.9	38.99
Biochemists and biophysicists	23.2	31.9	37.42
Athletic trainers	16.3	22.4	36.95
Veterinary technologists and technicians	79.6	108.1	35.77
Computer software engineers, applications	514.8	689.9	34.01
Medical assistants	483.6	647.5	33.90
Veterinarians	59.7	79.4	32.95
Self-enrichment education teachers	253.6	334.9	32.05
Environmental engineers	54.3	70.9	30.62
Pharmacy technicians	326.3	426.0	30.57
Computer software engineers	394.8	515.0	30.44
Personal financial advisors	208.4	271.2	30.13

Source: Employment Projections Program, U.S. Department of Labor, U.S. Bureau of Labor Statistics, http://www.bls.gov/emp/ep_table_103.htm.

 CHECK POINT Why are fewer office support workers needed now than in the past?

✳ WORKPLACE CONNECTIONS ✳

Many managers now do much of their own office work. Donna Komari is a product manager in the international division of a home appliance company. She spends much time traveling. Donna works for hours during a flight from New York to London. Using her laptop computer, she writes letters, accesses databases, and creates a spreadsheet. When she reaches London, she has completed a day's work. Donna commented about her way of working: "Before we had today's technology, I would have needed a full-time secretary to do the work I completed while on the flight from Newark to London."

> What challenges might a person face when working during a long flight?

Outlook for Employment of Office Workers

Increased use of computers and new technology will continue to have an effect on many office support jobs. This effect is shown in the modest rate of growth projected to 2018. However, many jobs will be available in this area. Many persons in this group will need to be replaced. Some workers will leave the field to enter new jobs or to retire. For example, about 4.8 million persons are expected to work as secretaries and administrative assistants by 2018. Figure 2-1.3 shows the job projections for selected jobs in this group.

Figure 2-1.3 Employment in Office Support Occupations

SELECTED OFFICE SUPPORT OCCUPATIONS 2008 AND PROJECTED 2018			
	Employment (Numbers in Thousands)		
Occupation	2008	2018	% Change
Secretaries and administrative assistants, total	4,348.1	4,819.7	10.85
Executive secretaries and administrative assistants	1,594.4	1,798.8	12.82
Legal secretaries	262.6	311.0	18.44
Medical secretaries	471.1	596.6	26.64
Secretaries, except legal, medical, and executive	2,020.0	2,113.3	4.62

Source: Employment Projections Program, U.S. Department of Labor, U.S. Bureau of Labor Statistics, http://www.bls.gov/emp/ep_table_106.htm.

 CHECK POINT How many workers are expected to be employed as secretaries or administrative assistants by 2018?

An Overview of Office Competencies

A wide range of activities make up office competencies. However, four major groups of activities based on primary skills reflect the overall nature of office work. These areas are:

- Word processing
- Data processing
- Information management and transmission
- General managing and communicating

You will now become acquainted with each of these areas. Pay attention to the basic skills needed for doing tasks effectively and efficiently.

Word Processing

Word processing is creating written documents, such as letters or reports, by using software programs and computers. Usually these documents are shared in printed form. However, they may also be shared and read online. Some word processing programs allow the user to save documents in HTML format. An example is shown in Figure 2-1.4 on page 40. These documents can be posted and viewed on a company intranet.

Desktop publishing is producing high-quality printed documents that include both text and graphics. It is closely related to word processing and requires many of the same skills. Examples of these documents include newsletters, brochures, and forms. Basic desktop publishing can be done using

word processing creating written documents, such as reports or letters, by using a computer and software

desktop publishing producing high-quality documents that include both text and graphics

Figure 2-1.4 Microsoft Word is a program used to do word processing and basic desktop publishing.

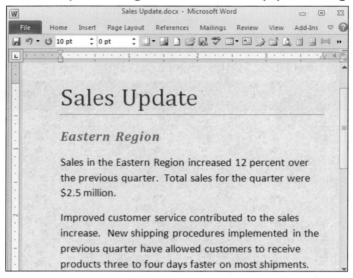

word processing software, such as Microsoft Word. Desktop publishing software programs, such as Adobe® PageMaker®, are used for advanced desktop publishing.

Basic Competencies

The efficient use of a computer in preparing many types of documents is the goal of skill development in this area. The essential skills include:

- Keyboarding with speed and accuracy
- Knowledge and skill in the use of software programs
- Skill in formatting and proofreading documents
- A large vocabulary
- Proficiency with grammar, punctuation, and spelling
- Ability to learn special vocabularies
- Ability to follow instructions
- Skill in preparing copy from audio recordings, if employed as a transcriptionist
- Skill in dictating text and commands if using speech recognition software

proficiency ability to perform at a satisfactory level

Workers Who Need These Competencies

Word processing skills are needed by many workers. Executives in many companies spend much time writing messages. Technical personnel, such as engineers, advertising designers, architects, and public relations specialists, are employees likely to use word processing and basic desktop publishing skills in their work.

Opportunities in Office Support Services

Some office support staff work full-time handling word processing and basic desktop publishing activities. Among the jobs in this category are typist, word processor, and transcriptionist. Such workers prepare drafts as well as final copies of letters, memos, and reports. They may assist one other worker or several workers. Some word processing workers assist an entire department.

Office support workers are considered for promotions to jobs in the same category. These jobs may require more advanced skills. For example, workers who quickly learn new software may be promoted to a supervisory or training job. Workers with good writing skills may become administrative assistants.

 CHECK POINT What skills are needed to handle word processing tasks?

Data Processing

Data processing is collecting, organizing, analyzing, and summarizing data. The data is generally in numeric form. Many jobs require such skills. This type of activity is usually done using spreadsheet or statistical computer programs. You may think of data processing as dealing with numbers and word processing as dealing with text. However, the two processes often blend with one another. The two processes together are often referred to as information processing. Many workers do this type of office activity.

data processing collecting, organizing, analyzing, and summarizing data

Basic Competencies

Among the skills important for workers who handle data processing activities are the following:

- Proficiency with spreadsheet, database, and related software programs
- Knowledge of arithmetic processes and statistical methods
- Ability to be consistently accurate
- Knowledge of methods of organizing and analyzing data
- Ability to interpret data
- Ability to prepare reports that give information in a meaningful way
- Ability to maintain an organized workstation

Workers Who Need These Competencies

Many types of workers in all kinds of organizations deal with data and prepare reports. Examples include accountants, budget analysts, brokers, and insurance salespersons. As new software programs make processing data faster and easier, these workers must learn to use new programs and methods in their work.

Opportunities in Office Support Services

Many workers continue to be employed in the data processing category. They include specialized clerks, such as accounts payable clerk, billing clerk, order clerk, payroll clerk, and shipping clerk. Such clerks prepare and process sales, purchases, invoices, payrolls, and other types of transactions. Their work is vital to the whole organization.

Companies need workers who can oversee automated systems for processing data. Workers who have an aptitude for understanding the total operation and have learned their jobs thoroughly are good candidates for promotions.

 CHECK POINT Give three examples of workers who need data processing skills.

Information Management and Transmission

Information management refers to organizing, maintaining, and accessing data. Transmission refers to sharing information both within and outside the organization.

Basic Competencies

The skills considered basic in this category are varied. They include the ability to:

- Find the information needed
- Maintain or develop an information system
- Give attention to details
- Use established procedures
- Apply knowledge of records management and basic filing rules
- Keyboard proficiently and work with databases
- Meet deadlines and solve problems
- Work with others

Workers Who Need These Skills

A wide range of workers need the skills in this area. Personnel such as buyers, real estate brokers, and property managers must have well-organized information systems. The details they need to make decisions often require them to design their own systems. Often their information must be available to others, too. Following a well-designed system is the key to easy use of information.

Opportunities in Office Support Services

People who find gathering and organizing data interesting will enjoy work in this area. Work in this area involves updating and sharing data promptly. Common jobs in this category include hotel desk clerk, mailroom clerk, records clerk, travel clerk, and communications center operator. Alert beginning employees in such jobs can learn much about the company. Such knowledge is a key to gaining promotions.

Managing electronic records is a vital function for many businesses.

ExaMedia Photography/Shutterstock.com

 CHECK POINT What skills are needed to perform information management tasks?

General Managing and Communicating

General managing and communicating are broad areas. Both involve handling work time and tasks efficiently. They also involve dealing with other employees and customers. Setting up schedules, meeting deadlines, and tracking the progress of tasks are aspects of general managing. Communicating with customers and coworkers is a common activity for many types of workers in a company. Reporting on the progress of projects or budgets is also an aspect of general managing. Often, these reports are given orally. They may be delivered with the use of a multimedia presentation.

Basic Competencies

The skills and knowledge needed to handle the activities in this category are varied. In general, they include the ability to:

- Establish priorities
- Establish schedules and meet deadlines
- Work in teams
- Motivate others to complete work
- Use a computer and manage files
- Handle telephone calls effectively
- Give attention to several tasks at the same time
- Determine the time required for completion of tasks
- Communicate effectively both orally and in writing
- Interact with many types of people at all levels

Workers Who Need These Competencies

General management and communication skills are critical for a wide range of employees. Executives, salespeople, and office support staff are examples of workers who need these skills. Office workers must be good managers of their own time. In addition, they must be skillful in guiding the work of any employees who report to them. They must be able to set priorities and follow schedules to complete tasks. They must communicate clearly and effectively to coworkers and customers.

✳ WORKPLACE CONNECTIONS ✳

Carlos Alvarez is the marketing manager of a packaged goods company. He commented about his work in these words:

Our staff of 10 employees is hard working. I set the pace. We have just developed a database to record far more information about product sales. We have staff members working on various ways to connect with our customers in an interactive way. As I think of our progress, I realize that basic managing skills, including establishing priorities, and communicating clearly what has to be done, are critical.

What type of information about each product sale might the marketing personnel want to know?

Opportunities in Office Support Services

Many office workers have duties found in the general managing and communicating category. The most common jobs include administrative assistant, secretary, customer service clerk, receptionist, and general office assistant.

Some positions in this category require specialized skills. The position of secretary, for example, may require high-level information processing skills. Receptionists must be at ease in meeting and talking with all types of people. General assistants learn to handle the special needs of the offices in which they work. Then they take the initiative in completing tasks in the proper manner.

Effective communication skills are essential for office workers.

Higher-level jobs are available to those who perform their initial tasks with success. There are many jobs in companies for those who have the ability to:

- Complete tasks with little or no supervision
- Use oral and written communication skills effectively
- Meet deadlines
- Organize tasks and work independently
- Evaluate their own performance objectively

CHECK POINT What are examples of management skills?

Your Future Prospects

Your education, including your study of business subjects, provides you with a background of value in many jobs. You can enter some jobs after your high school graduation. Others require further education.

Some openings for high school graduates will continue to be available. Many jobs, however, require skills and knowledge beyond those gained through high school studies. Some companies have on-the-job training to prepare employees for new tasks or new ways of doing their jobs. Business schools and colleges provide degree programs and continuing education programs. Continuing your education will add to your skills for jobs that interest you.

CHECK POINT What types of educational opportunities are available for high school graduates?

Work/Life Balance

The term *work/life balance* is commonly used to describe the need workers have to balance work with other aspects of life. In the last 20 years, the number of women in the workforce has increased significantly. This change has created more families with two working parents. Single-parent families are also on the rise. Many of the activities formerly handled by a nonworking parent must now be handled by a working parent.

When you think about a career, consider how your choice will affect all aspects of your life. Different careers make different demands on workers and their families. Some jobs may require much travel, overtime, or a long commute that will reduce your time for family or taking part in other activities. In many jobs, taking time off to care for a sick child or pursue a personal interest is very difficult.

When employees do not have enough time to take care of their personal matters, they bring stress to the workplace and are less productive. Many companies address this problem by creating a workplace that is supportive of workers' needs. For example, some companies have childcare facilities on-site or help pay for the cost of childcare. Other companies create positions with flexible work hours. Employees in these positions can choose to arrive and leave work earlier or later than the normal working hours to accommodate their schedules.

Another alternative that might be offered is a compressed workweek. Employees might work 10 hours a day for 4 days a week, then take the fifth day off. Some companies allow job sharing. This permits two part-time employees working different shifts to fulfill the duties of one full-time worker. Some companies provide benefits for part-time workers. Telecommuting on a part-time or full-time basis is a helpful option for some employees.

Companies find that employee loyalty increases when the company makes accommodations for workers' personal needs. Employees find that these accommodations contribute to their job satisfaction. When choosing an employer, consider whether the company fits your needs as well as whether you fit the needs of the company.

> Would you want to work a compressed workweek as described above? Why or why not? What type of job might require that you work this type of schedule?

21st Century Skills

Making Decisions

PARTNERSHIP FOR
21ST CENTURY SKILLS

Cleavon is soon to be a high school senior. He needs very few courses in order to graduate at the end of the school year. He has asked you and a couple of other friends to give him your opinions about what he should do about his school program. He has listed on a sheet of paper what he believes are his options. His list has these options, which are not in order of preference:

- Take only the courses required in the mornings. Relax in the afternoon until my friends are free.
- Take some extra courses, such as accounting, business law, or office procedures. Because I think I want to work in the business world or become a lawyer after college, these courses might be helpful.
- Get a part-time job at one of the local fast-food places.
- Really learn all about the new computer at home.

1. With a group of three or four other students, discuss the alternatives Cleavon has outlined. Select the alternative your group believes is best for Cleavon.
2. As a group, write a paragraph or two that identifies the alternative you think Cleavon should choose. Support your choice with reasons and be prepared to share your ideas with the class.

Making Academic Connections

Reinforcing Math Skills

Employees are planning next year's budget for the Accounts Payable Department. A study was done of how the work could be improved and costs reduced. The conclusion was that the office should operate with a supervisor and only two clerks, rather than the four clerks employed in the department last year. State-of-the-art software and equipment was purchased to help two clerks do the work formerly done by four clerks.

	Last Year's Expenses	Proposed Budget
Salaries	$133,000	$96,000
Supplies	4,000	3,800
Repairs and Maintenance	5,000	2,500
Depreciation	3,000	6,000
Telephone	3,500	3,900

1. Calculate the total expenses for the department for last year.
2. Using last year's figures, calculate the percentage of total expenses each of the expense items represents. Round percentages to one decimal place.
3. Calculate the difference in total expenses between last year's figures and the proposed budget.
4. Calculate the percentage decrease in total expenses if the proposed budget is used.

2-1 Activity 1
Employment Projections (Outcome 2-1a)

1. Review the employment projections for major occupational groups shown in Figure 2-1.1.
2. Access the website for the U.S. Bureau of Labor Statistics.
3. Find a table that gives information similar to the one shown in Figure 2-1.1. (The headings may be worded differently, but you should be able to find similar information.)
4. Save the table information in a spreadsheet file. This is typically an option on the website. If it is not an option, cut and paste the table.
5. Sort the data by the *% Change* column from highest to lowest, leaving out the *Total, all occupations* row.
6. Which occupational group is projected to have the highest growth? Which one will have the lowest growth?
7. Look at the projected employment number for the group with the highest growth. What percentage is the number for this group of the total projected jobs number?

2-1 Activity 2
Study an Occupational Field (Outcome 2-1b)

For this activity, choose an occupational field that interests you. Do some research to become acquainted with this field.

1. Use the Internet or the resources at your local library to get information about the occupation. A reference that is likely to be helpful is *The Occupational Outlook Handbook*. Find the following information for the occupation:
   - General responsibilities
   - Employment outlook (increasing or decreasing number of jobs)
   - Educational requirements

2. Interview a person working in this occupational field. In your interview, seek answers to these questions:
   - What are the primary duties of a beginner in this occupation?
   - What do you consider your primary duties?
   - For each primary duty, would you consider education, on-the-job experience, or training the best source of preparation?
   - To what extent do you use a computer in completing your job tasks?
   - What office skills do you find most valuable in your work?
   - What advice would you give a student who is thinking of preparing for a job in this field?

3. Create a report that summarizes the information you gathered. The final paragraph of your report should be your current opinion about the appeal of the occupational field as a career for you.

OUTCOMES

2-2a Explain how an organization's goals influence the expectations for employees.
2-2b Discuss general expectations related to employment competencies.
2-2c Discuss personal qualities and traits related to success on the job.

Goals Influence Expectations for Employees

Companies seek to hire the qualified workers who will help the company be successful. All workers are expected to help achieve company goals. If you were to read a dozen annual reports of major companies, you would find information about company achievements during the past year. You would also read about goals for the future. A primary goal of most businesses is to make a profit. Companies make predictions about level of earnings, new markets, new products, or improved customer service. The goals set by the company affect the work of all employees. Some companies post their goals on their company websites as shown in Figure 2-2.1.

Issues such as quality management, customer satisfaction, and teamwork affect how successful a company is in achieving its goals. These issues must be the concerns of all employees. The company expects all employees to be reliable and cooperative in efforts to increase productivity and meet company goals.

Figure 2-2.1 Company Goals

About Us

Company Goals

The goals of our company are to:

➡ Operate profitably in a manner that is socially, ethically, and environmentally responsible
➡ Meet the needs of our customers with the highest standards of value, quality and service
➡ Further research and development
➡ Promote the company's international presence
➡ Strength our domestic market presence in traditional and e-commerce channels
➡ Attract and retain quality employees by maintaining a rewarding and safe work environment with equal opportunity for promotion and success

© Cengage Learning 2013

Total Quality Management

The primary goal of all businesses is to make profits. In an effort to increase profits, many companies have adopted total quality management (TQM) plans. TQM means establishing and maintaining high standards in how work is done and in the creation and delivery of goods and services. All personnel, from the president to staff in the mailroom, are asked to view their work with an awareness of TQM.

The core idea behind TQM is that managing quality is everyone's business. Quality standards apply throughout the organization. For example, in one company, all office support workers were asked to keep track of the errors in their work. Two common errors were omitting an attachment with a letter and failing to answer the questions of callers. After recording such errors, the next step was to establish a new way of working so the errors would not recur.

In some companies, an executive is assigned to lead the company's efforts to improve quality. This person works with groups of employees to find out what will improve performance or products. Many companies have developed slogans, such as "Quality is everybody's business" or "We want to be the best in all we do," to highlight their quality goals.

Continuous Improvement

Over time, the policies and procedures used by a company may become outdated or inefficient. Companies seek to avoid this problem by applying the concept of continuous improvement. Continuous improvement means being alert at all times to ways of working more productively. This concept overlaps the principles of TQM. All employees are encouraged to take part in continuous improvement efforts.

Because of new technology, companies are finding that many aspects of their work require changes. Continuous improvement begins with looking at the work that is done and how it is being done. Improvements are often possible. The attitude reflected in the question "Could this be done in a better way?" helps workers think creatively about improvements.

Customer Satisfaction

"We are here to serve customers" is a message that many companies send to employees. Thinking through what you do in relation to what it will mean to customers is a key focus in many companies. TQM principles can be applied

total quality management establishing and maintaining high standards in how work is done

continuous improvement being alert at all times to ways of working more productively

Wavebreakmedia Ltd/Wavebreak Media (RF)/Jupiter Images

Many companies provide a telephone number that customers can call with questions about products or services.

to solving problems or improving operations that will increase customer satisfaction.

Companies often conduct surveys to see if they are delivering the value expected by customers. They study the results of such surveys and then make changes to improve customer satisfaction.

 CHECK POINT What is the core idea behind the total quality management concept?

WORKPLACE CONNECTIONS

The staff of a company is involved in a variety of ways in meeting the goal of customer satisfaction. One beginning worker, Kim Park, described his experiences in these words:

I serve as an assistant in our customer hotline office, which is open seven days a week, 24 hours a day. Among the team are members who speak English, Spanish, French, Chinese, and Japanese. Together, we are able to provide customers around the world with information about our products. We can quickly put a customer in touch with a technical person if additional assistance is needed.

Have you called a customer hotline for information? Were you satisfied with the service you received? Why or why not?

Ethical Standards

ethics moral standards or values reflected in behavior

Ethics are moral standards or values reflected in your behavior. Ethical standards require honesty, fairness, and justice in all business dealings. These qualities provide a foundation of trust. Company leaders should make clear their attitude toward standards of ethical behavior. Companies want to be considered trustworthy by their employees, their customers, the companies with which they deal, and the public.

Companies have developed standards of conduct for their employees, called codes of ethics or codes of conduct. Such codes are shared with all workers. Employees are generally informed about the code of conduct when they first join the organization.

From time to time, employees are called together to discuss what the code means in relation to specific behavior and actions. For example, all staff involved with purchasing may attend a meeting dealing with a new conflict of interest statement. Employees deal with many vendors who are eager to sell their products. The new statement makes clear that no employee is to accept gifts of any value from any vendor. Figure 2-2.2 shows a portion of a company's confidentiality policy that has been posted on the company intranet. This policy is part of the company's code of conduct.

Companies also have procedures for handling violations of ethical standards. Employees found guilty of violating the code of ethics may be subject to disciplinary action or dismissal.

Figure 2-2.2 A confidentiality policy is part of a company's code of ethics.

Employee Handbook

Confidentiality Policy

During the course of your employment, you will handle information sensitive to our company, partner companies, and clients. All information in both written and verbal form with which you come in contact in the scope of your duties is confidential. Please respect this trust that our partners and clients have given us. Confidentiality is critical. Communication of confidential matters may be grounds for corrective action or dismissal from the company.

© Cengage Learning 2013

CHECK POINT How does a company's code of ethics relate to the service it gives customers?

Responsible Teamwork

Some people work alone at the company's offices or at home. Frequently, however, employees must work in teams to complete tasks. Teamwork involves combining the efforts of two or more people to accomplish a task or achieve a goal. For a team to work effectively, each team member must understand the purpose or goals of the team. Each member of the team must accept responsibility for completing his or her duties and communicate clearly with other team members. For remote teams, in which team members may be located around the world rather than down the hall, communication is especially important.

Team members often are not from a single department. For example, customer collections were a problem in a relatively small company that makes shoes. The controller realized that those involved worked in the order entry, shipping, and billing departments. A team of several members of these departments was assigned the task of reviewing the policies and procedures involved. Through teamwork, the group recommended a new policy and related procedures. Soon thereafter, the problem was resolved to everyone's satisfaction.

CHECK POINT Why is effective teamwork considered so important in organizations?

Diversity in the Global Marketplace

The area in which a company does business is called its marketplace. In the past, many U.S. companies operated only within the United States. This is called the domestic marketplace. Many U.S. companies now have employees and customers in countries around the world. Some companies have moved into the global marketplace using only traditional sales methods, such as retail stores. Other companies have expanded using e-commerce. These companies sell goods and services online using the World Wide Web.

Moving into the global marketplace affects how companies do business. Employees must travel to other countries. Company personnel who live in other countries may visit the United States. Employee and customer groups are diverse. Diversity is the quality or state of having differences or variety. This term is often used to describe people from a wide range of ethnic and cultural backgrounds.

All company personnel must be sensitive to variations in cultures. Messages used for websites, advertising materials, and product instructions must

be available in many languages. Employees must communicate clearly with people of other nations. They must take into account varying time zones. They must find sources for information about travel and places for travelers to stay and work in other countries. Employees are expected to respect co-workers and customers

Having a diverse workforce can help companies serve a diverse group of customers.

from all backgrounds. In some companies, training programs help employees become aware of issues related to diversity.

General Expectations for Employees

A company expects the same basic work qualities in all employees. The way these qualities are shown will depend on the nature of the employee's work. Employers expect workers to be reliable and to cooperate with others in achieving company goals. They also expect them to be productive and to continue to learn the new skills and knowledge needed to be effective in their jobs.

Reliability

Reliable means dependable and trustworthy. Employers rely on employees to report to work on time. Employees are expected to devote their time on the job to completing their work. Companies expect employees to keep company business confidential and to protect the assets of the company.

Most office employees work with others daily. Information must be shared, and tasks often require more than a single worker. Being cooperative is an important quality for all employees. Employees must be prepared to learn new skills and handle new tasks as circumstances change. Most office workers have job descriptions, but seldom do such descriptions fully describe everything the employee will do on the job.

 CHECK POINT Are employees who believe they need to do only what is outlined in their job descriptions effective workers? Why or why not?

✳ WORKPLACE CONNECTIONS ✳

Alice Palmer, a manager in a real estate office, comments on employee reliability:

Employees who have to be watched every minute in order to keep them doing what they should do are worthless to us. We must have reliable employees. One of the most common reasons for dismissal is unreliability. For example, several times a new employee, Elena, failed to be at the office at eight o'clock on the mornings she was scheduled to open the office. The office was unattended. She didn't call to explain her lateness; she just arrived two hours later. This pattern continued in spite of several warnings. At that point, we had to dismiss her. We cannot run our office effectively without reliable employees.

How could unreliable behavior by employees affect a company's ability to achieve its goals?

Productivity

Productivity is a measure of the amount of quality work done in a certain amount of time. Employers expect workers to produce a reasonable amount of work. Often specific standards for a day's work are not practical. Managers, however, have some level of output that they believe is reasonable for an employee. Following a schedule that ensures you will complete the amount of work expected of you is important.

Valuable workers are aware of what they are accomplishing each day. They are able to evaluate their own work and make changes as needed. Some managers discuss productivity with their workers in informal ways from time to time. Other managers expect workers to decide on their own what changes are needed to improve productivity.

Workers should be careful to avoid these barriers to productivity:

■ Talking with friends on the telephone during working hours
■ Chatting with coworkers for long periods of time
■ Failing to keep an organized workstation
■ Failing to set priorities
■ Moving from task to task before completing any one task

> **productivity** a measure of the amount of quality work done in a certain amount of time

 CHECK POINT Think about the work you do for your school classes. Are there times or places when/where you are more productive than others? Explain.

Independence in Learning

As you may already realize, all you need to know to be an employee will not be learned while you are a student. Companies expect their employees to continue to learn. Learning must be a lifelong activity. Professional workers, such as lawyers, doctors, and accountants, for example, must have continuing education each year. As an office professional, you may need to learn to use new computer programs or follow new procedures to complete your work tasks. There may be other skills or knowledge specific to your job that you will need to learn.

Some continuing education may be in formal programs. Much learning, however, is self-directed. Workers can learn much from what they observe at work. Many companies have resources such as databases and libraries that are available to employees.

Reading current articles is one way an employee can continue to learn. Magazines, journals, and websites contain many articles and reports related to work. Many industries have associations that seek to provide current information to members. Many associations have yearly conferences or seminars that members can attend. Current trends, new equipment or methods, and issues of concern are discussed at these meetings.

 CHECK POINT What types of information, such as news reports or weather forecasts, do you regularly find online?

TECHNOLOGY CONNECTION

Many people see the value in continuing their education, either in an informal or a formal way. As mentioned in this chapter, reading articles in magazines and journals is a good way to learn about current trends or new methods related to your work. A great deal of information can also be found online. Websites for professional associations, online journals, and blogs are sources of career-related information. Online seminars are offered by professional groups and by some companies. For example, a software company might offer a seminar on ways using the software can increase your productivity. Some software companies also offer online tutorials for using the software. You can use these sources to continue your education in an informal and inexpensive way.

For more formal or structured learning, you can take courses online. Many colleges offer online courses. These courses typically last for one quarter or semester, just as courses do that are taken on campus. For some classes, you may need to attend a few class sessions on campus in addition to completing classes online. Some courses require only online work. This setup allows you to take classes from a college that is far away without having to travel to the campus. If you take classes from a few different schools, be sure the credits will transfer if you are working toward a degree.

Why might you want to pay to take online college courses rather than simply reading articles and other information that is free to access?

Many students take college courses online.

Developing Competencies

You are a student. What you have experienced as a student is of great value to you whatever career you choose. Your education has been focused on developing critical basic competencies. Those basics included skills for reading, writing, arithmetic, speaking, and listening. You have probably also studied math, literature, history, social studies, physical sciences, languages, and other subjects. In additions to these basic competencies, you can develop general and specific competencies for becoming an effective worker.

As a student, you are evaluated when you submit assignments and take tests. You have some idea of what you are able to do and what you would like to learn. Consider the competencies you have now. Think about the employment skills discussed earlier in this chapter. What skills and understandings do you have today that would be of value to an employer? What new skills do you want to learn? What skills do you want to improve? Set goals for improving or developing new competencies. You will develop many competencies as you study and complete the activities in this textbook. Your other classes and activities will also allow you to build your skills and knowledge.

 CHECK POINT What is one employment competency that you want to acquire as you complete this course?

Personal Qualities

For most people, working involves interacting with other people. Even those who work at home interact with others. The behavior of each person in a group influences how effectively the group will work together.

Each individual is unique. The combination of traits that distinguishes one person from another is called **personality**. Your personal traits influence how

personality the combination of traits that distinguishes one person from another

you think, what you say, and how you respond to the demands in your daily life. What is remarkable about your personality is that, to a far greater extent than many realize, you have control of who you are and what you believe. This means that you can make changes in your personality.

Character

character basic values and principles that are reflected in a person's behavior

The basic values and principles that are reflected in a person's behavior are referred to as **character**. Your parents, relatives, friends, or teachers have probably talked with you about issues such as character and ethics. This discussion, therefore, is not a new topic for you. You may want to use this opportunity, though, to review or reconsider some basic concepts related to character.

integrity honesty and trustworthiness

At the core of your character is what you believe about **integrity**. Honesty and trustworthiness are synonyms for integrity. Individuals with integrity are valuable at work because they can be trusted to use the resources of the company only for company purposes.

 CHECK POINT What would happen in a company if many people acted dishonestly?

Self-Acceptance

At the core of your personality is your attitude toward yourself. Experts in the field of mental health stress the value of accepting yourself. Many believe that you cannot change your personality without self-acceptance, which requires a realistic and honest view of who you are. To help bring about changes in areas of your personality:

- Be honest with yourself. Do not deceive yourself about your behavior and beliefs. Identify your weaknesses and your strengths.
- Understand that you are a unique individual. You share many of the same wants, needs, and fears of others. Remember that although others may not appear to have the same problems you face, they usually have problems of their own.
- Believe in your own worth, while respecting the uniqueness of others. Regardless of your failings, you are worthy. Every human being is. Self-acceptance means that you are willing to accept your faults but still have a feeling of confidence and a sense of security. For example, you can accept constructive criticism.

 CHECK POINT How might showing a lack of self-confidence at work affect how others treat you?

Maturity

A person in our society is expected to behave in a mature way by the end of adolescence. Of course, many young people show maturity earlier. A mature person has the emotional and mental qualities that are considered normal for a socially adjusted adult. To be mature means that you see beyond the moment

NotarYES/Shutterstock.com

A mature person accepts and learns from constructive criticism.

and understand the consequences of your choices. A mature person considers the rights of others and makes decisions based on such understanding.

You are mature when you are willing to:

- Accept criticism or disappointment tactfully
- Acknowledge that you do not know or understand something
- Admit that you made a mistake
- Learn from your mistakes
- Be considerate of others
- Demonstrate respect for the differences of individuals
- Be objective and honest in your relationships with others
- Value the worth of every person, and do not act superior to another person

A mature person can identify weaknesses and plan to overcome them. Think about your personality and the traits you have that will make you a valuable employee. Are you honest, reliable, and cooperative? Do you work well with others in teams? Do you try to learn new ways to complete tasks that will make you more productive?

Identify traits that you would like to improve or develop that will make you a more valuable employee. Create a plan for ways to develop or improve these traits. For example, suppose you need to improve your teamwork skills. Join a club, sports team, or other group that will give you opportunities to work in a team. Read books or articles about teamwork. Ask your teacher, coach, or friends to give you feedback on how you relate to others in team situations. Evaluate your progress from time to time and continue to try to improve until you reach your goal.

 CHECK POINT What is one personality trait that you would like to change or improve?

21st Century Skills

Interacting with Others

PARTNERSHIP FOR
21ST CENTURY SKILLS

Tanya, a manager in an advertising agency, called a meeting for three members of the staff—Jill, Chin, and Delores. Tanya explained that she had just received an exciting offer to submit a proposal for a new account. Tanya told them the project will require an intensive period of work. The proposal must be submitted within two weeks.

The project is complex. Tanya believes, though, that the three of them can do the job. They will be given some help from the department secretary. They must research the types of advertising campaigns used in the industry. They must also gain information about what the client's goals are and its present image in the marketplace. After they have gathered this information, they must develop what they believe are promising campaigns. Tanya told them that they can decide among themselves how to divide the work.

Jill, Chin, and Delores met immediately after leaving the supervisor's desk. Jill said, "Look, I feel rather tired and I just don't want to start work on this right away. Could I just beg off the research? Then I'll be happy to help you develop some plans for a campaign. I think I'm better in the creative part of such a project. I know that there will have to be many overtime hours during this first week of work. I just do not want to change my plans."

1. In a group with two or three other students, discuss what you would say to Jill if you were Chin or Delores.
2. Prepare notes on your response for use in a class discussion.

Making Academic Connections

Reinforcing English Skills

Companies have many different types of policies. These policies are often included in an employee handbook.

1. Open the data file 2-2 English Skills, which contains a workplace monitoring policy. Read the document. Correct errors in spelling, punctuation, and word usage.
2. Ask a classmate to review your work while you review his or her work. Make corrections based on the feedback you receive, if needed.

2-2 Activity 1

Checklist for Evaluating Team Projects (Outcome 2-2a)

As you have learned, the ability to work effectively in a team is a valued job competency. For this activity, work in a group with three or four students to develop a checklist for evaluating team project participation.

1. Search the Internet or other reference sources to find at least two articles about effective teamwork. Make a list of the main points of each article and share this list with the group.
2. As a group, prepare a list of factors to be included on an evaluation checklist. For example, one factor might be: Completed work on time.

3. Decide on a system to use in rating how well a student does on each factor on your list. (Hint: Should there be A, B, C grading? or 1, 2, 3, 4, 5? or Excellent, Good, Poor?)

4. Prepare a final copy of the checklist with the factors and rating scale. Use an appropriate title and format the document so it will be easy to read and use.

5. Participate in a class discussion and share the factors your team used on the checklist.

2-2 Activity 2

Professional Reading File (Outcome 2-2b)

Develop a file to record the source of newspaper, magazine, or online articles that will help you increase your knowledge of office work and related issues. Many articles that are published in hard copy newspapers and magazines can also be found online. Use your favorite search engine to look for articles online. Many major newspapers also have online sites where you can find some of their articles.

1. Create a file to store information about articles for professional development. This file can be in a word processing, database, or spreadsheet program. Name the file Reading File.

2. Create a table or other setup to store information. Include the following information for each article: title, subject, author, publication or website name, date, and web address for online materials. Also record your brief notes about the article.

3. Begin your reading file by finding one article related to any topic in Chapter 2. Read the article and enter the data for this article in your reading file.

4. Ask three classmates to share the data for the articles they have located. Enter data for the three articles in your reading file.

5. As you study each remaining chapter in this textbook, find at least one article related to topics studied in the chapter. Read the article and update your file.

Summary

2-1 Employment Outlook

- The U.S. Department of Labor does research to predict the need for workers in the future. The overall projected rate of increase in U.S. jobs to 2018 is 10.12 percent.

- Far more workers are doing office tasks than in the past. New technology is responsible for the shift.

- A modest rate of growth is projected for office support jobs in the United States to 2018. However, many jobs will be available in this area.

- Word processing skills are needed by many workers. Basic desktop publishing skills are included in this skill area.

- Data processing is collecting, organizing, and analyzing data. Many jobs require such skills.

- Information management and transmission skills are needed by a wide range of workers.

- General management and communication skills are critical for a wide range of employees, such as executives and office support staff.

- Many jobs require skills and knowledge beyond those gained through high school studies.

2-2 Employment Competencies

- Companies seek to hire the qualified workers who will help achieve company goals.

- Issues such as quality management, customer satisfaction, and teamwork affect how successful a company is in achieving its goals. These issues must be the concerns of all employees.

- Companies expect their employees to follow the company's code of ethics. Employees found guilty of violating the code of ethics may be subject to disciplinary action or dismissal.

- Many U.S. companies have employees and customers in countries around the world. All company personnel must be sensitive to the variations in cultures among a diverse group of customers and company employees.

- Employers expect workers to be reliable and to cooperate with others in achieving company goals. They also expect them to be productive and to continue to learn new skills and knowledge.

- Character, self-acceptance, and maturity are personality traits that relate to work behavior.

- Students should set goals for improving or developing competencies and improving personality traits that lead to success on the job.

Chapter 2 Activity 1

Unethical Behavior in Business
(Outcomes 2-2a, 2-2c)

Companies expect employees to behave in an ethical manner. The public expects companies to behave in an ethical manner. When ethics are disregarded, the company or the public often suffers. In this activity, you will do research to find examples of unethical behavior in business.

1. Search the Internet or other resources. Find an article that describes unethical behavior by a company or a person in business. Copy or print the article, if possible. Take notes of the important facts and points made in the article. Record complete source information for the article.

2. Write a short report using your research. Begin by explaining what is meant by ethical behavior. Then describe the unethical behavior from the article you found. Explain what happened to the company or the public as a result of the unethical behavior. Add your personal comments regarding the incident. Include the reference information for the article at the end of your report.

3. Format the report in an appropriate style. Proofread and correct all errors before printing the report.

Chapter 2 Activity 2

Employment Competencies and Traits
(Outcomes 2-1b, 2-2b, 2-2c)

1. Identify two specific competencies that would be required for an employee in a job that interests you. These should be skills you currently do not have or to need to improve. After each competency, write a statement that describes how you will learn or improve the skills.

2. Identify two expectations of employees, such as reliability, cooperativeness, or others listed in this chapter. For each one, write a sentence or two that describes how you have demonstrated this trait in the past.

3. Identify one or more personality traits that you want to acquire or improve. For each one, explain what you will do in an effort to acquire or improve that trait.

Fundamental Word Processing Skills Event

The purpose of the event is to evaluate skills in word processing and document production. The event covers knowledge and application of software functions, document formats, tables, graphics, proofreading, and editing. This event is in the administrative support assessment area.

After a few minutes for orientation, you will have one hour to complete a production test using Microsoft Office software. You are allowed to bring reference materials, such as a dictionary.

Performance Indicators Evaluated

The fundamental word processing skills event is in the administrative support assessment area. Sample performance indicators include the ability to:

- Apply intermediate-level keyboarding and word processing skills to produce business documents
- Demonstrate basic knowledge of word processing software functions, including formatting and keying text in columns
- Create and format tables; format and key letters, memos, news releases, agendas, and reports
- Insert graphics and special characters in documents
- Use paragraph formatting, tab settings, and text enhancements
- Proofread using edited copy
- Use electronic and hard copy references to assist in preparing documents

These performance indicators are from the Business Professionals of America guidelines as shown on their website. For more detailed information about this event, go to the BPA website.[1]

http://www.bpa.org

Think Critically

1. What are some jobs in which employees need fundamental word processing skills?
2. Which of the skills listed in the performance indicators do you have? Which ones would you like to learn or improve?

---

[1]"Business Professionals of America, Workplace Skills Assessment Program, Secondary 2011" (Business Professionals of America, 2011), http://www.bpa.org/download.aspx?dl=2011_WSAP_SECONDARY.pdf.

Manufacturing

The United States ranks high among nations that manufacture goods. Are you good at assembling parts and creating items? Do you like to design new ways to create things? Perhaps you are interested in repairing items or making sure they meet certain specifications. If so, a career in manufacturing might be right for you. Some workers in this field assemble parts or complete products, design ways to make things, assure quality in products, or maintain or repair products. Other workers are concerned with health, safety, and environmental issues related to making products. Still others work with inventory and movement of parts and products.

Jobs in manufacturing are found in many industries. Large items, such as airplanes and cars, to small items, such as jewelry and circuit boards, and many items in between all require manufacturing.

Employment Outlook

There are many jobs in the various areas of manufacturing. Many individuals are employees of a company. Others are entrepreneurs, running their own small businesses that produce products. The U.S. government provides job projections for 2008-2018. Jobs in this career area are expected to increase slightly over the next few years.[2]

Job Titles

- Assembler
- Machine operator
- Tool and die maker
- Design engineer
- Security system installer
- Quality inspector
- Traffic manager
- Health and safety coordinator

[2]*Occupational Outlook Handbook*, 2010–11 Edition, Bureau of Labor Statistics, U.S. Department of Labor, http://www.bls.gov/oco/ocos225.htm.

Needed Education/Skills

The education and skills needed in manufacturing jobs vary widely. They depend on the area of work. Product assemblers need different skills than traffic managers. For a product assembler or machine operator, a high school diploma and job-specific training may be all that are required. A certificate from a training program or a college degree and related work experience are often required for more specialized jobs. For example, a tool and die maker may need four or more years of education and apprentice training to prepare for this career.

What's it like to work in... Manufacturing?

Marcus works as a tool and die maker in a manufacturing company. Tool and die makers create and repair tools, dies, and holding devices. These items are used with machines to make many types of products. Marcus uses different types of machine tools and precise measuring instruments in his work. He must take into account the hardness and heat tolerance of the materials he uses to make items. He must also know how to operate various machines with great skill, read blueprints, and do complex math. He uses a computer-aided design program to design plans for some items. Much of Marcus's work is done in a tool room designed for this purpose. He wears protective gear, such as earplugs and safety glasses, during some operations.

When the company needs a new tool or part, Marcus works with an engineer to design and construct a prototype. Then he tests the prototype to see if it works as intended. In addition to making new tools and dies, Marcus often repairs items that have become worn or damaged through use. This work is sometimes done on the factory floor and helps keep operations running smoothly.

What About You?

Do you know someone who has a job in manufacturing? What does this person like or dislike about the job? What area of manufacturing seems most interesting to you?

Managing Information to Enhance Productivity

3-1 Information Management and Technology

3-2 Information Systems and Resources

scyther5/Shutterstock

To prosper and grow, an organization must make sound business decisions. To do this accurately, up-to-date information is needed. Information is simply facts that are organized in a meaningful and usable form. Information is a vital resource. It helps an organization serve its customers and operate smoothly.

As an office worker, you will deal with information daily. Understanding how it relates to the total organization can help you be more productive. As you study this chapter, you will learn about common information systems. You will also learn how technology can enhance information systems.

Wire_man/Shutterstock.com

OUTCOMES

3-1a Explain how businesses manage and use information.
3-1b Describe information technologies.
3-1c Describe networks and security measures for information systems.

Managing Information

Businesses use many resources in their daily operations. Raw materials, equipment, and employees are examples of these resources. One of the most important resources used in all businesses is information. It affects how other resources are used and the overall success of the business. Most of the work performed in offices involves processing, using, or managing information.

Processing Information

Information processing is putting facts or numbers into a meaningful and useful form. Basic facts made up of numbers, symbols, and letters are called raw data. This raw data becomes information when organized in a meaningful way. Consider these examples:

information processing putting facts or numbers into a meaningful and useful form

- A payroll manager prepares weekly payroll checks and a payroll register. Payroll tax reports are also prepared. The raw data used include hours worked, rates of pay, and payroll deductions.

- An office worker in a shipping department answers a customer's inquiry about a shipping date. The basic facts used are the customer's name, the invoice number, and the shipping date. Locating the specific invoice gives the office worker the information to answer the customer's question.

- A sales associate in a real estate office prepares for a business trip. The basic facts used are travel dates, destinations, flight numbers, and times. When the facts are arranged into a meaningful form, an itinerary is created.

Common forms of data include numbers, text, image, and voice. Examples of these data are identified in Figure 3-1.1. These individual forms of data are often used together.

Figure 3-1.1 **Common Forms of Data**

DATA TYPE	INFORMATION
Numbers	Amounts, quantities, sizes, weights, capacities, or ages organized to convey meaning, as in a table or list
Text	Words organized to convey meaning, as in letters or reports
Images	Charts, graphs, or photos
Voice	Messages conveyed in person or by telephone

© Cengage Learning 2013

Five types of activities or operations are typically involved in information processing. They include input, processing, output, distribution, and storage. These operations are summarized in Figure 3-1.2.

Figure 3-1.2 Information Processing

OPERATION	EXAMPLE
Input: Entering data into the information system	• Taking orders by phone and keying them into an order entry system to generate shipment and billing for the order • Entering data about a new employee to activate payroll and benefits • Writing product features and benefits for an advertising brochure
Processing: Handling data to create meaningful information	• Formatting and arranging text and graphics to create a newsletter • Generating a report from a database • Calculating and sorting data in a spreadsheet
Output: Retrieving information from the system	• Viewing a list of out-of-stock items from an inventory database • Printing labels and brochures for a customer mailing
Distribution: Sending information to the appropriate people	• Faxing product updates to sales representatives • Mailing price quotes to customers • Sending a report to a coworker as an e-mail attachment • Posting a survey on the company website
Storage: Saving information for future use	• Filing paper documents • Saving computer files

© Cengage Learning 2013

As you perform your duties, you will often proceed directly through all the operations. For example, you may enter numbers into a spreadsheet program, perform calculations, and create a chart. Next you may print 10 copies of the chart and distribute them to members of your department. Finally, you may store the file and printed copy. At other times, you may complete only some of the operations. For example, you may receive a request from a coworker for another chart using some of the figures in the spreadsheet. You can proceed to the processing operation because the data has been input earlier. Information can be stored and retrieved at any point.

 CHECK POINT Which phase of information processing involves sending information to the appropriate people?

Using and Managing Information

Many businesses gather data to use in making business decisions. Information enables businesses to answer some of their most important questions. Consider the questions listed in Figure 3-1.3. The decisions that may be affected by the information needed are also shown.

Figure 3-1.3 Using Information to Make Decisions

INFORMATION NEEDED	DECISIONS AFFECTED
What do our customers think of us?	Image to be built or points stressed through advertising
	Improvements to product quality or customer service
Who are our best customers and where are they located?	Placement of new branch locations
	Warehousing of goods to be shipped
	Areas or websites targeted for advertising
What are our best-selling products? Why are these products successful?	Products to keep and products to discontinue
	Changes for less successful products to make them more popular
Who are our best dealers? What are our most productive sales channels?	Reward plans for dealers
	Strategies for improving sales in other channels—retail stores, catalog sales, websites
Who are our biggest competitors? What do they offer customers that we do not?	Points stressed through advertising
	Improvements to product quality, product features, customer service

© Cengage Learning 2013

sales channels methods of marketing products, such as through retail stores or online

Complexity of Business

A company may process a large number of transactions each day. A transaction might be a business agreement, an exchange of data, or a sale. Operating even a small business can be quite complex. In a very small business, the owner may take care of all office activities. In many small companies, a few office workers handle all the daily work. Typically, all the information needed to operate the business is in one location, usually the business office. For a small business, good organization of information is important for success.

Well-organized information is even more important in large companies with many employees. Several workers may need to use the same information to process work or make decisions. Effective organization of information will help workers in all areas of the company be more productive.

Volume of Transactions

Some companies must deal with thousands of transactions each day. Effective management of information allows these companies to run smoothly. Consider the following examples:

- Banks process thousands of checks each day. They receive thousands of deposits and pay out thousands of dollars in cash each day.

- Manufacturing companies complete the production of thousands of products each day. They ship thousands of orders and receive payments from thousands of customers each day.
- Insurance companies receive thousands of payments each day. They issue new policies and send out notices to thousands of customers each day.

Think of the problems that would occur if these companies did not manage information effectively. The volume of transactions would be overwhelming. The access and retrieval of information would be slow and tedious.

Current and Accurate Information

For information to be valuable, it must be current and accurate. Outdated or incorrect information can be useless. Even worse, outdated information can cost a company money because poor decisions are made based on the incorrect information. Coworkers and customers expect to receive information quickly. They expect it to be accurate and up to date.

With the growth of e-commerce (buying and selling online), customers expect more current information. For example, a customer can buy from a traditional catalog. The customer completes an order form and mails it to the company. The customer does not know whether the item ordered is in stock or when the item will be shipped. For customers buying online, the website often indicates whether an item is in stock. It may also show when the item will be shipped. Many e-commerce sites provide order tracking. A customer can see the progress the order is making on the way to its destination.

Consider the value of current and accurate information in the following example. Airlines can provide a network of service because current data is available. Travelers can request a flight between two cities anywhere in the world. They can learn the number of seats available on the flight. Customers making reservations are not willing to wait days for a response.

 CHECK POINT Why is it important for businesses to use current and accurate information?

Customers who buy online expect to see current and accurate data.

nyul/iStockphoto.com

Obstacles to Managing Information

Information can help a company operate effectively. Yet, information can be difficult to manage. Data can be hard to organize and easy to lose or alter. It can be hard to locate and even incorrect. Obstacles to using information efficiently in an organization include:

- Uncoordinated procedures and files
- Duplication of information
- Incompatible databases (ones that are unable to work together)
- Outdated or inaccurate information
- Missing information
- Limited access to information

Office workers are often the employees best able to overcome these obstacles. Office workers gather or process information. An office worker is often the person who first recognizes that databases are incorrect or that critical information is missing.

Office workers should follow the company's procedures for reporting difficulties with using the company's data or software. If no procedures exist, a manager should be told about the problem. Include a description of the problem in your report. If a company can move quickly to correct problems with its information resources, the negative effects of these problems can be reduced.

 CHECK POINT As an office worker, what should you do if you have problems accessing data or think data is incorrect?

✳ WORKPLACE CONNECTIONS ✳

Using incompatible databases can make sharing data difficult. It may also increase errors. Gloria Santana works in customer service for small company. She handles calls about the status of customer orders. She also answers product questions or complaints. Before answering questions, Gloria must verify that the product was purchased from her company and when. That data is entered by an employee in another department when the product is sold. Data related to product complaints or questions is stored in a different database. The two databases are not compatible. Gloria must also enter the customer's name, product, and purchase date when the customer calls with a question or complaint.

How does having incompatible databases decrease Gloria's productivity?

Information Technologies

Information technology refers to both equipment and software. Together, they allow a user to create, store, and retrieve information. The information technology found in businesses varies. The telephone is the most common piece of equipment found in almost all offices. Photocopiers and computers are almost as common. Other technologies used in offices are described in the following list.

- Computers connected to networks, the Internet, and online services provide access to a wide range of resources.
- **Electronic imaging** of documents reduces paper files and needed storage space.
- Electronic mail and live video increase the flow of information and speed of responses.
- **Interactive voice response** systems allow access to data around the clock.
- Interactive reference media make retrieval of data quick and easy.
- Multimedia programs enhance training effectiveness. Figure 3-1.4 shows an example of a multimedia training program.

Businesses must handle large amounts of information in short time spans. To be successful, they must respond quickly to customer needs and wants. Effective use of information and technologies helps businesses meet these challenges.

electronic imaging converting paper documents to pictures that are stored and displayed by computer

interactive voice response a recorded message accessed and directed by the user to get or record information

Figure 3-1.4 **Many companies provide online training seminars.**

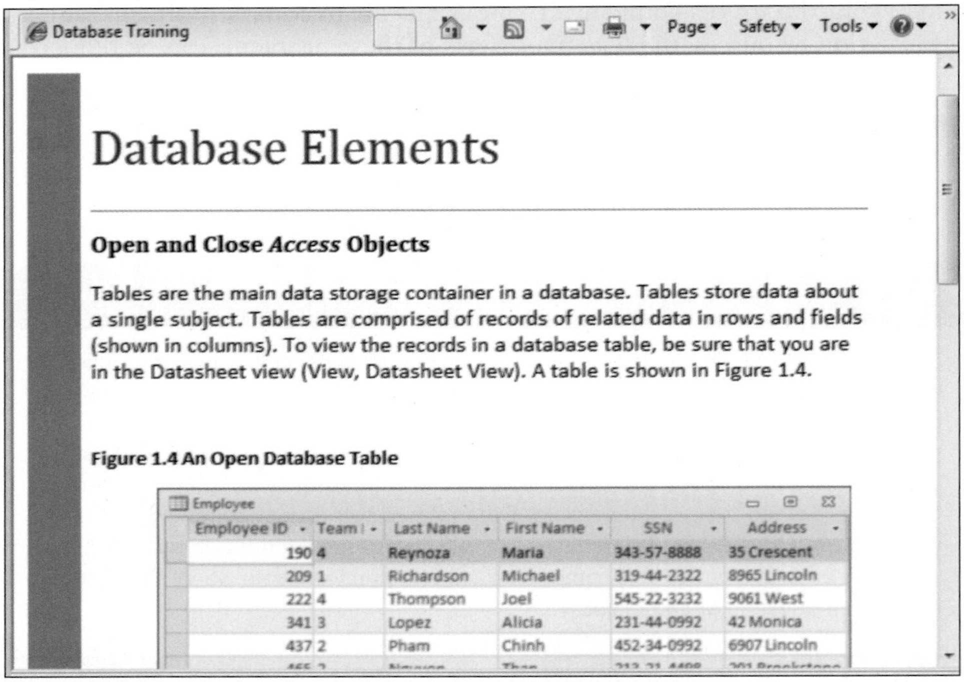

Hardware

Hardware refers to the physical parts of a computer or related equipment. Although we often speak of the "the computer," many types exist. Computers can be classified by their size, speed, and processing capabilities. The needs of an organization will determine the type of computers used.

hardware the physical parts of a computer or related equipment

Types of Computers

Mainframe computers are large, multipurpose machines. They have very high processing speeds. Mainframes can handle many users at once and process very large quantities of data. *Midrange* is another name used for powerful computers that can support a large number of users. These computers are typically used by large businesses and other organizations. E-commerce transactions for large companies are often handled by such computers.

A notebook computer is a type of microcomputer.

Microcomputers, also called personal computers, are the small, desktop variety. The system is made up of several parts such as the central processing unit, a keyboard, mouse, and monitor. A camera, microphone, and speakers are often part of the system. Microcomputers are used by people at all levels of a company.

Notebook (laptop) and tablet computers are other forms of microcomputers. These computers can be battery powered. They are especially helpful to employees who must work on the road or at locations where desktop systems are not practical. Notebook computers that are smaller than standard size are sometimes called mini computers.

A personal digital assistant (PDA) is a handheld computer, small enough to hold easily in one hand. These devices are also called *palmtops*. A PDA has a touch screen for entering data and giving commands. Some PDAs also have a very small physical keyboard. PDAs allow users to complete many of the same tasks and use some of the same programs as notebook computers. Some devices combine the features of a PDA with wireless telephone features. These devices are commonly called *smartphones*. As the processing power and storage space for PDAs continue to grow, they will become eve 82n more useful.

A PDA is a handheld microcomputer.

Input and Output Devices

Business transactions often involve handwritten, keyed, or printed data. Before being processed, however, the data must be entered into the computer system. Workers use input devices to enter data into computers. An input device is hardware that allows the computer to accept the data for processing. Common input devices that you probably use regularly include the keyboard and mouse. Other input devices include touch screens, digital pens, digital tablets, and scanners. Touch screens and digital pens are used to give commands, draw, or write input directly on a screen or digital tablet. Scanners are used to input text, graphics, and photos by "reading" printed documents. Speech recognition is also a form of input.

A computer system typically has at least one output device. An output device prints, displays, speaks, or records information from the computer. The most common output devices are monitors or screens and printers. Other output forms include speakers, disks, USB flash drives, tape drives, and microfilm.

Storage Devices

The amount of internal storage in a computer is limited. Additional external storage is often needed to store data. Storage devices such as optical disks (CDs, DVDs), USB flash drives, and magnetic tapes allow large volumes of data to be stored and retrieved easily. Storage media are described in more detail in Chapter 11.

Oleg Golovnev/Shutterstock.com

A USB flash drive is an example of an external storage device.

 CHECK POINT What are three types of microcomputers?

Software

Software is a program that gives instructions to a computer. Thousands of programs are available. Figure 3-1.5 lists common types of software you are likely to find in an office. Three broad categories of software are discussed below.

Operating system software controls the basic operations of the computer. It allows the computer to communicate with devices connected to it, such as a printer. Microsoft Windows is an example of popular operating system software.

Application software directs the computer to carry out specific tasks. The program may perform a single task, such as word processing, or it may include components to perform several kinds of tasks. Software that shares information between applications (such as word processing, database, and presentations) is known as integrated software. When these applications are packaged as one, they are commonly called a suite. Suites that contain a set of business programs are often called *office suites or productivity suites*. The programs typically look similar to one another and use similar commands.

Utility software is another type of program. You can use utility software to organize files, find computer viruses, protect data, or do other tasks. Some utility programs are included with the operating system software. Others can be bought separately. As the use of computers has grown, utility software has become essential in preventing data loss.

software a program that gives instructions to a computer

 CHECK POINT What are three broad categories of software?

Figure 3-1.5 Types of Software

SOFTWARE CATEGORY	SOFTWARE FUNCTION
Browser	Provides navigation and search tools to help you find topics and locations on the World Wide Web
Communications	Modem connections; fax; voice, electronic, and Internet mail; file transfers
Database management	Records creation and maintenance, records updating and editing, data querying, report creation
Desktop publishing	Page composition, use of features such as type style and fonts to product high-quality documents that contain text and graphics
Development	Tools for creating interactive applications including animations and pages for the Internet
Graphics and design	Clip-art images, photos, line art, and drawing and design tools for use in desktop publishing documents as well as computer-aided design
Finance	Checkbook, online banking, accounts receivable/payable, billing, financial reports, financial forecasting, tax planning, inventory, and job costing
Operating system	Controls the operation of the computer and communicates with devices such as printers, cameras, and scanners
Network	Server performance for networks, security, management, directory services, intranets
Presentation	Multimedia shows with graphics, sound, text, and animation
Project management	Timeline schedules, calendars, appointment reminders, travel guides, address books, prioritizing and task management, and employee performance evaluations
Specialized	Software developed for specialized needs such as medical, law, and real estate offices
Spreadsheet	Number calculations using formulas, sorting, charts, "what-if" analyses
Utility	Tools to scan and disable viruses, compress files, boost performance, recover lost files, repair disks, troubleshoot, protect, and back up data
Word processing	Document creation and editing, spelling and grammar checking, merging of text, data, and graphics into integrated documents

Networks

A **computer network** links two or more computers so they can share information. Networks are also used to link computers and other types of hardware, such as a printer or scanner. They help workers complete their daily tasks and share information.

To use a network efficiently, workers must first be trained. They must perform networking tasks, such as logging on and off, exchanging files, setting password security, sending and receiving messages, managing files, and viewing network printer queues. New workers may be introduced to networks in a variety of ways. Some organizations provide hands-on training by support staff. Others assign an experienced coworker to train the new user. Still others may give the user a network procedures manual to follow.

Local Area Networks

A network used to link computers that are close to each other—usually within several hundred feet—is a local area network (LAN). With a LAN, several computer users can share data files, software, and equipment such as printers or scanners. LANs are set up as peer-to-peer networks or server-based networks.

In a peer-to-peer network, computers can access software and data stored on all the computers in the network. Individual users and the company decide which data or software files will be made public for other network users to access.

In a server-based network, one computer fills requests for data and program files from network users. The central computer that performs this service is called a file server. Its primary task is supplying or "serving" files to computers on the network. In this type of network, every computer must have special software and hardware for networking.

Some LANs use cables to connect computers and other devices. Other LANs use wireless connections. Companies must consider cost, speed, efficiency, and reliability when choosing how to connect the network devices.

 CHECK POINT In which type of LAN can computers access software and data stored on all the computers in the network?

Wide Area Networks

A wide area network (WAN) links computers that are separated by long distances. A WAN for a small company may cover several cities or states. WANs for a large company may cover several countries. Wide area networks, like LANs, are used for file access, data exchange, and e-mail.

As you have learned, in a LAN data travels over cables or wireless connections. In a WAN, use of data transmission lines is purchased from a business that specializes in providing these services.

Microwave transmissions play an important role in a WAN. Microwave dishes and towers relay signals to each other directly. You have probably noticed imposing microwave towers on hillsides. The higher the dish or tower, the further the message can be sent. Objects between the two relay stations can interfere with the signal.

In a WAN, data travels by fiber-optic cable or telephone lines to the nearest microwave carrier. The data travels from carrier to carrier until it reaches the one nearest its final destination. Satellites may also play a role in sending the data. The satellite relay station sends the data to an orbiting satellite. The satellite sends the message to a receiving station on Earth. At the end of the process, the data is sent to the receiving computer.

WANs may use microwaves to transmit data.

Aquila/Shutterstock.com

Wireless Connections

The use of wireless devices to connect to a network and then to the Internet is growing. If you have recently been in a hotel, library, coffee shop, or airport, you have probably been in a hotspot. A hotspot is a public location that offers network access through a wireless connection. Some hotspots offer free access. For example, colleges typically have hotspots on campus to allow students to access the college network. Other hotspot providers charge a fee by the minute or hour. Some cities provide maps of hotspots in the area.

hotspot a public location that offers network access through a wireless connection

TECHNOLOGY CONNECTION

Electronic data interchange (EDI) allows the exchange of data or documents between computers. The use of wide area networks and electronic data interchange speeds business transactions. A B2B (business-to-business) network makes it possible to place orders with vendors electronically. Consider this example:

A clothing manufacturer in Atlanta needs silk fabric from a supplier in Hong Kong. A purchase order is sent from a computer at the factory in Atlanta to a computer in the warehouse in Hong Kong. The order is filled, the fabric is shipped, and an electronic invoice is sent to the computer at the factory in Atlanta. No paper has been exchanged. It could take weeks for the order to be received, filled, and billed without the use of electronic data interchange.

Communication speed is one advantage of using EDI. What might be some other advantages?

Connecting to the Internet

Many government offices, schools, and companies have direct Internet access through their local or wide area networks. Workers can easily gain access to the Internet if their LAN or WAN is connected to it.

Direct access is not the only way to get online. An Internet service provider (ISP) sells entry to the Internet, usually based on a monthly fee. Accessing the Internet through an ISP requires a computer, a modem, and telecommunications software. A dial-up access account also requires a phone line. With dial-up access, your computer contacts the ISP each time you want to go online. The ISP then provides you with a connection to the Internet. This service provides a slow connection to the Internet.

A broadband connection to the Internet provides much faster service than a dial-up connection. With a DSL (direct service line) account, your computer remains online and you can access the Internet at any time. The access is through telephone lines. Broadband access is also available through cable, wireless, and satellite connections. When selecting an ISP, evaluate the cost and quality of the service. Consider the types of services provided and the quality of customer service.

 CHECK POINT What public places in your community are hotspots that have wireless Internet access? (Search the Internet using the term *wireless hotspots* and your city name.)

Maintenance

Companies use and rely on computer systems daily. The computers and networks must be maintained properly to stay in good working order. Yet, a surprising number of businesses neglect to do proper maintenance on the systems. To work well, the systems must be serviced on a regular basis. Failure to maintain the equipment could result in lost data and even lost business.

When you use computers or other devices, follow the steps needed to maintain them. Read and follow equipment and software instructions so you do not accidentally harm the device or erase programs. Many companies instruct

---

✳ WORKPLACE CONNECTIONS ✳

Catrina received a phone call from a new customer requesting a rush delivery on an important order. She checked the inventory system. It showed that the needed items were in stock and could be delivered the same day. Little did Catrina know that the computer network had been shut down for unscheduled repairs earlier that morning. This shutdown prevented some shipments from being entered and deducted from the inventory count. The needed items were not really in the warehouse. The company lost a customer because accurate inventory information was not available when needed.

What could company personnel have done to avoid the problem described?

employees regarding how to care for computers and the routine tests that should be done. If you are responsible for the care of your computer, printer, or other devices, be sure you understand the procedures you are to follow.

 CHECK POINT What type of program could you use to perform routine maintenance on your computer's hard drive, such as compressing files or scanning for a virus?

Security

Businesses depend on their computer networks to process orders and provide needed data. Stored data must be kept safe from accidental damage or theft. As a result, security is a critical issue. Routine security risks and measures are discussed here. Disaster recovery relating to data and computers is discussed in Chapter 11.

Security Risks

Security for computer systems involves protecting against loss of data and loss of service. Unauthorized access and use of data or computers is also a concern. Loss of data can occur when a computer or network does not work properly because of hardware or software problems. To protect against loss of data, backup copies of the data are made and stored in another location. Data can also be lost through errors made by employees. For example, a file may be deleted or incorrectly updated in a customer database. Companies try to avoid losses of this nature through employee training.

Many companies have confidential data that are at risk of theft or misuse. The data gathered from customers and business partners are also at risk. Unauthorized users, called hackers, may be able to misuse or steal the data that are not protected.

A computer virus is a destructive program loaded onto a computer and run without the user's knowledge. Viruses are dangerous because they can quickly make copies of themselves. They can cause a computer to stop working or destroy data. Some viruses can travel across networks and sneak past security systems.

computer virus a destructive program loaded onto a computer and run without the user's knowledge

Computer viruses called Trojan horses may be used in creating distributed denial of service (DDOS) attacks. In a DDOS, hackers flood a system with so many requests for connections that the system cannot operate properly or at all. For an e-commerce site, this could mean lost sales while the site is not operating. A loss of customer confidence in using the site can also lead to lost sales in the future. DDOS attacks are illegal, but finding the person who launched the attack is very difficult. Companies can use filtering methods and adjust network settings to help protect against DDOS.

Not all security threats come from outside the company. Employee theft of company information, such as product designs, can be costly. Theft of other types of data, such as customer credit card numbers and addresses, can be costly for both the company and its customers.

Security Measures

US-CERT is a part of the U.S. Department of Homeland Security. Its purpose is to protect the nation's Internet systems and coordinate defense against cyber attacks. The US-CERT website provides security alerts and tips for general users and technical experts. It also has security publications. For example, you can read about how to set up your web browser for safer Internet surfing. This site can be helpful to both businesses and individuals. A page from the US-CERT website is shown in Figure 3-1.6.

Figure 3-1.6 US-CERT Website

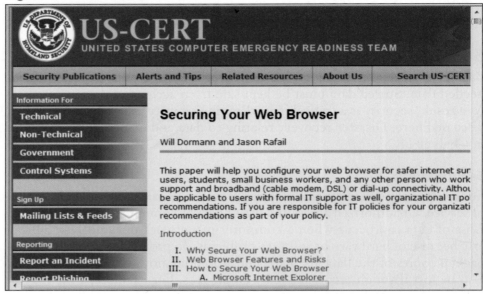

Source: US-CERT website, http://www.us-cert.gov/reading_room/ securing_browser/.

firewall software and equipment used to prevent unauthorized access to computers and networks

A variety of security measures are used to protect computer networks and data. Companies use software and equipment called **firewalls** to prevent unauthorized access to their computer networks. Many companies use data encryption when sending data. This process helps protect data, such as a credit card number, from being stolen during transfer of the data.

Antivirus software is used to help prevent data loss from computer viruses. Data scans are done routinely to find viruses and other threats. Norton Antivirus is a popular antivirus program that you can purchase. Effective anti-virus programs can also be downloaded from the Internet as freeware (programs for which there is no charge).

Many companies assign user IDs and passwords to employees. These data must be entered correctly to access the computer system. Entry to high-security areas may be restricted. An employee's badge or fingerprint may be scanned to verify the person's identity. All employees should follow the company's security procedures.

✓CHECK POINT What security procedures must you follow to gain access to your school's computer network?

REVIEW 3-1

21st Century Skills

Interacting with Others

PARTNERSHIP FOR
21ST CENTURY SKILLS

Kristin and Peng work together in a small office. One of Peng's main duties is updating customer account records. He enjoys talking with customers who call to report changes. However, he is not very prompt about updating the customer account database. Kristin's main duty is customer service. When responding to customer concerns, she accesses the customer database for information. Because Peng failed to update the customer database promptly, Kristin did not have up-to-date information available when she responded to three different customer calls.

1. Explain why it is important for Kristin to have up-to-date information when she responds to customer calls.

2. If you were Kristin, what would you say to Peng about this issue?

Making Academic Connections

Reinforcing Math Skills

You work for an organization that gives training seminars on various topics. Recently, the company completed a series of seminars in five cities. The fee for each person at three of the seminars was $1,000. At two of the seminars (Update on Virtual Meetings and Using PDAs) the fee for each person was $500. You were given the task of e-mailing the manager of each seminar site and getting enrollment figures for the courses. The details you recorded are shown below.

1. Record the title of each of the five seminars on a separate line. Calculate and record the following:
   • The total number of participants for each seminar
   • The grand total number of participants for all seminars
   • The total revenue earned from each seminar
   • The grand total of all revenue received
   • The total number of participants in each city

2. Identify the seminar with the largest total number of participants and the seminar producing the largest total revenue.

PARTICIPANTS

Seminar and Date	Boston	New York	Washington	Chicago	San Francisco
Data Mining, January 6–10	125	245	110	117	97
Managing Databases, February 15–18	105	325	175	130	110
Security for the Internet, March 1–4	78	110	45	72	70
Update on Virtual Meetings, March 19–22	170	295	140	110	115
Using PDAs, April 1–2	210	410	175	102	117

3-1 Activity 1

Using Data to Make Decisions (Outcome 3-1a)

You work for a small company that embroiders or prints names, logos, and art on various items. T-shirts, sweatshirts, uniforms, tote bags, and mugs are examples of these items. You are considering ways to improve sales by providing information to customers in better ways. Last month, which you consider a typical month, the company received orders in the following ways:

Sales Channel	Number of Orders
Company website	8,640
Telephone	3,262
Mail (using the company's printed catalog form)	98

1. What percentage of the total orders was made in each sales channel?
2. The company managers are considering three options for improving the order process:
   - Making the website more informative and easier to use
   - Adding another associate to handle telephone orders
   - Improving the company's printed catalog

   Based on the information you have, which option do you think would be best? Why?
3. In talking with the associates for telephone sales, you learn that many customers say they refer to the printed catalog when ordering by telephone. Does this information change your recommendation? Why?
4. What other information should be considered when making this decision?

3-1 Activity 2

Local Area Networks (Outcome 3-1c)

Learn about the local area network used in your school or in a local business. Find answers to the questions listed below regarding the LAN in your school. If your teacher so instructs, interview instead someone from a local business that uses a LAN. Create a short report that gives the name of the organization you are researching and summarizes your findings.

- What physical area does the LAN cover?
- Does the LAN use peer-to-peer or server-based networking?
- Are any wireless connections used on the LAN? If yes, describe.
- What types of equipment (computers, printers, scanners, etc.) are connected to the LAN?
- Approximately how many computers are connected to the LAN?
- Approximately how many people use the LAN?
- Are users required to enter a password to log on to the LAN?
- What other types of security measures are used with the LAN?
- Can users access the Internet through the LAN? If yes, is firewall software used?
- What are the primary uses of the LAN (storing data files, providing users with access to programs, etc.)?

3-2 Information Systems and Resources

Typical Systems and Resources

Information technology refers to the computer equipment and software used to process information. Technology is only one part of managing information. Managing information effectively also includes people who follow procedures to run the information technology efficiently. An information system is composed of people, the information technology and resources, and procedures used to process information.

Information Systems

Information systems help employees complete their daily work. The systems found in a company relate to business activities. Accounting and sales are examples of these activities. Three typical systems are described below. This information will help you understand how businesses use these systems. Often, the systems in a company work together or are part of an overall system.

Accounting Information Systems

An accounting information system is used to record transactions and create financial reports. These reports give information about many aspects of the business, such as expenses, accounts receivable, and income. The following list gives examples of how employees in a small business would use this information to make decisions or process work.

- A billing clerk prepares invoices and computes amounts due.
- The Credit Department manager approves credit for a customer.
- The controller prepares the annual budget and recommends ways to increase profits.

controller a person who supervises company accounting and financial reporting activities

Marketing Information Systems

A marketing information system helps the business keep track of customers. Data are recorded from an initial contact to the point of the sale or service. A follow-up to judge customer satisfaction may also be included. The data provided by this system identifies whether or not:

- A particular marketing approach is successful
- A customer is satisfied with the product or service
- A customer intends to make future purchases from the company

Product Information Systems

If a business manufactures a product, it must determine the cost of goods it sells. The activities that take place within the business to create the product are recorded in the information system. This system contains the cost of materials, labor, and overhead. The information stored in this system is used to help determine the cost of the product. The following examples illustrate how different people access the information system in a manufacturing firm:

overhead business costs not directly related to a product or service

- A stock control clerk checks the inventory of raw materials and processes a purchase order to replenish stock.
- A receiving clerk scans bar code labels on incoming shipments to create a record of goods received.
- A production manager locates purchase order data for goods used to calculate production costs.
- A production worker completes an assembly operation. A part number is scanned to enter the quantity of completed products.
- An accounts payable clerk verifies invoices and receipt of goods before approving payment for purchases.
- A department manager uses prior months' financial data in creating a budget.

✓CHECK POINT What kinds of information does an accounting system provide?

Dennis Hallinan/Alamy

Bar code labels are scanned to create a record of shipments received.

Traditional Resources

Companies can get information from many sources. Much of the information a business uses comes from within the company. You have already learned about some typical information systems. Businesses can also get information from outside sources. Some of these traditional sources are described in the following paragraphs.

Marketing Research Firms

Marketing research firms offer data in a variety of forms for business needs. They focus on the customer and the market. Marketing research firms use questionnaires and interviews to gather information about consumer behaviors and attitudes. They also look at marketing trends and collect valuable **demographic data**. Researchers collect a variety of data. They use computers to analyze huge amounts of data and forecast market conditions.

demographic data statistics that describe a population, such as age or income level

Companies often rely on the information provided by marketing research firms. Doing market research might be too costly for a small-business owner. A large company might be able to afford to do research. However, the company could save valuable time by using the information already gathered by a research firm.

Trade Publications and Associations

Many companies use trade publications, books, and journals to find facts about their industry. Products, markets, and other business topics are discussed in articles or research papers. Trade associations often conduct or sponsor research. Meetings and workshops allow you to talk with others who have similar interests or concerns. You can see new products at conventions or trade shows for the industry.

Government Agencies and Libraries

Data from government agencies are useful to many companies. Forecasts and research studies are provided in many areas. The Small Business Administration (see Figure 3-2.1) and the U.S. Census Bureau are examples of sources that provide information. The statistics and other data they provide are useful in making business decisions.

University libraries are a good source of information. Many libraries offer research services. They may also have specialized materials not found in other places. Some companies also have libraries. Many of these also report on research projects.

Figure 3-2.1 The Small Business Administration provides information helpful to businesses.

Source: U.S. Small Business Administration, http://www.sba.gov/content/using-technology -stay-competitive.

 CHECK POINT What are three types of traditional resources businesses can use to get information?

A company that makes toys is interested in the demographics of a particular region. The company considers data about the number of people within a certain age range in an area. This helps the company decide whether to advertise its products in that region. If a large number of people are under the age of 12, then toys could probably be marketed with success. On the other hand, if the number of people under the age of 12 is small, the advertising money might be better spent in another region.

What other demographic statistics would be helpful in deciding where to market these products?

Electronic Resources

With changes in information technology come new sources and new ways to access information. Electronic resources are often called online resources. These resources are those available via a computer or other device, such as a smartphone. Online resources are becoming more popular and widely used.

Electronic Databases

A database is a collection of related data. Use of electronic databases has grown rapidly in the past few years. Electronic databases are available on disks and the Internet. Online services are provided by various companies. These databases provide information on many topics useful to businesses. Most electronic databases have powerful search features. These features allow the user to find data quickly and easily.

Some databases support natural language searches. This means that the user simply enters a question in everyday terms. The database search feature interprets and answers the question. No special searching techniques or rules are needed. The Help feature of programs such as Microsoft Office allows users to search in this manner.

Companies often have relational databases as part of their internal information systems. A relational database allows the user to link data from a number of database tables to find data or generate reports. This linking capability means that data can be stored in relatively small tables that are easy to use. Data updated in one table or file can be used to update other tables easily.

Data mining is a process that helps businesses analyze the data contained in databases. With automated data mining, the program searches for interesting and significant patterns of data in the database. The data are then presented in graphs, reports, and so forth. The user can look at the data from several viewpoints. The results may reveal information the user never considered. Data mining can be used to help a business target consumers and predict market trends.

relational database a program that allows the user to link data from two or more tables to create reports

 CHECK POINT What are two advantages of using a relational database?

Personal Digital Assistants

A personal digital assistant (PDA) provides another means for retrieving information. PDAs can be used to store a variety of data, from a list of schedules and appointments to photos to a reference text. Versions of word processing, spreadsheet, e-mail, and other application programs are available for PDAs. E-mail and the Internet can be accessed through wireless connections. Some PDAs have built-in cameras or voice recorders.

Gene Blevins/LA Daily News/Corbis

PDAs can provide reference materials, contact databases, and Internet access.

CHECK POINT What types of information can be stored or accessed with a PDA?

✳ WORKPLACE CONNECTIONS ✳

Consider this example of how healthcare workers use PDAs:

Healthcare workers need access to clinical data. They also refer to medical resources, decision aids, and other professional information. A PDA can be used to access this data. A small memory card that fits into the PDA can be used to provide additional information or programs. A medical calculator program can be used for standard calculations. The healthcare workers have immediate access to reference material where and when they need it.

In what other types of jobs might workers use PDAs or other handheld computers to store or access data?

Intranets

Intranets are internal networks based on Internet technologies and standards. The intranet may reside on a company's local area network or be part of a wide area network. An intranet is designed for users within a company and is protected by a firewall. A firewall works in two ways. First, it blocks outsiders from entering the company's intranet. Second, it allows company intranet users to access the Internet. Only those users who have registered and/or received passwords are given access to an intranet.

Intranets allow workers to share data quickly and easily. The data can be used to make decisions and serve customers effectively. An intranet can be used to keep employees informed about the company's products, procedures, and activities.

Intranets have many uses within companies. They allow data such as production schedules to be updated quickly. They reduce the need for printed documents, which saves money. They provide quick access to data such as catalogs, price lists, product manuals, and shipping information. Job openings for which employees may apply may be posted on an intranet. Employees may be able to complete forms such as expense reports using an intranet.

The U.S. workforce is increasingly mobile. More than ever, workers are on the road on a regular basis or work from home offices. With a notebook computer and network access, these workers can easily use the company intranet to interact with coworkers. Consider these examples of intranet use.

Many workers can access a company intranet while away from the office.

Robert Harding World Imagery/Alamy

- Using an intranet, a company sends sales data daily to 400 salespeople. The data were previously sent by overnight mail.

- An import firm with offices around the world sends data on product availability to the home office via the intranet.

- A technology firm links research efforts by engineers in Europe, Asia, and the United States via the company intranet.

- Employees access training programs and find answers to frequently asked questions while away from the office via the intranet.

The technology needed to develop an intranet is getting less expensive and easier to use. In the future, more companies may make intranets part of their information systems.

 CHECK POINT What are some advantages to employees of using an intranet?

Intranets to Extranets

Many companies use intranets to provide current information to employees. Some businesses also use an extranet. An extranet is an information network like an intranet, but it is partially available to some outside users. An extranet uses a firewall to provide limited access to users outside the company.

Many extranets have grown from the use of a company's intranet. For example, FedEx began tracking the receipt and delivery of packages years ago. A customer could call and wait to find out tracking information. Now, FedEx customers can access tracking data via the Internet. Users enter their package ID number to retrieve the tracking information quickly.

Banks, insurance companies, investment firms, and schools are frequent users of extranets. In these instances, outside users look for information related to themselves. They gain access to the extranet with some form of password or ID number. The extranet can also link business partners with one another by linking their intranets. For example, a company may provide access to engineers from partner firms who are working on design projects.

By using the Internet, intranets, and extranets, companies can provide information to employees and customers. Changes can be made quickly to keep data current. Costs are lowered by reducing the number of paper documents. The use of intranets and extranets helps keep both employees and customers better informed.

> Have you used an extranet to track an order or get other information? Describe your experience.

The Internet

The Internet is a giant network of computers and smaller networks that spans the globe. It is the world's largest information resource. Using the Internet, businesses can connect to information resources quickly and easily.

The following examples describe a few ways that businesses use the Internet.

- Through electronic mail, coworkers are able to communicate with each other. Workers can send messages from their office or home or on the road.
- An office worker plans an out-of-state trip. The airline reservations are made using a travel service on the Internet.
- An investment broker accesses information on the Internet to get up-to-the-minute stock quotes.
- A small-business owner uses a website to sell sports items such as baseball trading cards, league pennants, autographed products, and T-shirts.
- A civic organization uses a website to provide information about the organization. It lists upcoming events and posts public service messages.
- A clothing maker provides product information on a company website. Customers can order products and track the progress of orders that have been placed.
- Employees access shared resources, such as software programs and information, on the Internet using computers and other devices rather than having the software programs on their computers.

extranet an information network like an intranet but partially available to some outside users

Finding and Sharing Information

The Internet is loaded with information about many topics. Finding the specific information you need among the large amount of data available may be a challenge. Programs are available to help you search for information on the Internet.

Web Browsers

Knowing where and how to look for information is basic to using electronic resources. With the increased use of the Internet, browser software programs have become very popular. Browsers provide navigation and search tools to help you find topics and locations on the World Wide Web. Though the programs vary in appearance, they offer many of the same features. Examples of browsers include Microsoft Internet Explorer and Mozilla Firefox.

hypertext information in electronic documents that is organized with links to information at other locations

URLs (uniform resource locators) are Internet addresses that can be understood by any Web browser as it searches for hypertext documents on computers around the world. URL addresses start with *http://*, which stands for *hypertext transfer protocol*. This is a set of instructions telling computers how to send and receive hypertext data and documents. The *www* in the URL stands for *World Wide Web*. Periods in the URL are separators and are pronounced *dot*. The last letters in the URL represent the domain name. Some common domain names are *edu* for education, *org* for organization, *com* for commercial, and *gov* for government. Other parts of the URL identify sections or levels within the website.

A two-letter country code is used at the end of some addresses. Every country has its own unique geographic domain code. For example, *uk* is used for the United Kingdom and *mx* is used for Mexico. If there is no geographic code in a name, then the domain is located within your own country. Some examples of URL addresses are shown below.

- http://www.dol.gov   (U.S. Department of Labor)
- http://canada.gc.ca   (Government of Canada, official site)
- http://www.whitehouse.gov/   (The White House)
- http://www.nps.gov/   (U.S. National Park Service)

When you want to visit a location on the Internet, you may do so by entering the URL address in your browser. Pay close attention to spelling, punctuation, symbols, and capitalization when entering the address. URLs are sensitive to the use of upper and lowercase letters. You may also move to a different location in the document or on the Internet by clicking a hyperlink. A hyperlink can be text or an image. When you use hyperlinks, the associated URLs are often invisible. You merely click on the hyperlink, and your browser takes you to the Internet address (URL) associated with that hyperlink. The U.S. Internal Revenue Service website is shown in Figure 3-2.2. The lines of text shown in blue and underlined in the figure are hyperlinks.

Search Tools

If you are looking for information about job opportunities, doing research for work or hobbies, or planning a trip, you might need help finding Internet sites that relate to these activities. Many search tools, often referred

Figure 3-2.2 The IRS website provides links to forms and publications.

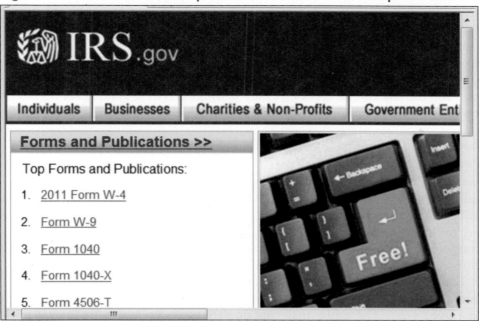

Source: U.S. Department of the Treasury, Internal Revenue Service, http://www.irs.gov/.

to as search engines, can help you locate sites. You may be familiar with some widely used search engines such as Yahoo! or Google. Once you find a website, you can use the site's search tool to find information on the site.

To perform a search on most websites, simply key two or three keywords related to the topic and then click the search button. The search tool will locate sites/documents, called *matches* or *hits*, which contain these keywords. Your search may result in no matches, several matches, or thousands of matches. If your search results in a large number of matches, you may want to use more specific keywords to locate the information. On the other hand, if you receive only a few hits, you may have to broaden your search by using more general keywords. You may need to use several search tools to perform a thorough search because not all search tools look at every site that may contain the information you need.

Depending on the search engine you use, you may see one or more sponsored links at the top of the search results list. These links may be in a colored box or indicated in some other way. These sponsored links are from companies or organizations that may have paid to have their names appear at the top of a search results list that relates to the keywords you entered as a form of advertising. These links are not necessarily the ones that will provide the information that best relates to your search terms.

Transferring Files

Millions of files are available on the Internet—research papers and data, software, pictures, sounds, and more. Perhaps a software vendor is offering a free update or "patch" to correct a problem for a software product. The publisher of your textbook may have a site offering student data files or special software tutorials. You may have to research a particular topic at work. You search for information about the topic with Yahoo!, Google, or other search tools. When you find sites with data you would like to use, what do you do? You can transfer or download many of these files from a distant computer to your computer by using something called FTP (file transfer protocol).

FTP (file transfer protocol) is a powerful tool that allows a copy of the file you request from a remote computer to be copied to your computer. There are two types of FTP transfers—private and anonymous. In a private FTP transfer, you must have permission to access and download files. A private user name or account number and password are needed before you can download files (copy from) or upload files (copy to) to the remote computer. In an anonymous FTP transfer, the site can be accessed easily without privately issued user names or passwords. Thousands of anonymous sites are open to everyone.

E-mail

One popular use of the Internet is electronic mail, or e-mail. E-mail is a method of sending and receiving electronic messages. LANs and WANs typically offer e-mail to all computers that are connected, whether they are in the same office or in different countries. Users are limited to sending and receiving messages only to and from those on their network unless their network is connected to the Internet. If they are connected to the Internet, they can send and receive messages outside the LAN or WAN.

E-mail messages contain text. Some programs also allow the message to contain audio and graphics. Files may be attached to an e-mail message as shown in Figure 3-2.3. These files may contain data such as research findings, corporate financial statements, or client databases. When an e-mail file is received, it is stored in a user's electronic mailbox. This mailbox is an online computer storage space. The messages may be read, saved for later reference, printed, or deleted. E-mail is inexpensive, fast, and easy to use for workers at all levels in organizations. However, e-mail should not be used to send sensitive or confidential information since the messages may not be secure. Messages with confidential or sensitive information should be sent in a printed letter or memo. You will learn more about using e-mail in Chapter 4.

Figure 3-2.3 **This e-mail message has a file attachment.**

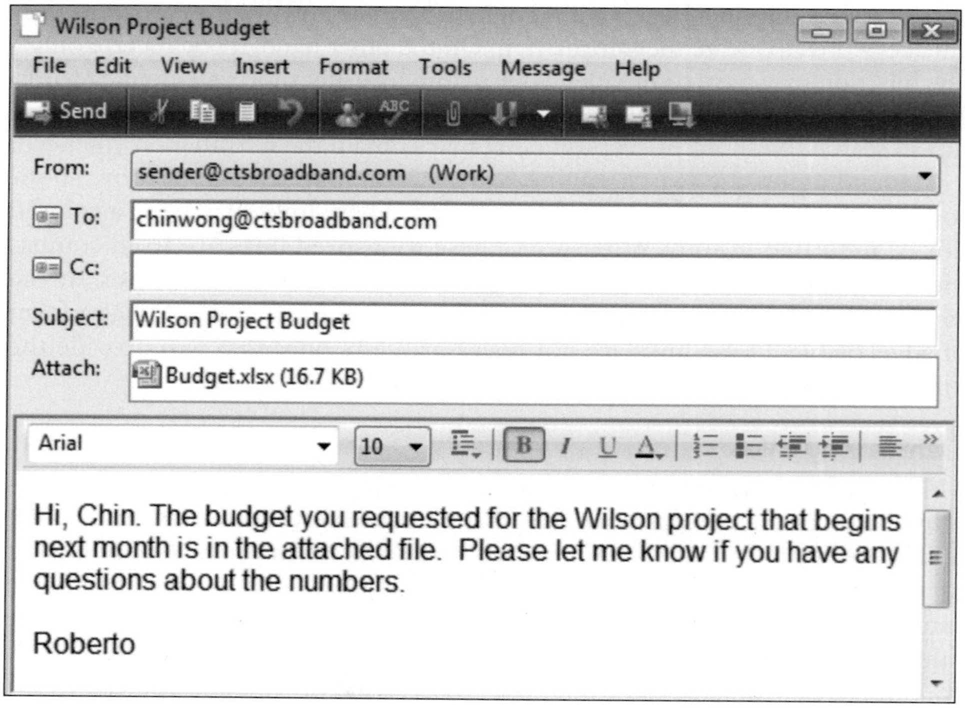

Discussion Groups

A discussion group is an online forum in which users discuss or monitor information on a specific topic. Discussion groups include mailing lists (e-mail newsletters), newsgroups, and web-based forums. A newsgroup consists of online articles and messages related to a topic. Users take part in online talks about the topic using newsreader software. A web-based forum is similar to a newsgroup except messages are posted or read via a web browser. Businesses use mailing lists and web-based forums to provide customer service and make customers aware of products and services. Employees can use discussion groups to stay updated with the latest information in their field.

discussion group an online public forum for articles and messages related to a certain topic

Wikis

A wiki is a website or group of web pages on which anyone can add, edit, or delete content. An example of a wiki is Wikipedia, a popular web-based free encyclopedia to which anyone can contribute. Wikis can be used in many ways. A company may host a wiki on its intranet to help work groups share information on work-related topics. A list of questions and answers or instructions for a procedure can be kept on a wiki and easily updated as needed. A personal wiki (that is not open to other uses) can be used to store notes and reminders that are easily updated and can be accessed from any computer with an Internet connection.

wiki a website to which anyone can add, edit, or delete content

Blogs

A blog, also called a *weblog*, is a web-based journal. The blogger (writer) expresses opinions and shares information in the messages. Posting to a blog is called *blogging*. Postings to a blog are listed by date. They generally follow topics or ideas called *threads*. A public blog may allow readers to post messages in reply to those posted by the blog host. Postings to a public blog may be monitored by the host and edited to remove inappropriate content. Examples of public blogs include those hosted by reporters and columnists at online news sites.

blog a web-based journal, also called a weblog

Businesses may use public blogs to create forums for sharing product information. An example of this type of blog is one hosted by a software company for the software users. Many individuals host blogs about various topics. You can create a blog using programs available on the Internet.

 CHECK POINT What are three types or formats of discussion groups?

Promoting Organizations

Many organizations are going online for promotion purposes. For example, many colleges have sites with information about their programs. Potential students visit the sites. They are able to compare courses, costs, and other aspects of campus life to help them choose a school.

Many states and cities have websites. The sites promote tourism and industry in the area. They typically include general information about the area and a calendar of events. Links to area hotels, restaurants, and other businesses are often included. Figure 3-2.4 shows a website for the U.S. National Parks Service.

Civic and charitable organizations also use websites. The sites provide information about the mission and goals of the organization. They advertise special events and encourage contributing to the organization. Some sites allow visitors to contribute online using a credit card.

Figure 3-2.4 **The U.S. National Parks Service promotes tourism on this website.**

Source: U.S. National Parks Service, Mammoth Cave National Park, http://www.nps.gov/maca/index.htm.

Many companies promote their products on websites. If the company does not sell products directly to consumers, the website usually gives a list of retail stores where the products may be purchased. The site may also show information such as the company's mission and goals, the history of the company, and the company's structure.

 CHECK POINT What types of organizations promote their products or services online?

E-commerce—Buying and Selling Online

Businesses are changing the ways they acquire, use, and share information. The amazing growth of the Internet is part of the reason for this change. For example, customers who buy online may provide data about themselves to the company. This data is called a customer profile. Companies may also build their store of data about online customers by using cookies. Cookies are messages exchanged by the user's web browser and the web server that the user visits. They can be used to track the user's identity and online behavior.

The data from online customers allow the business to study buying habits. Then the company can suggest related products that may be of interest to a customer. Amazon.com, one of the most successful e-commerce companies, uses this technique. When you purchase a book or movie from the company's website, the site suggests other titles that may be of interest to you. Using customer data to target advertising can increase sales.

Consumer trust in the company is very important in e-commerce. Companies want to build customer trust and loyalty. They offer services such as online support and order shipment tracking. Online newsletters about their products may also be offered. By using the Internet to share information with customers, companies can strengthen their relationships with customers.

Privacy of customer data is an area of concern related to e-commerce. Will the company share data such as a customer's name, e-mail address, and buying habits with other companies? Many companies have privacy statements on their websites. A sample is shown in Figure 3-2.5. A privacy statement tells how customer data will be used. These statements can reassure customers and help build their trust.

Figure 3-2.5 A website's privacy policy discusses how customer data will be used.

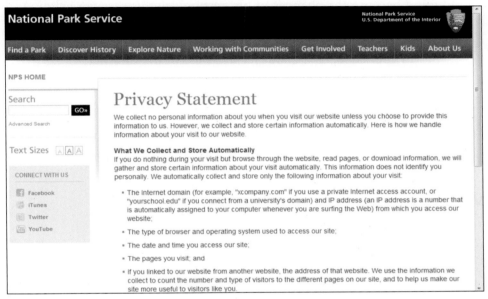

Source: U.S. National Parks Service, http://www.nps.gov/privacy.htm.

E-commerce has created a lack of geographic boundaries for many businesses. This brings new challenges in communicating and sharing information with people of many countries and cultures. Websites must be designed to be attractive and easy to use for all customers. Product instructions, warranties, and customer support may be needed in several languages. Marketing personnel may need to study the cultures of their new customers to learn how to create appealing advertisements.

Just a few aspects of information related to e-commerce have been described in this section. As Internet use and e-commerce continue to grow, companies will need to adapt to new ways of acquiring, using, and sharing information.

 CHECK POINT   What is the purpose of a privacy statement on a website?

21st Century Skills

Interacting with Others

PARTNERSHIP FOR
21ST CENTURY SKILLS

While completing some tasks to meet a deadline, you noticed that a member of your sales team, Jerome, was using the computer at his workstation to download copyrighted clip art. You observed him pasting the clip art into the department's online newsletter and posting it on the company's website. When you asked Jerome about his activities, he shrugged and said that no one should mind because the chances of his getting caught were very slim. And besides, he was not really hurting anyone. What should you do?

- Let the matter drop and ignore his illegal actions.
- Inform your supervisor about Jerome's use of the Internet.
- Send an e-mail message to Jerome condemning him for his actions.
- Talk with Jerome again and list reasons why you think his behavior is inappropriate.

1. Prepare a written response to each of the four suggested actions.
2. If you think there is another action that would be more effective, describe the action.

Making Academic Connections

Reinforcing English Skills

You have been asked to review information about shared workspaces for an intranet article.

1. Open the file 3-2 English Skills found in the data files.
2. Proofread and edit the information to correct errors in spelling, punctuation, and word usage.

3-2 Activity 1

Information Resource (Outcomes 3-2a, 3-2b)

The U.S. Census Bureau is a traditional source of data for organizations. The information it provides about the country's population can help determine issues such as where a new business will be opened or whether a new school will be needed. Since much of the information it provides is available online, it is also an electronic resource.

1. Work with a classmate to complete this activity. Access the U.S. Census Bureau website.
2. Select the link for *publications*.
3. Select a link for publications related to population and housing.
4. Open one of the reports or tables that are available on this topic.
5. Record the name of the document or table and describe the type of information it contains. If the document is long, review the table of contents to see what it contains.
6. Give an example of the type of business decision for which you think this data might be used. For example, knowing the number of children ages five to nine years in a city might help a company decide whether to advertise products for young children in that area.

3-2 Activity 2

Discussion Group (Outcome 3-2c)

A web-based forum is a discussion group accessed with a web browser. In this type of online forum, users discuss or monitor information on a specific topic.

1. Use an Internet search engine to find a list of web-based forums. Search using the term *forum directory*.
2. View the directory to find an area of interest to you. For example, you might select a topic such as *business*, *health*, or *sports*.
3. View the forums available for this topic. Select a forum and read at least three messages.
4. Write a brief summary of this experience to include:
   - The forum area or topic
   - The forum name and web address
   - The name of the organization or group that sponsors the forum
   - A sentence or two that tells what each message you read is about

Summary

3-1 Information Management and Technology

- One of the most important resources used in all businesses is information.
- Activities typically involved in information processing include input, processing, output, distribution, and storage.
- Many businesses gather data to use in making decisions and answering questions. For information to be valuable, it must be current and accurate.
- Information technology refers to both equipment and software. Together, they allow a user to create, store, and retrieve information.
- Hardware refers to the physical parts of a computer or related equipment. Software is a program that gives instructions to a computer.
- A computer network links two or more computers and related devices so they can share information.
- The use of wireless devices to connect to a network and then to the Internet is growing.
- Computers and networks must be maintained properly to stay in good working order.
- Security for computer systems involves protecting against loss of data and loss of service. A variety of security measures are used to protect computer networks and data.

3-2 Information Systems and Resources

- Information systems relate to business activities, such as accounting or sales.
- Businesses can get data from outside sources. Examples include marketing research firms, trade associations, libraries, and government agencies.
- Electronic (online) resources are available via a computer or other device, such as a smartphone.
- Electronic databases are available on disks and the Internet. They provide valuable information to companies.
- A personal digital assistant (PDA) can be used to store a variety of data and to access the Internet.
- Intranets are internal networks based on Internet technologies and standards. An intranet may reside on a company's LAN or be part of a WAN.
- The Internet is the world's largest information resource. Organizations use the Internet to find and share information, promote groups, and buy and sell products and services.

Chapter 3 Activity 1

Equipment Inventory
(Outcome 3-1b)

Office workers are often responsible for keeping an inventory of the computers, software, and other equipment used in the office. Because theft is a serious problem in some companies, having an accurate record of items purchased and assigned to the office is important. Equipment inventories are also used in scheduling equipment maintenance and upgrades. Because you probably do not currently work in an office, you will create an inventory of the hardware, software, and other equipment found in your classroom.

1. Use spreadsheet software to create a table named Equipment Inventory.
   - Include the following column headings: Item, Quantity, and Description.
   - Enter data to create a record for each item (hardware, software, and other equipment) found in your classroom.
2. Sort the data in the report in ascending order by the Item column.
3. Save the table as Equipment Inventory (Date). Use the current date in the name.
4. Print the table.

Chapter 3 Activity 2

Password Tips
(Outcome 3-1c)

Many networks and websites require you to use a password. Effective passwords help prevent unauthorized users from accessing data. You have been asked to create a list of tips for creating passwords to post on your company's intranet.

1. Use the Internet and other sources, such as magazines, to find tips for creating effective passwords. The US-Cert website is one that provides this kind of information.
2. After reading several sources of information on this topic, write a list of tips for creating passwords in your own words.
3. Use an appropriate title for the document. Format the tips as a bulleted list. Include reference notes for articles or websites you used as sources of information.
4. Save the document as a single file web page. View the document in a browser. Make adjustments to the format, if needed, so the document can be easily read in the browser.

Computer Applications Event

In this competitive event, you will be judged on your skills and knowledge of computer applications. The event involves word processing, graphics, presentation, spreadsheet, and database applications. The event includes a written test lasting one hour and a production test lasting two hours. Reference materials, such as a dictionary, are allowed.

Performance Indicators Evaluated

Participants will demonstrate skills related to the information technology career cluster. Sample indicators include showing an understanding of:

- Basic computer terminology and concepts
- Presentation, publishing, and multimedia applications
- Security
- Basic application knowledge and word processing
- E-mail, integrated, and collaboration applications
- Netiquette and legal issues
- Spreadsheet and database applications
- Formatting, grammar, punctuation, spelling, and proofreading

For more detailed information about this event, go to the FBLA website.[1]

http://www.fbla-pbl.org/

Think Critically

1. Which do you think is a better indicator of computer application skills—a written test or a production test?

2. In which skill areas included in this event are you proficient? In which areas do you need to learn or improve skills?

---

[1]FBLA-PBL, "FBLA Competitive Events, Computer Applications," 2010, http://www.fbla-pbl.org/docs/ct/gdlrs/FBLA/computer%20applications.pdf.

Do you enjoy working with computers and electronic devices? Are you detail oriented? Are you good at explaining technical information in a way that is easy to understand? If the answer to these questions is yes, then a career in information technology might be right for you. Jobs in this field are varied. Some workers install and maintain computer networks and related devices. Others write software programs, create games, or develop web pages. Still others write instructions or manuals to explain how equipment and software works. Help desk specialists, who talk with customers in need of assistance, are also employed in this career area.

Employment Outlook

There are many jobs in the field of information technology. Employees in this field work for businesses, schools, government agencies, and other organizations. The U.S. government provides job projections for 2008-2018. Jobs in this career area are expected to increase faster than average for all jobs.[2]

Job Titles

- Network administrator
- PC support specialist
- Database administrator
- Technical writer
- Help desk specialist
- Computer programmer
- Software engineer

Needed Education/Skills

A college degree is typically needed for jobs in information technology. Special certifications may be required for some jobs, such as network associates. Degrees in areas such as computer science, information science, or technical support prepare workers for jobs in this career area.

What's it like to work in . . . Information Technology?

Linda works as a technical writer for a company that makes software applications. While earning her college degree, Linda took courses in computer science and technical writing. She needs knowledge and skill in both of these areas to do her job well.

Much of Linda's work involves writing passages for the Help section of a software program. She also writes articles for the information database that the company makes available online to software users. The same database is used by customer support associates who answer questions for customers by phone.

Before Linda can write instructions for using a program, she must first explore and learn how to use the program. She uses software that is almost fully developed for this task. The final software sold to users will contain the Help entries Linda writes. While writing instructions for using the software, Linda sometimes finds features that do not work quite as they were intended. She reports these issues to the software development team to be fixed. Linda's biggest challenge is explaining technical information in a way that is easy for software users to understand. She knows that having clear, correct, and complete Help entries is important for the success of a software program.

What About You?

Does a job in information technology sound appealing to you? What type of job in this career area would you find rewarding?

---

[2]*Occupational Outlook Handbook*, 2010-11 Edition, Bureau of Labor Statistics, U.S. Department of Labor, http://www.bls.gov/oco/ocos319.htm.

Communicating Effectively

Vadym Andrushchenko/Shutterstock.com

Effectively managed and shared information helps a company serve its customers better and operate more efficiently. Employees need accurate information for use in making decisions and handling work tasks. The information must be communicated in written, visual, or oral forms. In this part you will learn about ways that reading and writing are used at work. You will review common types of business correspondence and reports. You will learn strategies for developing messages. You will also learn about telephone equipment and procedures for effective telephone communications.

Dmitriy Shironosov/Shutterstock.com

Communicating in Written Form

4-1 Reading and Writing at Work

4-2 Business Correspondence

4-3 Business Reports and Related Documents

Sung-Il Kim/Canopy/Corbis

This chapter focuses on reading and preparing written messages at work. Many business messages are in written form. Since their preparation is a time-consuming task, it is important to prepare them efficiently. The ability to read and understand written documents is a vital skill for all types of office workers.

In this chapter, you will learn strategies for improving your reading skills. You will also learn to create effective business documents. You will prepare business letters, memos, reports, and related documents.

Wire_man/Shutterstock.com

OUTCOMES

4-1a Identify ways reading and writing are used at work.
4-1b Describe and apply ways to improve reading skills.
4-1c Describe and apply ways to improve writing skills.

Written Communication at Work

On many occasions you will need to read and write on the job. You will find that these skills are vital to understanding the company in which you work. You will also need to read and write to complete your work tasks.

Reading at Work

Employees who want to understand how their work relates to the total company can read about the company in memos, newsletters, and other documents.

Many policies and procedures related to your job will be available in written form. A manager may explain how a particular task is to be done or what policies are to be followed. You will find it helpful, though, to read the written version of what was presented. Reading will help you get a thorough understanding of what you are to do. From time to time, memos related to ways of doing tasks or changes in policies are sent to employees. Such correspondence should be read and filed for easy reference later.

An informed employee works more efficiently.

iofoto/Shutterstock.com

Understanding Instructions

Employees are often provided new equipment and software at work. They must read and follow the written instructions for these items. For example, an employee may need help learning to prepare a database report. The report **wizard**, shown in Figure 4-1.1, provides instructions regarding how to complete this task.

wizard a software feature that gives the user dialog boxes with instructions for completing a task

Figure 4-1.1 This wizard screen gives instructions for completing a database report.

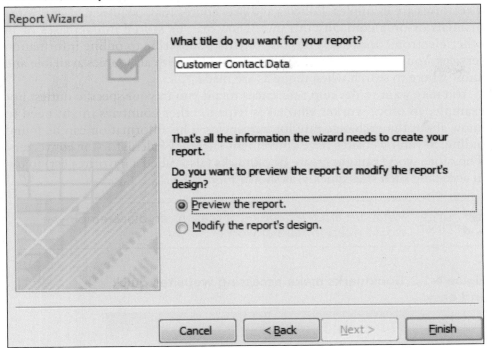

Businesses develop forms to use in collecting data. You will find forms for tasks such as recording telephone messages, reporting travel expenses, and submitting time reports. Reading all instructions on forms is very important. Try to provide all information requested when completing a form. If some data are not needed or are not available, a comment stating that fact should be added.

Responding to Inquiries

Many employees must respond to questions from other workers or customers. The questions will vary. Employees are not expected to know every answer from memory. They are expected to know where to find the answers promptly. Once the material is located, the worker needs to read quickly and accurately to find the information.

☀ WORKPLACE CONNECTIONS ☀

Linda works in customer services for a mail-order company that sells a variety of items related to books, such as bookcases, lamps, and reading tables. Linda often receives specific questions. For example: "I have a bookcase that is not the exact size as the one you advertise. I need a bookcase to place on top of the one I have. So I need to know the exact dimensions of your bookcase. Can you help me?" Linda is able to access the product database quickly and provide the caller with the correct information.

Have you been frustrated when you called a business and the employee could not answer your questions about a product or your account? Describe the situation.

Using Written References/Databases

Office workers use a variety of references. Dictionaries, atlases, and telephone directories are examples. Policies and procedures may be provided in printed manuals or on a company intranet. Data may be stored in databases or in other electronic formats. The company may subscribe to online information services. You will be expected to become familiar with all sources available and know where to search when requests are made.

You may want to develop references to aid you in your specific duties. For example, an office worker who takes trips to other countries might need to know about the exchange rate for currencies. This information can be found online. Several websites have convenient currency calculators or converters. The office worker might create bookmarks (also called a Favorites list) to use in accessing such sites quickly, as shown Figure 4-1.2.

bookmark a link to a website stored for quick access

✓**CHECK POINT** What are three examples of reasons an office employee would need to read at work?

Figure 4-1.2 **Bookmarks make accessing websites quick and easy.**

Writing at Work

The extent and nature of your writing duties are related to the nature of your job. However, all office workers need strong writing skills. Among the common writing tasks for an office worker are the following:

- Summarizing written messages
- Writing notes of actions and decisions at meetings
- Revising others' writing and making changes
- Preparing communications for others to review
- Composing messages and revising them before they are distributed

Like most activities in business, business writing is purpose driven. A practical reason exists for all writing activity at work. Some of the most common purposes are described in the following list.

- **Communicating policies and procedures.** People must be informed about the company and their work. Many written messages relate to the policies and procedures in a company.
- **Reporting on plans in progress.** Business managers know that planning for the future is important for success. Meetings are held where workers think carefully about what lies ahead for the company. Written reports are

valuable for informing everyone about plans or the progress of various projects.

- **Seeking or giving information.** Detailed data is often required to make a business decision. Messages asking for data may be sent to outsiders and employees.

- **Sending messages to customers.** Companies send messages to customers to encourage greater demand for their products and services. Letters, brochures, flyers, catalogs, and websites all require careful writing. Messages are also required to remind customers to pay overdue bills. Efforts to get payment are done in a friendly manner so that the customer will continue to buy from the company.

- **Following up oral discussions.** Discussions may take place in group meetings, person-to-person, by telephone, or by teleconferences. A written record of what was discussed is often required for those in the meetings and others. Such a report serves as a summary of what happened and as a preview for further discussions.

Written reports are valuable for communicating plans or progress on projects.

Reviewing the Writing of Others

Revising is often required to create an effective message. Office workers are often asked to review the messages written by others. Some executives expect their assistants to act as editors. An editor is a person who reviews written messages to suggest changes in wording, organization, and content. Workers with editorial duties perform tasks such as those listed below.

editor a person who reviews written messages to suggest changes in wording, organization, and content

- Consider the writer's goal for the message.
- Review the message to ensure that it meets all the requirements for effectiveness.
- Make candid and tactful suggestions for improving the message.
- Review the suggestions of others in an objective manner.

Read the message prepared by a human resources manager shown in Figure 4-1.3. Note the suggested changes made by a colleague. Consider the changes proposed. Do you think they improve the message?

Figure 4-1.3 A paragraph marked for revision using Word's track changes feature.

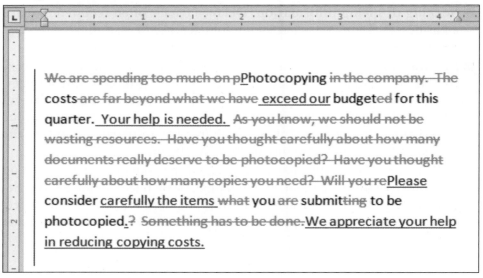

Composing Messages

Messages may reflect the point of view of a department or the company. Often, one person is assigned to prepare a draft, which is then reviewed by others. Staff at all levels may take part in writing tasks.

 draft a rough or preliminary version of a written message

In some companies, administrative assistants and secretaries read incoming messages addressed to coworkers. They prepare drafts of responses to the messages. Then the executive reads the incoming messages and the suggested responses at one time. Often executives are satisfied with their assistants' suggestions. Little editing is needed. Final copies can be prepared quickly. Recipients will have responses within a relatively brief period.

You may have complete responsibility for certain writing tasks. You will want to be at ease when you write messages on your own. Little time may be available to get reviews from others and rewrite what you want to say. You will want to develop the skill of writing a message appropriately with few revisions needed. When you are doing the entire job of composing and signing memos and letters, you must be your own editor. If you are objective, you will be a good editor of your own work.

CHECK POINT Do you think it would be easier to revise and improve your own writing or a message written by another person? Why?

Improving Reading Skills

High-level reading skills will help you be more productive at work. For this reason, adopt a positive attitude toward improving your reading skills. Strive for reading skills that are so natural you need not give deliberate attention to the reading task itself. Instead, you can focus on the content of what you are reading. Critical skills for high-level reading are comprehension, vocabulary, and speed.

Comprehension and Vocabulary

Comprehension is the ability to understand what you have read, seen, or heard. In the case of reading, it involves a transfer of information from the printed page or the computer screen to your memory. A simple example is keeping in mind a number that you have just found in the telephone directory. A more complex example is reading about a supplier's new product. You must remember what you have read to be able to tell whether the product appears to be better than the brand your company is currently using. Some techniques you may find helpful as you work to increase reading comprehension are listed in Figure 4-1.4.

Figure 4-1.4 Techniques for Improving Reading Comprehension

IMPROVING READING COMPREHENSION	
Focus	Put aside anything else on your mind when you begin to read.
Identify purpose	Before you begin, ask: "What do I want to know when I have completed this reading?"
Scan	Get an overview of the page, the chapter, article, or book before you read carefully.
Summarize	Mentally summarize as you move from one paragraph to another, particularly if you are reading to gain information for handling a task.
Sequence	After reading several paragraphs, try to think of the ideas in an appropriate order.
Draw a mental picture	Attempt to imagine what it is that is being discussed.
Checkup	Determine, through a fast review of key points, whether you have learned what you expected to learn.
Reread	Begin anew to read what you have just read if you are not satisfied with your checkup process.

© Cengage Learning 2013

Your **vocabulary** consists of words you know and understand how to use. A large vocabulary increases your understanding of what you read. Words that are unfamiliar to you are a barrier to your reading. Certain techniques can expand your vocabulary and help you to be an effective reader. Consider using some of these techniques as you study the content of this book:

1. When you read an unfamiliar word, try to determine its meaning from the way it is used in the sentence. After you have a meaning you think is correct, check the dictionary. If you were right, you will now be more confident as you consider what unfamiliar words might mean.

2. When you read an unfamiliar word, try separating the word into parts to see if you can guess a meaning for one or more of the parts. You read, for example, the word *rearrange*. You know from earlier experience that *rekey* means that you must key again. You know the meaning of *arrange*. You then guess that *rearrange* means to put in a new or different order. You check the dictionary and find that your guess is right.

3. While reading, have at hand a notepad and pencil to record words you do not know. Write down your best guess of what the word might mean. Also, record the page on which the uncertain word appears.

When you pause to reflect on what you have read, check the words on your list in a dictionary. As you read a definition, compare what you thought the meaning was with the dictionary's definition. You may want to refer back to the place where the word is found. Reread the passage and assure yourself that you understand what is being said. If there is more than one definition provided, be sure to select the definition that fits the context in which the word appeared. Context refers to the parts of a sentence or paragraph around a word that can help you understand the word's meaning. You may find it useful to record new words and review your list from time to time. Try using new words in your conversations as a way of reinforcing your learning.

You may find that a specialized vocabulary is required in your work. You will want to be alert to such terms. You may have available a specialized dictionary or other reference that will help you master new words.

CHECK POINT Why is the context in which a word appears important?

Speed

Another aspect of reading skill relates to speed—the time required for reading a passage. Problems with comprehension or vocabulary can slow the rate at which you read. The rate at which you read can be merely a habit. You probably can learn to read more quickly. Some strategies that can be useful in increasing reading speed are described below.

1. Focus your attention on a whole paragraph at one time. By doing so, you are forcing yourself to break a common habit of deliberately pausing at each word or each sentence as you read. When you have finished reading the paragraph, try to summarize it in a sentence or two. If you realize that you have not grasped the meaning, read it again. Again, attempt to summarize it. You are likely to improve on your second attempt.

Practice techniques to improve your reading comprehension and vocabulary.

Elena Elisseeva/iStockphoto.com

2. Time your reading. Set a goal such as: "I will read this page, which has approximately 350 words, in three minutes." Check to see if you reached your goal. If you did, try the same passage in a shorter time.

3. Deliberately force yourself ahead as you read. Do not set a specific time goal. Note the extent to which you return to your slower way of reading. Think about why you do not continue reading quickly. Try to change your reading habits so that you read quickly while still understanding the passage.

 CHECK POINT Which of the techniques for improving reading comprehension do you think would be most helpful to you? Why?

Reading as a Single Process

The critical areas of comprehension, vocabulary, and reading speed have been discussed separately. When you are actually reading, however, these areas interact. In some cases, you may make up for a weakness in one area by strength in another. For example, you may comprehend well what you read. If you see an unfamiliar word, you figure out its meaning from your understanding of the rest of the sentence or paragraph. In another example, perhaps you read rapidly but your comprehension is limited. By reading rapidly, you have time to reread the material to improve your comprehension. Ideally you want to have high skill levels in all three areas.

As you consider the variety of reading tasks you may handle at work, you will come to realize how much good skills are worth. As you complete the varied assignments in your study of office procedures, regularly assess your reading skills and think of ways to improve them.

 CHECK POINT Which area of reading skill, comprehension or speed, is stronger for you? How can you improve the weaker area?

Improving Writing Skills

Messages written for business purposes should contain all the needed information. They should be written in a style that is easy to understand and appropriate for the audience. Writing tasks must be managed so they are completed on time.

Characteristics of Effective Writing

Unlike a poem, for example, where meaning can be obscure, business writing is expected to be clear and meaningful to all who read it. Common characteristics of good business written messages are listed below. As you write or edit a message, check to see that the message has these characteristics.

- **Clear.** A clear message is logically arranged with the information in an order that is natural for the recipient to follow. To prepare a clear message, you must know why you want to communicate, what you want to say, and who your recipient will be. A clear message eliminates the need for requests for additional comment.

- **Concise.** A concise message states what you want to say in the fewest and most direct words possible without being abrupt. The recipient will waste no time reading words and thoughts that add nothing to understanding the message.

- **Courteous.** Written messages are courteous when they conform to the expected polite, considerate behavior of the business world. Expressions such as "thank you," "please," and "you are welcome" are commonly used in business correspondence. Using the recipient's name and the words *you* or *your* direct the focus of the message toward the receiver.

- **Complete.** A complete message provides all the information needed. Think of the recipient by asking yourself, "Does this answer all the questions the recipient might raise about this matter?"

- **Correct.** A correct message is accurate and up to date. Details provided in messages should be verified before the final copy is prepared.

Effective business writing reveals good command of the English language. To create effective messages, follow these guidelines.

- Check sentence structure and be sure all sentences are complete.

- Use proper grammar. Check grammar references as needed. Use the grammar check feature of your word processing software.

- Follow rules of punctuation and capitalization. Check reference sources as needed.

- Spell words correctly. Use the spell check feature of your software and have a dictionary at hand. Remember that a spell check program does not find misused words such as "two" for "to" as shown in Figure 4-1.5.

✳ WORKPLACE CONNECTIONS ✳

Changes are common in business. Workers should take care to see that all messages have current information. Using incorrect or outdated information can cause problems. Additional messages are often required, and the goodwill of customers can be lost.

Part of Kim Yung's job is to answer inquiries about whether products are in stock and when they can be shipped. A customer asked whether a certain product could be shipped at four dates throughout the year. Kim knew that the company kept good inventories. He responded by e-mail that there would be no problem meeting the customer's order. Only after the customer sent the order with the dates for delivery did Kim check on the items ordered. At that point, he learned that the company would stop making the item within the next two months.

What should Kim have done before answering the customer's question? What may be the result of Kim's error?

Management of Writing Tasks

Writing tasks must be managed wisely if they are to be completed successfully and on schedule. The management of writing tasks has two aspects. One relates to the actual writing task itself. The other relates to scheduling the task properly to meet deadlines.

Figure 4-1.5 A spell check program often does not find misused words.

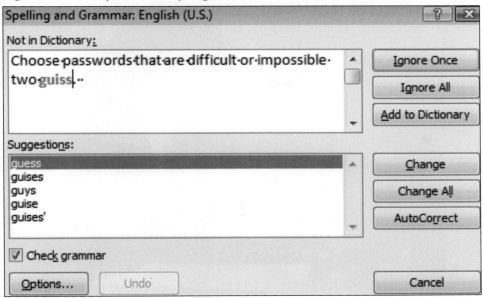

Managing the Task of Writing

The following steps will prove useful to you in completing a writing assignment.

1. Identify the reason for the written message. Write a single sentence that states the goal of the message.

2. Consider the audience for the message. The **audience** is the recipient(s) for whom the message is intended.

3. Secure all the information required for the message and compose a draft. Prepare an outline if the message is long. Key or dictate your message directly at your computer using your outline as a guide.

4. Review your message. Is it clear, concise, courteous, complete, and correct? Make changes or corrections if needed.

5. If required, submit your draft to a colleague or manager for review and approval.

6. Prepare a revised copy of your message.

7. Proofread carefully and make final corrections.

8. Prepare the final message (printed or electronic) for distribution.

audience the recipient(s) for whom a message is intended

Managing the Schedule for Writing Tasks

In most instances, you will have a deadline for the completion of a writing task. This means that when you accept a writing task, you must review how much time is required for each aspect of the work you must do.

One strategy is to review the steps in the preceding section, noting just how much time is needed to do the task well. For example, having the required information at hand in a letter eliminates the need for time to search for information. A schedule may be needed for a major writing task to ensure that you work within the time period allowed. The time available must be scheduled so that each aspect of the task can be done properly.

Complete each part of a large writing task on schedule to meet the final deadline.

nyul/iStockphoto.com

You will have many occasions during your study of office procedures to develop your writing skills. Remember that all written messages do not need to be of the same quality. For example, a message to the manager of the stockroom, whom you know personally, might be written informally and e-mailed without editing. On the other hand, a letter to thousands of customers might be rewritten several times, with others reviewing the drafts, to make sure the letter will attract customer attention.

With practice, you will improve your skill in preparing simple messages in a first draft. Also, you will gain a sense of what a good message should be and how to prepare one. With practice, you will develop skill in evaluating and improving your writing.

REVIEW 4-1

21st Century Skills

Interacting with Others

PARTNERSHIP FOR
21ST CENTURY SKILLS

Tomasine works as an assistant manager in the office of a warehouse facility where she interacts with a number of employees. The office is a busy place because an inventory of over 11,000 items is maintained. On several occasions, Juan, a part-time employee, asked Tomasine to help him with instructions for incoming merchandise. Tomasine began to realize that Juan did not understand instructions. Then Tomasine began to wonder if Juan was having problems with reading. One evening after work, Tomasine and Juan were leaving at the same time. The two began to talk. Juan said to Tomasine: "I think I should give up this job; it is too hard for me. I guess I don't really want to work."

1. If you were Tomasine, what would you say to Juan?
2. What resources are available in your community to help adults who have trouble with reading?

Making Academic Connections

Reinforcing English Skills

1. Read the following sentences and identify the errors in noun and verb agreement.
2. Key the sentences, correcting the errors.

Simple rules of writing applies to e-mail. This type of writing seem informal, but it is still business communications. Experts points out that brisk and brief writing are fine. Considering this type of communicating impersonal is not wise. Insensitive and discourteous statements should not be in your messages. The ease in corresponding via e-mail have led to many unclear and confusing messages. Reviews of e-mail has discovered all types of inappropriate and irrelevant material that are really clutter.

4-1 Activity 1

Reading and Writing at Work (Outcome 4-1a)

The way in which employees are required to read and write at work varies depending on the employee's job.

1. Interview someone who works in an office. The interview can be by phone, by e-mail, or in person. Ask the following questions related to reading and writing at work.
   - What is your job position?
   - What types of activities are involved in your work?
   - What types of materials do you read at work? Are they mostly in print or electronic format?
   - Do you typically have trouble understanding what you read in these materials?
   - Do the materials have a specialized vocabulary? If yes, describe the type of words used.
   - What types of documents do you typically write at work?

- Are the documents distributed in print or electronic format?
- Do you review or edit the writing of others?

2. Write a short summary that gives the name and job position of the person you interviewed and the answers to the questions you asked.

4-1 Activity 2

Improving Reading Skills (Outcome 4-1b)

1. Open the file 4-1 Rules from the data files. This document shows a portion of the rules regarding early withdrawal costs for a bank at which you work.

2. Read this document at a comfortable rate, noting the amount of time it takes you to read the document.

3. Identify any words or terms about which you are unsure of the meaning. Look up the meaning of these words or terms.

4. Read the document again, trying to complete the reading in less time than your first reading.

5. Test your comprehension and memory of the passage by answering the following customer's questions from memory.

- **Customer A:** My one-year deposit will mature in eight months. Could I withdraw the money next month?
- **Customer B:** I would like to add money now to my certificate of deposit that matures in three months. May I do this?
- **Customer C:** I have an 18-month certificate of deposit that matures in six months. What penalty will I pay if I withdraw all the money now?

6. Now read the document again. Did you answer the questions correctly? Update the answers if needed.

OUTCOMES

4-2a Describe and apply steps for preparing effective business documents.
4-2b Describe and create effective business correspondence.
4-2c Apply guidelines for preparing documents using desktop publishing.

KEY TERMS

tone p. 116
direct approach p. 116
indirect approach p. 117
revising p. 118
proofreading p. 119
protocol p. 121
spam p. 129
font p. 129
resolution p. 129
white space p. 130

Preparing Effective Documents

Office workers often compose business letters and memos or e-mail messages. Employees may prepare letters or memos for or with coworkers as well as for themselves. The ability to compose and prepare effective business messages will make you a more valuable employee. As you study this chapter, you will review document parts and standard formats. You will also study some guidelines for using desktop publishing to prepare documents such as newsletters or flyers.

As you learned earlier, effective business documents are clear, concise, courteous, complete, and correct. These traits are known as the *five Cs* of business writing. They are your guidelines to preparing business documents. You can quickly check the effectiveness of your documents by considering these factors.

An effective document is planned well and prepared carefully. Preparing a document includes three stages. First, a draft of the document is written. Then the document is revised or edited as needed. The last stage is proofreading and correcting the document for final presentation.

Drafting

Your first draft of a document will probably not be your final or finished version. It is considered a rough draft. Your goal in preparing the rough draft is to record your ideas. Do not try to make each sentence perfect. You will refine your document during the editing and proofreading stages. To help focus your writing as you develop your document, ask yourself these questions:

1. What is your purpose in writing?
2. Who and where is your audience?
3. What are the main points of your message?
4. What details should you include in your message?
5. What response do you want from the reader?

Purpose

Fix the purpose of the document clearly in your mind before you begin writing. Business documents are often written to inform. For example, you may want the reader to know about a new product or a new procedure. Business documents are also written to persuade or describe. Although these purposes may overlap, you need to have a clear understanding of why you are writing the document before you write the first draft.

Audience

Knowing certain things about your reader(s) is important to how you develop your document. Is the reader already familiar with the topic? Knowing this will help you determine how much information to include. Is your document going to one reader or many? Is the document meant for external or internal use? These factors may influence how formal your writing needs to be, whether confidential topics may be mentioned, and how responses may be requested.

tone style, manner of writing or speaking that shows a certain attitude

Considering the audience will help you write messages that are appropriate and effective.

Antenna/Jupiter Images

Message

Determine the points you need to make. What do you need to say to get your message across? What information do you need to include to build support for your position? The **tone** of your message can be as important as the content. Keep these points in mind as you draft your message:

■ Prepare an outline of the document, particularly for longer documents. An outline will help you prepare the message in a logical sequence. The better you organize your points, the easier it will be for you to write the message and for your reader to understand it.

■ Focus on the reader as you write. Avoid using too many "I" and "we" words. Instead, use "you," "your," or the recipient's name frequently. This technique is called the *you* approach.

■ Give your message a positive tone. Avoid using negative words or a negative tone. Always be courteous. Make an effort in your writing to be helpful to the reader.

Business messages may be written with a direct, indirect, or persuasive approach. To determine which approach you should use, consider the effect the message will have on the receiver.

Direct Approach

direct approach a style of writing in which the main point is stated early in the message

A reader will not be disappointed with a **positive message** or **neutral message**. For these messages, give the good news or neutral news to the reader early in the document using a direct approach.

Examples of positive or neutral messages include:

- Placing or confirming an order
- Placing or filling a request for information
- Filling or extending a request for credit
- Making, approving, or adjusting routine claims

Follow the guidelines below to prepare positive or neutral messages. Note how the message in Figure 4-2.1 follows these general guidelines.

- Use the direct approach.
- State the main point directly and early in the message.
- Include specific, complete information as appropriate.

Figure 4-2.1 **Use a direct approach for a positive message.**

Dear Ms. Racine

Congratulations! Your request for a car loan was approved by our loan officer this morning.

Your loan for $10,000 is now being processed and will be available for your use within 24 hours. Please contact our loan officer, Jan Truong, at 555-0134 for an appointment to sign the final papers and to discuss your monthly payments.

Thank you for your business, Ms. Racine. Please let us know if you would like to discuss other services offered by our bank.

© Cengage Learning 2013

Indirect Approach

Negative messages typically involve a refusal or other news that the reader will find disappointing or upsetting. For this type of message, use an indirect approach. For example, tell the reader why a request is being refused. Give reasons for the disappointing news before stating it directly. Try to keep the reader's goodwill. Examples of negative messages include:

> indirect approach a style of writing that gives reasons or details to support a main point that comes later in the message

- Refusing a request for an adjustment, a credit, or a favor
- Canceling a service
- Reporting unfavorable results

Negative messages require the writer to take considerable care in preparing the document. Figure 4-2.2 gives an example of a negative message. Follow these guidelines to prepare a negative message.

- Use an indirect approach.
- Begin the message with a neutral statement that lets the reader know the message is your response to the request or to a situation that has arisen.
- Build your position by stating the reasons for your decision.
- State the refusal or other negative news.
- Close on a positive note and suggest alternatives if appropriate.

Figure 4-2.2 Use an indirect approach to prepare a negative message.

Dear Mr. Ortiz

Thank you for considering the Trust Bank for your car loan. Our loan officers met this morning to consider your loan application.

After a careful review of your application, they determined that your monthly income must be higher to support a loan of $10,000 with your current debt liability. Therefore, we cannot approve your loan at this time. Please consider resubmitting your loan application once your monthly payments of $250 on your existing loan are finished.

Your patronage is important to us, Mr. Ortiz. We at Trust Bank hope you will continue to consider us for your future banking needs.

© Cengage Learning 2013

An indirect approach is often used to prepare a persuasive message. In this type of message, the writer wants to influence the reader to take a desired action. Sales letters, collection letters, and donation requests are all examples of persuasive messages. When you write a sales letter, for example, you want to influence the reader to buy your product or service. When you write a donation request, you want to persuade the reader to donate to your cause. The basic steps to preparing a persuasive message are as follows:

■ Gain the reader's attention.
■ Stimulate the reader's interest or desire.
■ Give the reader an opportunity to act.

Response

Consider how the reader will use the document or message you are preparing. Will it be used to make a decision? To gain information? If you want a response from the reader, let the reader know the specific action you want. Make it easy for the reader to respond by stating your message and the desired response clearly.

 CHECK POINT When writing the first draft of a document, what four factors should you consider to help focus your writing?

Revising and Editing

Many business documents are changed one or more times between the rough draft and the final document. This process of making changes to refine a message or document is known as editing or **revising**.

The primary purpose of revising is to make certain the message is accurate and says what the writer intends. In this stage of preparing your document, focus on the details of your writing. Read your draft carefully and consider the

revising making changes to refine a written message

five Cs of effective documents. This is your chance to polish your writing by making changes in response to these questions:

- Can you improve your word choice?
- Are the transitions smooth, flowing logically from one topic to another?
- Should the order of the points be changed?
- Are there inconsistencies in the writing that need to be corrected?

To mark changes that can be understood easily by others, writers often use standard proofreaders' marks as shown in Figure 4-2.3 when writing on printed copy. Popular word processing programs have features that allow you to mark changes and make comments in a document file. Once the changes are identified and marked, you can review the changes and accept or reject them.

Figure 4-2.3 **Proofreaders' marks are used in revising printed documents.**

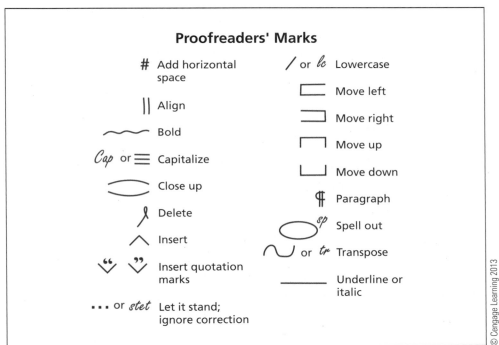

Proofreaders' Marks

#	Add horizontal space	/ or *lc*	Lowercase
‖	Align	⌐	Move left
～	Bold	¬	Move right
Cap or ≡	Capitalize	⌐	Move up
⌒	Close up	⌐	Move down
ℓ	Delete	¶	Paragraph
∧	Insert	*sp*	Spell out
❝ ❞	Insert quotation marks	～ or *tr*	Transpose
••• or *stet*	Let it stand; ignore correction	___	Underline or italic

© Cengage Learning 2013

Proofreading, the last phase of preparing a document, is your careful, overall check of the document for errors and mechanical issues. During this process, verify that the changes you marked in the editing phase have been made correctly. Check all numbers and unusual spellings against original documents. Use a spell checker and a grammar checker if available with your software. Then complete a detailed manual proofreading. Remember that the spelling feature of your software is limited in the errors it can identify. For example, errors such as "there" for "their" will not be detected.

Proofreading requires your complete attention. Your goal is to produce error-free documents. When a document is very important or complex, you may need to revise and proofread the document several times before it is final.

proofreading checking a document carefully for errors and mechanical issues

CHECK POINT What is the difference between revising and proofreading?

Preparing Business Correspondence

Business correspondence consists mainly of letters, printed memos, and e-mail messages. Each type of correspondence has appropriate uses. A business letter is a considered a more formal communication than a memo or an e-mail message.

Business Letters

A business letter is a written message to a person(s) or an organization. Letters are usually written to someone outside the company. As the writer of a business letter, you are your company's representative. Your letter helps the reader form an opinion about your company.

Letters provide a long-lasting record of your message. They can be read many times and can serve different purposes. Reasons for writing business letters include:

- Requesting information or an action
- Giving information or fulfilling a request
- Being courteous or maintaining goodwill (congratulation and thank-you notes)
- Explaining or stating a position or persuading the reader
- Selling goods or services

Presentation of Business Letters

The primary purpose of a business letter is to convey a message. However, even before the message is read, the reader makes a judgment about the letter and its sender. An attractively presented letter on quality paper will encourage the recipient to read the message with care. On the other hand, a carelessly presented letter on smudged paper may fail to get close attention.

A letter makes a good first impression if it has the following characteristics:

- The margins and spacing are pleasing to the eye.
- Each letter part is correctly placed within the letter.

- Appropriate stationery is used.
- There are no obvious errors.
- The print is neat and clear.
- There are no smudges or fingerprints.

Make your letters attractive as well as complete and correct. If the appearance of the letter is pleasing to the eye, the receiver will be encouraged to read what you have written.

Letter Parts

Business letters represent a form of communication within the business world that follows a standard protocol. That is, those who receive business letters expect to see them written using certain letter parts. Of course, few letters will include all these parts. Some parts are included in most letters. Other parts are included only when needed. The standard letter parts that should be included in most business letters, as well as optional parts, are listed in Figure 4-2.4.

protocol generally accepted customs or rules

Figure 4-2.4 **Standard and Optional Letter Parts**

STANDARD LETTER PARTS	OPTIONAL LETTER PARTS
Letterhead	Subject line
Date	Enclosure notation
Letter address	Copy notation
Salutation	Postscript
Body	Reference initials
Complimentary closing	Multiple-page heading
Signature, printed name, and title	

© Cengage Learning 2013

Occasionally, a letter will require more than one page. In such instances, a multiple-page heading is prepared to identify each page. As shown in Figure 4-2.5, the heading includes the name of the addressee, the word *Page* and a page number, and the letter date. Other letter parts are illustrated in Figure 4-2.6.

Figure 4-2.5 **Multiple-page Letter Heading**

Miss Laureen DiRenna
Page 2
February 20, 20--

apply the credit toward a future purchase. Be sure to include your membership number on the account credit form provided and return the form with the survey. This will ensure that your account is credited properly.

Sincerely

© Cengage Learning 2013

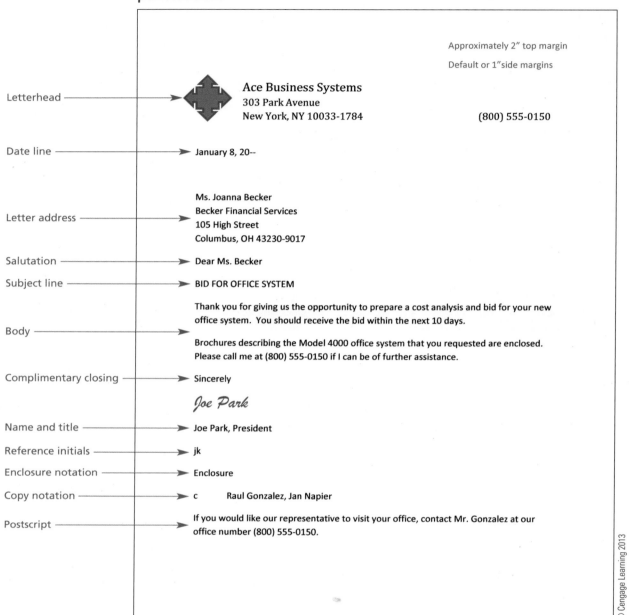

Letterhead

Date line

Letter address

Salutation

Subject line

Body

Complimentary closing

Name and title

Reference initials

Enclosure notation

Copy notation

Postscript

Approximately 2" top margin

Default or 1"side margins

Ace Business Systems
303 Park Avenue
New York, NY 10033-1784

(800) 555-0150

January 8, 20--

Ms. Joanna Becker
Becker Financial Services
105 High Street
Columbus, OH 43230-9017

Dear Ms. Becker

BID FOR OFFICE SYSTEM

Thank you for giving us the opportunity to prepare a cost analysis and bid for your new office system. You should receive the bid within the next 10 days.

Brochures describing the Model 4000 office system that you requested are enclosed. Please call me at (800) 555-0150 if I can be of further assistance.

Sincerely

Joe Park

Joe Park, President

jk

Enclosure

c   Raul Gonzalez, Jan Napier

If you would like our representative to visit your office, contact Mr. Gonzalez at our office number (800) 555-0150.

© Cengage Learning 2013

Business Letter Formats

The arrangement of the letter text on the page is referred to as its format. Using a standard format for letters increases efficiency for both the writer and the recipient. For the writer, extra time is not needed to decide how to arrange the letter. For the recipient, the task of reading and comprehending is simplified because the format of information is familiar.

Many companies have procedures manuals that contain standard format instructions and examples for frequently prepared documents. If examples are not available, you will be expected to make format decisions. These decisions should reflect your desire to produce attractive, easy-to-read documents.

Writers frequently use the block and modified block letter formats. In block format, all lines begin at the left margin. Paragraphs and other letter parts are not indented. The letter in Figure 4-2.6 is in block format. Block format is efficient because it saves time in moving from one part of the letter to another.

In modified block format, the date, complimentary closing, and signature block (writer's signature, typed name, and title) begin at the horizontal center of the page rather than at the left margin. The letter in Figure 4-2.7 is in modified block format.

Two punctuation styles are typically used in business letters. These styles are open punctuation and mixed punctuation. In open punctuation style, no punctuation marks are used after the salutation and the complimentary close. See Figure 4-2.6 for an example. In mixed punctuation style, a colon is placed after the salutation and a comma after the complimentary close. Either punctuation style may be used with a block or modified block letter.

Figure 4-2.7 This business letter is in modified block format with open punctuation.

Approximately 2" top margin

Default or 1" side margins

Ace Business Systems
303 Park Avenue
New York, NY 10033-1784

(800) 555-0150

January 8, 20--

Ms. Joanna Becker
Becker Financial Services
105 High Street
Columbus, OH 43230-9017

Dear Ms. Becker

Thank you for giving us the opportunity to prepare a cost analysis and bid for your new office system. You should receive the bid within the next 10 days.

Brochures describing the Model 4000 office system that you requested are enclosed. Please call me at (800) 555-0150 if I can be of further assistance.

Sincerely

Joe Park

Joe Park, President

jk

Enclosure

c   Raul Gonzalez, Jan Napier

© Cengage Learning 2013

Writing in the business office often involves preparing similar messages that are used again and again. The same letters may be sent to hundreds of people. Employees who prepare such documents often use technology to speed the preparation. Standard text, which is used in all the letters, can be combined with other data to form a finished document. The writer assembles the document by using custom text (the person's name and address) with selected standard paragraphs. Standard text is also called boilerplate text. Custom text is also called variables. The variable data may be stored in a table or a database file, such as a customer address file. A special feature of word processing software, often called mail merge, allows users to combine standard text and variables automatically. Once the document is assembled, it is printed and saved in the same manner as other documents.

Have you received a document that was personalized for you and probably created by merging your information with standard text? Describe the document.

Envelopes

Most business letters are written to individuals outside the company. They require an envelope for mailing. The receiver begins forming an opinion of the document when he or she views the envelope. For this reason, the same care should be used in preparing envelopes as in preparing letters. The letter-head stationery and the envelope stationery should be of the same quality and color. The print should be clear, and the envelope should be free of smudges. A sample envelope is shown in Figure 4-2.8.

Figure 4-2.8 Envelopes should include the recipient's address and a return address.

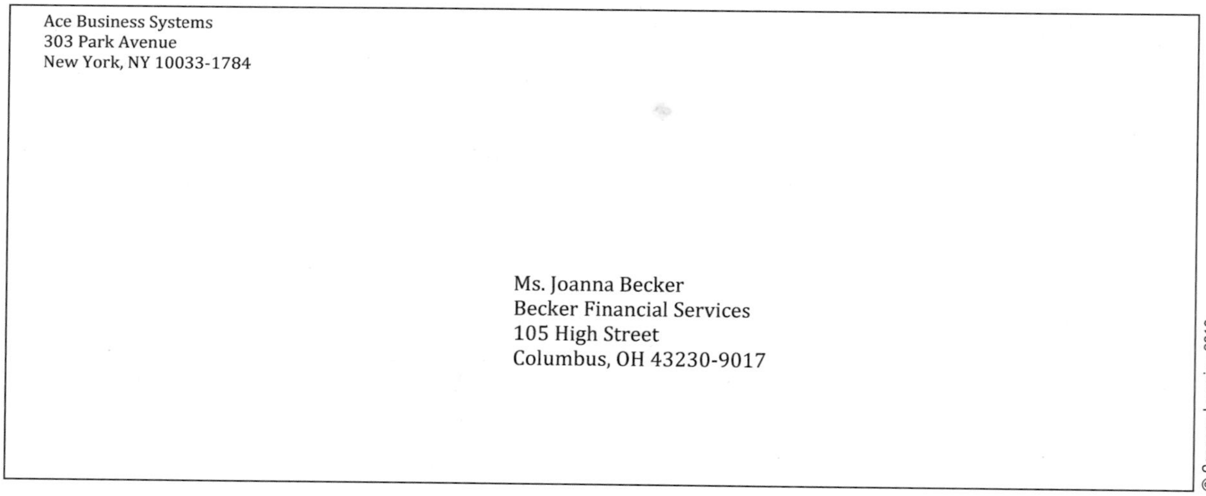

Ace Business Systems
303 Park Avenue
New York, NY 10033-1784

Ms. Joanna Becker
Becker Financial Services
105 High Street
Columbus, OH 43230-9017

© Cengage Learning 2013

The envelope must be a proper size and made of material acceptable to the United States Postal Service (USPS). To ensure prompt delivery, envelopes should include the recipient's name and address and the sender's return address. Use the envelope or mailings feature of your word processing software to create envelopes. The letter address will be lifted from the letter. You can set a default return address for the company name and address. The software will automatically place the letter address and the return address in the proper location. (The return address should be placed in the upper left corner of the envelope. The letter address should be placed about 4 inches from the left and 2 inches from the top of the envelope.) Once the envelope has been added to the letter file, you can place any special addressee notations, such as CONFIDENTIAL, just below the return address.

 CHECK POINT What standard letter parts should be included in every business letter?

Memos

A memo is an informal document. It is typically used to communicate with people within an organization. However, a memo can also be sent to someone outside the organization. A memo is more formally called a memorandum.

Memos are useful for giving the same information to several people. They can be used to give instructions or explain procedures. A personnel director, for example, may send memos to tell employees of holiday schedules. A credit manager may send memos to sales staff giving new credit terms for customers.

Memos and e-mail are the most commonly used written messages within an organization. A memo rather than an e-mail message should be used when the message contains confidential information. Memos can also be used for messages to workers who do not have access to e-mail at work, such as factory workers.

The headings and body are the standard parts of a memo. Other parts, such as copy or enclosure notations, are optional. An example memo is shown in Figure 4-2.9 on page 126. When a memo is sent to a large group of people, do not list all the recipients after the *To* heading. Instead, enter *Distribution List* after the *To* heading and list the recipients at the end of the memo under the heading *Distribution List*.

If the person receiving a printed memo is located nearby, the memo may be placed in the person's in-basket or mailbox. In this case, an envelope may not be needed. If the receiver is in a different location, the memo typically is sent in an interoffice envelope. A confidential document should always be placed in an envelope marked *Confidential*.

Each memo you write makes an impression on the receiver. If the memo is prepared well, the reader forms a positive image of you as an employee. When preparing a memo, follow the five Cs of effective writing and use a positive tone.

 CHECK POINT What is the purpose of a memo? How does it differ from a letter?

Figure 4-2.9 **A memo is an informal document.**

Approximately 2" top margin

Default or 1" side margins

TO: Raul Gonzalez

FROM: Joe Park

DATE: January 8, 20--

SUBJECT: Project Bid

Joanna Becker, of Becker Financial Services in Columbus, has requested a cost analysis and bid for a new office system. I have indicated to Ms. Becker that we will have our bid to her within 10 days.

Offhand, I think the Model 4000 will be the best option for this company. I have sent Ms. Becker brochures describing this system. Please review the attached documents that describe the company needs and be ready to offer your recommendations at our regular meeting on Friday.

Attachment

c   Jan Napier

© Cengage Learning 2013

E-Mail

E-mail is a message sent electronically. Local and wide area networks can provide e-mail service to their users. Users who are connected to the Internet can send and receive messages all over the world. Workers use e-mail for routine messages with people inside and outside the company.

E-mail is appropriate for short, informal correspondence. Files containing more information may be attached to an e-mail. E-mail is inexpensive, fast, and easy to use for workers at all levels in a company. Remember, however, that e-mail messages are recorded. They may be viewed by people other than the person to whom you wrote. Your e-mail may be read by your employer or coworkers. At work, never write an e-mail message that you would not want other employees or your supervisor to read.

Yoshi works in the Human Resources Department of a large company. He has access to data about employees such as salary data. Yoshi uses e-mail to send messages to managers in the company. He takes for granted that his e-mail messages will be read only by his intended recipient.

Ellen Wilson, a company employee, was being considered for a promotion. Ellen's manager, who was new to the company, sent an e-mail message to Yoshi. The message asked for Ellen's current rate of pay and the date of her last salary increase. Yoshi wrote an e-mail to Ellen's manager giving the data requested. By mistake, Yoshi's sent the message to everyone in his department, including Ellen. Yoshi was called to his supervisor's office. He was reprimanded for sending confidential employee information via e-mail.

Would Yoshi's behavior have been correct if he had sent the message only to Ellen's manager? Why or why not?

E-Mail Addresses

Before you can send and receive e-mail, you must have a unique e-mail address. E-mail addresses begin with a user ID (identification). The ID is a unique identifier such as *dsmith* (for Diane Smith). The user ID is followed by the @ sign and the domain name. To understand a domain name, read from right to left. The highest level of the domain appears at the right and identifies the type of organization. Consider the address *dsmith@eng.unlv.edu*. Starting at the right, the *edu* identifies this address as being located at an educational institution. The next section, *unlv*, identifies the specific one, such as University of Nevada, Las Vegas. The *eng* identifies the department, such as English or Engineering. The last part, *dsmith*, identifies an individual.

When you pronounce an e-mail address *Djones@cmu.com*, you would say, "d jones at c m u dot com" rather than spell out each letter. Be careful when recording an e-mail address. Addresses are often case sensitive. If you key an address incorrectly, your message will not be delivered to the intended address.

E-Mail Features

E-mail software varies somewhat in look and features from one program to another. However, certain features are found in most e-mail programs. E-mail messages contain headings and a section for the body of the message. An example is shown in Figure 4-2.10 on page 128. E-mail programs allow the user to read mail, check for new messages, compose and reply to messages, delete messages, attach files to messages, and send new mail.

An e-mail address book is provided to store the user's most frequently used addresses. The Inbox collects incoming messages. A user alert, such as a tone or flashing icon, often accompanies the receipt of new mail. The Outbox holds e-mail messages to be sent to others. It may also hold messages that have already been sent, or these messages may be stored in a separate Sent box or folder. Because these messages are actually stored on your hard drive, you should frequently delete messages that are no longer needed. Most mail programs will allow you to prioritize an e-mail message, that is, to rank it in importance, usually from urgent or high to low.

Figure 4-2.10 **E-mail makes sending messages fast and easy.**

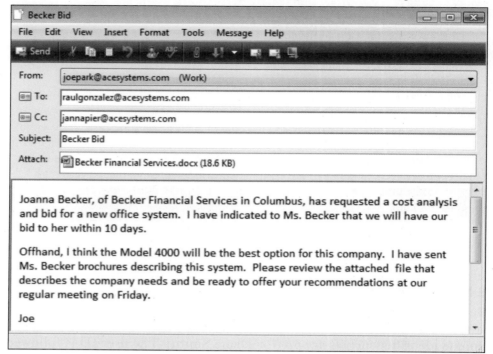

E-mail Guidelines

Consider these guidelines for improving e-mail messages:

- Keep the message short. Attach a report to the message if more details are needed.
- Use a descriptive subject line so the recipient can see the topic of your message immediately.
- Follow a logical sequence in presenting the information.
- Write using a positive tone. Be tactful when expressing personal opinions in your writing. Handle sensitive situations positively.
- Follow the same strategies as you would for a business letter to deliver positive, neutral, negative, or persuasive messages.
- Carefully read your message, checking for application of the five Cs. Is the message clear, concise, complete, correct, and courteous?
- Use the spell check feature of your software and proofread carefully.
- Check for messages regularly and reply to your messages promptly. Do not, however, send a message quickly in frustration or anger that you may regret later.
- Send messages only to people who really need to read the message. When replying to a message, reply only to the sender—not to everyone who received the message—unless everyone needs your answer.
- Take steps to safeguard confidential information. Never send confidential information in an e-mail message. Prepare a memo or printed report instead.

- Consider carefully before forwarding messages you receive to others. Honor others' rights of privacy. Never forward chain messages or send spam.

 CHECK POINT List four guidelines that you think are the most important ones for improving e-mail messages.

Desktop Publishing

Not all business correspondence follows standard formats as letters do. Product brochures, newsletters, and flyers may each use a unique format and design. These documents often contain graphics (clip art, photos, or other images) as well as text. They may use fancy fonts or banner headings to draw the reader's attention. Word processing or desktop publishing software is used to create these documents.

Desktop publishing programs, such as QuarkXPress and PageMaker, contain features for creating complex documents with text and images. These programs allow the user to control type settings and page layouts. They also allow full-color output. The text and images appear on your computer screen almost exactly as they will when printed. The images are often created or edited with drawing or illustration programs. They are then placed in the document using the desktop publishing program. Word processing programs usually have basic desktop publishing features. Programs such as Word may be used to create documents with multiple columns (Figure 4-2.11), text, and graphics.

Figure 4-2.11 **Some programs, such as Word, allow users to create documents with multiple columns.**

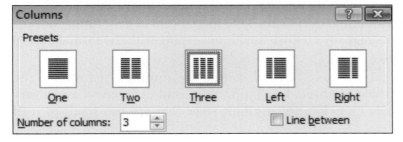

Resolution

True desktop publishing results in high-resolution printed documents. Printed text and images are made up of many tiny dots of color. Resolution is the number of dots per inch (dpi) in a printed document. The greater the dpi, the higher the resolution and the sharper the printed image. Professional printers use around 2,400 dpi for many documents. Many businesses do not have high-resolution printers. They create the document files and send them to an outside company for printing. For in-house or informal documents, 600 dpi is considered acceptable. Many businesses have printers that can produce this resolution.

 CHECK POINT What is print resolution? How does it relate to clarity of printed material?

Desktop Publishing Guidelines

When creating documents to be desktop published, follow the five Cs of effective writing. Consider the purpose of the document. Is it to inform, to persuade, or to request information? Also consider the audience for the document. Is in-house (probably low-resolution) printing acceptable? Should a professional printer be used? If printing will be done by a professional printer, obtain details from the printer about how the file must be created to print successfully. Use copyrighted text or images in your documents only with proper permission from the copyright holder.

Your goal is to create a document that makes a good impression. It should be attractive and deliver your message effectively. Consider these guidelines for creating desktop published documents:

■ Use consistency in the design. For example, format all heads of the same level in same way. If the company logo appears on each page, place it in the same location on every page.

■ Use ample **white space** to rest the eye and identify the beginning and end of each section. Effective use of white space keeps the text and images from looking cramped on the page.

■ Create a pleasing balance of elements (headings, body text, and images) on the page. Documents with a balanced format (with roughly the same amount of material on each side of the page) have a formal, traditional look. Documents with an unbalanced format have a more informal look.

■ Create contrast in the design by placing different objects next to each other. A graphic placed next to text, for example, creates contrast on the page.

■ Include artwork or photos that are relevant to the message. Place them near the text to which they relate. Use decorations or other artwork that are appropriate for the document. Take special care in very formal or serious documents that any artwork used is in keeping with the formal tone of the document.

■ Use fonts that are easy to read. Limit the number of fonts in the document to two or three. Use bold, italic, and different sizes to vary the font appearance. Do not use font sizes that are too small to read easily.

■ Use all capitals sparingly because text in all caps is hard to read.

■ Avoid widow lines. A widow line is one that appears alone at the beginning of a page or column, separated from the rest of the paragraph. Adjust the spacing or rewrite the sentence if necessary to prevent widow lines.

■ Use printer's curves for apostrophes and quotes (' and " rather than ' and ").

■ Avoid large horizontal spaces between words, which look unattractive. Using a ragged right margin and hyphenating words helps avoid this problem.

white space the area on a printed page that is empty, having no text or images

---

CHECK POINT List five guidelines to follow when creating desktop published documents.

REVIEW 4-2

21st Century Skills

Thinking Critically

PARTNERSHIP FOR
21ST CENTURY SKILLS

Selena, an administrative assistant at a travel agency, wrote this draft:

We are happy to announce that The Traveler's Agency will now offer a full range of travel services. In addition to our regular travel services, we are now promoting three travel discount packages that we designed for the business traveler. Please contact our offices for more information. Our website also provides details.

Selena's manager reviewed the draft and had these comments: "This draft includes all the needed information, Selena, but the approach isn't quite right. Please revise the draft using a reader-focused approach."

What changes do you think Selena should make? Revise the messages to use a reader-focused approach.

Making Academic Connections

Reinforcing English Skills

A coworker at Computer Corner Furniture needs your help with answering a letter to a customer. The customer has had difficulty assembling a computer workstation. The tone of the response written by your coworker is too negative.

1. Open the file 4-2 English Skills from the data files. Revise the excerpt from the letter to give the message a more positive tone.
2. Spell-check, proofread, and correct all errors before printing the message.

4-2 Activity 1

Personalized Form Letters (Outcome 4-2a, 4-2b)

A draft of a letter to be used as a response to routine inquiries for employment has several errors in spelling, capitalization, and word usage. These errors must be identified and corrected before the form letter is merged with the data source.

1. Open and print the file 4-2 Activity 1 found in the data files. This file contains handwritten text to be used as standard text for a form letter.
2. Key the standard text for the form letter. Assume the letter will be printed on company letterhead. Use the current date, block letter format, and open punctuation. Add an appropriate salutation and closing. Correct errors as you key; then spell-check and proofread the message. Save the letter as 4-2 Form Letter.
3. Create a new word processing or database file named 4-2 Contacts. Create a table named Contacts that contains the following column heads or fields: Record ID, Title, First Name, Last Name, Address, City, State, ZIP Code, and Position. If you are using a database table, make Record ID the primary key and a number field. Make all other fields text fields.
4. Enter data for five records in the Contacts table. The records are shown below the standard text in the 4-2 Activity 1 file.

5. Open the standard letter you created earlier (*4-2 Form Letter*). Begin the process to merge the standard text and the five records. Select the file that contains the table you created as the data source for a mail merge. Enter fields from the table for the variables. Complete the merge steps to create personalized letters. View the merged letters and make corrections, if needed, before printing the letters.

6. Perform a merge to create personalized envelopes for the letters. Make corrections, if needed, before printing. (Use paper cut to envelope size if envelopes are not available.)

4-2 Activity 2

Netiquette Flyer (Outcomes 4-2a, 4-2c)

Guidelines for interacting with others courteously online are called *netiquette* (derived from *network* and *etiquette*). Prepare a flyer on netiquette related to e-mail to distribute to coworkers.

1. Search the Internet or other reference sources for several articles or websites that provide information about netiquette. For each article or website, record the source information. Include the author for articles, the article or web page name, the publication or website name and address, and the date of the publication or the date you view the website.

2. After reading about netiquette, write in your own words a list of 8 to 10 netiquette rules that relate to e-mail.

3. Create a one-page flyer to communicate your netiquette rules. Follow the design guidelines found in this chapter for creating effective documents.

4. List the source information for three articles or websites you reviewed as sources of additional information on netiquette.

OUTCOMES

4-3a Describe types of business reports.
4-3b Prepare reports in formal and informal formats.
4-3c Create visual aids used in reports.

Types of Business Reports

Business reports are used to share information. Reports may be prepared for employees or people outside the company. The types of reports workers prepare will depend on their job duties. In many companies, office workers write, edit, assemble, and distribute business reports.

Reports can be prepared in various formats and for various reasons. You will explore reports with different purposes in this chapter. In addition, you will explore special features of reports such as tables and graphs. You will learn to gather, organize, write, and present information in a standard report format. You can easily adapt this format to other reports you may encounter on the job. Reports can be saved as web pages and shared with others using an intranet.

Informational Reports

Informational reports are typically based on data gathered within the normal operations of the company. The company relies on employees to gather or enter the data accurately and on time. In many companies, routine reports are created on a regular basis. For example, workers at a company use a screen similar to Figure 4-3.1 to clock in and clock out each workday. A report is generated each week that shows the hours worked by each employee. This report is used to create the weekly payroll.

Some companies use handheld computers to gather data that are later used to create reports. For example, utility company workers use devices to read meters that monitor use of electricity. The data gathered are copied to a central computer. Office workers use the data in creating reports and customer bills.

When writing an informational report, follow the guidelines used for a direct approach message. State the purpose early and clearly. For example, use the subject line in a memo report or the title in a formal report to help focus the reader to your purpose.

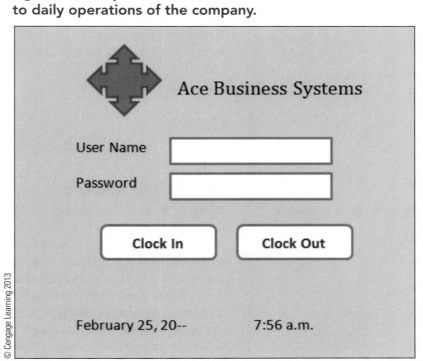

Figure 4-3.1 **Reports are created from data related to daily operations of the company.**

© Cengage Learning 2013

Stan Bridge works for a package delivery service. He uses a handheld computer device to gather data. When each package is delivered, Stan scans the package bar code label that identifies the package and the delivery location. The customer signs for the package entering his or her signature on the touch screen of the computer device. At the end of each day, Stan places the handheld device in a unit that allows the data to be downloaded to a computer. The data are used to create a report that shows the number of deliveries Stan made that day, the number of pounds the packages weighed, and the types of items (overnight letters, small packages, large boxes) delivered.

The data collected by several drivers are also used to create reports. These reports address issues such as how long a route should be assigned to various drivers. The number of drivers needed in a particular delivery area might also be discussed.

▶ **What is an advantage of creating reports from scanned data rather than gathering data from paper documents?**

Consider the audience in deciding how formal a report should be. Consider whether to use technical terms or confidential information. Make certain the reader knows why the report is being written. State clearly the response or action required. Provide complete and correct supporting data. Write the report in a positive tone.

Organize the report by outlining the points that should be covered. If you are expected to follow a standard format, the organization is already determined. If, however, you can develop your own reporting format, organize your thoughts in a logical way.

Present only data that relate to the topic of the report. Do not clutter the report with unnecessary data. You may be expected to add your own comments about the data. Identify these comments clearly.

Give attention to the formatting and final presentation of the report. The report represents you or your company. It can make a positive or negative first impression affecting how the content of the report will be received.

 CHECK POINT What guidelines should a writer of an informational report follow?

Analytical Reports

analytical involving detailed study

Analytical means involving detailed study. An analytical report is generally a longer, more complex report than an informational report. Such a report is normally prepared as a formal business report. It often requires much research and information gathering. An analytical report takes more time to write and may require in-depth analysis of situations.

The data presented in an analytical report are often used to make important company decisions. Typically, an employee is asked to research a specific problem or issue. Several employees may work in a group to research and write the report. The employees gather data related to the problem. Then they write a report that presents the data they have collected. The report may also include interpretations of the data. The writers are often expected to draw conclusions and make recommendations.

Gathering Data

Reports are often completed under the pressure of deadlines. Employees are expected to gather data quickly and accurately. You may be asked to contribute to a formal business report. These guidelines will help you gather and process data quickly, accurately, and with attention to detail:

- Record complete source details for all data you locate. Include the title of the publication or website and address, author, publisher, date, and page.
- If information must be keyed during the data-gathering stage, key it as it is collected.
- Use a scanner with optical character recognition (OCR) software, if available, to reduce the amount of time needed to enter large quantities of previously keyed data. If scanning is not possible, photocopy the material (such as tables) to be sure that the details are accurate.
- If your duties include creating many reports, consider using speech recognition software to speed data entry. A typical office worker might enter text using the keyboard at 50 words per minute (wpm). After a little practice using speech recognition software, the same worker could probably dictate text at 120 wpm.
- If a document has sections that are often repeated, save time by using boilerplate text.
- Use tablet PCs or handheld computers to collect data as an alternative to keying data. These devices allow the user to handwrite notes on a touch screen or scan bar codes. The handwriting can be converted to text and downloaded to a desktop computer. This process can be much faster than recording data manually on note cards or forms and then keying the data.

optical character recognition (OCR) scanning text printed on paper and translating the images into words

speech recognition software programs that allow voice input, also called voice recognition

Scanning text and graphics can save time when creating reports.

Lusoimages/Shutterstock.com

Voice Recognition Systems

Voice recognition systems allow users to input data by simply talking to a computer. This process is also called speech recognition. As the user speaks into a microphone, the spoken words appear on the computer screen. Current software versions allow the user to speak up to 160 words per minute with good accuracy. This type of software has improved greatly in recent years. Voice input is now a practical alternative to keyboarding.

Using voice input helps workers be more productive. Data are input directly in one step rather than recorded on tape and then keyed later by the same or another person. This process reduces the time needed for the work to be completed. It also reduces the need for outside transcription services.

Using voice input reduces the need for clicking a mouse. Many commands can be given by voice instead. Documents, databases, or the Internet can be searched using voice commands. This can help reduce the instances of repetitive strain injuries.

In the future, more programs for voice input will likely be developed for portable and wireless computer devices. For example, some smartphones allow users to enter voice commands. Users can look up contacts, start programs, make phone calls, and do other tasks using voice input. Such programs provide greater freedom and higher productivity for users.

Do you think keying skills will become less important for some office workers as use of voice input becomes more common? Why or why not?

Researching Information Online

The Internet and private information services provide access to data that can be used in reports. Many of the sources available on the Internet are free for all users. Private information services, however, usually charge a connect fee. They may also charge according to time used or the number of searches made. Many businesses find using an information service more efficient than using staff time to search for data.

By using the Internet or an information service, data can be searched quickly. Company financial profiles, investment advice, text of magazines and journals, U.S. Census data, and government regulations are a few examples of the data that can be found.

Pay attention to the sources of the information you find on the Internet. Does the information come from a person, group, or organization that has expert knowledge on the subject? Is the information biased? Are facts and figures backed by reputable research? Answering these questions will help you determine whether a source is reliable.

Writing the Report

When report data have been gathered, organized, and analyzed, you are ready to begin writing the report. As a writer, you will need to consider and use an appropriate tone and degree of formality in the report. If the report is for your coworkers, an informal style may be used. If the report is for a broad audience or readers outside the company, however, your writing style should also be more formal. Read the examples in informal and formal styles in Figure 4-3.2.

Figure 4-3.2 **Use an appropriate style for each report.**

Message in Informal Style

Jason, this report contains the information on the delivery routes and schedules you requested. You're right, two of the three delivery schedules overlap. This leaves the third route only partially covered on Tuesdays and Thursdays. No wonder we have had complaints from our customers on the third route. I'm taking immediate steps to correct this schedule.

Message in Formal Style

In July 20--, the Board of Directors authorized a study to determine the effect of downsizing on the production capability of the Houston plant. Several additional factors were identified that contributed to the 20 percent overall production drop.

© Cengage Learning 2013

Use a formal style when the report will be read by a larger number of people or when the topic is complicated. To achieve the formal style in the second example, note that the writer:

- Did not use first names (*The Board of Directors* vs. *Jason*)
- Did not use contractions (for example, *you're* or *I'm*)
- Used passive voice (*were identified* vs. *report contains*)

> passive voice a style of writing in which the subject is acted upon rather than performing the action

Use the general guidelines presented in Figure 4-3.3 on page 138 to begin creating the report. If several drafts of the report are required, cycle through step 4 as often as revisions are required. These steps are common to all business reports.

Distributing or Posting Reports

Once a report is completed, you may need to make one or more copies and deliver or mail the report to persons who need it. You will learn about mail delivery services in Chapter 12.

A report might be sent as an attachment to an e-mail message. Reports that are prepared to be used in printed form may also be posted on a company intranet. Word processing and spreadsheet programs have features and commands that allow documents to be saved as web pages. Always preview the document in a web browser to check the format before posting. You may need to make adjustments to the layout of documents saved as web pages.

Figure 4-3.3 Report Guidelines

GUIDELINES FOR ORGANIZING AND WRITING REPORTS

1. Focus the report.
   - Identify the purpose of the report.
   - Identify your readers.
   - Determine why readers will want to read the report.
   - Identify data needed for the report.
   - Identify information resources.

2. Plan the message.
   - Identify the main topics and subtopics.
   - Prepare an outline of the report.
   - Identify potential visuals and graphics.

3. Write the first draft.
   - Write a draft of the text.
   - Develop related visuals and graphics.

4. Revise your first draft.
   - Revise the outline if necessary.
   - Edit or revise text of the first draft.
   - Verify and document sources used.
   - Finalize visuals and graphics.

5. Present your report.
   - Use a standard format to prepare the final draft.
   - Check headings and subheadings.
   - Prepare preliminary report pages.
   - Proofread the final copy.

© Cengage Learning 2013

 CHECK POINT When is a formal writing style appropriate for reports?

Business Report Formats

Several acceptable formats are can be used for business reports. Your company, however, may have a preferred format. Look at previous reports or a company procedures manual to see formats that have been used for reports. Two common business report formats are the unbound and leftbound formats.

An unbound report is fastened in the upper left-hand corner with a paper clip or staple. No extra space is provided in the margin for fastening the report together. This format is useful for short reports that will be distributed internally.

In a leftbound report, the left margin contains one-half inch of extra space. The extra space allows for binding the report at the left. All other margins are the same as those of the unbound report. Writers use this format for longer, more complicated reports. Leftbound format is also useful for reports that require a formal presentation or are being sent outside the company.

The formats presented to you in this topic represent acceptable business report formats. Refer to Figure 4-3.4 for a summary of report formatting guidelines.

Figure 4-3.4 Report Format Guidelines

BUSINESS REPORTS FORMATS				
FORMAT	TOP MARGIN	BOTTOM MARGIN	LEFT MARGIN	RIGHT MARGIN
Unbound				
First page	2 inches	1 inch	1 inch	1 inch
Other pages	1 inch	1 inch	1 inch	1 inch
Leftbound				
First page	2 inches	1 inch	1.5 inches	1 inch
Other pages	1 inch	1 inch	1.5 inches	1 inch
The body of the report may be single-spaced or double-spaced.				

© Cengage Learning 2013

 CHECK POINT How do unbound and leftbound reports differ?

Formal Business Reports

A formal business report includes standard parts. These parts help readers understand the report. A formal report generally explains the reason for the report. The report data and an explanation of their meaning follow. Conclusions or recommendations are given last. The writer also documents the sources of information used to write the report. A formal business report may contain all or some of the common report parts. Typical report parts used in a formal business report are listed in Figure 4-3.5 on page 140.

Report Pagination

Pagination is the process of dividing a document into individual pages for printing. Page breaks are set by the software as the page is filled. These breaks are called soft page breaks. When revisions are made, the page endings will change and the pages will be renumbered automatically.

> **pagination** the process of dividing a document into individual pages for printing

The user can enter a command for a page ending. This type of page ending is called a hard page break. This page ending will not shift when edits are made to the document. A hard page break is useful for beginning a new chapter or section of a report. A hard page break can also be used to prevent paragraphs from dividing at an inappropriate place.

Paragraphs divided between pages should contain at least two lines on each page. A first line of a paragraph printed by itself at the bottom of a page is called a widow line. The last line of a paragraph printed by itself at the top of a page is called an orphan line. Avoid widows and orphans by reviewing the page breaks in the report and adjusting them as needed. Your word processing software may allow you to set options that help prevent widows and orphans.

Use the automatic page numbering feature of the software to number report pages. The title page of a report is considered page 1, but it should not display a page number. Pages coming before the body of the report, such as a table of contents, are numbered with lowercase Roman numerals. The numbers are centered in the page footer. Pages in the body of the report, the references section, and any appendices are numbered in the header at the right margin. See Figure 4-3.6 on page 141 for examples of page numbers.

> **footer** information that appears below the body text on pages of a document

> **header** information that appears above the body text on pages of a document

Figure 4-3.5 **Formal reports can have several parts.**

PARTS OF A FORMAL REPORT	
Title page	Contains the report title, the writer's name, the name of the organization, and the report date. The company address may also be included.
Table of contents	Contains a listing of the report headings and their corresponding page numbers. Can be created from headings marked in the body of the report in some word processing software.
Summary	Contains a brief overview of the report. The summary may also be called an *executive summary* or *abstract*.
Body	Contains the text or message of the report. In long reports, the body will be divided into chapters or sections. Use the default spacing (1.15 or 1) for the body. Place a blank line between paragraphs if the software does not add space after each paragraph.
Quotation	Material from another source that is identified in the body of the report. A quotation of more than three lines is set off from the rest of the text. Indent long quotations 0.5 inches from the left margin.
Documentation	Source information for quotations or material adapted from other sources. Two common methods are endnotes and textual citations.
References	A list of the sources used in preparing the report. The list should include the sources for direct quotes, paraphrased sources, and sources used to obtain ideas or background information. This section may also be titled *ENDNOTES*, *BIBLIOGRAPHY*, or *WORKS CITED*. Use hanging indent format for reference entries.
Appendix	Contains more detailed data (usually in the form of a chart, graph, table, or text) to support the body of the report. The appendix (or appendices if several are included) is placed at the end of the report. If more than one appendix is included, number or letter each in order.

© Cengage Learning 2013

CHECK POINT How are the title page and other preliminary pages of a report numbered?

Report Headings

The main heading is the title of the report. Use the heading to introduce the reader to the report's topic. Give the title on page 1 of the body a prominent position by using title style. (If a title style is not available, use bold type and a slightly larger type size or a different font style.) The secondary heading, if used, provides additional information. If a secondary heading is used, give it less prominence in your report than the main heading. Capitalize only the first letter of key words. Use the same font style, perhaps in a smaller size, as used for the main heading.

Use side headings to divide the main topic into subdivisions. Key side headings in capital and lowercase letters on a separate line beginning at the left margin. Use the default heading styles in the word processing software to format report side headings. When these heading styles are used, the word processing software can generate a table of contents for the report that includes the headings.

Figure 4-3.6 **Unbound Report Pages**

Internet Use

Alberto Diaz
Office Communications Consultants

August 5, 20--

Table of Contents

ii

Internet Use

Internet use is growing quickly. Currently, approximately 1.9 billion people worldwide use the Internet (Internet Stats, 2011). One of the primary uses of the Internet for many consumers is shopping online. More and more companies are selling products, providing customer support, and doing market research via websites.

Market Research

Marketing research firms make data available in a variety of forms for business needs. They focus on the customer and the market. Marketing research firms use questionnaires and interviews to gather information about consumer behaviors and attitudes. They also look at marketing trends and collect valuable demographic data. The U. S. Census Bureau (2011) describes the demographic data it provides:

> The Population Estimates Program publishes total resident population estimates and demographic components of change (births, deaths, and migration) each year. We also publish the estimates by demographic characteristics (age, sex, race, and Hispanic origin) for the nation, states, and counties.

Computer technology makes it possible for researchers to collect a variety of data, analyze huge amounts of information, and forecast market conditions. For example, customers who buy online typically provide information about themselves to the company. This information is called a customer profile. Companies may also build their store of information about online customers by using cookies. Cookies are messages exchanged by the user's web browser and the web server being visited. They can be used to track the user's identity and online behavior. The information acquired from online customers allows the business to analyze customer buying habits. Then the company can suggest related products that may be of interest to a customer.

Mailing Lists

A mailing list is a directory of Internet user addresses of people who want to have information about a topic delivered regularly to their addresses. Some mailing lists are maintained by businesses while other lists are private. The user subscribes to the mailing list to receive messages. Mailing lists can be used to gather market data or to advertise products. Many websites that sell products have an option users can select to be added to a mailing list. Reputable sites also have a method that allows users to unsubscribe from the mailing list.

Figure 4-3.6 **Unbound Report Pages** (*continued*)

2

E-commerce

E-commerce has created a lack of geographic boundaries for many businesses. This brings new challenges in communicating and sharing information with people of many countries and cultures. Websites must be designed to be attractive and easy to use for all customers. Internet users by world region are shown in the following chart.

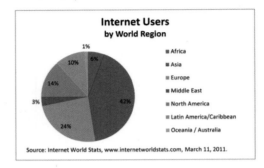

Internet Users
by World Region

- Africa
- Asia
- Europe
- Middle East
- North America
- Latin America/Caribbean
- Oceania / Australia

Source: Internet World Stats, www.internetworldstats.com, March 11, 2011.

Electronic Mail

One popular use of the Internet is electronic mail, or e-mail. E-mail is the electronic transfer of messages. LANs and WANs offer e-mail to all computers that are connected, whether they are in the same office or in different countries. Users are limited to sending and receiving messages only to and from those on their network unless their network is connected to the Internet. If they are connected to the Internet, they can send and receive messages all over the world.

E-mail messages may contain not only text, but also audio and graphics. Messages advertising products or sales can include photos or links to a company website. When an e-mail file is received, it is automatically stored in a user's electronic mailbox. An e-mail mailbox is an online computer storage space designated to hold electronic messages. These messages are stored for the owner of the mailbox and may be read, saved for later reference, printed, or deleted. E-mail is inexpensive, fast, and easy to use for workers at all levels in organizations.

Web Browsers

A web browser is a software program that provides navigation and search tools to help users find topics and locations on the World Wide Web. URLs (Uniform Resource Locators) are Internet addresses that can be understood by any web browser as it searches for hypertext documents on computers around the world. URL addresses start with *http://*, which stands for *hypertext transfer protocol*. This is a set of instructions telling computers how to send and receive hypertext data and documents. The *www* in the URL stands for *World Wide Web*. Periods in the URL are separators and are pronounced *dot*. Ending

5

References

Internet Word Stats, "Internet Usage Statistics, The Internet Big Picture."
http://www.internetworldstats.com/stats.htm (accessed March 11, 2011).

U.S. Census Bureau. "Population Estimates." http://www.census.gov/popest/overview.html (accessed March 11, 2011).

Report Documentation

Giving credit to the sources of information you used in a report is called documentation. One common method uses endnotes. When the endnote method is used, a superior (raised) reference figure is placed at the appropriate point in the copy. The matching numbered reference is then listed at the end of the report in a section titled *Endnotes*.

When writing the report, credit must be given for material quoted either directly or indirectly from other sources.[1]

If using endnotes, use the footnote feature of your software to create the endnotes. If text that contains an endnote reference is moved, the endnotes will be renumbered. Endnotes numbers will also be adjusted when new endnotes are inserted.

Another common method uses textual citations. When the textual citations method is used, part of the source information is placed in parentheses within the text. This information includes author(s), date of publication, and page number(s).

When writing the report, credit must be given for material quoted either directly or indirectly from other sources (Tilton, Jackson, and Rigby, 2011, 395).

If the source is identified by name within the report copy, only the publication date and page number are used.

According to Tilton, Jackson, and Rigby, credit must be given for material quoted either directly or indirectly from other sources (2011, 395).

The matching reference is listed at the end of the report in a section titled *References* as shown in Figure 4-3.6. The entries are listed in alphabetical order by the author's last name. Entries are in hanging indent format with a blank between them. Each reference should provide all the data needed for the reader to locate the source. Data included will vary depending on the type of source. Consult a current reference manual for example entries. The company may identify a reference style or guide that employees should use. Examples of reference manuals include:

- *The Chicago Manual of Style*
- *MLA Handbook for Writers of Research Papers*
- *Publication Manual of the American Psychological Association*

 CHECK POINT What are two common methods used to give credit to the sources of information used in a report?

Memo Reports

Short, informal reports are often prepared in memo format, as shown in Figure 4-3.7 on page 144. The subject heading is used to identify the topic of the report, just as the main heading is used for an unbound report.

Side headings, like those used for unbound report format, may be used to identify sections of the report. A memo report frequently has more than one page. In such instances, the page number is part of the heading that appears on all pages after the first page. Review multiple-page headings in Figure 4-2.5 on page 121. Use the header feature of your word processing software to automatically print the page number and the rest of the heading at the top of succeeding pages.

 CHECK POINT How is the topic of a memo report indicated? How are sections of the report indicated?

Figure 4-3.7 **Memo Report**

TO: Alma Yung, Manager

FROM: Alberto Diaz

DATE: August 5, 20--

SUBJECT: Marketing and the Internet

Internet use is growing quickly. More than a billion people worldwide use the Internet. One of the primary uses of the Internet for many consumers is shopping online. More and more companies are selling products, providing customer support, and doing market research via websites.

Market Research

Marketing research firms make data available in a variety of forms for business needs. They focus on the customer and the market. Marketing research firms use questionnaires and interviews to gather information about consumer behaviors and attitudes. They also look at marketing trends and collect valuable demographic data.

Computer technology makes it possible for researchers to collect a variety of data, analyze large amounts of information, and forecast market conditions. For example, customers who buy online typically provide information about themselves to the company. This information is called a customer profile. Companies may also build their store of information about online customers by using cookies. Cookies are messages exchanged by the user's web browser and the web server being visited. They can be used to track the user's online behavior. The information acquired from online customers allows the business to analyze customer buying habits. Then the company can suggest related products that may be of interest to a customer.

Mailing Lists

A mailing list is a directory of Internet user addresses of people who want to have information about a topic delivered regularly to their addresses. Some mailing lists are maintained by businesses while other lists are private. The user subscribes to the mailing list to receive messages. Mailing lists can be used to gather data or advertise products. Many websites that sell products have an option users can select to be added to a mailing list. Reputable sites also have a method that allows users to unsubscribe from a mailing list.

Newsgroups

Newsgroups publish online articles related to many topics. Users participate in public discussions about a topic by sending messages that all users in the newsgroup can read. Newsgroups are available for thousands of topics. Some companies sponsor newsgroups related to their products. Users can ask

Visual Aids

Visual aids consist of the tables, graphs, and other illustrations, such as maps, which are used to present data in a report. The purpose of using visual aids is to help make the report easy to understand. They may also reduce the amount of text needed, presenting the data in a chart or table instead.

Tables

table data arranged in a format of rows and columns

A **table** contains facts, figures, and other information arranged in rows and columns. Tables can be used to summarize information and make comparisons. When developing a table to be used in a report, be certain that it relates directly to the report. The table should have a clearly defined purpose and should focus the reader's attention on a specific aspect of the report.

A report table should be self-explanatory. That is, the reader should not have to refer to text that may accompany the table to understand the table's contents. This is especially important when a table appears on an electronic slide. Look at the table in Figure 4-3.8. Is it self-explanatory? Which employee received the highest commission? How much were his or her total sales for the first quarter? Which employee received the lowest commission? How much were his or her total sales for the first quarter?

Most word processing programs have a table feature that automatically determines column spacing and prepares the table layout. You may wish to start with this table style and then make adjustments as needed. Figure 4-3.8 displays the standard parts of a table. Some simplified tables will not include all these parts. More complex tables will include other parts, such as a source note indicating the source of the data. Ruled lines may be used to separate the data visually. Dot leaders may be used to aid in reading across the table from one column to the next.

Spreadsheet software can also be used to create tables. Using spreadsheet software is best when the table contains numbers that must be totaled or used in formulas. Your goal is to create a table that is easy to read and highlights the appropriate information. The following guidelines can be used when formatting tables.

- Key the main headings in all capital letters using a 14-point font. Apply bold and center alignment to the title. The title may be placed as the first row in the table grid or above the table grid as shown in Figure 4-3.8. If the table has a secondary heading, key it in bold below the main heading.
- Key column headings in bold and center the headings.
- Key data in the cells in the default font or the one provided in the table style. Data in cells can be aligned left, aligned right, or centered. Usually, numbers are aligned right and words are aligned left.
- Center tables horizontally on the page. Center tables vertically on a page or use a top margin of two inches. When a table is placed in a memo or report, leave one blank line above and below the table.

Figure 4-3.8 **Basic Table Format**

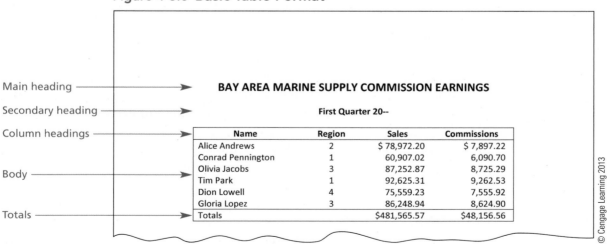

Name	Region	Sales	Commissions
Alice Andrews	2	$ 78,972.20	$ 7,897.22
Conrad Pennington	1	60,907.02	6,090.70
Olivia Jacobs	3	87,252.87	8,725.29
Tim Park	1	92,625.31	9,262.53
Dion Lowell	4	75,559.23	7,555.92
Gloria Lopez	3	86,248.94	8,624.90
Totals		$481,565.57	$48,156.56

BAY AREA MARINE SUPPLY COMMISSION EARNINGS

First Quarter 20--

Main heading
Secondary heading
Column headings
Body
Totals

Graphs or tables may be included in electronic slide shows.

Fancy/Veer/Corbis/Jupiter Images

■ Tables can be formatted with the cell borders (gridlines) hidden, with all cell borders showing, or with selected borders showing. Shading or automatic table styles can also be used.

■ The body of the table may have default spacing or double spacing. Tables are often double-spaced for improved readability. When the table is placed within the text of a report, use the space available on the page to determine how you will space the table body. The table width should not exceed the left and right margins of the report body.

■ Data in a table are often summarized or calculated with the results shown at the end of the table. *Total*, *Average*, *Maximum*, and *Minimum* are common summary lines included in tables. The last entry in a column is often underscored to separate the table data from the summary lines.

 CHECK POINT When is it best to use spreadsheet software to create a table rather than word processing software?

Graphs

graph a picture that represents data

A **graph** is a picture that represents data. Graphs can make a report more interesting and informative. In many cases, data are easier to interpret in a graph than when shown in columns of figures. Graphs, therefore, are used frequently in business reports to display supporting information.

As you prepare business reports containing graphs, study previous reports from the company to determine style preferences. If the graph is half of a page or less in size, include it in the body of the report. Leave a blank line before and after the graph to separate it from the text. Position the graph as near as possible to the portion of the report in which it is mentioned, ideally on the same page. If the graph is larger than half a page, place it on a separate page and include a reference to the graph's page number.

Spreadsheet programs are commonly used to prepare charts and graphs. A pie chart (so called because the graph wedges look like pieces of a pie) is a display of how the parts contribute to the whole. The whole circle represents 100 percent, and each wedge represents a portion of the whole. Each wedge should be identified with an appropriate label, color, or pattern. A pie chart is shown in a report in Figure 4-3.6.

A bar graph is used to show comparisons, as displayed in Figure 4-3.9. Use bars of equal width and space the bars equally across the graph. If more than one set of data is included in the graph, use different colors or patterns to identify

Figure 4-3.9 **Bar graphs are used to compare items.**

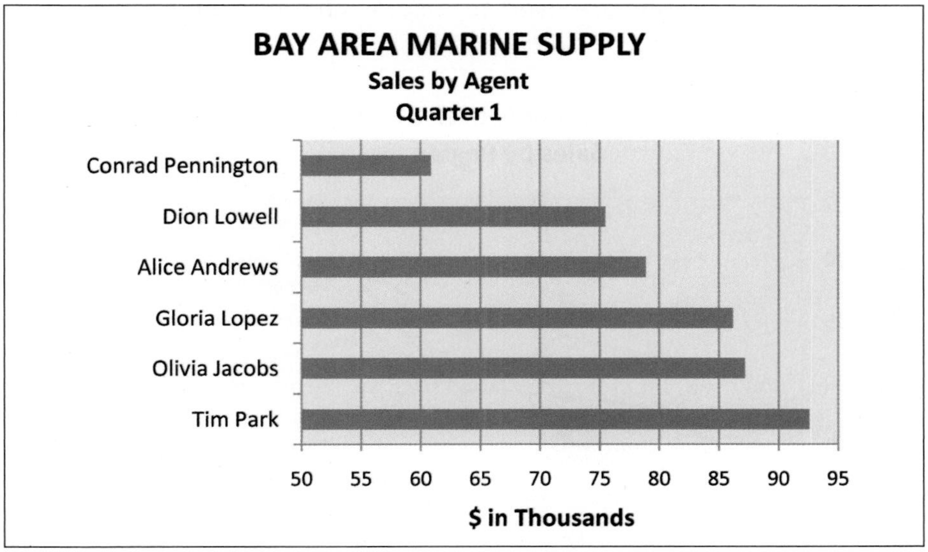

© Cengage Learning 2013

the sets of data. Stacked bars, three-dimensional bars, and gridlines may be used to make the data easier to read or understand. The number scale should be adjusted to show an appropriate range. For example, if the numbers graphed range from 75 to 103, the graph scale might begin at 70 rather than at 0. Consider carefully the point you intend to make with the graph. Adjusting the graph scale can make differences in the data appear smaller or larger.

A line graph is used to display trends that emerge over a period of time. An example is shown in Figure 4-3.10. Monthly sales, for example, are frequently represented in line graph form. In preparing such a graph, place the time categories across the horizontal axis and the amounts along the vertical axis. If more than one set of data is shown on the graph, use lines in different colors to distinguish each set.

CHECK POINT What type of graph is used to compare parts to a whole?

Figure 4-3.10 Line graphs are used to display changes over a period of time.

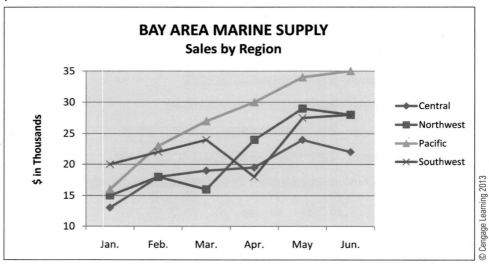

REVIEW 4-3

21st Century Skills

PARTNERSHIP FOR
21ST CENTURY SKILLS

Interacting with Others

You are working on a special research project with Lionel Moore. He was supposed to e-mail you a lengthy attachment that you need to complete the project. He promised to send it to you by noon yesterday. At 4:30 p.m. you have not heard from Lionel. You are becoming very concerned because the deadline for the report is only one week away. You must study Lionel's material carefully before you can complete your part of the project. By your estimate, it will take you about nine hours to review Lionel's data.

1. Compose and key an e-mail message to Lionel that is appropriate for the situation described above. If you do not have e-mail software, key the message as a memo using your word processing software. If using e-mail software, key your teacher's e-mail address after the *To* heading.

2. State your concerns and the action that you want Lionel to take. Follow proper guidelines for preparing e-mail messages as you compose your message. Make the tone of the message positive.

3. Save and print the message. Send the message if using e-mail software.

Making Academic Connections

Reinforcing Math Skills

You work in the Accounting Department of Ace Computers, a small retail computer store. Your supervisor, Mrs. Lowell, has sent you a file containing part of the data needed for a report. She asked you to complete the spreadsheet.

1. Open the Excel file 4-3 Math Skills from the data files, which contains the report data.

2. Enter the column headings Total Sales, Cost of Units Sold, and Gross Profit in columns F, G, and H.

3. Enter formulas to calculate the total sales for each product to Wayne Middle School for the current year.

4. Enter formulas to calculate the cost of units sold for each product. (Multiply units sold by the wholesale price.)

5. Enter formulas to calculate the gross profit for each product. (The gross profit is the difference between the total sales and the cost of units sold.) Add the gross profit column to determine the total gross profit figure. For the total gross profit amount cell, use a single top border and a double bottom border.

6. Adjust the table titles to extend across all the columns with data. Save your work; you will use it in another activity.

4-3 Activity 1

Memo Report with Table (Outcomes 4-3a, 4-3b, 4-3c)

Your supervisor at Ace Computers, Mrs. Lowell, has asked you to prepare a table using the spreadsheet you created earlier. The table will be included in a short memo report.

1. Create a memo form for Ace Computers that includes the company name and the appropriate memo heading lines. Address the memo to Carlos Morales, Vice President of Sales. The memo is from Virginia Lowell, Accounting Supervisor. Use an appropriate subject heading. Date the memo using September 4 of the current year.

2. Open and print the file 4-3 Activity 1 found in the data files. Begin the body of your memo report by keying the text shown. Add figures from your spreadsheet to complete the sentences. Next, inform Mr. Morales that you are including a table that shows a complete list of the products Wayne Middle School has purchased this year.

3. Refer to the spreadsheet you completed earlier. (If you did not complete the *Reinforcing Math Skills* exercise before, do so now.) Hide these columns in the spreadsheet: Wholesale Prices and Cost of Units Sold. Copy the spreadsheet data and paste it into the memo report. Adjust the table format, as needed, to create an attractive table.

4-3 Activity 2

Memo Report with Graph (Outcomes 4-3a, 4-3b, 4-3c)

Mrs. Lowell has asked you to prepare a graph using data from the spreadsheet you created earlier. The Gross Profit column shows the dollar amount of profit on each product. Mr. Morales would like to know the markup percent this amount represents for each product.

1. Open the spreadsheet you edited in Activity 1. Insert a new column between columns E and F. Enter Markup Percent for the column head.

2. Enter formulas in column F to find the markup percent for each product. (Subtract the wholesale price from the selling price and divide by the wholesale price.) Format the cells for percent and show zero decimal places in the percents.

3. Sort the table rows by the Markup Percent column. Create a bar graph that compares the markup percents for all the products. (Hide columns B, C, D, and E to make creating the chart easier.) Enter MARKUP PERCENT for the graph title. Do not include a legend.

4. Add a paragraph at the end of the memo report you created in Activity 1. Introduce and explain what is shown in the bar graph. Tell which product has the highest markup percent. Insert the graph into the report.

5. Keep the last paragraph that introduces the graph and the graph on the same page. Add a second-page heading in the header on page 2.

Summary

4-1 Communicating in Written Form

- Reading and writing are vital skills for office workers.
- Reading skills are used at work for understanding instructions, responding to inquiries, and using written references and databases.
- Writing skills are used at work to summarize written messages, record notes of actions and decisions, revise others' writing, prepare communications for others to review, and compose messages.
- Critical skills for high-level reading are comprehension, vocabulary, and speed.
- Well written business messages have common characteristics. The messages are clear, concise, courteous, complete, and correct.
- Writing tasks must be managed if they are to be completed successfully and on schedule.

4-2 Business Correspondence

- Preparing a document includes three stages: writing, revising, and proofreading for final presentation.
- When preparing a draft, identify the purpose of the message, consider the audience, outline the main points, and note the desired response.
- Use a direct approach for neutral or positive messages. Use an indirect approach for negative messages.
- Revise the initial draft of a message to refine the content and organization of the message.
- Proofreading, the last phase of preparing a document, is your careful, overall check of the document for errors and mechanical issues.
- Business correspondence consists mainly of letters, printed memos, and e-mail messages.
- Desktop publishing is used to create documents such as brochures, newsletters, and flyers that may each use a unique format and design.

4-3 Business Reports and Related Documents

- Informational reports are typically based on data gathered within the normal operations of the company. When writing an informational report, follow the guidelines used for a direct approach message.
- An analytical report is generally a longer, more complex report than an informational report. It often requires much research and may require in-depth analysis of data or situations.
- Reports can be written in a formal or informal style. Use a formal style when the report will be read by a large number of people or when the topic is complicated. Unbound and leftbound are popular styles for formal business reports. Informal reports may be prepared as memo reports.
- Visual aids consist of the tables, graphs, and other illustrations that are used to present data in a report.

Wire_man/Shutterstock.com

Chapter 4 Activity 1

Press Release
(Outcomes 4-1c, 4-2a, 4-2b)

Assume that you are an assistant manager in the Public Information Department of Laughlin & Mead Corporation. The company's Board of Directors met yesterday to appoint a new vice president for technology. The public information director has asked you to prepare the draft for a press release. The release will be sent to local newspapers as well as to business periodicals.

1. Open the file 4 Activity 1 from the data files, which contains a sample press release. Read the document to learn about writing and formatting a press release.

2. Compose and key the draft of a press release for review by the department manager. Use the current date and your name as the contact person. Other details that should be included in the release are given on page 2 of the data file.

3. Work with a classmate. Act as the department manager and review your classmate's press release. Use proofreaders' marks or the editing feature of your word processing software to add comments and corrections to the document.

4. After your classmate has reviewed your document, make corrections and print a final copy of the press release.

5. Save the document as a single file web page appropriate for posting online. View the document in your browser software. Make corrections to the format as needed for an attractive online document. Save and print the web page version of the press release.

Chapter 4 Activity 2

Leftbound Report
(Outcomes 4-3a, 4-3b, 4-3c)

In this activity, you will format text for a leftbound report. Review report guidelines and examples shown earlier to help you complete this activity.

1. Open the file 4 Activity 2 found in the data files. Format the text as a leftbound report with a title page, table of contents, body, and references page.

2. Use a cover page style found in your word processing software for the title page or format it similar to the title page shown in Figure 4-3.6. Use a title style for the table of contents heading, the report title on page 1, and the references page heading. Use a heading style available in your software to format the side headings. Adjust the style, if needed, for attractive spacing.

3. Create a header to number the pages in the body of the report. The second page of the body should be page 2.

4. Generate a table of contents using the appropriate features of your software. Delete any lines that are not needed, such as the report main title. Only the side headings and the References page should be listed.

Wire_man/Shutterstock.com

Visual Basic Programming Event

In this competitive event, you will be judged on your skills and knowledge of Visual Basic programming logic, system design concepts, databases, and objects. The event involves an application test lasting up to 90 minutes. The contestant must supply a computer to use in the event. The contestant must complete the setup of the computer in the allotted orientation time period. Written reference materials are allowed.

Performance Indicators Evaluated

Participants will demonstrate skills related to programming and design with Visual Basic. Sample indicators include showing an understanding of:

- Object oriented concepts and techniques
- General computer concepts and computer language
- Visual Basic programming language, concepts, and syntax
- Native Visual Basic designers and tools
- Database concepts and Access 2007
- Structured design techniques, algorithms, and object-oriented concepts
- Reports within a Visual Basic application that use a database as source data
- Programs using variables, looping, controls, logical operations, calculations, totals, sequence, data structures, selection, and I/O operations

For more detailed information about this event, go to the BPA website.[1]

http://www.bpa.org/

Think Critically

1. Which aspects of working with Visual Basic do you find most challenging?
2. In which skill areas included in this event are you proficient? In which areas do you need to learn or improve skills?

---

[1]"Business Professionals of America, Workplace Skills Assessment Program, Secondary 2011" (Business Professionals of America, 2011), http://www.bpa.org/download.aspx?dl=2011_WSAP_SECONDARY.pdf.

Are you interested in all the news all the time? Do you like digging for the details of a story? Are you good at talking with people and getting them to open up about their feelings and experiences? If the answer to these questions is *yes*, then a career as news reporter or broadcast journalist might be right for you.

Employment Outlook

Employees in news reporting and broadcast journalism work for radio and TV networks, broadcast stations, newspapers, and magazines. The U.S. government provides job projections for 2008–2018. Jobs in this career area are expected to decline moderately, so workers will face strong competition for jobs.[2]

Job Titles

- News analyst
- Reporter
- Correspondent
- Broadcast journalist
- News writer
- News commentator
- News columnist

Needed Education/Skills

A college degree in journalism or mass communications is typically needed for jobs in broadcast journalism. Special degrees may be required for some jobs. For example, a person who reports on weather conditions may need special training in this field. Experience gained at small broadcasting stations, newspapers, or magazines may also be required.

---

[2]*Occupational Outlook Handbook*, 2010-11 Edition, Bureau of Labor Statistics, U.S. Department of Labor, http://www.bls .gov/oco/ocos088.htm.

What's it like to work in . . . Broadcast Journalism?

Rhonda works as a news reporter for small broadcasting company. A college degree in journalism and experience at a local cable station while in school prepared Rhonda well for her career. She worked as a news writer and did reports on location before becoming the morning news anchor. Her friendly presence and thoughtful manner when presenting the news have made Rhonda popular with viewers.

Since the morning news show begins at 6 a.m., Rhonda arrives at work very early in the morning. When she reaches the station, she reviews all the stories that are scheduled for the show. She asks questions of the news writers about aspects of a story that she thinks need more explanation. Then she's off to makeup and wardrobe. As Rhonda reports the news on camera, she takes cues from the show's director and introduces other reporters who give on-location reports or discuss sports or the weather.

Later in the day, Rhonda may make a personal appearance, such as at a school program or community event. She also does interviews and investigates stories that will appear as special features on future news programs. Rhonda works long hours and often has an irregular schedule. However, she enjoys meeting people and reporting about events in her area. Being a local celebrity isn't bad either!

What About You?

Does a job as a news reporter or broadcast journalist sound appealing to you? What skills would you need to develop to be effective in this career area?

Communicating Orally

5-1 Listening and Speaking

5-2 Planning and Preparing a Presentation

5-3 Delivering a Presentation

ColorBlind Images/conica/Getty Images

You will need to express yourself clearly in your speech at work so others will understand you. This is true whether you are talking with a coworker, addressing people at a meeting, or giving a presentation. In some cases, you will speak to motivate and influence people. In other cases, the purpose of your spoken messages will be to inform and educate. You will also need to listen effectively so you can give appropriate feedback, answer questions, or carry out instructions.

This chapter focuses on speaking skills and their importance to your success at work. In this chapter, you will learn how to improve your listening and speaking skills for both communicating with coworkers and giving formal presentations.

Wire_man/Shutterstock.com

OUTCOMES

5-1a Apply strategies for listening effectively.
5-1b Apply strategies for speaking effectively.
5-1c Describe elements of nonverbal communication.

KEY TERMS

modulated p. 156
listening p. 156
barrier p. 157
bias p. 157
enunciation p. 160
colloquialism p. 161
slang p. 161
body language p. 164

modulated adjusted to a proper level

listening hearing and focusing attention to understand sounds

Listening Effectively

Regardless of the career you choose, you will want to be confident about your listening and speaking skills. These oral communication skills will play a role in many aspects of your responsibilities. Imagine you are walking along a hall in a high-rise office building. You notice that many conversations are underway. You cannot hear what is being said because voices are **modulated** so that only persons nearby hear the actual words. You would undoubtedly see workers talking by telephone and others in conference with other people. In every instance, listeners are taking part in the communication process.

The Listening Process

Listening involves a mental process as well as the physical aspects of hearing. You may hear a speaker but not actively listen to the speaker by giving your full attention to what is being said. Focusing your attention on the message is a critical part of listening. The listener must think about what is being discussed. When you listen, your mind processes the information you hear through reshaping what is already known about the topic and storing the information for future use.

Effective listening skills are important for every office worker.

Image copyright Monkey Business Images, 2010. Used under copyright from Shutterstock.com.

Listening is required to gain an understanding of what is being said. Conversations, meetings, lectures, answering machines, and voicemail will be meaningless if you fail to listen. You will need to listen at work countless times. When you listen effectively, you will be able to:

■ Follow through on oral instructions correctly.

■ Consider the additional information as you continue your work and make decisions.

■ Use time productively.

 CHECK POINT How does listening differ from hearing?

Barriers to Effective Listening

Think carefully about how you react when someone begins to talk with you. Even though you are attempting to listen, barriers can hinder your understanding of the message. Barriers to effective listening may be external or internal.

barrier an obstacle or obstruction

External Listening Barriers

External barriers include things in the environment that distract you from listening. A room that is too warm or cold, an uncomfortable chair, and noise in the nearby hallway are examples of external barriers.

To overcome an external barrier, try to change the condition that is distracting you. For example, adjust the temperature in the room or move to a different room that is not near a noisy hallway. If you are listening in a large group setting, you may not be able to control the environment. In this case, put extra effort into focusing your attention on the message.

Internal Listening Barriers

Internal listening barriers may be more difficult to control than external barriers. Examples of internal barriers include:

■ Your attitude toward the speaker. If you do not like the speaker or think the speaker is not qualified to deliver a message on the topic, you may be distracted by these thoughts.

■ Ideas or biases you have about the topic. If you have strong ideas about the topic that are different from those offered by the speaker, you may have trouble accepting the information presented.

bias preconceived notion or prejudice

■ Your knowledge of the topic. If you have a great deal of knowledge about the topic, you may have trouble listening because you think the speaker will have nothing to add to what you already know. On the other hand, suppose the speaker assumes that you know more about the topic than you actually do. You may have trouble understanding the message as presented.

■ Physical distractions. If you are tired, sleepy, or not feeling well, you may have trouble focusing on the message. If you are worried about some important issue, this can also distract you from listening effectively.

The following strategies will help you overcome internal barriers and improve your listening skills:

- Set aside feelings or preconceived ideas about the speaker. Focus on the message rather than the speaker.

- Show respect for the ideas and experiences of others. An attitude of respect for others is important for good listening. Remember that no two persons have had exactly the same experiences. Respecting the ideas and backgrounds of others will help you listen attentively.

- Keep an open mind. Assume that some new information may be presented even if you know a great deal about the topic. If you think you can learn from others, you are likely to listen with a sincere wish to know what the other person thinks. You are likely to follow up comments made by others with a closely related question or further comment.

- Focus your attention. Try to block out distracting thoughts that come from worry or your physical condition. If you are really not well, try if possible to postpone the discussion or meeting until a later time when you are feeling well.

 CHECK POINT What listening barriers are the most difficult for you to overcome? Why?

Listening to Instructions

You will often use your listening skills at work to receive instructions. The instructions may be for a specific task or more general information that you are to apply to your work. Mentally reviewing the information and asking questions, when appropriate, will help you understand such messages.

Mentally Summarize and Review

If possible, anticipate what you will hear and prepare for listening by mentally creating an outline. For example, if you know that the manager often gives you assignments, you should set up a mental outline with the following

---

⁕ WORKPLACE CONNECTIONS ⁕

Adanna worked in a busy office as an industrial engineer. At times, he had to be on the factory floor. Often he would return from the factory to find a number of messages in his voice mailbox. He would retrieve the messages. He found, however, that even though he heard the messages, he wasn't listening. His mind was wandering to thoughts of a stressful situation in his personal life. He had to play the messages again. Adanna realized he was wasting valuable time because of his failure to listen effectively. He made a promise to himself: "I will focus my attention and listen carefully the first time, so I do not need to repeat messages." He listened to his own promise. He was surprised at his success.

> What could Adanna do to be sure he has understood each message?

sections: What is to be done? Why must it be done? What is the deadline? At what points does my manager want to know about my progress? With such a mental outline, you can listen to your supervisor and put what is said in its proper place. A quick review of your mental outline will ensure you that you have all the information you need or help you identify what is missing.

Pause, even momentarily, to review what you have heard. Determine whether you have clearly understood what you heard. Does it make sense? Do you have all the information you need? This review acts as a reinforcement of new information. Mentally reviewing a conversation and your notes assures you that you have gained what you needed to move ahead with your work or undertake a new assignment.

Take Notes and Ask Questions

Frequently, details are given with instructions when talking with someone in person or by phone. Make a note of details, such as dates, figures, telephone numbers, and scheduling requirements, to supplement your careful listening.

The person talking with you wants you to understand clearly what is being discussed. In most cases, he or she will welcome your questions. By listening carefully and raising questions, you can confirm that you understand the message. Your questions can also focus on points that were not clearly explained.

 CHECK POINT Why is it important to take notes on details given in instructions?

Speaking Effectively

The companion skill of listening is speaking. You will have many occasions when you must speak to coworkers or customers about your work and what is to be done. On such occasions, you will want to speak with ease and confidence.

To communicate your thoughts effectively, you must show your listeners that you are interested in what you are saying. Have you ever listened to a speaker who seemed to be reading a speech with no understanding of the words? If you have heard such a speaker, do you recall whether you enjoyed what you heard or learned much? You probably did not.

On the other hand, you may have heard someone who seemed very interested in what was being said. Your attention was captured because of the way the person spoke as well as by the content of the message. The interest of the speaker in communicating with the listeners increased the effectiveness

Doreen Salcher/Shutterstock

A speaker who shows interest in the topic will capture the listeners' attention.

of the communication. Expressing ideas clearly, using an appropriate tone and language, and considering your audience will also help you speak effectively.

Express Ideas Clearly

Thinking must precede speaking, if only by a brief moment. Try asking a mental question such as: "What do I really need to say to communicate my meaning?" Consider the purpose you are trying to accomplish with your communication. You are not likely to be misunderstood if you think about what you want to say before speaking.

Speak Clearly in an Appropriate Tone

enunciation pronouncing words clearly and correctly

Your spoken words are worthless if the listener is unable to hear and understand them. Speaking clearly requires that you say each word carefully. This is referred to as proper enunciation. When you enunciate words properly, your listener is more likely to hear them correctly. Listeners have trouble understanding speech when speakers run words together and when syllables are not sounded fully. Note the examples in Figure 5-1.1.

Figure 5-1.1 **Enunciate clearly to avoid mispronouncing words.**

COMMONLY MISPRONOUNCED WORDS		
'preciate	for	appreciate
cam	for	calm
didya	for	did you
gimme	for	give me
gonna	for	going to
granite	for	granted
labatory	for	laboratory
libary	for	library
nothin'	for	nothing
'r	for	our
winda	for	window
winnin'	for	winning

© Cengage Learning 2013

Speaking at an appropriate volume level and using an appropriate tone are important for clear communications. Consider the situation in which you are speaking and the distance your voice must carry. Regulate the volume level of your voice so listeners can hear you clearly, but so you do not disturb others who may be working nearby.

Make the tone of your voice match the message you are trying to convey. Speak in a warm and friendly tone when complimenting a coworker on a job well done. Use a questioning tone when asking for information. When giving a warning, let your tone of voice convey caution or danger. Remember that the tone of voice and expression you use in speaking can be as important as the words you say in communicating your message.

Use Standard Language

Standard language uses the words taught in English courses in schools. These words are explained in current dictionaries. However, most dictionaries also show some common terms that are not standard language.

Office workers should use standard language and correct grammar at work. Use of standard language helps others understand spoken messages. Increasingly, workers talk with others from around the world. Many people have learned English as a second language. For these people, using standard language helps ensure that your message will be understood.

Colloquialisms are informal words and phrases. These words are used among people who know each other well or among people from a specific geographic area. For example, in some parts of the United States, a soft drink in called *pop* while in other areas it is called *soda*. Some colloquialisms are commonly used at work among employees who know each other well and tend to speak informally. A few of these terms are shown in Figure 5-1.2.

colloquialism informal word or phrase used among a particular group

Figure 5-1.2 Colloquialisms may not be understood by everyone.

COLLOQUIALISMS		
bearish	for	pessimistic
finish off	for	complete
get out of line	for	fail to conform
head up	for	serve as chairperson
put it to bed	for	finish something
right off the bat	for	immediately
the bottom line	for	the end result
touch bases	for	discuss a matter
walk the talk	for	carry through what you say
under the table	for	hidden or secret

© Cengage Learning 2013

Slang is another type of informal language. For example, the word *hot* means having a high temperature. When used as slang, *hot* may mean stolen, as in a *hot car*. It might also mean something or someone who is very attractive or exciting, as in *that bike is hot*. Discovering the meaning of slang words is difficult for those outside the group in which such words are popular. Slang expressions are often short-lived. Most of the time, slang expressions are inappropriate when communicating with others at work.

slang informal language used in casual conversation

 CHECK POINT What is standard language and why is using it at work important?

Consider Your Audience

Audience is another term for listeners. Whether you are talking with a few people or a large group, you will want to consider the interests and needs of your audience. These interests will affect how you accomplish

Focus on *BUSINESS*

Greetings and Introductions

There may be times at work when you need to greet visitors or coworkers or introduce people. You will want to confident and effective in these situations.

Greeting coworkers and colleagues is customary when arriving at and leaving work. Phrases such as "Good morning, Alice" and "Have a nice evening, Mr. Chang" are appropriate. Using names makes the greetings more personal. Use a first name for a coworker, manager, or customer only if you have been invited to do so. Observe the customs followed in your office. Typically, workers at the same level of the organization will be on a first name basis. Managers and subordinates may be more formal in their communications, using last names and titles.

If you deal with clients or customers as part of your job, greet each person promptly when he or she arrives, if possible. Use the person's name if you know it. If you are helping one person, indicate that you will be with the next person who has arrived as soon as you can.

When you introduce people in business situations, show respect to the person of higher status by mentioning his or her name first. Then present the person of higher status to the person of lower status. For example, suppose you need to introduce a new employee to the company manager. You might say, "Mrs. Diaz, this is Mr. Tom Park, our new employee in the Accounting Department. Tom, this is Mrs. Elena Diaz, our general manager." Note that each person's first and last names and relevant titles or job positions should be mentioned.

There may be times when you will introduce two people of about the same status. If one person is significantly older than another person of the same status, mention the older person's name first. If both people are about the same age, use other logical ways to decide which person's name to mention first. For example, you might mention the name of a long-time employee first when introducing a new employee to him or her. If one person is speaking at a meeting and the other person is a member of the audience, you might mention the speaker's name first. In social situations, traditionally, men are introduced to women. (The woman's name is mentioned first.) However, in business situations, gender is not considered a factor in determining status.

When you are introduced to someone, make an appropriate reply and mention the person's name. For example, you might say, "I am pleased to meet you, Mrs. Diaz." Extend your hand to the other businessperson for a handshake. Make eye contact with the other person and shake hands firmly but briefly. If you are seated, generally you should stand to take part in an introduction and shake hands. In some cases, such as in a meeting with several people, this may not be appropriate.

> Is it appropriate to address your supervisor by his or her first name? Why or why not? How should you determine which person's name to mention first when introducing two people?

your purpose for communicating. Talking with a single person or a small group usually permits you to be more informal than when you are speaking with a large group.

You want to consider: (a) what your listeners want to know; (b) what they might already know; and (c) how what you are saying can relate to their experiences. You also want to be sensitive to how listeners are reacting to what you are saying. Are they looking away with a lack of interest? Do they seem impatient with the length of your comments? Are they confused? Do they seem eager and attentive while you are talking? Do they seem ready to move on to another topic?

When speaking, allow time for interaction, if possible. Give listeners a chance to respond. One of the major advantages of oral communication is that there can be immediate feedback. When talking with others, be interested in getting questions, comments, and reactions to what you say. A skillful speaker is also a good listener.

 CHECK POINT Why should you consider the interests and needs of your audience?

※ WORKPLACE CONNECTIONS ※

Leon was asked to instruct a new employee, Abby, in the use of a spreadsheet software program. Leon sat at the computer with Abby, beginning the explanation as though she knew nothing about the computer.

Leon did not inquire about Abby's experience at the computer and with spreadsheets. If he had, he would have learned that Abby had considerable experience with spreadsheets, even though she didn't know the feature Leon was explaining. Abby would have a more positive impression of Leon if he had been considerate of what she already knew.

How would Leon's instructions have been different if he had asked some questions about Abby's skills?

Nonverbal Communication

Communicating a message often involves more than words. Facial expressions, gestures of hands and arms, posture, and other body movements also communicate to listeners.

Understanding Nonverbal Behavior

Nonverbal behavior can be difficult to understand. For example, glancing at a clock might mean that a person is eager to leave a meeting as quickly as possible. However, perhaps the person wants to remain until the last possible minute before going to another meeting. Making eye contact and smiling when someone comes to your workstation may show an interest in being helpful. It might also merely reveal pleasure in having an excuse to stop work and take a break.

Be aware of the nonverbal behavior that you display. Make sure it agrees with the intent of the words used. Nonverbal behavior should reinforce what is said, not distract from its meaning. You may have heard the saying, "Actions speak louder than words." This saying can be quite true in the case of nonverbal communications. Do not confuse your listeners by saying one thing and having your nonverbal behavior communicate something else.

 CHECK POINT Why is it important to be aware of your nonverbal behavior when talking with coworkers or customers?

Body Language

body language facial expressions, gestures, eye movements, and postures used to communicate without words

Nonverbal communications are commonly called **body language**. Many studies have been done on nonverbal behavior. Meanings people assign to different kinds of body language vary. Nonverbal behaviors do not always speak as clearly as words. Be aware of the possible meaning of nonverbal cues. This awareness can help you understand others and deliver your messages more effectively.

Facial expressions are important nonverbal cues. A smile can convey understanding or support for what is being said. A frown, on the other hand, may indicate lack of understanding or disagreement. A smile at an inappropriate time, however, may convey smugness or insensitivity. Raised eyebrows may convey surprise or disapproval.

Eye movement can signal that you are paying attention. Making eye contact frequently shows your interest in what is being said. It implies that you are being honest or open when speaking. Letting your eyes roam around and seldom making eye contact can signal that you are not paying attention when listening or that you are being evasive when speaking.

Posture and gestures are important elements of body language. Good posture when sitting or standing shows confidence. Slouching or stooping shows an indifferent attitude or lack of self-confidence. Leaning closer or nodding conveys interest. Leaning or turning your body away conveys discomfort or disagreement with what is being discussed. Crossed arms show a defensive or unwelcome attitude. Sitting calmly with hands folded in your lap shows an openness to listen. Placing your hand to your cheek generally indicates that you are evaluating or considering. Placing your hand over your mouth generally indicates your disapproval.

Fidgeting while talking or listening shows a lack of focus. Constantly glancing at the door or at a clock while speaking with a coworker can show that you are not really interested in the discussion. This behavior may reduce the effectiveness of what you are saying.

Facial expressions and gestures are elements of nonverbal communication.

Tony Metaxas/Glow Images, Inc.

When talking with coworkers or taking part in meetings, notice the body language of the speaker and those around you. Paying attention to body language will help you understand better what others are trying to say. When talking with coworkers or giving a formal presentation, be aware of your body language. Use your body language to reinforce the message you want to communicate. Body language that is consistent with the words you use will enhance your message.

 CHECK POINT Posture is an important element of body language. What nonverbal message does good posture send? What message does slouching or stooping send?

REVIEW 5-1

21st Century Skills

 **PARTNERSHIP FOR 21ST CENTURY SKILLS**

Interacting with Others

Three classmates were talking together after school one afternoon. One of them, Gloria, said to the other two: "Listen, can I talk with you about my problem? I will confess to you that I don't want to give a talk in class next week. I'll just pretend that I am sick and not come to school for a few days. Sitting here and talking with you is fine. But I can't get up before the class. I have figured out a way to get out of doing this all through high school. I'll be honest with you. I remember having to stand before the class in the seventh grade to recite part of a poem. I was so scared that after the first two lines I couldn't remember a word. Oh, was I embarrassed. Aren't these assignments ridiculous? I'm not going to have to stand up before anyone and talk when I am out of school and earning a living. Do you agree with my scheme for next week?"

1. What would you say to Gloria? What decision do you think would be best for her?
2. What tips can you give Gloria to help her overcome her fear of public speaking?

Making Academic Connections

Reinforcing English Skills

You overhear the following conversation between two colleagues who are standing at the photocopying machine. Both of your colleagues have made a number of errors in their use of pronouns.

1. Key a copy of the conversation between Melissa and Steve, changing all pronouns used incorrectly.
2. Underscore all the pronouns you substituted for those in error.

Melissa:	"Do you plan to take the continuing education class for we staff people that Ms. Wong discussed at the meeting yesterday? Do you think she means for us to attend?"
Steve:	"I don't know if I'll go. Both me and Earl wonder if we would be better off taking a course later in the year. The topics are interesting though, aren't it?"
Melissa:	"Well, between you and I, I think there are likely to be some good courses later; but Aina and me have pretty much decided we will go. We believe Ms. Wong would like we to go."
Steve:	"Melissa, if you go, will you tell us what them said at the meeting?"
Melissa:	"Of course; the instructor will be good, I guess. I won't be as good as her, but I'll do my best."

5-1 Activity 1

Speaking and Listening (Outcomes 5-1a, 5-1b)

Office workers must often present ideas or plans at small group meetings. Practice organizing your ideas and presenting them at a meeting in this activity.

1. Work with two classmates to complete this activity. (Read all the instructions for the activity before you begin completing the steps. You will repeat some of the steps so that each student will be a speaker, listener, and observer.)

2. As a team, create a form or checklist to use in recording notes about the effectiveness of communications during a meeting. List important points for listening and speaking on the form. Also include a place to comment on the body language of both the speaker and listener. A sample form is shown in the following page.

3. As the speaker, choose a topic from the following list to develop into a three- to five-minute talk. List the main points you want to convey and then place the points in logical order. Be specific and give examples or supporting information as appropriate. Present your talk to the listener as if the two of you were in a meeting. Answer your listener's questions.

Topics

Why you need new equipment or software

How you want to change a procedure and why

Why your company should sell a new product or service

Instructions for a work project the listener is to complete

4. As the listener, pay careful attention to the speaker. Using two or three minutes after the speaker finishes, note the main points of the talk. Then ask questions relevant to the information presented.

5. As the observer, pay careful attention as your classmates role-play the meeting. Then note what you observed on the form. Discuss your observations with your classmates.

6. Repeat steps 3–5 so each person plays each role—speaker, listener, and observer. Give your teacher a copy of your notes for the talk as a speaker, notes and questions as a listener, and the form you completed as an observer.

LISTENING

Yes	No	
____	____	The listener seems to be focused on understanding the speaker.
____	____	The listener does not seem to be distracted by internal or external barriers to listening.
____	____	The listener gives verbal or nonverbal feedback to the speaker.
____	____	The listener asks appropriate questions.

Comments:

_____

_____

SPEAKING

Yes	No	
____	____	The speaker seems to be interested in the topic she or he is discussing.
____	____	The speaker speaks clearly in an appropriate tone.
____	____	The speaker uses standard language.
____	____	The speaker seems to consider the audience members and relate to their experiences and knowledge.
____	____	The speaker's body language and other nonverbal communication reinforce the message.

Comments:

_____

_____

© Cengage Learning 2013

5-1 Activity 2

Nonverbal Communication (Outcome 5-1c)

Nonverbal communication is an important part of sending and understanding messages. For three days, note each instance you observe of nonverbal communication. Describe each situation and the message the behavior was intended to communicate. Note whether or not you think the behavior was a good way to communicate the intended message.

OUTCOMES

5-2a Plan effective presentations.
5-2b Develop the message and visual aids for a presentation.
5-2c Describe strategies for effective team presentations.

Planning Presentations

Regardless of your job, you will need to express yourself clearly to others at work. Presentations may not be a part of your daily work. Occasionally, however, you may need to present information to others. The situation may require you to speak to a small group of your peers or to a large audience. Regardless of the size of your audience, you must keep your goals and your listeners' interests in mind as you develop your presentation.

Identify the Purpose of the Presentation

When you have an opportunity to prepare a presentation, it will likely be for one of two purposes. You will either want to motivate and influence your listeners, or you will want to inform and educate them. The message of your presentation will include the main ideas and supporting details you want to present.

When you are speaking to motivate or influence, your message needs to be persuasive. Your purpose is to get your listeners to take a course of action. When you are speaking to inform, your message should be clear and concise. Your purpose is to communicate information so your listeners can understand and use the information. Identifying the overall purpose of the presentation and the specific goals you want to accomplish is the first step in preparing a presentation.

You should show listeners how your message is important to them.

Jupiter Images/Goodshoot

Profile Your Listeners

Your message must be important to your audience if you are to hold their attention. Developing a profile of your listeners is the next step in preparing a presentation. You must determine your listeners' interests or needs. Then you can relate your message to something they want to hear about.

profile description or picture

To determine what is important to your listeners, you must first describe them in as much detail as possible. Put yourself in their shoes. Write down everything you know about them:

- What do the listeners like or dislike?
- What do the listeners need?
- What is the expertise of the listeners?
- What biases do the listeners have?
- What responsibilities do the listeners have?
- Are the listeners decision makers?

Developing a listener profile helps you identify the interests of your listeners. At first this may seem difficult, but if you try to think as they think, you should be able to do so.

CHECK POINT Why is it important to prepare a profile of the expected listeners for a presentation?

✴ WORKPLACE CONNECTIONS ✴

Roberto is planning a presentation for office personnel in his department. The purpose of his presentation is to tell about new office procedures that are to be used by the department. The new procedures have been adopted to help workers be more productive. However, Roberto's message to the office staff must address their concerns and interests.

Roberto knows that several workers update the customer database. As a result, some customer records are overlooked because one person assumes another employee made the updates. Workers are never sure customer records are accurate. Better procedures are needed for updating customer records. When Roberto makes his presentation, he can discuss how the procedures will affect this situation that is of interest to his audience. He will explain how the new procedures will make their jobs easier.

Is Roberto likely to know much about the personnel in his department? How will this help or hinder him in making the presentation?

Organize Your Ideas

After you have identified the ideas or main points to be included in the presentation, organize them in a logical way that your listener will understand.

Create Storyboards

Sketching out and organizing your thoughts is called creating **storyboards**. Creating storyboards involves considering several ideas and then organizing them to create an outline and notes about the topic. The notes can be just words or phrases, or they can be complete sentences.

To create a storyboard, you can complete a worksheet page for each element or idea for your presentation. Figure 5-2.1 shows a sample of a storyboard worksheet. The worksheet helps you organize your thoughts about a specific idea. You begin by stating the purpose of the presentation. Next, you describe one of the main ideas and provide information that supports your idea. Then you identify a listener interest. You also list listener advantages. Don't be concerned right now with the worksheet box labeled "Visual Element." You'll learn about that shortly.

To complete the storyboard, you fill out a worksheet for each idea in your presentation. Once all your ideas are written down, you can improve the flow by rearranging the pages. The storyboard provides the basic organization of the presentation. Through this planning process, you organize the key concepts and define the overall presentation.

An alternative to completing storyboard worksheets is to use a software outline feature to create the storyboard pages. Create the main topics (or ideas) and then break down each main topic into subtopics. Once you key

Figure 5-2.1 Using storyboard worksheets helps you organize a presentation.

Sheet # ____1____

Storyboard Worksheet

Purpose	Motivate and influence sales staff to increase sales during the fall campaign
Main Idea	Commission and bonus opportunities will increase
Support for Idea	Commissions on sale items raised from 10% to 15% $500 bonus for top 10 total sales
Listener Interest	Commissions and bonuses that may be earned during the campaign
Listener Advantage	More income for the staff member
Listener Objection	Large number of clients to be handled during the sale Counter: The extra effort required will be rewarded with higher income
Visual Element	Growing dollar sign graphic

© Cengage Learning 2013

your ideas, you can edit and rearrange them quickly and easily. Be sure to include listener interests, support for your ideas, and listener advantages for each idea.

Consider Listener Advantages and Objections

Once you have developed your ideas and your listener's interests, list the advantages for your listeners if they accept your ideas. If possible, prioritize these advantages in order of importance to the listeners.

Consider all the objections your listeners may have regarding your ideas. When you anticipate the listeners' objections, you can decide how to address them. You may be able to offer solutions or alternatives to what the listeners see as a problem. Your goal is to minimize the objections so the listeners no longer see them as a problem.

objection reason to disapprove or reject an idea

 CHECK POINT How many main ideas should go on each page of the storyboards for a presentation?

Develop the Message

Your ideas, or the main message of your presentation, must accomplish the purpose of the presentation. The message must also relate to your listeners' needs or interests. During the planning phase, you have developed a list of major points or ideas you must include to accomplish your purpose. Consider how you can relate each major point or idea to the interests of your audience.

Message Parts

Your presentation message will have three main parts: the opening, the body, and the closing. Each one plays an important part in achieving the goal you have set for the presentation.

Opening

The opening or beginning statements of your presentation should get the listeners' attention and indicate the topic of the presentation. You can begin with a statement, such as "Today you will learn about some new procedures for updating customer records that will make your job much easier." You could also begin with a question, such as "Would you like to know how you can update customer records more quickly and easily?" In both examples, the opening remark is designed to get attention and let the listeners know that the message is important to them.

During the opening, you should briefly introduce yourself if the audience does not know you well. You could include remarks that show your qualifications to speak on the topic. Keep this part brief, especially if you have already been introduced to the audience by someone.

Body

The body is the main part of the presentation where you present the points of the message. Refer to the storyboards you created earlier as you write the message. The storyboards may contain only words or phrases to indicate the content you planned to include. Write the body in complete sentences similar to how you would write a report. Remember, however, that you will want to speak in a conversational style and tone that might be less formal than that used for a business report.

Whenever possible, provide evidence or details that support your ideas. For example, you can state facts or offer statistics to back up a proposal. You can use examples and comparisons to confirm a need. You can use expert opinions to endorse a recommendation. You can relate a situation to the personal experiences of your listeners or experiences of your own. For example, in a presentation on new office procedures, you could describe an embarrassing situation you experienced recently. Perhaps you were talking with a customer on the phone, and the information in the customer database was not up to date. As a result, you were not able to handle the customer's questions. Other members of the office staff could probably easily identify with this experience.

Closing

During the closing, first summarize the main points you have presented. The summary should be brief and should include only the most important main points of the presentation. Next, tell the listeners what you want them to do. For example, you might want them to take some action, such as voting to accept a proposal. Finally, thank the listeners for their attention.

✓ CHECK POINT How can you provide information to support your ideas during a presentation?

During the closing of a presentation, tell listeners the action you want them to take.

Erik Snyder/Jupiter Images

Visual Aids

 visual aid an object or image that illustrates a point or concept, such as photos, posters, or slides

Images are very powerful. Visual aids (also called simply *visuals*) stimulate the listener and keep the listener's attention. Studies show that we remember about 10 percent of what we hear in a presentation and about 20 percent of what we see. However, we remember about 50 percent of what we both see and hear. Even in one-to-one communications, visual aids are extremely effective. Not only will the visuals help you present your content, they will also make your listeners feel important because you took the time to create them.

Plan a visual aid for each main idea (each page in your storyboard). This will help provide direction for your presentation. Each visual you create should be designed for consistency and simplicity. Carry out the theme of the presentation in all visuals. The first visual aid should introduce the topic and set the tone for the presentation as shown in Figure 5-2.2. All visuals should support the overall message and should address the interests of and advantages to the listeners.

Figure 5-2.2 **This visual aid introduces the topic and the speaker.**

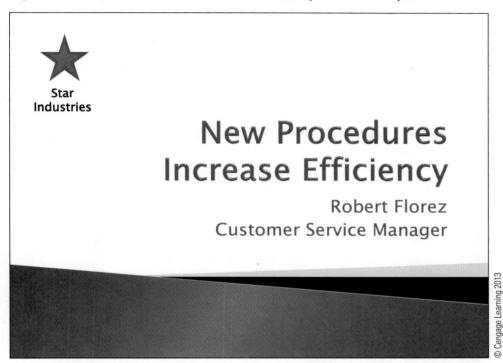

© Cengage Learning 2013

The media you choose for your visuals will depend on your budget and the equipment you have available. Your audience and whether the presentation is formal or informal will also influence your choice of media.

media materials or means used to communicate

Transparencies

Overhead transparencies are effective for presentations to small groups. They are inexpensive to create and can be in black and white or in color. If you have access to a copier that can handle transparency film, you can copy text, photos, and illustrations and turn them into transparencies quickly and easily. If you reorganize your presentation, you can easily rearrange the order of the transparencies. You can also write on them and add to them during a presentation.

Electronic Slides

Presentations that use electronic slides are appropriate for both large and small groups. With programs such as Microsoft PowerPoint, you can create electronic slide shows quickly and easily. Slide shows that also use sound are called multimedia presentations. If you need to show images that are from printed photos or film, you can use a scanner to convert these images to digital form. Most computers can display high-quality images and play sound. You can enhance a presentation by including video, **animation**, and audio.

animation moving pictures or graphics

Handouts

The audience will only remember a small part of the content of your presentation. Provide handouts for your listeners so they can be used later for reference and as reminders of the key points in your presentation. Consider using a color copier to make handouts for an important presentation. Color copies will add impact to your presentation.

The intent of the handouts will determine how you design them and when you give them to the audience. Handouts containing the outline of your presentation can be useful in guiding your listeners through the presentation. Distribute this type of handout at the beginning of the presentation. The outline will help your audience follow the presentation and stay involved. Throughout the presentation, the handout can be used for note taking.

Handouts can be used to supply your listeners with detailed information that is too long to place on transparencies or slides. These details or references can add credibility to your presentation. Handouts can also be used to summarize the main points of a presentation. Distribute a summary handout after you have given the presentation.

✳ WORKPLACE CONNECTIONS ✳

In his talk on new office procedures, Roberto provided a handout containing the outline of his presentation. He removed the details of the outline and replaced them with blank lines. As he presented the new office procedures, the staff members took notes to help them remember the information.

One of the handouts contains detailed descriptions of the new office procedures. The office staff will review this information later when they begin using the new procedures.

Why do you think Roberto removed the details of the presentation outline when making handouts?

Posters and Flip Charts

Posters that you have prepared ahead of time are very effective for small, informal groups. Posters can be used to reinforce the content of a presentation. A slide, photo, or handout can be enlarged into a poster-size print. Display the poster to restate key points, introduce a new product, or review a visual element.

Large paper flip charts or whiteboards allow you to write notes or draw illustrations during a presentation. Flip charts and small whiteboards are inexpensive and easy to use.

Electronic Whiteboards

electronic whiteboard a device that allows users to write text or draw images and print or save them

An **electronic whiteboard** allows you to capture the notes or images you create on the board in digital form. The notes and images can be sent to a printer or saved in a computer file. A more advanced version of the electronic whiteboard is called an interactive board or panel. You can write and draw on it as you do with an electronic whiteboard. However, this type of board also allows you to display a computer screen on the board. You can use an electronic pen like a mouse to give commands to the computer. Some electronic whiteboards have a built-in printer. These boards are very effective when you want to record input from the audience or use computer programs during the presentation.

An electronic whiteboard is effective for displaying a computer program during a presentation.

CHECK POINT What are three examples of media you might use as visual aids during a presentation?

Design Strategies

People remember graphics better than words. Whenever possible, use a graphic or picture to reinforce words. Keep the graphics simple. Make sure the visual element you choose reinforces what you want to communicate. Do not use images that are unrelated to the content of the message. Use the storyboard worksheets to describe your visual element(s) as you plan and organize your presentation.

Many programs are available for working with clip art, graphs, illustrations, and photographs. However, the graphics you use in a presentation do not need to be elaborate. They can be simple creations that you draw or clip art that comes with your presentation software. For example, you can use a clock to represent "time" or an up arrow to represent "increase" as shown in Figure 5-2.3 on page 176.

Limit your design to one main idea per visual, and use plenty of white space. Use the same orientation (slide directions) for all of the visuals. Visuals in landscape orientation are wider than they are tall. Visuals in portrait orientation are taller than they are wide. Transparencies and slides are usually created in landscape orientation. The visual in Figure 5-2.3 is in landscape orientation.

Figure 5-2.3 **Simple graphics can be used to illustrate an idea.**

Text

Limit text on visuals. If the text on a visual is crowded, it results in a confusing appearance. If you have too much text, the audience becomes involved in reading the content of the visual instead of listening to what you are saying. Limit the use of different text styles, sizes, and colors throughout to avoid a confusing appearance. Lowercase text is easier to read than all capitals. As a general rule, use all caps sparingly.

Use bullets to help the audience follow the presentation. Bullets are effective for presenting important points and specific terminology. Indent bullets to establish a hierarchy of points or details. The visual in Figure 5-2.3 has two levels of bullets. Make the wording on visuals parallel. On a slide, for example, begin each bullet line with same part of speech, such as a verb or a noun. Use active voice. Whenever possible, make the points short and concise.

Writing on the visual as you use it in your presentation is very effective. Not only does this draw the listeners' attention to the visual, but it also enables you to create a visual memory for your audience. For example, some presentation programs allow you to underline or circle important information on a slide as you discuss the information.

Color

Use color effectively. Just because color is available does not mean it has to be used extensively. In fact, limiting the number of colors used is often best. A blending of colors or graduated colors instead of a solid background can help to guide the viewer's eyes to a focal point. Borders are effective for adding and using color wisely. They help guide the viewer's attention and give the visual a professional look.

bullets small graphics, such as circles or diamonds, used to draw attention to a line of text

The colors you choose will depend on the media you are developing for the presentation. Choose your background color, text colors, and image colors to complement one another. You want to create a pleasing effect that will not distract your audience from the message. Some presentation programs have design themes you can use to give the slides a professional look as shown in Figure 5-2.4. Coordinating colors for background, text, bullets, and other design elements are part of the design theme.

Figure 5-2.4 **Design themes give slides a coordinated color scheme.**

© Cengage Learning 2013

Motion

You can add motion to electronic slides in a variety of ways. Cascading bullets, transitions, video, and moving images can all be used to add interest to your electronic slides.

When creating electronic slides, bullet lines can be set to cascade or appear on screen one at a time. Using this technique is effective when you want to emphasize each point as you present it. Your listeners cannot read ahead to the next point you plan to discuss as they can when all bullets appear on screen at once. Your command (usually a mouse click or key stroke) that brings on the next bullet also signals to the audience that you are ready to move ahead to a new point.

In an electronic slide show, the screen images that appear when moving from one slide to the next are called transitions. A variety of transition styles are available. Transition effects can be set to move slowly or quickly and can be accompanied by sound in some programs. Transitions can add interest to a slide show.

You can place links in electronic slides to videos you want to play during the presentation. You might include a video of a company executive who could not attend the meeting in person, for instance. You might play a video that shows technical details or the operation of a piece of equipment. You might want to include videos of customers commenting on a product. A video of a warm sunny beach with swaying palm trees can set the mood for a discussion of a winter sales meeting held in Florida. As with other images, be sure the video is appropriate for the content of the message and that it is fairly short so you do not lose the attention of the audience.

CHECK POINT Give one design strategy related to text and one related to color on visual aids.

Team Presentation Strategies

Office workers often give presentations as part of a team. Different team members bring different skills and knowledge that can be used to complete the task. Working together, team members may be able to provide broader coverage of the topic than one person could provide.

Roles of Individuals

The first step in preparing a team presentation is to select or identify the team leader. The leader will ensure that the team stays focused on accomplishing its objectives.

Each team member must have a valid role. All team members might not be involved in delivering the presentation, but each should make a significant contribution. Those contributions can vary. For example, one or more team members may research and develop content for the presentation. Another person may create the visuals. One or more members may deliver the presentation.

 CHECK POINT What are two advantages to working in a team to prepare and deliver a presentation?

Working as a Team

All members of the team should agree on the purpose or objectives of a team presentation. Everyone's efforts will be directed toward accomplishing these objectives. Team members can share ideas and develop storyboards or an outline of the points to be presented.

Developing the content of a team presentation requires some special efforts. Several people may have contributed content to be covered. The team should make sure the tone and the terms used are consistent throughout the presentation. All the content should be presented in a way that addresses the listeners' interests or needs. Listener advantages should be stated clearly. Comments should be prepared to counter listeners' objections that the team members think may be mentioned.

The visual aids must also be consistent in style and content. Using compatible media for visual aids can help create a smooth transition from one presenter to another. For example, all presenters should use the same design theme and color scheme for electronic slides.

Individuals must work together to prepare a team presentation.

The team should review the entire presentation to make sure all the content and visuals flow together well. Team members should be chosen to deliver each part of the content. A specific amount of time should be set for each part. As a last preparation, the team should practice giving the presentation as a group. Practicing and delivering a presentation is covered later in this chapter.

 CHECK POINT What can team members do to make a smooth transition from one presenter to another?

REVIEW 5-2

21st Century Skills

PARTNERSHIP FOR 21ST CENTURY SKILLS

Thinking Critically

Assume that you are part of an office team assigned the task of improving the company's schedule for employee breaks and lunchtimes. The schedule was revised to prevent overcrowding in the cafeteria at various times throughout the day. The team recently submitted a proposed schedule to management and has just received approval. The new schedule will be effective the first of next month.

You have been asked to present this new schedule to the personnel in your department. You know that some people in the department are slow to accept changes. You also realize that some of the employees currently enjoy sharing their breaks and lunches with employees from other departments. Unfortunately, this may no longer be possible for some. Before you present the new schedule, you must be ready to address the concerns and needs of the personnel in your department.

1. Describe how you would introduce this new schedule with the listener in mind. What listener needs or interests would you address? What listener advantages would you present?
2. List some complaints and objections you might expect to hear from your coworkers. Explain how you would attempt to minimize these objections.

Making Academic Connections

Reinforcing Math Skills

At a recent presentation, you asked your listeners to complete evaluation forms. Listeners scored each item on a scale of 1 to 10. Evaluators are identified by letter because the evaluation was anonymous. Compile and average the ratings to determine an overall evaluation score.

1. Calculate the average score given by all evaluators for each item.
2. Calculate the average score given on all the items by each evaluator.
3. Find an overall evaluation score by averaging the average scores from the 10 evaluators.

	EVALUATORS									
EVALUATION ITEMS	A	B	C	D	E	F	G	H	I	J
1. The coverage of the topic met my expectations.	8	9	7	9	10	10	9	7	8	9
2. The topic was of interest to me.	6	10	8	10	8	9	7	9	8	8
3. The length of the presentation was appropriate.	9	9	10	10	10	9	8	6	10	10
4. The presenter addressed the topic effectively.	8	9	8	9	8	9	9	7	10	10
5. The concepts were presented clearly.	8	9	8	9	8	9	9	7	10	10
6. The presenter related the information to my experiences.	6	8	9	9	7	7	7	5	8	8
7. The information presented will be useful to me.	6	8	8	8	8	7	8	6	7	9
8. The visuals used were helpful and appropriate.	9	10	9	9	8	9	8	7	10	10

5-2 Activity 1

Plan and Organize a Presentation (Outcome 5-2a)

In this activity, you will plan and organize a five-minute presentation to inform and educate your classmates. In later activities, you will prepare the visuals you plan here and give the presentation to your class.

1. Choose a hobby, sport, or activity that you really enjoy and about which you are knowledgeable. Get your teacher's approval for the topic. Plan a presentation about this topic.
2. Create a storyboard worksheet for each main idea in your topic. See Figure 5-2.1 for an example storyboard worksheet. Complete all parts of the storyboard worksheet, including ideas for the visual elements. (You will write the message and create the actual visuals in a later activity.)

5-2 Activity 2

Create a Presentation (Outcome 5-2b)

In this activity, you will write the message and prepare visuals for the five-minute presentation you planned for 5-2 Activity 1.

1. Using your storyboards created earlier, write the message for the presentation. Begin with an opening that will get the attention of the listeners. Next, discuss each point of your message following your storyboards. Give appropriate details and examples. Finally, write a strong closing that summarizes the message and tells the listeners the action you want them to take.
2. Choose the media you will use to create the visuals depending on the equipment and materials available. Ask your instructor for the media options available to you. Create the visuals indicated on the storyboard worksheets you prepared earlier. (You will learn how to practice and deliver your presentation later in this chapter.)

OUTCOMES

5-3a Apply strategies for practicing and preparing for a presentation.
5-3b Demonstrate methods for delivering an effective presentation.
5-3c Gather feedback for a presentation through questions and evaluations.

Practice and Prepare

Now that you have prepared your message, you are ready to put your ideas in motion. You may think that with all this preparation, you are ready to deliver the message. The content of your presentation may be right on target, but if you cannot communicate the content effectively, your efforts will not be rewarded. You must practice and prepare for the delivery with the same care you prepared the content.

Practice

The more experienced you become in speaking to others, the less practice you will need. If you're new at making presentations, you will definitely want to practice. You can practice before friends or colleagues, or you can rehearse the presentation on your own.

Review each of your visuals and the notes you have created to accompany them. Rehearse out loud exactly what you plan to say. However, do not attempt to memorize and later recite the message. Instead, review the message until you know it well and can discuss the points with just a few reminders from your notes or visuals. Make sure you state each idea from the listeners' point of view. Also be sure to provide listener advantages.

For team presentations, each presenter must know the content he or she will present. Although each member should use his or her own style of speaking, everyone should reflect the overall theme. It is a good idea for all team members to be present, even if some of them do not present. The team should practice the presentation as a group.

Record your presentation if possible. You could use a **webcam** or a digital video camera. Review the

webcam a video capture device connected to a computer

Creating a video is a good way to practice a presentation.

Getty Images

video and consider the ways you can improve the delivery of your message. If necessary, practice and video yourself again. Remember, you will most likely be much more critical of yourself than anyone in your audience will be. Also, consider getting constructive criticism from friends or coworkers.

 CHECK POINT   Describe two strategies for practicing a presentation.

Prepare

One of the best ways to ensure that you will make a successful presentation is to prepare well. The visuals you have prepared will guide you through the outline of the presentation. Use notes to remind you of the key points and the facts relevant to your presentation. You can use note cards or the notes feature of your presentation software to record details, ideas that each visual presents, content prompts, and reminders. If you have practiced at length, you will probably find you no longer need to look at your notes because you know the content and know what you plan to say. When you have done a thorough job of preparing your message, you can feel confident and remain calm during the presentation.

Prepare the Meeting Room

There are many factors to consider regarding the meeting room. Make sure the seating arrangement is appropriate. A semicircular, or "U," arrangement is good for an audience that will focus on visuals at the front of the room. This arrangement also helps the presenter control the focus of the group. If the presenter is standing before the audience, a rectangular seating arrangement also works well. A circular or oval arrangement is helpful for small group discussions.

Arrive early to set up equipment and support materials. Practice ahead of time with the specific equipment to be used in the presentation, such as a computer or projector. Even if you are familiar with operating a similar piece of equipment, make sure you practice on the one you plan to use. This will allow you to discover any differences or problems with the equipment. Test the audio equipment and get comfortable with the microphone. Know whom to call if you should need a technician.

Check the lighting in the room and determine the best light level to use for the presentation. Even though your visuals may look good in a dark room, you want the lighting to be sufficient so your audience can clearly see you as you speak. Also, check the room temperature. Remember that a room may become warmer as more people enter it. Setting the temperature to about 68 degrees will usually provide a comfortable environment when the room is filled with people.

Consider Your Appearance

Your appearance makes an impression on your audience and can influence how they receive your message. Dressing appropriately can help you gain their respect and hold their attention. When inappropriate, your appearance can distract your listeners.

Good grooming is important. Be neat and clean in your appearance. Get a good night's rest before the presentation so you can look and be alert. For formal presentations, business suits are appropriate. For informal presentations, your attire can be more casual depending on the audience. Dress comfortably but conservatively.

 CHECK POINT   How should you adjust the room lighting and temperature for a presentation?

Pablo is inexperienced at giving presentations and is a bit nervous about addressing a group at next week's sales meeting. When deciding what he plans to wear for the presentation, Pablo considers the information he knows about the meeting. The sales team meets each winter in an area likely to be warm and sunny, such as Florida or southern California. The salespeople enjoy this break in their normal routine of visiting clients. They take this opportunity to dress in business casual attire at this company meeting rather than in business suits.

Pablo considers dressing in business casual attire. After further consideration, however, he decides to wear a business suit. He believes the salespeople will take his presentation more seriously if he dresses formally. He will wear business casual attire when he attends presentations given by others and wants to be seen as part of the group.

If a speaker's dress is not appropriate for the situation, how may this affect how the presentation is received by the audience?

Deliver the Presentation

In a small- or large-group presentation, another person may introduce you to your audience before you deliver your presentation. You should also introduce yourself. In your opening remarks, be sure to state your purpose. Your opening remarks help to set the tone for your presentation. You may choose to use a visual for this introduction.

Always remember that your remarks should be appropriate for the occasion. For example, some people like to begin with a joke or with a note of humor. This sets a friendly tone and makes you more comfortable with your audience. Jokes should always be in good taste and appropriate for the audience. If the topic of your presentation is very serious in nature, however, a joke may not be appropriate.

Communicate Effectively

To deliver your message effectively, you must communicate with your audience. Although you will not be carrying on a two-way conversation with members of your audience, a sharing of ideas and information must take place. For this to happen, you must get your audience involved.

Your listeners will likely be involved in your presentation if you appear relaxed and comfortable. Being nervous is normal. Naturally, you want to do well, and you may experience some nervousness. Take deep breaths, concentrate on talking slowly, and think about what you're going to say next. You may think that you are talking too slowly, but that is generally not the case. The listeners will find you to be more **credible** because they can tell you are giving thought to what you are about to say. Maintain a positive self-image and an upbeat attitude. Remind yourself that you are well prepared and can deliver the message effectively.

credible believable, reliable

Maintain Eye Contact

Making eye contact with one person in the audience helps all members of the audience feel as if you are talking to them. Until you become experienced, you may find it difficult to make eye contact with your listeners. If this is a problem for you, try to maintain eye contact with one individual for at least five seconds before making eye contact with another person in the audience. Maintaining eye contact helps you involve your listeners and know whether your audience is following you. You can judge their reactions to what you are saying, and your listeners will feel more involved and important.

Avoid Non-Words

Sounds or words that do not contribute to the meaning of the presentation are often called non-words. Examples of non-words are shown in Figure 5-3.1. The use of non-words is a habit many of us need to break. Often we don't realize we say non-words such as "uhh" and "ah." Review your videotape or have a friend help you identify non-words that you use. Count the number of non-words you say throughout your presentation. You may be surprised to find how frequently you use non-words.

Usually we say non-words because we are thinking about what we want to say next, and we do not want to allow a period of silence. Actually, a non-word does not fill up much time as we speak. Having quiet pauses between our statements is preferable to using non-words. The non-words can be much more annoying to listeners than a pause with silence.

If you know you use too many non-words, video your presentation a second time. This time, consciously pause instead of saying a non-word. Review your video and count the occurrences of non-words again. Hopefully, you were able to reduce them significantly. Don't be concerned if you cannot eliminate all non-words initially. Habits are difficult to break. Consciously work on avoiding non-words in your daily communications as well. You will soon see you can speak without them.

non-words spoken sounds with no meaning, such as "ah"

Figure 5-3.1 **Avoid the use of non-words in your presentations.**

NON-WORDS		
ah	okay	yeah
all right	uh-huh	you know
and	well	you see
and ah		

© Cengage Learning 2013

Show Enthusiasm and Speak Convincingly

Speak with enthusiasm and conviction. A sure way to get your audience involved is to convince them that you are excited about the topic. If you believe in what you are saying, let your listeners know. Let your enthusiasm be genuine, however. Most listeners will know if you're not being honest, and that is a sure way to lose their attention.

Show a sincere interest in helping your listeners meet their needs. Use key words that your listener wants to hear and to which they can relate. Describe experiences or examples with which your listeners can identify. In doing so, you can be very convincing as you share your ideas.

Control Your Posture and Gestures

Watching speakers who constantly pace back and forth or who shuffle their feet and shift weight from one leg to the other can be very distracting. Instead of becoming involved in your presentation, listeners start concentrating on your posture and gestures. You want them to think about your message, not your gestures.

Gestures can enhance or detract from a speaker's words.

Ghislain & Marie David de Lossy/Cultura RM/Alamy

Stand with your feet slightly apart and firmly planted, moving or shifting your weight only occasionally. Leave your hands at your sides until you use them for natural gestures that enhance your words. For example, if something is really big, show it by opening your arms really wide. If something is minor, use a gesture with your hands to show the problem is small. Make sure your gestures do not contradict your words. When your hands drop below your waist, your gestures are not effective.

Avoid other distracting gestures such as rubbing your hands together or crossing your arms. These forms of body language communicate nervousness. Your listeners will be watching your body language as they listen to you speak. Make sure your posture and gestures are not communicating something different than the message you want them to receive.

Use Good Intonation

No one likes to listen to a person speaking in a monotone. As you review your practice video, close your eyes and listen to your voice. Do you use good **intonation**? Does your voice show your enthusiasm? Is it easy to listen to? With practice, you can learn to speak with a pleasant voice that is neither too high nor too low. Your voice should sound relaxed and have an even tone.

Learning to relax can help you control your voice. If you are tense, your voice may sound shaky and high-pitched. Concentrate on speaking loudly enough without straining your voice or shouting. Enunciate clearly and don't speak too quickly. If the meeting room and audience are large, use a microphone so you can speak normally and still be heard by everyone.

intonation the rise and fall in voice pitch

Keep the Audience Focused

Watch the reactions of your audience. Make sure they are focused on what you are saying. If they seem confused or distracted, back up and rephrase your point. If you sense that you are losing their attention, try to focus again on listener interests and advantages.

Do not panic, however, if the audience does seem to lose focus. Keep in mind that this topic is something that you know and understand very well. Your listeners may need more time to think about the information and ideas you are presenting.

 CHECK POINT Why is maintaining eye contact with your listeners important when delivering a presentation?

Use Visuals Effectively

If you've prepared well, you have some great visuals to help you communicate your ideas. These visuals, however, are not the key to your presentation. You are the key element. Begin by drawing the listeners' attention to yourself. Then, when appropriate, direct their attention to the visuals to make your message more powerful.

One way visuals can make your message more powerful is by creating anticipation. Do not reveal the visual too soon. As you display the visuals, look at your listeners, not at the visuals. Continue to maintain eye contact. Stand to the left or right of the display of your visuals. Do not let the visuals replace you. Be sure your listeners can see both you and the visuals.

Pause to allow listeners time to view and think about the visuals. You have seen them and studied them, but your listeners have not. Also, use pauses to allow for listeners' reactions. Allow listeners time to laugh if the visual is humorous, or give them an opportunity to read and evaluate a proposed solution displayed on a visual. During this pause you can study their reactions to your visual. For example, look for nods of agreement or expressions of disagreement. If appropriate, ask for their feedback before continuing.

 CHECK POINT Describe two strategies for using visuals effectively during a presentation.

Gather Feedback

Gathering **feedback** after a presentation is important. You want to know whether the listeners understood your message and what questions they may have about the information presented. You also want to know whether you were effective in the way you delivered the message, used visuals, and answered questions.

feedback reactions, opinions, or comments

Answer Questions

Allowing the audience to ask questions is appropriate for many presentations. Question-and-answer sessions are valuable to you as well as the audience. They provide you an opportunity to hear from your listeners as they share what they are thinking.

Anticipate Listener Questions

Many speakers become anxious about receiving questions from an audience. They are afraid they will not be able to answer the questions. The key to feeling calm and confident when receiving questions is preparation. Anticipate what the listeners may ask you. If you have prepared well, you have probably addressed many of their concerns in the presentation. However, you may get questions about content you have already covered. This means that the listener either did not understand or did not retain that information.

✳ WORKPLACE CONNECTIONS ✳

Cathy Park is preparing a talk on the reassignment of sales territories. She considers anticipating questions an important part of preparing for the presentation. She knows members of the sales team will have lots of questions. They may ask about how the change will affect workloads, commissions, and follow-up on needs of customers in the territory previously assigned to a salesperson. Cathy keys each question she thinks someone is likely to ask. Then she keys a complete and concise answer to the question. Cathy will use these notes for reference if needed during the question-and-answer portion of the presentation. Preparing questions and answers in advance helps Cathy feel confident that she will be able to answer most of the questions that arise.

What do you think Cathy should do if she does not know the answer to a question someone asks?

Perhaps when you give your audience the opportunity to ask questions, no one will raise a question. This situation happens frequently. Initially, you may think the listeners are not interested in the topic and just want to leave. If you have been effective as a speaker, they have been listening and thinking about your ideas. You have been directing their train of thought. Perhaps they have not had time to think about their own ideas and questions to ask. Just in case no one in the audience asks a question, have some questions ready. This will help to fill the time you have allotted for questions and may prompt some questions from the audience.

Restate the Question

When you receive a question from the audience, the entire group needs to hear the question. Generally, the person asking directs the question to the speaker, and the entire audience does not hear the question. Restate the question for everyone to hear. Doing so gives you time to think about the answer and lets you confirm to the listener that you understand the question.

In one-to-one situations, you may wish to rephrase a question to let the listener know you understood it. Incorporating part of the question in the beginning of your answer can also be helpful. Be careful, however, not to offend your listener by rephrasing all the questions. Instead, allow yourself time to think about the answer by making comments such as, "I can understand your concerns" and "I, too, have experienced that, and this is what I've learned."

Respond to the Question

Respond to all questions in a courteous and sincere manner. Keep your answers brief to maintain the exchange between you and the audience. Direct your answer to the entire group, not just the person who asked the question. Maintain eye contact to keep the audience focused on the discussion. When appropriate, provide supporting details or evidence to back up your answer.

Be honest if you do not know the answer to a question. You will gain more credibility with your audience if you are honest than if you try to bluff your way through the answer. If appropriate, offer to find the answer and communicate it to the individual later.

Do not become frustrated if the question relates to information you have already covered. If one listener missed details or became confused, chances are that others did, too. Provide the details or explain the point again briefly. Use different words to explain the idea or data. Offer to provide more details later if appropriate.

Sometimes one individual will ask more than one question. That person may begin to dominate or take over the question-and-answer session. The other listeners often become aggravated when this happens. They can begin to feel unimportant or unnoticed. If this happens, you can quickly lose the audience's attention. If one individual begins to dominate the questions, break eye contact with that individual before he or she has an opportunity to ask another question. After giving an answer to that individual's question, establish eye contact with another person and ask, "Does anyone else have a question to ask?"

In a team presentation, the team members should decide in advance how they will handle questions from the audience. For example, they may decide that one team member will direct the questions to the appropriate person for an answer. All presenters should be included in the question-and-answer session.

Present Closing Remarks

Following the question-and-answer session, you have one last chance to get your point across. Your closing remarks should be a concise review of the major points in your presentation. Be careful, however, to word your closing so that you do not repeat exactly what you have already said. Restate the specific points. Then close the presentation, thanking your audience for listening.

 CHECK POINT Why should a speaker anticipate questions the listeners may ask at the end of a presentation?

Evaluate Your Presentation

You can ask for feedback from your audience by using an evaluation form. Evaluation forms are valuable tools that can help you improve your speaking skills. To be effective, though, the form has to gather appropriate information from your listeners. Be specific about the feedback you want from the audience. Figure 5-3.2 on page 190 shows a sample evaluation form. You will get the most accurate feedback if you ask your listeners to complete the evaluation right after the presentation. Their reactions are fresh, and their comments will be more specific.

Learn from the evaluation comments and use the information constructively to improve the content and/or the delivery of your message. Each time you speak before a group, you will grow in confidence and ability.

After each presentation, you should also evaluate yourself. Consider the strong points of your presentation and what seemed to be effective. Think about what you could do to improve it. Did you forget to mention something? Could you have used more visuals, or did you use too many? What would you do differently the next time? If you have the opportunity to give the same presentation again, you can refine and improve it using the feedback you receive and your own evaluation.

CHECK POINT When is the best time to get feedback on a presentation from listeners?

Figure 5-3.2 **Evaluation forms provide valuable feedback.**

Presentation Evaluation

Speaker: _____   Date: _____

Topic: _____

Please check one of the options at the right for each of the statements below. Place your completed form on the table by the door on your way out. Thank you for your feedback.

	Very Much	Somewhat	Not at All
The coverage of the topic met my expectations.			
The topic was of interest to me.			
The length of the presentation was appropriate.			
The presenter addressed the topic effectively.			
The concepts were presented clearly.			
The presenter related the information to my interests or experiences.			
The information presented will be useful to me.			
The visuals used were helpful and appropriate.			

Comments:

_____

_____

_____

REVIEW 5-3

21st Century Skills

Interacting with Others

After you completed a presentation about how to operate a new copier, you asked for questions from the listeners. One person in your audience, Jason, thinks he knows this topic well. He is dominating the question-and-answer session. During one of his questions, he implies that the information you have presented is not correct.

1. How would you respond to the suggestion that your information is not correct?
2. What can you do to prevent this person from dominating the session?

Making Academic Connections

Reinforcing English Skills

Your colleague Latoya has asked you to review her ideas for a presentation she will give to train new employees in using the company e-mail system. She plans to create electronic slides for her presentation. A partial list of her ideas is provided below step 3.

1. Restate Latoya's key ideas in short, concise phrases. Use strong, active verbs and limit the use of adjectives, adverbs, and prepositions.
2. Key the text to be contained on each slide. Use bullets to help organize the information.
3. Plan the flow of the presentation. Rearrange the information to place it in a logical order.

This e-mail system offers many advantages that will improve your efficiency and reduce the amount of time you are online. For example, you have lots more options that you can set. You can customize these settings for your particular needs. You get faster delivery times.

The features include the following: You can upload and download files. You can automatically retrieve new incoming mail and send new outgoing mail. You can also get to the address book and retrieve data quickly and easily.

Let's take a close look at the address book. You can store multiple e-mail addresses within an individual record. You can sort the records in the address book in alphabetical order. Or you can organize the address book to first display the addresses you use most frequently.

5-3 Activity 1

Create a Presentation Evaluation Form (Outcome 5-3c)

In this activity, you will create a presentation evaluation form to use in evaluating presentations given by your classmates. Work with three or four classmates to complete this assignment.

1. Review the information from this chapter related to effective speaking and presentations. Think about the information that a listener might want to comment on. Also think about the information a speaker would find useful for judging the effectiveness of the current presentation and for improving future presentations. Then create a list of evaluation points or questions to be included on the evaluation form.

2. Key the form using a format that will be easy to use for both the evaluators and speakers. A sample evaluation form is shown in Figure 5-3.2. Include an appropriate title for the form and blanks to record the speaker's name, topic, and date of the presentation. Also include a place for the evaluator to make comments on the form.

3. Print copies of the form for use in 5-3 Activity 2. You will need forms to evaluate all the other students in your group.

5-3 Activity 2

Practice and Deliver a Presentation (Outcomes 5-3a, 5-3b, 5-3c)

In this activity, you will practice and deliver the presentation created in 5-2 Activity 2. You will also evaluate your performance and that of your classmates.

1. Work in the same group as you did for 5-3 Activity 1 to complete this assignment. Take turns with the other students in your group so that all students complete steps 2 and 3.

2. Practice your presentation using the strategies described in this chapter. Video your practice session if possible.

3. Deliver your five-minute presentation to the group. Include a question-and-answer session at the end of your presentation. Ask fellow students to evaluate your presentation using the form created in 5-3 Activity 1.

4. Review the evaluations of your presentation prepared by your classmates. Then write a brief self-evaluation of your presentation. Comment on your overall performance, areas where you performed particularly well, and areas where you will try to improve for future presentations.

Summary

5-1 Listening and Speaking

- Listening and speaking skills are important for office workers.
- Listening involves a mental process as well as the physical aspects of hearing.
- Listening barriers can hinder your understanding of a message. You can apply strategies to overcome these barriers.
- When listening to instructions, mentally review the information and ask questions to help you understand the message.
- When speaking with coworkers or customers, express ideas clearly, speak in an appropriate tone, and use standard language.
- Facial expressions, gestures, and posture communicate to listeners. Nonverbal behavior should reinforce what is said, not distract from its meaning.

5-2 Planning and Preparing a Presentation

- Presentations for work are typically given to motivate and influence listeners or to inform and educate them.
- When planning a presentation, identify your goals and profile the listeners.
- Use an outline or storyboards to record the main ideas for a presentation. Note listener advantages, objections, and ideas for visual aids.
- Use the outline or storyboards to develop the opening, body, and closing for the presentation.
- Create visual aids, such as electronic slides or handouts, to reinforce the message. Use design strategies to make visual aids interesting and effective.
- Team presentations require individuals to work together to research, plan, prepare, and deliver the message.

5-3 Delivering a Presentation

- To practice for a presentation, review your notes and rehearse what you plan to say. Video your practice session, if possible.
- To prepare for a presentation, consider the seating arrangement, lighting, and temperature in the meeting room. Practice with the specific equipment you will use.
- Be neat and clean in your appearance and dress appropriately for the presentation.
- When delivering the presentation, make eye contact with listeners, avoid using non-words, show enthusiasm, and speak convincingly. Control your posture and gestures.
- Use visuals effectively to reinforce the points of a presentation.
- Gather feedback for a presentation by having a question-and-answer session and asking listeners to complete an evaluation form.

Chapter 5 Activity 1

Research for a Presentation
(Outcomes 5-2b, 5-3a)

When you must prepare a presentation, the topic may be a familiar one about which you know a great deal. Often, however, you will need to do research to find the latest information or supporting details related to the topic. Practice your research skills in this activity.

1. In a later activity, you will create a presentation related to flextime. Use the Internet or other reference sources to find three articles or reports about flextime. Print or copy the articles, if possible.

2. For each article, key the name of the article and complete source information. Then compose and key a summary of the main points you learned from reading the article.

Chapter 5 Activity 2

Team Presentation
(Outcomes 5-2a, 5-2b, 5-2c, 5-3b, 5-3c)

You work in the Accounting Department for a large insurance company. There are approximately 25 workers in your department. They have diverse ages and lifestyles. You and several coworkers created a plan for flextime options. Recently, management decided to test the flextime schedule with a two-month pilot program. The program will be for employees in your department only. If the pilot program is successful, flextime options will be offered to most employees.

You and a team of coworkers have been asked to prepare and deliver a 10-minute presentation. Your goal is to motivate the coworkers in your department to take part in the flextime pilot program.

1. Work with a team of three classmates to complete this assignment.

2. Open and print the file 5 Activity 2 found in the data files. This file contains specific details about the flextime program.

3. Plan the presentation. Create storyboard worksheets and develop an outline of the main points of the presentation.

4. Develop the detailed contents of the presentation. Use information found in articles from your research in Chapter 5 Activity 1 to provide supporting details. Develop the visual aids. Anticipate questions and plan sample answers.

5. Decide who will present each part of the presentation and practice with your team.

6. Deliver the presentation to your class or to another team as directed by your teacher. Include time for a question-and-answer session.

7. Ask your listeners to complete an evaluation form such as the one you developed in 5-3 Activity 1. Review the evaluation forms and write a summary of how the listeners rated your presentation and what you need to improve in future presentations.

Business Law and Ethics Event

In this team decision-making event, you and your teammate will be judged on your skills and knowledge related to business law and ethics. The event includes a written test (to be taken individually by each team member) and a case study. The team will analyze the case study and make decisions regarding the situation. The team will present the decisions or solutions to the judge, who will portray a business executive. The team will also answer questions posed by the judge. Teams moving to a final round will have a second case study situation. No reference materials are allowed. You may use notes made during preparation time when giving the presentation.

Performance Indicators Evaluated

Participants will demonstrate skills related to the business management and administration career cluster and human resources management pathway. Specific performance indicators are given during the event and may include indicators such as the following:

- Knowledge of business law in the United States, including topics such as contracts, product liability, employment, and types of business ownership
- The ability to explain workplace regulations
- The ability to evaluate competing ethical and social values
- The ability to defend ideas objectively
- The ability to identify possible resolutions to ethical issues

In addition, the following general skills will be evaluated:

- Communication (writing, speaking, reading, or listening)
- Analyzing data to form conclusions and recommendations
- Critical thinking and problem solving
- Teamwork skills
- Setting priorities and managing time

For more detailed information about this event, go to the DECA website.[1]

http://www.deca.org

Think Critically

1. Why do you think the ability to defend ideas objectively is evaluated in this event?
2. How could having a teammate benefit you when addressing ethical issues?

[1]DECA, "High School Competitive Events Guidelines" (DECA, 2011), http://www.deca.org/competitions/highschool.

This career area includes a wide variety of jobs. Lawyers, judges, and legal aides are all part of this vital career area. Many employees, such as court reporters and judges, work for government agencies. Others, such as legal secretaries and paralegals, work for private companies. Some people, such as lawyers, are self-employed.

Employment Outlook

The U.S. government provides job projections for 2008-2018. Many jobs in this career area are expected to increase about as fast as the average for all jobs.[2]

Job Titles

- Lawyer
- Judge
- Paralegal
- Legal assistant
- Court reporter
- Case manager
- Legal secretary

Needed Education/Skills

The education and skills needed in this career area vary widely. They depend on the type of work to which the job relates. For example, a judge needs different skills than a court reporter.

---

[2]*Occupational Outlook Handbook*, 2010-11 Edition, Bureau of Labor Statistics, U.S. Department of Labor, http://www.bls.gov/oco/ocos114.htm.

For some positions, a high school diploma and job-specific training may be all that are required. Higher level jobs and specialized jobs require education and experience appropriate to the job. A college degree and related work experience are often required.

What's it like to work in... Legal Services?

Kim works as a paralegal (also called a legal assistant) at a small law firm. She prepared for her career by earning a college degree in business administration and a paralegal certification.

Kim's job involves duties that assist the firm's lawyers in doing their work. Much information must be gathered to prepare for events such as hearings, trials, and corporate meetings. Kim does research on the Internet and in a law library. She analyzes and organizes information for the lawyers' use. She also prepares legal documents, such as motions to be filed with a court, for a lawyer's approval.

Typically, Kim works about 40 hours per week. However, overtime is sometimes required when the firm is working on an important case and tasks must be completed quickly. Kim finds her job fulfilling and believes that she helps provide important services for the firm's clients. She appreciates the confidence the lawyers show in her abilities.

What About You?

Does a job in law and legal services sound appealing to you? What might be some rewards of working in this career area other than job pay?

Telephone Communications

6-1 Telephone Technology and Services

6-2 Effective Telephone Communications

StockLite/Shutterstock

The telephone plays a key role in communicating at work. Data, text, images, and video as well as voice can be transmitted across the country or around the world using telephone channels. Mobile phones allow users to place calls easily from many locations away from the office.

You will use the telephone and related technologies for sharing information at work. As these technologies change, you must learn about the new equipment and features that are available. In this chapter, you will become familiar with telephone equipment and services. You will learn to use effective telephone procedures and become aware of available telephone technology.

Wire_man/Shutterstock.com

OUTCOMES

6-1a Describe channels and equipment for transmitting data by telephone.
6-1b Describe features available through telephony technology.
6-1c Describe common telephone features and services.

telecommunications   the electronic transfer of data over a distance

Transmitting Data by Telephone

Office workers often need to share information with others quickly and reliably. This information is often shared using telecommunications technology. **Telecommunications** is the electronic transfer of data over a distance. This data can be in the form of voice, video, text, or images. Because voice transmission by telephone is a common form of telecommunications, the technology is often simply called telephone technology.

Telephone Channels

Telephone technology allows workers to send data across the country or around the world. Workers often place telephone calls or transfer data to a remote computer. The data usually travel over telephone channels. Many companies are replacing older lines that send data in analog (wave) form with lines that send data in digital form. Electronic data that can be read by a computer is in digital form. Digital signals can transmit large quantities of data at speeds much faster than analog signals. This means your electronic message (a letter, a long report, or a chart) is received quickly and reliably.

Norman Chan/iStockphoto.com

Some communications systems use only analog signals. They require a device called a **modem** to send digital data. This device is used to convert the digital data into analog signals that can be transmitted over telephone channels. A modem can be an internal device installed inside the computer case. It can also be an external device that is attached to the computer.

modem   a conversion device for digital and analog data

A modem is used to send electronic data over traditional telephone lines.

Satellites play an important part in worldwide telecommunications systems. Satellites send voice, video, and other data in the form of microwave signals. A communications satellite is a data relay station that orbits the earth. A satellite dish is a data relay station that remains stationary, on earth. Data from your telephone or computer may travel through telephone lines to a satellite dish. From a satellite dish, data can be sent to an orbiting satellite. The orbiting satellite transmits the data to another satellite dish in another part of the world. Data from the second satellite dish may travel through telephone lines to the receiving telephone or computer.

 CHECK POINT What is the purpose of a modem?

Facsimile Technology

Facsimile technology, often called fax, sends images (text, photographs, drawings) using telephone channels. A fax machine works by combining scanning technology with telephone technology. The sending machine scans a page and encodes (electronically "takes a picture of") the data to be sent. The data are transmitted over telephone channels to a receiving fax. Within seconds, the document is received.

facsimile technology used to send images (text, photographs, drawings) using telephone channels

Fax machines are easy to use and are commonly found in offices. A company may have one or several fax machines. Portable models may be used to send documents while workers are away from the office. Fax machines are also found in some homes for personal use. They provide an inexpensive, fast way to send and receive information.

John A. Rizzo/Jupiter Images

Fax machines allow users to send and receive messages quickly.

Fax machine to fax machine is not the only method of sending documents as images. An image can also be sent from a computer directly to a fax machine or another computer. The computer must have a fax card and software to control the process.

Features

Fax machines offer many features. Among the more common features are:

- Laser or full-color printing
- Store-and-forward capability
- Automatic dialing and redialing if the receiving number is busy
- Automatic answering
- Automatic document feed
- Activity-reporting of date, time, and number of pages sent and received
- Small screens that display messages such as data about sending and errors or problems with the system

The automatic answering feature makes fax systems almost self-operating. Many users leave their machines on 24 hours a day, unattended, for receiving messages.

Procedures

Procedures for using fax machines vary from office to office and from machine to machine. Many procedures depend on the sending and receiving equipment to be used. When you send a fax, include a cover sheet or note. Figure 6-1.1 shows the top portion of a fax cover sheet. The cover sheet should contain information such as the following:

- Current date
- Total pages being sent, including the cover sheet
- Name, company, and fax number of the recipient of the message
- Name, company, address, telephone number, and fax number of the sender
- Subject of the document or message
- Special remarks as needed

Check the accuracy of your count of the number of pages to be sent and the number of pages you recorded on the cover sheet. Confirm the number carefully before dialing the fax number of the recipient. Enter your name, department, date, and number of pages sent or other required data on a fax log sheet if one is used in your office.

You may hear a series of beeps after all pages have been sent. A message may be displayed telling you that your message has been received at the location you dialed. If a report form is printed, attach it to the fax cover sheet and return it with the original materials to the sender. The report may include data such as the date, start time of the message, fax number dialed, number of pages sent, and time used to transmit pages.

✓CHECK POINT What information should be included on a fax cover sheet?

Figure 6-1.1 A cover sheet or note should be sent with each fax.

NOUVEAU INVESTMENT COMPANY		
800 Elm Avenue		
Mt. Vernon, NY 10500-3113		
Phone: 914-555-0122		
Fax: 914-555-0121		

FAX

To:	John Mayfield	From:	Anna Wong
Fax:	513-555-0098	Pages:	3
Phone:	513-555-0096	Date:	April 2, 20--
Re:	Quarterly Report	Time:	11:35 a.m.

Comments:
Please review this report and send me your comments.

© Cengage Learning 2013

Lana Perez works for an environmental waste firm in Phoenix. The company has branch offices in Denver, St. Louis, and Salt Lake City. This morning she receives a typical assignment. An engineer in her office needs to send a copy of project plan changes as soon as possible to a worker. The worker is on location at a customer's construction site outside Denver. Using the office fax machine, Lana is able to send the document within minutes from her computer to the portable fax machine at the work site.

What fax machine feature might Lana use if the receiving fax machine is busy when she dials?

Telephony

As technology changes, businesses are using new equipment and procedures to improve communications. The integration of computer and telephone technologies is called telephony. In a modern communications system, a computer may be used to control and access telephone functions. Such a system may also allow users to access computer functions by telephone. Telephony technology offers features such as:

telephony the integration of computer and telephone technologies

- Two-way video, audio, and computer communications that let callers open, view, and edit computer files and send notes to each other as they talk

- Computer software that lets users manage telephone activity at a personal computer

- Caller ID service that allows the user to see the number of the caller and allows incoming calls to be screened—whether from within or outside the company

- Conference calling that can be placed by using names from the user's computer phone directory

- Access to the Internet and World Wide Web

- Management of all voice, fax, or e-mail messages with either a touch-tone phone or a personal computer

- Multimedia tutorials that help users learn how to use advanced system features

Voice over Internet Protocol

Some businesses take advantage of current technology by using voice over Internet protocol (VoIP). VoIP, also called Internet voice, allows users to make telephone calls using a high-speed Internet connection instead of standard telephone channels. A traditional telephone with an adaptor or a computer with a modem is used to place calls.

VoIP a service that allows users to make telephone calls using a high-speed Internet connection

An advantage of using VoIP is that it can help a business save money. The business can use a broadband Internet connection and other equipment that is already in place for sending data to make phone calls. The business may be able to reduce or even cancel the services purchased from a standard telephone company. Some VoIP providers offer plans that allow unlimited local and long-distance calls to anywhere in the United States for one set fee. Also, some VoIP providers offer features such as caller ID, call waiting, and voice mail at no added charge. These services often involve an extra charge when purchased from standard telephone companies.

A disadvantage of using VoIP is that service may be lost during a power outage. Problems with the company's network or high-speed Internet connection may also mean that service will be disrupted. Backup power supplies and network servers can be used to help avoid these problems. Using the 911 emergency number with VoIP from remote locations is also a concern. If the caller is using VoIP, the 911 service may not be able to find the location of the caller in some cases.

 CHECK POINT How does using VoIP to make a call differ from using regular telephone channels?

Videoconferencing

Videoconferencing is communicating with people at two or more locations using two-way voice and video data. A special conference room equipped with microphones, television cameras, and screens may be used. Data, text, voice, and documents may be exchanged during the conference.

Video conferences, sometimes called web conferences, may also be conducted by computer. In a web conference, people communicate using private computer networks or the Internet. These conferences are sometimes called virtual meetings. The users' computers must have speakers, microphones, and webcams. A connection to the Internet is also required.

Web conferences are becoming more popular as they become more affordable. Skype is a popular program used to hold web conferences. Both businesses and individuals use Skype to make video and voice calls. Users access Skype through their computer web browsers or compatible mobile phones. A webcam, an Internet connection, and Skype software are also needed. Group video calls can involve three or more people. A user calling from a computer can share images from the computer screen. This allows callers to show a presentation or chart, for example, during a call. Skype users can also send instant messages and share files.

At the time of this writing, Skype video calls to another Skype user are free. A fee is charged for other services, such as making calls to mobile phones or group video calls.[1]

 CHECK POINT What equipment and services are needed to make a web conference call?

[1] Skype, "Make the Most of Skype," 2011, http://www.skype.com/intl/en-us/features/.

Dalmar Aaron, Director of Sales, is located in Detroit. Dalmar called a meeting with local managers, managers located at headquarters in San Francisco, and a third group of managers located at a branch in Hong Kong. Using videoconferencing, they could see and hear each other. Dalmar wrote on an electronic whiteboard as he discussed sales projections. Dalmar's notes from the board appeared on a video monitor at the remote locations. The data were sent and later printed for the managers at each location. This meeting was very cost effective.

Explain how having a video conference can save Dalmar's company money.

Centralized Telephone Systems

In a small company, the telephone system may be as simple as having one or two telephone lines for the company. In other companies, the telephone system may include many lines and be integrated with a computer system. Centralized telephone systems route calls coming into and going out of an organization. All calls in a centralized system are handled by a single computer or operator switchboard that routes calls to the requested location. Older systems required the assistance of a human switchboard operator to answer and transfer calls. Some systems that are handled by computer give callers the option of speaking to a person.

Many telephone systems in businesses today are answered by an automated attendant. An automated attendant is a computerized system for handling telephone calls. When an incoming call is answered by an automated attendant, a recorded message is played. Messages vary depending on company needs. However, the message usually instructs the caller to dial the extension number of the person being sought. It may provide the caller with various menu options. Callers make selections using the telephone number keypad. Some systems also allow users to select menu options by speaking a word or term into the receiver. A computer will identify the spoken command and perform the chosen action. This feature is called speech recognition. Additional messages may then instruct and direct the caller.

automated attendant a computerized system for handling telephone calls

Speaking with a person is no longer always a choice for the caller. Many callers have adjusted to computerized systems. However, some callers become frustrated with systems that seem to block human contact. These callers prefer to speak with a person rather than give responses to an automated attendant. Some callers may not have a touch-tone phone, which is usually required for the automated system. This is another reason why having an option to speak with a person is helpful. Businesses must deal with these issues and do their best to meet callers' needs and preserve goodwill.

✔CHECK POINT How do callers make selections to get information or reach a person when using an automated attendant?

Voice Mail Systems

Voice mail is a messaging system that uses computers and telephones to record, send, store, and retrieve voice messages. Voice messaging systems are popular because they eliminate the problems of time lost in playing "telephone tag." Most voice mail systems operate 24 hours per day. They are an important communications tool.

Each user of a voice messaging system has a voice mailbox. A voice mailbox is a space reserved in a computer to hold recorded voice messages. A caller leaves a voice message that is recorded by the computer. The message is held in storage until the recipient of the message chooses to access it. Unless a message is deleted, it remains in storage and can be accessed later for reference. Effective voice mail greetings and messages are discussed later in this chapter. Some of the voice mail features that may be used by companies include:

- Long-term incoming message storage
- Message prioritizing
- Ability to broadcast recorded messages to multiple or all users of the system
- Creation of multiple greetings that can be selected as needed

 CHECK POINT How does a voice mail system differ from an automated attendant?

Telephone Features and Equipment

Many features are available that allow users to customize a telephone. Different features are available on different telephones or systems. A user's manual is generally provided. The manual gives steps for using the features available. To activate call forwarding, for example, you may be instructed to tap the * (asterisk, or "star") and other keys, listen for a tone, dial the number to which you want all incoming calls routed, and hang up. Your incoming calls will then be forwarded and will ring at that number. Figure 6-1.2 on page 205 lists common features of telephones or telephone systems.

Conference Calls

At times it may be necessary to place calls that will have three or more participants speaking at different locations. These calls are known as conference calls. Conference calls may be handled in several ways: with the user's own equipment, operator-dialed service, or dial-in service.

With some company telephone systems, users may be able to place a conference call. No outside help is needed from a telephone company service provider. The person setting up the call lets all those who will take part know the time to expect the call. At the appointed time, the user calls each person in turn and adds them to the call, following the appropriate steps for the phone system.

Figure 6-1.2 Common Telephone Features and Services

FEATURE	DESCRIPTION
Auto redial	Redials automatically the last number dialed when the user presses a key
Call block	Restricts callers from making toll calls or calls for which an extra charge is made
Call forwarding	Sends calls automatically to another telephone number
Caller ID	Records or displays the telephone number of the caller
Call queuing	Reestablishes the connection after a busy signal when both parties are free
Call return	Allows users to press a code number, such as *69, to dial the number of the last incoming call
Call waiting	Signals an incoming call is waiting while a call is in progress
Conferencing	Allows the user to set up conversations with three or more people at the same time
Memory	Allows the user to store numbers and then dial a number with one button
Speakerphone	Allows the user to speak into a microphone on the telephone rather than the handset
Camera	Allows the user to transmit pictures as well as voice
E-mail access	Allows users to send and receive e-mail messages
Internet access	Allows users to access websites
Text messaging	Allows users to send text messages on mobile phones
Application programs	Allows users to perform various tasks on smartphones

© Cengage Learning 2013

With operator-dialed service, a long-distance operator handles the setup and connections. You inform the operator of the date, time, time zone, and estimated length of the call. The operator performs tasks that you request, such as the following:

- Informs all participants of the time that the conference call will take place
- Makes all the necessary connections at the prescribed time
- Calls the roll to make sure all callers are connected
- Can provide specialized services such as a recording or written transcript of the conference

Dial-in service allows participants to call a number at a prearranged time without operator assistance. They may call from any telephone rather than wait for an operator to call them at one specific number. Several telephone companies provide this type of service. Effective procedures for planning and taking part in a conference call are discussed later in this chapter.

 CHECK POINT What are three ways that employees may be able to hold conference calls?

Special telephone equipment and services are available for people who have hearing, vision, or speech difficulties. A teletypewriter (TTY) device has a screen and a keyboard. Using this device, messages travel over the telephone lines. They are typed on the keyboard and read on the screen.

In some cases, a person serves as an interpreter between the callers. The interpreter may be an employee of a telephone company or of a state or other agency. The messages are relayed by the interpreter by typing the spoken words. The message is relayed to a TTY or a phone that allows users to read and key Braille. Braille is a system that allows the user to read by feeling a pattern of raised dots. The visually impaired person reads the Braille; the hearing impaired person reads the screen. Other features for impaired callers include:

- Large-button phones
- Headsets or speakerphones for hands-free operation
- Speech amplifiers to make voices louder
- Loud bells and flashing light indicators to signal incoming calls

What special telephone equipment and services are available for the visually or hearing impaired?

Mobile Phones

Mobile devices are commonly used for both personal and business communications. Mobile phones use wireless, radio frequencies to transmit data across geographic areas called cells. These phones are also called cellular telephones or cell phones. When you dial a mobile telephone number, the radio signal "switches" from cell to cell until the right number is reached. Mobile service providers furnish the user with the transmission. Because modern cell phones use digital technology, they are sometimes referred to as digital phones.

Mobile phones are designed to be portable, lightweight, and small. You may use them in your car or carry them in your briefcase to use wherever you are. In some areas, cell phones may not be close enough to a transmission tower to receive a signal. A *no signal* message may be displayed to indicate that a call cannot be made from that location.

Mobile phones that also have features of a handheld computer are called smartphones.

mbbirdy/iStockphoto.com

In Chapter 3 you learned about handheld computers called PDAs (personal digital assistants). These small, portable computers are used to track appointments, record contact data, take notes, access the Internet, send e-mail, and perform many other tasks. A device that combines the features of a PDA and a mobile phone is called a smartphone. With a smartphone, users have one device (rather than two) to handle calls and manage data. Some smartphones have a small keyboard on the outside of the device. Other smartphones have an on-screen keyboard and use handwriting recognition. Some smartphones can be placed in a docking station that contains a keyboard. Many smartphones have built-in cameras. When buying a smartphone, the user should be aware of the device's operating system and additional programs available that can be loaded onto the device.

smartphone a device that combines the features of a handheld computer and a mobile phone

 CHECK POINT What are some features of smartphones?

Purchasing Equipment and Services

Telephones and systems may be purchased from many vendors at various prices. Some vendors will customize features to meet user needs. Some vendors will also conduct training and offer product support after the sale.

When purchasing mobile phones, the phones should be tested in the areas where they will be used often. If the areas do not receive a strong signal, users may have trouble making calls. Some companies allow users to borrow a mobile phone for a short trial period before purchasing a phone. This allows the user to test the phone in various areas.

A local telephone company provides services to users within a set local area. A business may have no choice as to which company to use for local service through standard telephone channels. Companies can choose a long-distance company and optional features. A wide variety of features and pricing plans is available. Companies should carefully compare services and prices when choosing a telephone service provider. For mobile phones, the service area and variable charges are important considerations when choosing a provider.

 CHECK POINT Why should a business compare services and prices when choosing a telephone service provider?

21st Century Skills

PARTNERSHIP FOR
21ST CENTURY SKILLS

Interacting with Others

Your sales team member, Joe Park, is letting voice mail answer his phone the majority of the time, even when he is at his desk. You and Joe share sales and service duties for several accounts. Your clients have complained to you that Joe seems never to be at his desk. Also, they complain that he takes several days to answer their voice mail messages. You realize that this is a problem situation. What should you do?

1. Should you inform your supervisor about Joe's voice mail procedures? Why or why not?
2. Should you apologize to clients for Joe's poor voice mail habits? Why or why not?

Making Academic Connections

Reinforcing English Skills

Your knowledge of punctuation rules will be helpful as you prepare written messages on the job. Write or key each sentence, inserting the proper punctuation.

1. She faxed a report from Cheyenne Wyoming to Tucson Arizona
2. Our account was credited with two months interest
3. Did you place the call to Jeorge my friend from Mexico City
4. On Tuesday January 23 we began using our new computerized telephone system
5. To qualify for a position you must have a years experience using a computer telephone system
6. Showing you our new voice mail system was a pleasure we have a training session planned for all new users
7. We prefer using voice mail for recording messages not an answering machine
8. Conferencing lets you set up conversations with three four or more people at the same time
9. A speakerphone allows hands free speaking capabilities
10. Is the toll free number an 800 or an 888 number

6-1 Activity 1

Fax Procedures (Outcome 6-1a)

You work at the headquarters of Prudent Development Corporation. Your supervisor, Dalila Waters, asks you to prepare a well-designed one-page list of common procedures to be followed for successful fax transmissions. The procedures list is to be faxed to the office manager at the Denver branch. She also wants you to compose a short memo to include with the procedures.

1. Compose and key a document that lists procedures for successful fax-to-fax transmission. Follow effective document design guidelines.

2. Create a memo form for the company using appropriate headings. Compose a memo to Edwardo Cruz, Office Manager. In the memo, explain that this list is to be distributed to all fax users at the Denver location. Also ask him to write any additions or comments on the list and return it to you within three days.

3. Create a fax cover sheet to send with the memo and the fax procedures document. Use the cover sheet in Figure 6-1.1 as an example, or use a fax cover sheet template from your word processor software.

YOUR COMPANY'S INFORMATION:	MR. CRUZ'S INFORMATION:
Prudent Development Corporation	Prudent Development Corporation
8700 Martin Luther King Blvd.	Fax number: 303-555-0102
Austin, TX 78765-0800	Telephone number: 303-555-0122
Fax number: 512-555-0139	
Telephone number: 512-555-0142	

6-1 Activity 2

Telephony Report (Outcome 6-1b)

In this activity, you will do research and prepare a short report about a topic related to telephony. Work with a classmate to complete this project.

1. Select one of the topics below for your report.
   - VoIP
   - Videoconferencing
   - Centralized telephone systems
   - Automated attendants
   - Voice mail systems

2. Review the information presented in this chapter and do research to find additional information about your chosen topic.

3. Working with your teammate, prepare a short report about the topic. Review the format for a report in Chapter 5. Include a title page, report body pages, and a page with references for the sources of information you used for the report.

OUTCOMES

6-2a Describe skills required to make a favorable impression over the telephone.
6-2b Apply telephone techniques and procedures to handle incoming calls effectively.
6-2c Apply telephone techniques and procedures to handle outgoing calls effectively.

Making a Favorable Impression

Employees in a company may receive and place many calls each day. Workers talk with others both inside and outside the company to discuss common concerns, place orders, or request information. Messages must be taken and recorded either manually or electronically. Telephone calls are often less time-consuming than a memo, a letter, or even an e-mail message.

All office workers should use proper techniques when answering or placing calls. When you place a call to a business, your first impression of the company is often based on how you are treated by the person answering your call. If the person is courteous and interested in helping you, you will probably form a good impression of the company. If the person is abrupt, rude, or unwilling to help, you probably will form a negative impression. When you answer the telephone or place an outgoing call, you may be making an initial customer contact. You will want to give callers a positive impression by what you say and how you say it.

When you handle telephone calls at work, you are representing your company. To the individual who is calling, you are the company. To create a positive image, you should develop good communication skills. Your voice, pronunciation, grammar, and vocabulary, as well as your attitude, contribute to the impression you make when using the telephone.

Your Voice

When you talk with others in person, you make them feel welcome by smiling and perhaps by shaking hands. You show interest and alertness by making eye contact with them during the conversation. When you talk by telephone, however, all you have to convey interest and courtesy is your voice. Elements of your voice that you must pay attention to include tone, pace, and volume.

Tone

The tone of your voice refers to the changes in pitch used to emphasize words and get your meaning across to the listener. You have, no doubt, listened to speakers who talked in a monotone. Paying attention is difficult when someone is speaking in a monotonous voice. The listener may become bored or perceive the speaker as indifferent or inattentive. Vary the tone of your voice to express feelings and emphasis of ideas but avoid using extremes. An animated voice reflects interest in the caller and helps you achieve successful communication. Avoid speaking in a very high-pitched voice, a very low-pitched voice, or with an up-and-down, "singsong" manner.

You represent your organization every time you place or answer a call.

When you speak to someone over the telephone, all you have is your voice to give information and express your feelings. Even though you may not be seen by the person with whom you are speaking, your attitude is reflected in your speech and tone of voice. Any boredom, anger, or indifference you are feeling may be obvious to the person on the line. On the other hand, a smile and an upbeat, caring attitude are also clearly projected to the person with whom you are speaking on the phone. You should put any negative feelings aside and respond to the caller with a sincere, positive attitude.

Pace and Volume

Pace is the rate or speed of speech. The rate at which you talk to someone on the telephone can affect the ability of the listener to understand your message. If you speak too rapidly, the listener may not hear all the information. This is true especially if the information is technical or detailed. On the other hand, if you speak too slowly, the listener may become bored, insulted, or inattentive.

Consider the listener when determining a proper pace for speech. You may be speaking with people from different parts of your nation and or from countries all over the world. You may be conversing with people who, even though they speak the same language as you, have speech patterns and regional **dialects** that are different from your own. You must learn to adjust your pace to fit the needs of the listener.

dialect speech patterns or vocabulary used by people from a specific area or group

Extremes in volume should be avoided when speaking on the telephone. Do not shout or speak so softly that the listener cannot hear what you are saying. Control the volume of your voice so that you are speaking neither too loudly nor too softly. Speak directly into the telephone receiver or mouthpiece.

✓ CHECK POINT How does the tone of your voice affect the impression you make on a caller?

Your Speaking Skills

Your voice and speaking skills are put to the test when you speak on the telephone. Speaking skills such as word pronunciation, grammar, and vocabulary usage affect the impression you give over the phone. Although you may have a pleasant tone, good pace, and well-modulated voice, communication is difficult if the person you are speaking with cannot understand your words.

Pronunciation

Correct pronunciation of words is essential for understanding. Proper enunciation is also important. When you enunciate effectively you pronounce words clearly and distinctly. For example, you should say *what do you* instead of *whaddaya*, and you should say *going to* instead of *gonna*. Always enunciate word endings such as *ing*, *ed*, possessives, and plurals.

You will find that many people speak with a regional accent. An accent involves a certain rhythm, speed, and pronunciation of vowels that is native to a particular region. You probably have an accent even though you may not be aware of it. If you find that you have trouble communicating because of an accent, several strategies can help you succeed:

■ Pronounce words correctly and enunciate clearly.

■ Speak slowly, but not so slowly that you insult or annoy the caller.

■ Avoid long words, complicated phrases, or long sentences.

■ If you are unsure of any word's pronunciation, look it up in a printed or online dictionary. Figure 6-2.1 shows an example of an online dictionary.

Figure 6-2.1 Online dictionaries provide a quick way to learn the meaning and pronunciation of a word.

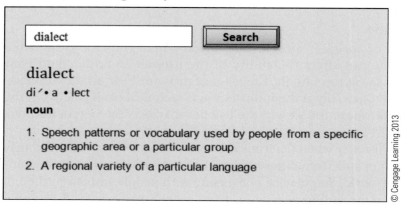

Grammar

Although some rules of grammar are relaxed for spoken communications, you should follow basic grammar standards. Doing so will help you project a favorable impression of yourself and your company. Avoid the use of slang or regional expressions that may not be widely known or understood, especially if the call is an international one. Other people may use terms that you do not recognize. When you do not understand an expression or phrase, always ask for an explanation.

Vocabulary

You should strive to improve your professional and personal vocabulary. You can learn new terms that relate to your position or your company. You can also learn words that will help you express your feelings, ideas, and needs. Remember that clear and courteous communication is always your goal. Avoid using trendy, slang expressions in formal business communications. State your ideas simply without using highly technical terms or lengthy words.

Many companies deal directly with clients, customers, or suppliers from other countries. Your company may even be an international one whose owners or headquarters are located outside the United States. Learn some simple courtesy phrases to use when speaking with international callers. Your attempts at learning and using some simple, basic phrases will be appreciated by foreign callers. Using these terms will help you make a favorable impression. Keep a list of basic phrases along with their translations and pronunciations. Practice them and make sure that you are saying them correctly.

 CHECK POINT Why is it important to use standard English (not slang) and pronounce words correctly during business calls?

Incoming Telephone Calls

Handling incoming telephone calls requires skill in using proper telephone techniques and effective procedures. When answering the telephone, you usually do not know who is calling or what the caller wants. Your work may be interrupted, or you may have a visitor in your office. You should know how to handle a variety of situations and take care of caller requests, needs, and problems.

Answering and Ending Calls

You have learned that your voice, your speaking skills, and your attitude all affect a caller's impression of you and your company. Your call may be an initial customer contact—the first time the customer has spoken with someone at your company. How well you handle the call may determine, at least in part, whether the customer will do business with your company. Using proper telephone techniques will help you make a positive impression.

Answer Promptly

Answer all incoming calls promptly and pleasantly. If possible, answer the telephone after the first ring. When you reach for the receiver, have ready a pen and a notepad or message form, also. You may need to take notes or a message. If you prefer to key messages using your computer, place a shortcut on your desktop that will allow you to open a form for notes or messages quickly.

Identify Yourself

Many companies use automated telephone systems that answer the calls and route them to the requested person. In this case, you may not need to identify your company when you answer a call. Otherwise, you should identify first the company, then yourself.

A telephone conversation cannot begin until the caller knows that the correct number, department, or person has been reached. Figure 6-2.2 shows examples of improper and proper responses for answering the telephone.

Figure 6-2.2 Using improper responses when answering the telephone can create a negative impression.

IMPROPER RESPONSES	PROPER RESPONSES
"Hello," or "Yes?" (These greetings do not identify the person or of the company.)	"Marketing Department, Leon DiMarco." (Use this greeting when you are answering an inside or outside call in a company where all calls are routed through a switchboard operator or an automated attendant that has already identified the company.)
"Good morning. International Electronics. Our company is number one in the field of international electronics, products sales, and service. Pat Lopez speaking. May I be of help to you?" (This greeting is too long and distracting.)	"Good morning. International Electronics, Pat Lopez." (Use this greeting when you are answering an outside call.)
"Hello, hold please." (This greeting does not identify the company. Abruptly placing the caller on hold is rude and abrasive.)	"Hello, this is International Electronics. Can you hold, please?" (This greeting identifies the company and asks the caller to hold.)
"Heh. This is Lisa." (This greeting does not give enough information.)	"Ms. Yamaguchi's office, Lisa Stein speaking." (Use this greeting when you are answering the telephone for a coworker.)

© Cengage Learning 2013

Conclude the Call

As a general rule, the person who places a call is the one who should end the call and hang up first. If you follow this rule, you avoid making the caller feel as if the conversation has been "cut off."

Use the caller's name as you end the conversation. For example, say: "Yes, Ms. O'Toole, I will mail a copy of our latest catalog to you today," or, "Thank you for calling, Mr. Haliz. I will give Ms. Schmidt the information." Such a practice personalizes the conversation.

 CHECK POINT How should you answer your phone at work if outside calls come directly to you?

Focus on BUSINESS

Voice Mail

Voice mail is a computerized voice messaging system. It has many features that can be modified to meet individual needs. A standard personal computer, a special voice processing card, and voice software are needed. Both the sender and the receiver use the telephone push buttons to activate and use the features of voice mail.

Because of the convenience and efficiency of voice mail, its use has become widespread in business. Still, with all its advantages, voice mail does not replace human contact. Follow proper procedures to ensure that the negatives of voice mail are reduced and the full benefits are realized. When using your voice mail system:

- Prepare a message that presents you as a professional and delivers appropriate information and instructions to the caller. Include your name, department, and other necessary information.
- Give instructions as to how to get immediate assistance if the caller cannot wait for you to return the call.
- Record the message yourself. Speak clearly and distinctly. Pronounce words correctly and use correct grammar.
- If you are going to be out of the office for one or more days, refer callers to another worker who can provide help while you are away, if appropriate.

- Check your voice mail several times a day. Return all calls as soon as possible.
- Answer your telephone when you are at your desk unless you have visitors in your office or are involved in an important work project. Do not let voice mail answer your phone for you the majority of the time.

Follow these procedures when leaving messages for others on their voice mail systems.

- Leave your name, telephone number, company, and a brief reason for your call.
- Make your message neither too lengthy nor too brief. You want the person you called to have enough information to return your call promptly and efficiently.
- Speak slowly and distinctly. Spell out any difficult names (your name, your company's name).
- Do not communicate bad news or negative statements in the voice message. Wait until you actually speak with the person to give negative information.

> What procedures should you follow when creating a greeting for your voice mails? What procedures should you follow when leaving a message on voice mail?

Assisting Callers

Your job is to help the caller as efficiently as you can. Never assume that you know what the caller wants. Instead, listen attentively to the caller's questions and comments. Make sure you give accurate information to callers. If you do not know the answer to a question, admit it. Tell the caller that you will obtain the information and call back or offer to transfer the call to someone who can answer the question. If you know that it will take several minutes to find the information needed for the call, do not keep the caller waiting. Explain the situation to the caller. Ask if the caller wishes to wait on the line or receive a return call later.

Placing a Caller on Hold

Hold is a feature that allows a telephone caller to remain connected but waiting for the other person to come back on the line. At times, you may

hold a feature that allows a telephone caller to remain connected but waiting for the other person to come back on the line

place a caller on hold while you find an answer to the caller's question. At other times, you must place a caller on hold while you answer another call. Ask the first caller if you may place him or her on hold. Then answer the second call. Ask permission to place the second caller on hold while you complete your conversation with the first caller. When a caller is on hold, check back frequently to reassure the caller that he or she has not been forgotten.

Transferring Calls

Calls are usually transferred when the caller has reached a wrong extension or has a request that can be handled more effectively by another person. The caller may request the transfer, or you may determine that the transfer is necessary. Always tell the caller why the transfer is necessary. For example, you may say: "I'm going to transfer your call to Mr. Bakari. He will be able to provide you with the information you need."

You may prefer to place the caller on hold while you speak with the person to whom you intend to transfer the call. This will allow you to confirm that this person can help the caller and to introduce the caller. Calls can sometimes become accidentally disconnected during a transfer. You may wish to give the caller the extension number or name of the person to whom the call is being transferred. Then if the call is accidentally disconnected, the caller can reach the appropriate person or extension when he or she calls again.

Handling a Disconnected Call

Occasionally, you will be disconnected while you are talking on the telephone or while you are waiting on hold. In general, the person who placed the call should call back immediately after the disconnection. That person has the telephone number of the party being called and should, therefore, be able to redial the call quickly.

The caller should report a disconnected long-distance call to the telephone company. Depending on the telephone company used, an adjustment may be made in the long-distance charge.

Handling Difficult Calls

On occasion you may receive calls from persons who are angry, unreasonable, rude, or demanding. These calls may be few, but they can be very stressful and difficult to handle. You must control yourself and remain professional when dealing with difficult calls. Your goal is to diffuse the situation and to maintain goodwill with the caller, if possible. Follow these guidelines when dealing with difficult telephone calls.

- Try to resolve the matter if possible. Usually the caller wants the company to solve a problem or fix a mistake. Do not hesitate to apologize to the caller for any problems or inconveniences the caller has experienced.
- Always present a helpful, positive, and sincere attitude, even in an adverse situation.

When a call is unintentionally disconnected, the caller should place the call again.

© Tetra Images/Alamy

- Remain outwardly calm and do not display defensive behavior. Usually, the caller is not upset with you but with the company or its actions. Do not take the caller's anger personally.

- If the caller is abusive or uses profanity, identify the caller and end the conversation quickly. Record the caller's name and number and a brief summary of the abusive behavior. Share this information with your supervisor or follow other procedures your company has in place for dealing with abusive callers.

✓ CHECK POINT What should you do if you have placed a caller on hold and you learn that several minutes will be needed to find information the caller has requested?

Screening Calls and Taking Messages

Answering the phone for coworkers and taking messages may be part of your duties as an office worker. You will want to be tactful in managing calls for others and accurate in recording messages. You should also consider what information is appropriate to give callers.

Screening Calls

In some offices, you may be asked to screen calls. Screening incoming calls is a procedure used to determine who is calling and, at times, the purpose of the call. For example, your supervisor may instruct you to screen calls and take a message from all salespeople who call. You may inform the caller that you will relay the message. However, do not promise a return call. Your

screen calls determine who is calling and the purpose for the call

supervisor may be in an important meeting and ask you not to interrupt except for certain callers. Screening can save you and the caller time because you may be able to help the person yourself or transfer the call immediately to another person.

When screening calls, find out who is calling. Be tactful, yet direct. To learn the caller's name, ask questions such as "May I have your name?" or "Who is calling, please?" Sometimes callers refuse to give their names. If your company requires you to identify each caller by name before transferring the call, you must be courteous, yet firm. Explaining the policy to the caller will usually encourage the caller to give you his or her name. Even if the caller becomes rude or still refuses to tell his or her name, you should at all times be courteous. Remain firm, however, in following the company's policies.

Giving Information

You may take calls for a manager or coworkers who are out of the office or in a meeting. In these situations, you must tactfully tell the caller that the person is not available and offer to take a message or assist the caller yourself. When coworkers are unavailable to receive calls, give the caller enough information to explain the person's absence. However, do not give unnecessary or sensitive details. Improper and proper responses are shown in Figure 6-2.3.

Figure 6-2.3 **A proper response to a caller gives only appropriate information.**

IMPROPER RESPONSES	PROPER RESPONSES
"Ms. Fox has a hair appointment this afternoon."	"Ms. Fox is not available until tomorrow morning. May I take a message or ask her to call you?"
"Mrs. Barnes is away on a trip with her son."	"Mrs. Barnes will be out of the office until May 1. May I transfer you to her assistant, Ms. Potter?"
"Mr. Chandler is playing golf with a prospective client."	"Mr. Chandler is in a meeting this afternoon and won't be available the rest of the day. May I take a message or ask him to return your call?"

© Cengage Learning 2013

Taking Messages

In many companies, the use of voice mail eliminates some of the need for taking written messages. Even with voice mail, it will be necessary for you to record information for yourself such as the caller's name, telephone number, and purpose of the call.

Message forms are usually available in offices for recording telephone messages. When you record a message, it is essential that it is accurate and complete. Verify names and telephone numbers by reading back the information to the caller. Ask for accurate spellings of names if you are in doubt. Key or write the message carefully. If the message is handwritten, make sure that your handwriting is legible so you do not waste time rewriting it later or fail to be able to read it. Each message should include the following data:

- Date and time of the call
- Name of the caller with the caller's company
- Caller's telephone number, including area code if needed
- Details of the message
- Your name or initials

Your office may have software that can be used to complete an electronic message. A sample electronic message form is shown in Figure 6-2.4. Using a computer message offers these advantages:

- Less time is needed to key a message than to write it.
- The number of lost messages is reduced because messages can be transferred immediately to the intended receiver.
- Printed message forms are not needed.

Figure 6-2.4 Electronic message forms make taking messages quick and easy.

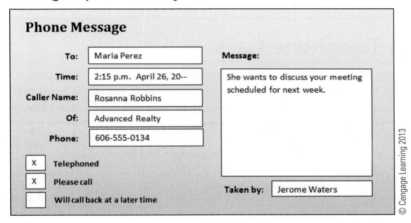

Each computer message you key should include the same basic information as a handwritten message. As you key the message, make sure it is accurate and complete. Verify all names and numbers. The current date and time may be entered automatically by the system into the onscreen form, or you may need to enter this information. The message may be transferred to the receiver's computer screen by keying in the correct extension number. A reminder or some form of electronic notation will appear on the receiver's screen showing that a message is waiting. In some offices, e-mail is used to record and forward telephone messages.

CHECK POINT   What should you do if a caller refuses to give his or her name when you are screening calls?

Answering the telephone in an appropriate manner and taking accurate messages is important for effective telephone communications. Notice how the office worker answering this call gives enough information to satisfy the caller but does not give inappropriate information.

Office Worker:	"Hello. Ms. Perez's office. Jerome speaking."
Caller:	"May I please speak with Ms. Perez? This is Rosanna Robbins from Advanced Realty."
Office Worker:	"I'm sorry, Ms. Perez is out of the office until Thursday. I am her assistant. Could I help you, or may I ask her to call you when she returns?"
Caller:	"Yes. Please ask her to call me at 606-555-0134 regarding our meeting scheduled for next week."
Office Worker:	"Thank you, Ms. Robbins. To confirm, your number is 606-555-0134. I will give Ms. Perez the message."

What are two methods Jerome might use to prepare a message for Ms. Perez?

Outgoing Telephone Calls

As with incoming telephone calls, outgoing calls may be made to a person outside or inside the company. Calls may be interoffice, local, or long distance. You should understand the process and procedures for placing all outgoing calls. Your goal is efficiency and economy.

Planning Calls

Every business call you make requires some preparation and planning. Most calls may be simple; however, others may require detailed planning. When preparing for any call, confirm the name and number of the person you are calling. Identify clearly the main purpose of the call. Outline briefly the points you want to cover during the call. Gather other information or items you need to have available before making the call, such as:

- Dates and times of any meetings or planned events that relate to the call
- Documents that relate to the topic discussed
- Questions that you want to ask
- Pen and paper or your computer to take notes during the call

Personal Telephone Calls

Follow your company's policy regarding making or receiving personal telephone calls at work. Many companies permit a limited number of personal calls. Other companies discourage personal calls. Workers may be expected to use their cell phones to make calls during break times. Generally, brief urgent or emergency calls are permitted. Long or frequent personal calls are typically not considered acceptable at work.

Calls on Mobile Phones

Many employees who spend a lot of time away from the office keep in touch with the office and customers using a mobile phone. Plan to place and receive calls on a mobile phone at appropriate times and places. Do not use your mobile phone in an area where you will disturb other people. Meetings and restaurants are examples of places where using mobile phones can disturb others. Confidential information should not be discussed in a public area.

Use caution when talking on the phone while driving a car, as this may distract your attention from driving. Be aware of the laws regarding cell phone use while driving in your area or wherever you travel. Some states have laws that prohibit drivers from using handheld cell phones while driving. Many drivers use hands-free headsets to talk on the phone while driving. Others use devices that act as a speaker for cell phones.

shutswis/Shutterstock.com

Headsets can be used to talk on a cell phone while driving.

Time Zones

Be aware of time zone differences when placing long-distance calls. Note the current time in the location you are calling. Avoid calling when the time is before or after business hours or during lunch at that location. The continental United States and parts of Canada are divided into five standard time zones: Atlantic, Eastern, Central, Mountain, and Pacific. As you move west, each zone is one hour earlier. For example, when it is 1 p.m. in Washington, DC (Eastern zone), it is noon in Dallas (Central zone), 11 a.m. in Denver (Mountain zone), and 10 a.m. in Los Angeles (Pacific zone). If you are in San Diego and need to speak to a coworker in the New York City office, you will need to place the call before 2 p.m. Pacific time. Otherwise, the New York office may be closed because it will be 5 p.m. (Eastern time).

time zone a geographical region that has the same standard time

Twenty-four time zones are used throughout the world. A time zone map of the United States is included in most telephone directories. Several websites display the current time in all U.S. or world time zones. You can find such a site by searching the Internet using terms such as *U.S. time zones* or *world time zones.*

You may need to place calls to people outside the United States. To place a call to London, England, for example, you would dial the following sequence of numbers: 011 (international access code) + 44 (country code) + 20 (city code) + local phone number. You can consult the International Calling or similar section of your local telephone directory for country codes. You can also find several websites that provide information on international calling. Search the Internet using terms such as *international calling* or *international area codes.*

Salima works for Castor Imports. The company recently began doing business with a company in Mexico. Salima has tried to phone her contact at the company, Pedro Martinez, several times. Salima and Pedro cannot seem to find one another in the office. Salima usually calls Pedro between 1 p.m. and 2 p.m. when she returns from lunch. Pedro is always out. Pedro returns Salima's calls between 5 p.m. and 6 p.m. and finds that she is not in. Salima and Pedro need to learn about one another's customs and work schedules. For example, in Mexico during the hours of noon to 3 p.m., many offices are closed. Workers return at 3 p.m. and often remain in the office until 7 p.m. or 8 p.m. In the United States, the typical office work day ends at 5 p.m. Understanding these customs will help Salima and Pedro find a time to talk that is convenient for both of them.

How can Salima learn about work hours and customs in other countries?

Conference Calls

A conference call is placed when it is necessary to talk with persons at several different locations at the same time. Methods for placing conference calls were discussed earlier in this chapter. Successful conference calls require advance planning to ensure that all the necessary information and equipment are at hand. Follow these guidelines in planning a conference call:

- Inform all participants of the date, time, and proposed length of the call.
- Verify everyone's telephone number.
- Send any needed information or items for discussion to all participants in advance.
- Identify the objectives and intended outcomes of the call.
- If using a service provider, call in advance and give accurate numbers, names, date, time, and the expected duration of the call.

Participating in a conference call requires the use of your best communication skills. Think of the conference call as a type of meeting where you will both contribute to the conversation and listen to others. Follow these procedures during the call:

- Take roll. Call out the names of all participants.
- Lead the call by presenting the agenda and conference guidelines.
- Have participants identify themselves when speaking.
- Speak clearly, spelling out difficult or unusual names and terms. Repeat numbers.
- Avoid interrupting other speakers. Only one person should speak at a time.
- Take notes of important points and comments.
- Apply good listening skills.
- Encourage discussion and participation from everyone.

Participants should use effective listening skills during a conference call.

Brand X Pictures/Jupiter Images

CHECK POINT   What steps should you take to plan a business call?

Using Directories

Many resources are available for you to use when planning a call. Your local telephone company publishes a yearly **directory**. Local as well as national organizations publish a variety of business and professional directories. National telephone directories are available on CD. Directory information also is available on the Internet. Users can search for telephone numbers using a simple interface. You should become familiar with the wide range of information contained in these resources.

directory   a list of items, such as names and corresponding telephone numbers

Local Directories

Local telephone companies usually provide directories to their customers free of charge. The front section of most directories is actually a user's guide for the directory itself. It may also contain a "how-to" guide for telephone users. Some of the information you will find here includes the types of telephone services provided by the company, local emergency numbers, and directions for how to make many types of calls. You should read and become very familiar with this section.

You may want to find the telephone number of an individual or business in your local area. You can usually find the number in the white pages of the local directory. Names are arranged alphabetically in the **white pages** and have the corresponding numbers shown.

If you are searching for a particular service or product, you may find the number in the **yellow pages** section of the directory. Names are arranged alphabetically under section headings and have the corresponding numbers shown. The section headings relate to the products or services offered by the organization.

white pages   part of a telephone directory with an alphabetical list of names and related telephone numbers

yellow pages   part of a telephone directory with names and related telephone numbers arranged by subject headings

Large directories may include another section called the *blue pages* or *green pages*. This section may contain numbers for government offices or another special group of numbers. You should become familiar with all sections of the local telephone directory.

Personal and Company Directories

You should make a list of all numbers that you call often. You may be able to program a limited number of frequently dialed numbers into your telephone. Your company may provide you with a directory of employees working at a particular location. The directory may also include procedures for using the features of the telephone system. Tips for proper telephone techniques as well as how the company wants you to identify yourself and your department may also be included.

Electronic Directories

toll-free requiring no payment

The types of data contained in the paper directories can also be accessed using a computer. National telephone directories can be purchased on CD. Several websites provide telephone numbers for individuals and businesses. Some sites also provide other services, such as reverse lookup or a directory for toll-free numbers. Reverse lookup service allows users to enter a telephone number and find the person or company to which the number is assigned. A sample reverse lookup screen is shown in Figure 6-2.5.

Figure 6-2.5 Reverse lookup service can be helpful in identifying names for phone numbers.

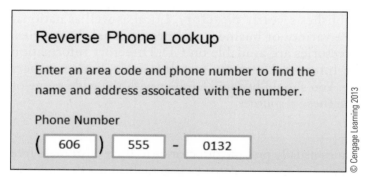

Reverse Phone Lookup

Enter an area code and phone number to find the name and address assoicated with the number.

Phone Number

(606) 555 - 0132

© Cengage Learning 2013

Directory Assistance

If you are unable to locate a telephone number, call the directory assistance operator for help. Dial 411 for a local directory assistance operator. For long-distance directory assistance, dial 1, the area code, and 555-1212. A directory assistance operator will ask you what city you are calling. Be prepared to supply the operator with as much information as possible about the person or business for which you need the number. Be prepared to give the correct spelling and street address if known. After giving the information, there will be a pause; then you will hear the number repeated twice. Make a note of the number for future reference. Because you may be charged for using directory assistance, use this service only as needed, not as a convenience.

Long-Distance Service

Long-distance calls are made to numbers outside the service area of your local telephone company. The length of the call and type of long-distance service used may affect the cost of the call. Long-distance carriers provide a variety of pricing plans. The consumer or company chooses a long-distance provider. Do research online to learn about the varied long-distance programs and prices available before selecting a carrier.

As an office worker, you will be expected to help control telephone costs. Follow any guidelines provided by your company regarding telephone use. Plan your calls so the time spent during a long-distance or any other call is used efficiently.

Direct-Dial Calls

Direct-dial calls, also called station-to-station calls, are those placed without assistance from an operator. To make a direct-dial call, first dial 1, which gives you access to a long-distance line. Then dial the area code and the number you are trying to reach. Charges for these calls begin as soon as the telephone is answered. If you make a direct-dial call and the person you need to speak with is unavailable, your company still will be charged for the call.

Specialized Long-Distance Calls

Specialized long-distance calls are more expensive than those you dial directly. Person-to-person and collect calls are types of special long-distance calls.

Person-to-person calls are an expensive type of operator-assisted calls. To place a person-to-person call, dial 0 (zero), the area code, and the telephone number of the individual or business you are calling. When you have finished dialing, you will be asked what type of call you wish to place, such as a person-to-person or collect call. You will say "person-to-person call" and will then be asked to supply the name of the person you are calling. Pronounce the name clearly and accurately. You may have to spell it for clarity.

Charges for a person-to-person call begin only after the person you have requested is on the line. If that person is not available, you will not be charged for the call. If you must call repeatedly before reaching the person, or if it takes the person several minutes to get to the phone, this type of call may be less expensive than a direct-dialed call. You do not pay until you begin speaking with the person you have indicated.

The charges for a collect call are billed to the telephone number being called, not to the number from which the call was placed. To place a collect call, dial 0 (zero), the area code, and the telephone number. You will be asked what type of call you are placing. Speak clearly into the phone, answering "collect." You will then be asked to give your name. The call will be completed, and the recipient will be asked whether or not the call and the charges will be accepted. People who travel for a business may find it necessary to make collect calls to their offices. Customers or clients may be invited to call collect.

Prepaid Phone Cards

Another way to make long-distance calls is using a prepaid phone card. This card is purchased in advance and used to pay for a certain number of minutes of phone use. The user receives a PIN (personal identification number) and a toll-free access number. The phone system will inform you of the amount of calling time remaining for the card. Prepaid phone cards may be purchased in many locations, such as airports and convenience stores, or from your long-distance carrier.

A prepaid phone card provides a convenient way to purchase long-distance phone service.

Toll-Free Service

As a convenience to customers who call long-distance, a company may subscribe to toll-free service for callers. This discounted service applies to incoming calls only. No charge is made to the caller. For toll-free numbers, users dial 800 or 888 rather than an area code. To determine whether a company in the United States has a toll-free number, dial 1-800-555-1212 and give the company name. Several websites provide a lookup service for toll-free numbers. The Internet 800 Directory is an example of a site that offers this service. To find other sites, search the Internet using the phrase *lookup service for toll-free numbers*.

As with other telephone services, rate plans and regulations for toll-free service plans vary widely. Compare price plans and features from several companies to find the plan that will be most cost-effective for your company.

REVIEW 6-2

21st Century Skills

PARTNERSHIP FOR
21ST CENTURY SKILLS

Thinking Critically

You are employed in a growing computer sales and service business, Computer Corner. Several calls are received daily for the 15 sales associates, 7 service technicians, and 4 office services employees. The owner is considering the purchase of an automated attendant telephone system. The office manager, Ms. Lin Chang, would like to hear your suggestions before deciding whether to purchase a system. You are aware of both the advantages and disadvantages of using these systems. What do you recommend?

1. Make a list of the pros and cons of using an automated attendant at Computer Corner.
2. Prepare a memo or e-mail message to Lin Chang. Include your list of pros and cons. Give your recommendation as to whether or not you think the company should install an automated attendant. Give reasons for your recommendation.

Making Academic Connections

Reinforcing Math Skills

You work for a company that has offices in Seattle, Houston, and St. Louis. You are responsible for monitoring the costs of the various forms of telecommunications used by the company. A table showing the monthly long-distance telephone charges for each regional office for a period of six months is shown below. Do manual calculations or prepare a spreadsheet to answer these questions:

1. What are the total charges for the three offices for each month?
2. What are the total charges for each regional office for the six-month period?
3. What are the total charges for the six-month period for all regional offices?
4. What are the average monthly charges for each regional office?
5. What are the average monthly charges for all offices?

MONTHS	SEATTLE	HOUSTON	ST. LOUIS
January	$201.56	$58.67	$250.78
February	190.45	75.34	277.56
March	175.66	68.90	265.19
April	188.34	92.51	281.40
May	205.22	61.61	275.37
June	199.29	74.27	259.39

6-2 Activity 1

Telephone Techniques Presentation (Outcomes 6-2a)

You supervisor has asked you to prepare an electronic slide show with information about making a favorable impression when communicating by telephone. Work with a classmate to complete this activity.

1. Review the information presented in this chapter about effective ways to communicate by telephone. Do research online to find additional information.
2. Create an electronic slide show that can be placed on the company's intranet.

   - Include a title slide and at least six other slides.
   - Place the main points on the slides using text. Add graphics (photos, shapes, or clip art) to at least three slides.
   - Record comments for each slide to discuss the points on that slide. Set up the slides so the comments will play automatically when the user transitions to that slide.

3. Save the presentation in a format that can be viewed in a web browser. Play the presentation in a web browser to be sure the slides are attractive and work as you intended. Make changes or corrections, if needed, and save the show again.

6-2 Activity 2

Telephone Conversations (Outcomes 6-2b, 6-2c)

Role-playing telephone conversations will help you develop your telephone skills. For the role-playing activities, work with another member of your class. Rotate in each situation between being the caller and being the person answering the telephone.

1. Open and print the file 6-2 Activity 2 from the data files. This file describes several dramatic situations that you will role play.
2. Select two dramatic situations. Work with your teammate to prepare a script. Compose the dialog that each person might say in this situation and print a copy for each of you.
3. Practice the telephone conversations. If possible, record the calls. Evaluate yourself and your teammate using the form provided in the data file.
4. Present the calls to the class or another team. Have classmates complete an evaluation form for each presentation. Your classmates will also be acting out the situations, and you will complete forms to evaluate them.

Summary

6-1 Telephone Technology and Services

- Telecommunications is the electronic transfer of data over a distance. This data can be in the form of voice, video, text, or images.

- Facsimile technology, often called fax, works by combining scanning with telephone technology to send images using telephone channels.

- The integration of computer and telephone technologies is called telephony. VoIP, videoconferencing, automated attendants, and voice mail are all types of telephony.

- Many features are available that allow users to customize a telephone or telephone system. Users should compare features and prices for equipment and services.

- Mobile phones and smartphones are commonly used for both personal and business communications.

6-2 Effective Telephone Communication

- How you communicate by phone can make a favorable or unfavorable impression on the caller. Your voice tone, pace, volume, and speaking skills contribute to the impression you make.

- Handling incoming telephone calls requires skill in using proper telephone techniques. You should know how to answer calls, assist callers, screen calls, and take messages effectively.

- Because of the convenience and efficiency of voice mail, its use has become widespread in business. You should use effective procedures in creating voice mail greetings and leaving voice mail messages.

- Making business calls, especially conference calls, requires preparation and planning. Plan to use mobile phones in ways that are safe and do not disturb others.

- Local, national, and online telephone directories provide a wide range of information that can be helpful to business callers.

- Direct-dial and specialized long-distance calls are often made by business callers. Learn about the services available and use the most cost-effective telephone services available.

- Your company may subscribe to a toll-free service, which allows customers to call the company at no charge.

Chapter 6 Activity 1

Telephone Features and Services
(Outcome 6-1c)

The small business for which you work has decided to purchase smartphones for the five employees of the company. You have been asked to do research and report on the features and services of three smartphones.

1. Use the Internet or local service providers as your sources of information.
2. Prepare a table that compares the three phones. Include the phone brand or maker, model/name, phone features or services, and price for each phone. Consider both the purchase price for the phone and the cost of service plans.
3. Prepare a memo from you to the company manager, Helen Patel. Use the current date and an appropriate subject line. Let Ms. Patel know that you have completed the research she requested on smartphones. Tell which phone you think would be the best choice for the company's employees. State reasons to support your recommendation. Attach the table to the memo.

Chapter 6 Activity 2

Directory Research
(Outcome 6-2c)

Telephone directories provide a wealth of information for your use in planning telephone communications and locating people and services. Use your local telephone directory or online directories to find the information requested. Key and print your answers.

1. Number of the nearest Federal Bureau of Investigation office
2. Number to call to report telephone problems on your line
3. Number to call if you have questions about your telephone bill
4. Number for the nearest U.S. Post Office
5. List of all area codes for Illinois, Colorado, and Washington, D.C.
6. The time zones for Nashville, Tennessee; Prince Edward Island, Canada; Seattle, Washington; and Wichita, Kansas
7. The country codes for dialing the following countries: Japan, Mexico, Kenya, and Greece
8. Number for your state's motor vehicle department
9. Number for the local public schools
10. Subject in the yellow pages where you would find:
    - Agencies that supply temporary office workers
    - A vision center that sells eyeglasses
    - A service station that will change your car's oil
    - A company that will repair your computer
    - A company that sells voice mail equipment
    - A doctor who specializes in eye surgery

Business Communication Event

In this competitive event, you will be judged on your skills and knowledge of business communications. The event covers a wide variety of skills including those related to reading, writing, nonverbal communications, and digital communications. The event includes a written test lasting one hour.

Performance Indicators Evaluated

Participants will demonstrate skills related to the business management and administration career cluster. Sample indicators include showing an understanding of:

- General communication concepts
- Nonverbal and oral communication concepts
- Written and report applications
- Grammar
- Reading comprehension
- Editing and proofreading
- Word definition and usage
- Capitalization and punctuation
- Spelling
- Digital communications, such as e-mail and messaging, and netiquette

For more detailed information about this event, go to the FBLA website.[2]

http://www.fbla-pbl.org

Think Critically

1. What topics do you think might be covered under *general communication concepts*?

2. In which skill areas included in this event are you proficient? In which areas do you need to learn or improve skills?

---

[2]FBLA-PBL, "FBLA Competitive Events, Computer Applications," 2010, http://www.fbla-pbl.org/docs/ct/gdlrs /FBLA/business%20communications.pdf.

Agribusiness Systems

Agribusiness is a term used to describe the many activities involved in growing, distributing, and marketing agricultural products. These products include items such as foods that come from plants and animals. People who sell items such as fertilizer and other chemicals and equipment used in growing food, grain, and livestock are also part of this career area.

Many people in this career area own the farms and ranches where they work. Others work on large farms or ranches owned by companies. Businesses that sell products related to agriculture employ many workers.

Employment Outlook

There are many jobs in agribusiness systems. The U.S. government provides job projections for 2008-2018. The number of jobs for some occupations, such as farmers, is expected to decrease. Other jobs, such as for ranch managers, is expected to increase slightly. This change is due in part to the trend toward fewer but larger farms and ranches, often owned by companies.[3]

Job Titles

- Farm/ranch owner
- Farm worker
- Ranch manager
- Farm supply store manager
- Livestock buyer/seller
- Fertilizer salesperson
- Agricultural loan officer
- Commodities broker
- Aquaculture farmer

Needed Education/Skills

The education and skills needed in agribusiness jobs vary widely. They depend on the area of work to which the job relates. For example,

an agricultural loan officer needs different skills than a livestock buyer. For many farm and ranch workers, job specific training may be all that is required. Farmers and ranchers gain skills through work experience, often while growing up on a family farm or ranch. They may also earn college degrees in business management or agribusiness. Other employees in agribusiness may need training specific to their jobs. For example, a farm commodities broker may have a college degree in finance.

What's it like to work in . . . Agribusiness Systems?

Sara owns a small farm where she raises vegetables. She sells her produce at a local farmers' market and to local restaurants. She also sells to many people in the community who come to her farm to buy produce. Sara learned many practical aspects of growing vegetables from her parents, who also were farmers. To be better prepared to manage the finances for the farm, Sara attended college and earned a degree in business management. She also took courses in botany and chemistry.

During the planting and harvesting seasons, Sara works long hours six days a week. She must prepare the soil for planting during the early spring when she also grows plants from seeds in a small greenhouse. These plants are moved outside to the garden after the danger of frost has passed. During the growing season, she tends the plants. They must be watered and the area kept free of weeds and pests. Sara has two employees who help with these tasks. She sets up a stall at the farmer's market each Saturday to sell vegetables. She also make deliveries of produce to local restaurants at scheduled times. Being a produce farmer is hard work, but Sara enjoys it.

What About You?

Do you know someone who works in agribusiness systems? What type of job does this person have?

Which do you think is more important for success as a farmer—practical experience or a college degree? Why?

[3]*Occupational Outlook Handbook*, 2010-11 Edition, Bureau of Labor Statistics, U.S. Department of Labor, http://www.bls.gov/oco/ocos176.htm.

Processing and Understanding Financial Information

Vadym Andrushchenko/Shutterstock.com

CHAPTER 7
Banking and Payroll

CHAPTER 8
Financial Reports and Procedures

Making a profit is a goal of most businesses. Recording and tracking financial information lets the company managers know whether this goal is being achieved. Financial reports may also be used by investors or creditors of the company. An as office employee, you may be involved in banking transactions or handling payroll records. You may prepare financial reports or make purchases or payments. You will need to understand the financial documents and procedures used in these activities, as discussed in this part.

Dmitriy Shironosov/Shutterstock.com

Banking and Payroll

7-1 Banking Procedures

7-2 Payroll and Employee Benefits

Joern Wolter/vario images/Alamy

Wire_man/Shutterstock.com

Sound financial information is very important to the success of a business. Many day-to-day business decisions are based on financial information. Data are needed to answer questions such as: How much do we owe our suppliers? How much cash is on hand? Will this expense exceed our budget? Businesses need current and correct financial information to make informed decisions.

In this chapter, you will learn about the procedures used in handling cash and banking activities. You will also study payroll procedures and learn about employee benefits.

OUTCOMES

7-1a Describe procedures for safeguarding cash and handling a cash drawer.
7-1b Describe procedures for deposits, checks, and electronic funds transfers.
7-1c Apply procedures for completing a bank account reconciliation.

Handling Cash

A business must keep track of cash receipts carefully to avoid losing money or recording customer payments incorrectly. In business terms, cash refers to currency (coins and bills), checks, money orders, and funds in checking accounts in banks. Some businesses accept only currency or money orders. Other companies, such as supermarkets and retail stores, handle large volumes of currency. In still other companies, almost all transactions are paid by check, credit card, debit card, or electronic funds transfer.

If you work in a small office, you are likely to have some duties related to cash transactions. If you work in a large company, you may work in a department where many cash transactions are processed. In this chapter, you will learn about safeguards for cash, processing cash receipts, and preparing checks. You will learn about procedures of making payments in Chapter 8.

> **check** a written order to a bank to make a payment using funds from the depositor's bank account

> **debit card** a kind of bank card used to make payments from a depositor's bank account

Safeguarding Cash

Cash is a valuable asset of the business. It must be safeguarded in all its forms. Currency is generally considered to be owned by the person who has it. Currency stolen from a business can be spent easily. Checks can be stolen and cashed using forged signatures. The overall method a business uses to safeguard assets is known as internal control. Internal control methods fall into three categories—preventive, detective, and corrective.

> **forge** imitate or counterfeit for illegal purposes

Preventive Internal Control

The goal of preventive internal controls is to reduce loss of cash due to employee error or theft. Dividing the duties for handling cash among two or more employees is usually a part of this control. In Figure 7-1.1, note that tasks are given to different workers. This helps ensure that all checks received

Figure 7-1.1 Separation of duties helps provide internal control of cash.

PREVENTIVE INTERNAL CONTROL		
MAIL CLERK	**CASHIER**	**ACCOUNTING CLERK**
Delivers checks to cashier	• Makes a list of checks received • Prepares deposit slip and makes bank deposit • Forwards a list of checks to an accounting clerk	• Records the customers' payments • Verifies that the total of customers' payments equals the total of checks listed

© Cengage Learning 2013

by the company are properly deposited and recorded. Accuracy checks also help prevent error. Preventive internal control is the most important category because it is designed to avoid loss of cash.

Detective Internal Control

Another type of internal controls tries to find losses that have taken place. Losses may be found by reviewing reports and customer accounts. A bank reconciliation is an example of this type of detective control. It can be used to find missing deposits or other errors. Some companies have employees who do **audits**. Audits are done to see whether internal controls are being applied correctly. You may be expected to assist the employees who do internal audits.

audit to verify or check facts or procedures

✳ WORKPLACE CONNECTIONS ✳

Jill Wong, a staff member in the Internal Audit Department, was asked to determine whether the procedures for recording customer payments were being followed. Jill requested a list of the checks that were received on a particular day from the cashier. She looked at the records for each customer from whom a payment was received on that date to verify that the payment was recorded correctly. Jill found no differences between the list of payments and the customers' records. It seems that all the procedures were followed correctly, so the audit revealed no problems.

▶ **What possible misuse of checks did Jill's audit fail to consider? Hint: Refer to Figure 7-1.1.**

Corrective Internal Control

Corrective internal control is used to restore assets after a loss has occurred. For example, changing poor procedures that lead to a loss is a form of corrective internal control. Money received from insurance policies may be used to replace losses caused by employee theft. This is another type of corrective internal control.

One method used to protect cash is **bonding** for employees. Bonding is insurance for financial loss due to employee theft or fraud. Bonding is effective because the company that insures bonded employees makes a search of the employee's work history and criminal record. They check with former employers and other references. This search, which is generally more thorough than that done by the company at the time employees are hired, is the major advantage of bonding.

bonding insurance for financial loss due to employee theft or fraud

---

✔**CHECK POINT** Which type of internal control is the most important and why?

Handling a Cash Drawer

A cash register drawer is assigned to an employee who deals with customers in person, receiving payments and making change. When the employee is assigned the cash drawer, it contains currency and coins to use in making change. As transactions are completed, currency, coins, checks, and credit card and debit card receipts from customer payments will be added to the drawer. Each sale is recorded in the cash register electronically. The cash register will show the total sales made during the time the worker used the cash drawer or at other times, as needed. For example, the manager may want to limit the maximum amount of cash held in the register drawer. The cash report lets the manager check the cash amount quickly.

An employee who is issued a cash drawer is required to verify the amount of cash in the cash drawer when he or she receives the drawer. When the drawer is turned in, the employee must verify that the proper amount of currency, checks, and bank card receipts are in the drawer. This procedure is known as proving cash or balancing the cash drawer. It is an important type of internal control.

Balancing cash is done at closing time or at the end of a work shift for the cashier. The procedure should be done in an office or other secure area. To prove cash, an employee would add total sales (as shown on the cash register for the employee's shift) to the beginning balance (the amount in the drawer when received). This total should match the amount in the cash drawer. In some businesses, employees may be required to list the contents of the drawer in detail by type of item (currency, coins, checks, and bank card receipts).

In some companies, the employee must make up shortages when the cash drawer does not balance. Even if employees do not have to make up shortages, frequent shortages of a significant amount in an employee's cash drawer may lead to a poor job evaluation. These workers may not receive a promotion or even be fired if the problem continues.

Enigma/Alamy

Accounting for cash and other receipts is an important internal control procedure.

CHECK POINT What steps are taken to balance a cash drawer at the end of the cashier's work shift?

Depositing and Transferring Funds

Many companies receive checks in payment for goods and services. These checks must be deposited in the company's bank account. Companies also receive and make payments by transferring funds electronically. Employees must understand and follow the proper procedures for both types of transactions.

Making Deposits

Businesses commonly deposit cash in a bank shortly after it is received. In some organizations where many payments are received, deposits may be made several times a day. In other companies, deposits may be made only a few times a month because payments are not received often. If your tasks include going to the bank with deposits, be sure all checks, currency, coins, and deposit forms are in proper order and in an envelope before you leave the office.

Deposits can be made electronically at some automated teller machines (ATM) at banks or at other convenient locations. If you make this type of deposit, follow the instructions provided and get a receipt. Verify that the receipt shows the amount of your deposit.

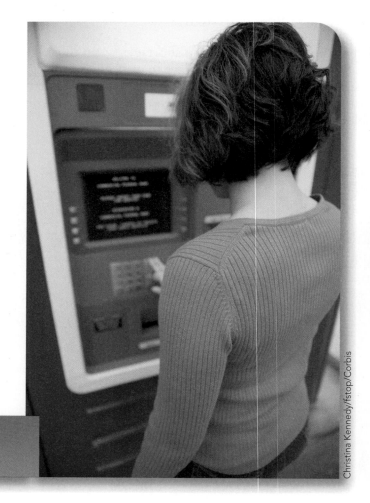

Christina Kennedy/fstop/Corbis

This employee is making a deposit at an ATM machine located near the office.

Endorsements

endorsement a name placed on the back of a check that authorizes a bank to cash or deposit the check

Employees who prepare bank deposits should verify that all checks are properly endorsed. An **endorsement** is a signature or instructions, stamped or written on the back of a check. It authorizes the bank to cash or deposit the check. An endorsement is required before a check may be transferred from the company or person to whom the check is written to another person, company, or bank. In many companies, office workers who prepare deposits also endorse the checks using a stamp.

Many checks have an endorsement area printed on the back of the check. Be careful to write, print, or stamp the endorsement within the area provided. If no endorsement area is indicated or the back of the check is blank, place the check face up. Grasp the left edge of the check and turn it over, keeping the same edge at the left. Carefully stamp or write an endorsement on the left edge of the check or other marked endorsement area. Endorsements vary. Some provide more protection or instructions than others. The most commonly used forms of endorsements are blank, restrictive, and special. Look closely at Figure 7-1.2 as you read about each form of endorsement.

Figure 7-1.2 Endorsements can be stamped or handwritten on checks.

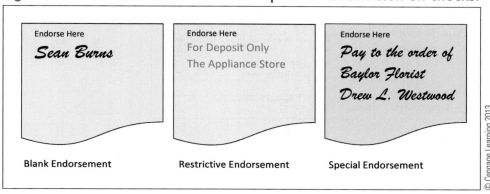

Blank Endorsement   Restrictive Endorsement   Special Endorsement

© Cengage Learning 2013

- **Blank endorsements.** For a blank endorsement, the signature of the payee is written on the back of the check. The signature should be in ink. This endorsement provides little protection because anyone who has the check can easily transfer it to another person or cash the check. Generally, use this endorsement only when you are at the bank ready to cash or deposit the check immediately.

- **Restrictive endorsements.** In a restrictive endorsement, the purpose of the transfer of the check is indicated in the endorsement. For example, the check may be marked *For Deposit Only*. Restrictive endorsements are often made with a rubber stamp or a stamping machine.

- **Special endorsements.** In a special endorsement, the signature of the payee is placed after the name of the person or company to whom the check is being transferred. In some instances, a special endorsement is referred to as an *endorsement in full*.

Deposit Forms

A deposit form (slip) is used to record currency, coins, and checks to be added to a bank account. On a deposit form, *cash* refers to the total of currency and coins. A sample deposit form is shown in Figure 7-1.3 on page 240. When completing a deposit form, do the following:

- Write the current date in the space provided.

- Write the amount of each item to be deposited. For each check, identify the bank on which the check is drawn. This is done by recording the bank's number, which is the upper portion of the three-part number noted on each check. A bank number example is shown on the deposit form in Figure 7-1.3.

■ Write the amount of cash received from the deposit, if any, and sign the space to indicate that cash is received.

■ Write the net deposit amount. This amount includes all checks listed on both the front and back of the deposit slip minus any cash received.

Figure 7-1.3 **A deposit form lists items to be added to a bank account.**

To verify the accuracy of the total deposit, add the checks and currency to be deposited. Verify that this total is exactly the same as the total listed on the deposit slip. If the totals match, the list is correct and includes all items.

☀ WORKPLACE CONNECTIONS ☀

One of Inez's daily tasks is preparing deposit slips for receipts to be taken to a local bank. Inez works in a systematic fashion so that she makes no errors. She verifies that each deposit slip is correct by totaling the amounts carefully. Inez is proud that the bank has never sent her company a notice that an error had been made in a deposit she submitted.

What are some common errors that you might make when completing a deposit slip?

Lockbox Deposits

Some banks offer a service to businesses called lockbox deposits. With this service, the company directs customers to send payments to a post office box rather than to the company's physical location. A bank employee collects the payment from the post office box and processes the deposit. The bank then updates the company's account balance. This service is typically used by companies that receive a large number of customer checks as payments, such as utility companies.

Having the checks sent directly to the bank improves internal control by reducing the possibility of employee theft or errors. Company employees do not have to spend time processing checks and are free to complete other duties.

CHECK POINT How does a blank endorsement differ from a restrictive endorsement?

Preparing Checks

In some offices, especially small ones, a checkbook similar to one an individual uses for personal check writing is used to prepare checks. Checks may be handwritten or printed on a check form. The check register may also be handwritten or prepared in a spreadsheet program. In other offices, checks are computer generated by entering data into an accounting or check writing program.

Checks Prepared Individually

If you are responsible for writing checks using a checkbook or by printing on check forms, these suggestions will be helpful.

1. Read carefully the name of the company or individual to whom payment is to be made as well as the amount of the check. (The complete process and documents related to making payments are discussed in Chapter 8.)

2. Enter data into the check register. (See Figure 7-1.4.) The check register should show the check number, date of the check, the payee, and the amount of the check. The register may also have a column for the balance forward.

Figure 7-1.4 Check Register and Completed Check

Item No.	Date	Payment to or Deposit	Payment Amount	✓	Deposit Amount	Balance Forward
	10/25/--				2,500.00	10,485.75
2267	10/25/--	Just Shades Invoice No. 5479	4,469.68			6,016.07

Check Register

The Lampshade Store   2267
426 Monroe Street   69-439
Cedar Falls, IA·50613-3467   October 25, 20 --   515

Pay to the order of Just Shades--- $ 4,469.68

Four thousand, four hundred sixty-nine and 68/100 ------------------------- **Dollars**

Memo Invoice No. 5479   _____

⑆051504393⑆ 3 8953 4⑆   0226   ↑

Check   **Authorized signature here**

© Cengage Learning 2013

3. Prepare the check. (See Figure 7-1.4.) Note that the amount is written in numbers as well as in words. Notice how the space between the name and the dollar sign and the space between the amount in words and the word "dollars" is filled in so that changes cannot be made easily. Notice that the purpose of the payment is shown on the face of the check on the memo line.

Computer-Generated Checks

Many companies use computer-generated checks. If you prepare checks, you likely will be issued a password to access the company's accounts payable system. Security measures are taken to safeguard both the information used to prepare the checks and the printed checks.

You may need to refer to the files in the accounts payable system to obtain the information needed to complete the checks. For example, you will need the payee's name and address, the amount to be paid, and the purpose of payment. In automated systems, you may need to enter only a vendor number or name. Other information, such as the address, will be entered automatically by the system. Then, by selecting a menu option such as Print Checks, checks will be printed. Checks and related documents are sent to an authorized person to be signed. In some systems, the signature is printed on the check.

Special Checks

From time to time, special checks that provide guarantee of payment are used by businesses. A certified check is an ordinary check that the bank marks "certified." This is done after the bank determines that the funds are in the account of the party writing the check. The funds are immediately subtracted from the depositor's account. A cashier's check is a check written by a bank on its own funds. Such a check can be purchased with cash or with an ordinary check.

 CHECK POINT What information should be entered into a check register when preparing checks manually?

Transferring Funds Electronically

Deposits and payments can be made electronically rather than using paper documents, such as checks and deposit slips. Electronic funds transfer (EFT) is the use of a computer network to transfer funds from one party to another. EFT is used for transactions between companies and for those between companies and individuals.

Many companies allow customers the option of having payments deducted directly from a bank account. This process eliminates the need to write and mail a payment check. It may be done for a one-time payment or for regular monthly payments. For example, a customer can provide a utility company with his or her bank account number and related information. Each month, the amount of the customer's utility bill will be deducted from the customer's bank account. The amount will be transferred to the utility company. Many companies allow customers to set up automatic payments or pay a bill using the company's website. An example screen is shown in Figure 7-1.5.

electronic funds transfer using a computer network to send money from one party to another

Figure 7-1.5 **Online payments can be transferred using a customer's bank account information.**

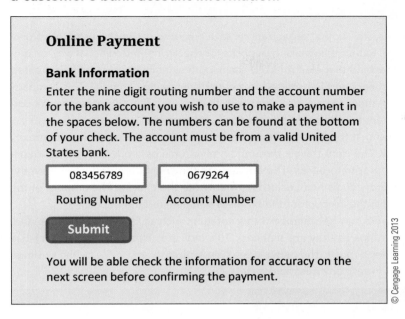

As with payments, deposits can also be made directly to a bank account. No check is sent to the company or individual receiving the money. However, a document showing the amount deposited, the date, and other related information may be sent. The document could be in paper or electronic form. Many companies use this method to deposit wage and salary payments for employees. The U.S. government deposits Social Security benefit payments for many people using this procedure.

Use caution when entering your bank account number on any website or paper form. Make sure the organization to which you give the number can be trusted to take reasonable precautions to keep the information secure. Your bank and other reputable organizations should not ask you to send this information in an e-mail message.

 CHECK POINT Give two examples of payments that can be made using electronic funds transfer.

Reconciling a Bank Account

Companies need to be sure that receipts and payments shown in their records are also reflected in the bank's records. You may have the task of comparing these records to prepare a **bank reconciliation**. This document is prepared using a statement from the bank as well as the company's records.

Cash is a valuable resource for all businesses. Knowing the exact status of the cash account, therefore, is important. By completing a bank reconciliation, you will fulfill the following purposes:

bank reconciliation a report used to compare bank and company account records

- Determine that all deposits made have been recorded by the bank, as indicated on the bank statement.
- Verify that all the checks that cleared the bank were written by authorized persons in the company.
- Determine which checks have not yet cleared the bank.

Many businesses and other organizations save time and money by using electronic check processing. Rather than making deposits for checks in the traditional way, an employee uses a machine that electronically scans both sides of checks. A file is created for the batch of checks and transmitted to a check processing company. This company reviews the file. If there are any problems with the scanned file, the company will correct them or contact the depositor for additional information.

When everything in the file appears to be in order, the check processing company transmits the file. The data travels through an electronic network for financial transactions to the appropriate banks. The amounts of the checks are deducted from the accounts of the individuals and businesses that wrote the checks. The amount of the deposit is placed in the account for the business that initiated the deposit.

The paper checks may be stamped with a notation, such as *Electronically Processed,* by the check machine as they are scanned. This indicates clearly that the check has been processed for deposit. The paper checks are typically kept on file by the business for a few months in case any questions arise.

How might using electronic check processing save time or money for a business?

■ Identify additional bank charges, as indicated on the bank statement, that need to be recorded in the books of the company.

■ Determine the cash balance as of the date of the bank statement.

Bank Statement and Company Records

A bank statement provided by the bank shows the activity in each account on a regular basis, usually monthly. The statement may be a paper statement that is mailed to the company. It might also be an electronic statement that you access using the bank's website. As you will note in Figure 7-1.6, a bank statement gives the following information:

■ The balance as of the opening date of the statement

■ Checks listed by number and amount that the bank has received and honored

■ Automated teller machine transactions and miscellaneous charges

■ Automatic withdrawals, if any

■ Deposits and/or transfers

■ The balance on the closing date of the statement

On the bank statement shown in Figure 7-1.6, the automated teller transactions are coded AW for ATM withdrawals, AC for ATM deposits and credits, and PD for preauthorized electronic deposits.

With the bank statement, some banks return canceled checks or photocopies of canceled checks. Other banks may provide only the statement. Copies of checks that have been scanned may be provided on request. Notices reporting changes in bank policies may also be included.

The bank statement shown in Figure 7-1.6 shows that a check deposited was returned by the bank on which it was drawn. Because the person writing the check did not have enough funds to cover the amount of the check, the check was not honored. Such checks are referred to as NSF (not sufficient funds) checks. Figure 7-1.6 shows that Adler Knitting's balance was reduced by the amount of the check that was not honored.

Figure 7-1.6 This bank statement is for Adler Knitting Manufacturing Co.

Neches Bank
Cincinnati, Ohio

ADLER KNITTING MANUFACTURING CO   Account No.   32921-6
658 TEAKWOOD AVENUE
CINCINNATI OH 45224-4578   Statement Date   08/31/--

Balance from Previous Statement	Number of Credits	Amount of Deposits and Credits	Number of Debits	Amount of Withdrawals and Debits	Total Activity Charge	Statement Balance
22,890.75	4	26,962.10	20	29,255.96	25.00	20,596.89

Date	Code	Transaction Description	Transaction Amount	Account Balance
22-Jul	AW	0248 634	200.00	22,690.75
23-Jul		Deposit	6,790.40	29,481.15
		Check 187	3,750.00	25,731.15
		Check 189	1,890.25	23,840.90
27-Jul	AW	0248 634	2,500.00	21,340.90
28-Jul		Check 190	6,590.70	14,750.20
29-Jul	PD	Rae's Sweater Corner Deposit	7,980.70	22,730.90
3-Aug		Check 191	3,875.00	18,855.90
4-Aug		Check 192	1,870.70	16,985.20
		Check 194	580.90	16,404.30
5-Aug		Check 193	450.00	15,954.30
6-Aug	AC	ATM Deposit	4,280.90	20,235.20
9-Aug	AW	0248 634	1,000.00	19,235.20
10-Aug		Check 197	2,975.25	16,259.95
		Check 195	1,800.00	14,459.95
11-Aug		Check 196	290.20	14,169.75
12-Aug	PD	Rae's Sweater Corner Deposit	7,910.10	22,079.85
		Check 198	378.28	21,701.57
16-Aug		Check 202	150.50	21,551.07
		Check 201	95.70	21,455.37
		Check 199	110.98	21,344.39
17-Aug		Check 206	525.00	20,819.39
18-Aug		NSF Check	197.50	20,621.89
19-Aug		Service Charge	25.00	20,596.89

Generally, there are no documents included that relate to automatic teller machine (ATM) transactions. These are deposits and withdrawals made at electronic machines. Keep the slips generated at the time these transactions are made. They provide your receipt of the transaction. If you transfer funds from one account to another online, save or print the screen indicating that the transfer was made successfully.

Steps in Preparing a Reconciliation

To complete a reconciliation, you will need the company's checkbook or check register, which records all checks written and all deposits made. You also will need the reconciliation from the previous month.

The company will have procedures for preparing bank reconciliations. You will want to learn these specific procedures. Assume that you are working in an office where a bank statement is received monthly and a reconciliation is prepared at that time. The steps described here are likely to be similar to the ones you will learn on the job:

1. Prepare a spreadsheet similar to the one shown in Figure 7-1.7. Record the balance from your check register as of the last day of the month in the spreadsheet.

2. Record the ending balance as shown on the bank statement in the spreadsheet.

3. Compare each deposit shown on the bank statement with the deposits recorded on the check register. A partial check register is shown in Figure 7-1.8. Enter a check mark in both places if the amount and date agree.

4. Record on your spreadsheet any deposits shown in the check register that are not on the bank statement. Deposits made near the end of the statement period may not have been processed by the bank by the date of the statement. These deposits are called deposits in transit.

Figure 7-1.7 Bank reconciliation for Adler Knitting Manufacturing Co.

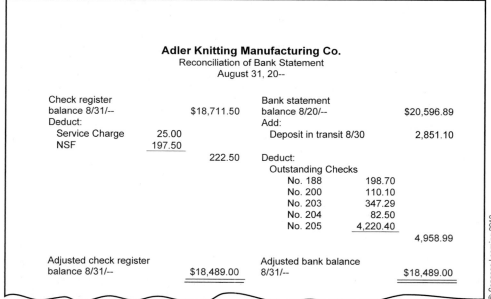

Adler Knitting Manufacturing Co.
Reconciliation of Bank Statement
August 31, 20--

Check register balance 8/31/--		$18,711.50	Bank statement balance 8/20/--		$20,596.89
Deduct:			Add:		
Service Charge	25.00		Deposit in transit 8/30		2,851.10
NSF	197.50				
		222.50	Deduct:		
			Outstanding Checks		
			No. 188	198.70	
			No. 200	110.10	
			No. 203	347.29	
			No. 204	82.50	
			No. 205	4,220.40	
					4,958.99
Adjusted check register balance 8/31/--		$18,489.00	Adjusted bank balance 8/31/--		$18,489.00

© Cengage Learning 2013

Figure 7-1.8 Check register for Adler Knitting Manufacturing Co.

Adler Knitting Manufacturing Co.
Check Register

Item No.	Date	Payment to or Deposit	Payment Amount	✓	Deposit Amount	Balance Forward
						28,681.15
187	7/17/--	Taylor Brothers	3,750.00	✓		24,931.15
188	7/16/---	Elman and Stone Co.	198.70			24,732.45
189	7/18/--	Marshall Gomez	1,890.25	✓		22,842.20
190	7/25/--	Leitz Mfg. Co.	6,590.70	✓		16,251.50
	7/29/--	Deposit		✓	7,980.70	24,232.20
191	8/1/--	Yarns, International	3,875.00	✓		20,357.20

© Cengage Learning 2013

5. Compare the amount of each check with that shown on the bank statement. Record any differences noted. Follow up on any differences before preparing your final reconciliation.

6. Compare each canceled check (or photocopy) with related information in the check register. Place a small check mark in the register if there is agreement.

7. Record on your spreadsheet the number, date, and amount for each check that was written but had not cleared as of the bank statement date. These checks are referred to as outstanding checks. The total of the outstanding checks will be subtracted from the bank balance.

8. Review last month's outstanding checks to determine which ones are still outstanding. List these on your spreadsheet also.

9. Record on your spreadsheet any charges shown on the statement that are not recorded in your company's records. For example, any checks returned for insufficient funds (NSF checks) must be subtracted from the balance in your check register. Bank charges, such as ATM fees, also must be subtracted.

10. Enter formulas for the calculations required on your spreadsheet. Note that the two balances are the same in the reconciliation shown in Figure 7-1.7. Having the same balances means that your bank account has been properly reconciled.

When you have completed a bank reconciliation, obtain any required approval signatures. Once the reconciliation is approved, file it so that it can be retrieved when needed. When you receive the next bank statement, you will refer to this one to determine which checks were outstanding and should be in the next batch of canceled checks.

 CHECK POINT What amounts on a bank reconciliation should be the same?

21st Century Skills

PARTNERSHIP FOR
21ST CENTURY SKILLS

Thinking Critically

You work in the office of a small company that manages rental property. Residents of the rental apartments and homes the company manages sometimes come into the office to pay their rent. You and a coworker, Tom Wu, handle these transactions. Each customer is given a receipt for the rent paid. Cash and checks are kept in a lockbox in the office and deposited at the end of each day. Yesterday a customer, Ms. Latoya Jones, came in to pay her rent. Tom handled the transaction. The rent amount was $750, which the customer paid in cash. Tom gave Ms. Jones a receipt before she left. Tom counted the money a final time before recording the amount and placing the money in the lockbox. "Wow!" he exclaimed. "That lady gave me an extra hundred dollar bill. This is great. Now I will have enough money to make it until we get paid on Friday. Oh, do you want half?"

1. What would you say to Tom in this situation?
2. What should you do if Tom keeps the money?

Making Academic Connections

Reinforcing English Skills

Write or key each sentence, correcting errors in number and symbol usage.

1. Dion bought 2 new tires for his car.
2. 11 members of the team were ill and could not play.
3. The amount of the payment was four dollars and sixty cents.
4. On Tuesday, January twenty third, we began using our new computer system.
5. Only 60% of the students completed the test on time.
6. You will need 1/2 yard of fabric to make this pillow.
7. The meeting will begin at 2 o'clock.
8. Several 100 people voted for the new ordinance.
9. Please order two boxes of pencils and 15 reams of paper.
10. 2 customers returned merchandise today.

7-1 Activity 1

Reconciling a Cash Drawer (Outcome 7-1a)

Tomasine works part-time as a cashier at a convenience store. When she went on duty and received her cash drawer, it contained $80 in bills and coins. During her work period of three hours, sales on her register were $194.99. She has the items listed below in her drawer at the end of her work period. Does her cash drawer balance? If not, by what amount is it over or short?

$1 bills	23	Dimes	16
$5 bills	5	Nickels	4
$10 bills	4	Pennies	34
$20 bills	7	Check 238	$23.40
Quarters	15	Check 1290	$18.45

7-1 Activity 2

Making a Deposit (Outcome 7-1b)

Your tasks as an office assistant at Vine Associates include preparing bank deposits. The list of checks the company has received is shown below. These checks will be deposited in one of two banks. The checks from L. T. Mills, Olsen Corp., Yaroff Bros., Susi & Karlin, Rice Corp., Caputa & Zinn, and Prevetti Co. will be deposited at the Penn Avenue Bank; the remaining checks will be deposited at the Smithfield Bank.

1. Open and print the file 7-1 Activity 2 from the data files. This file contains deposit slips for the two accounts.
2. Prepare a deposit slip for checks to be deposited at the Penn Avenue Bank.
3. Prepare a deposit slip for checks to be deposited at the Smithfield Bank.
4. Endorse the back of one check (shown on your data file printout) to show how you would endorse all checks for the two deposits. Use the company name in a restrictive endorsement to indicate that the checks are being submitted for deposit only.

FROM	BANK NO.	AMOUNT	FROM	BANK NO.	AMOUNT
L. T. Mills	18-419	4,200.50	Rice Corp.	12-407	81.18
Olsen Corp.	18-426	6,592.60	Rabinowitz & Sons	07-190	2,668.61
Mars, Linwood & Co.	73-258	2,540.15	Caputa & Zinn	26-317	848.88
Gomes & Co.	18-403	985.40	Beilens, Lutz & Co	12-508	129.50
Yaroff Bros.	73-259	1,965.95	Prevetti Co.	18-403	8,912.50
O'Brien & Wickes	18-419	3,691.21	Jay F. Sterling	73-286	819.19
Susi & Karlin	18-419	6,296.45	W. N. Neeley	26-317	6,819.12

OUTCOMES

7-2a Describe common plans for paying employees.
7-2b Describe typical employee benefits.
7-2c Apply procedures for completing payroll records.

Employee Payment Plans

In some companies, all employees are paid in the same way. In other companies, different plans may be used for different groups of workers. The typical ones include salary, hourly wages, commission, and combination plans.

Salary and Wages

gross pay salary or wages earned before deductions are made

Under a salary plan, an employee is paid a certain amount per week, month, or year. The **gross pay**, which is the salary before any deductions, is the figure quoted. A salary quoted on a yearly basis is divided into the number of pay periods per year. Thus, a person who earns $35,000 yearly and is paid twice each month will have gross pay of $1,458.33 each pay period. Later in this chapter, you will learn about various deductions from gross pay.

Business executives are often paid under a salary plan.

StockLite/Shutterstock

In some jobs, employees are paid a wage rate per hour. The hourly rate applies to the hours considered standard. The standard hours per week may be 35, 37.5, or 40 hours. When workers paid on an hourly basis work more hours than those set as the standard, they generally earn a higher rate for the **overtime** hours. Overtime rates are commonly 1.5 to 2 times the standard hourly rate. Thus, a worker who earns $10 per hour at the standard rate would earn $15 per hour for overtime (at a rate of 1.5 standard pay).

overtime hours worked beyond the set standard hours per week

CHECK POINT Under which type of payment plan, salary or hourly wages, are employees paid overtime for work beyond the standard hours per week?

Commission and Other Plans

Some workers' earnings are based on a percentage of the price of what they sell. This payment is called a **commission**. The percentage may vary by volume of sales. This method is commonly used for the payment of salespersons. For example, salespersons for a computer supplies company are assigned sales territories. Because their earnings depend on the sales they make, they are motivated to please customers and secure new orders. For a salesperson who earns a 10 percent commission on each sale, a $1,000 order would result in a $100 commission.

In some jobs, a combination payment plan is used. For example, a commission, often referred to as a bonus, may be given to employees who are successful beyond some established standard. Such a bonus is often a percentage of sales or production. For example, a factory worker who assembles products may be paid an hourly wage. If the worker assembles more than a certain number of products per day, the worker may be paid a bonus for each item assembled above the set number.

commission payment based on an amount of items sold or produced

 CHECK POINT Give an example of how a commission or bonus payment might be calculated.

✳ WORKPLACE CONNECTIONS ✳

Lauren works as a salesperson for a furniture store. She is paid according to a combination plan. She earns a weekly salary of $500 plus a 5 percent commission on weekly sales exceeding $5,000. Last week Lauren's sales were $8,000. She earned $500 in salary plus $150 ($3,000 x 5%) in commission for a total of $650. Lauren likes the combination pay plan because the weekly salary assures her of a steady, basic income. At the same time, the bonus portion of the plan rewards her for using her sales skills to make higher sales for the company.

What might be a disadvantage of being paid on a salary plus commissions plan?

Employee Benefits

In addition to pay for work, employees often receive other benefits. These benefits, such as vacation pay and insurance coverage, can be a valuable part of the employee's total **compensation**.

compensation pay or benefits given for a service or a loss

Paid Time Off

Some companies include paid time off as part of the employee benefits package. Vacation days and holidays fall into this benefit category. Many employees appreciate having paid time away from work to relax, travel, or take part in other activities.

Holidays and Vacation Days

Many companies give employees several paid holidays per year. For companies in the United States, these holidays may include:

- New Year's Day
- Martin Luther King, Jr. Day
- President's Day
- Memorial Day
- Independence Day
- Labor Day
- Columbus Day
- Thanksgiving Day
- Christmas Day

Employees may also have one or two floating holidays. These floating holidays can be used whenever the employee wishes (with prior approval). This allows employees to be away from work on special days that are not on the company's holiday list.

Employees may receive vacation days each year in addition to paid holidays. The number of vacation days may be the same for everyone or it may vary. Job position and the number of years of service are often a factor in the number of vacation days an employee will receive. In some companies, all employees must take their vacations at the same time. This is often the case in companies that shut down operations for one or two weeks per year. In other companies, the employee can request to have vacation scheduled on certain days.

Vacation days give employees time for travel and leisure activities.

Gorilla/Shutterstock

Sick Days

Some companies give employees a certain number of hours or days per year for paid sick days. These days are to be used to recover from an illness or to have medical appointments or tests. Some employers also allow sick days to be used to care for a close family member who is ill. Paid sick days can be a valuable benefit. Many employees, especially part-time workers, do not have paid sick days.

 CHECK POINT Which type of benefit, paid vacation or paid sick days, would be more important to you? Why?

✴ WORKPLACE CONNECTIONS ✴

Latrice has been considering which of two jobs she should accept. Both jobs have similar duties and work hours in a pleasant office environment. The office for Monticello Manufacturing is a few miles farther from her home than the office for Somerset Products. However, Latrice considers this a minor factor in her choice. She is thinking about the pay and benefits she will receive. At Somerset Products, Latrice's salary would be $3,000 more per year than at Monticello Manufacturing. However, Monticello Manufacturing offers better employee benefits in the form of group insurance, paid vacation, and paid sick days. The company will also match the money she places in a retirement account up to certain amount. After careful consideration, Latrice decided to accept the job at Monticello Manufacturing.

Do you think Latrice made the right choice? Why or why not?

Group Insurance

Insurance is a process in which a company agrees to pay compensation for loss due to damage, theft, illness, or death in return for payments by the individual or company that is covered. Health and life insurance are often less expensive when purchased as part of a group. Many employers offer group insurance plans as an employee benefit.

> **insurance** a process in which a company agrees to pay compensation for loss in return for payments by the insured

Health, Life, and Disability Insurance

Health insurance helps pay for costs related to a personal injury or illness. Doctors' bills, medicine, and hospital stays are example of expenses covered by health insurance. Some companies pay a portion of the employee's **premiums** for the group health insurance. At other companies, the employee pays the entire cost. However, the cost of the insurance at a group rate is typically lower than what the employee would pay for an individual plan. The employee may also be able to include family members in the insurance coverage. Dental and vision care expenses are also covered by some plans.

> **premium** the payment for an insurance plan

Some companies offer life insurance as an employee benefit. Life insurance pays a benefit to a designated person or company in the event of the employee's death. The company may pay for the insurance, or the employee may be required to pay for the policy if it is optional.

Disability insurance pays benefits when the insured person is injured or ill and cannot work. Both short-term and long-term disability policies are available. Short-term policies are typically for six months or less. The benefit paid is generally a percentage of the insured person's normal income. The money is paid directly to the insured person to be used for whatever purposes are needed.

COBRA

Many people have health insurance through group plans offered by employers. When people change jobs or are unemployed for some time, they can take steps to see that their health insurance coverage is not interrupted or canceled. COBRA (the Consolidated Omnibus Budget Reconciliation Act) is a law that makes it easier to accomplish this. COBRA gives many workers the right to continue their health insurance through a former employer's group plan. The coverage time can vary, but it is typically for 18 months. The worker usually must pay the full cost of the insurance premium. However, that cost may be lower than paying for an individual plan. Not all employees are entitled to COBRA benefits. For example, the law generally covers companies with 20 or more employees. You can find other rules and information about COBRA on the U.S. Department of Labor website.

 CHECK POINT Why is the option to purchase insurance under a group plan a valuable benefit for many employees?

Retirement Plans and Other Benefits

Retirement is a time, usually later in life, when people stop working. They may stop working because they no longer want to work or because of poor health or other reasons. Retirement plans are designed to help workers set aside money to pay for living expenses after they no longer have an income from working. Many employers include some type of retirement plan as part of their employee benefits.

Defined Benefit Pension Plan

Some employers offer retirement accounts that are paid for by the employer. These accounts are called *defined benefit pension plans* or simply *pensions*. With some plans, the employee may also contribute money to the account. Employees are usually required to work for the company for a set number of years to qualify for the plan. Benefits paid at retirement may depend on the number of years worked, the employee's salary, and other factors. Taxes must be paid on the benefits received. Because pension plans are costly for the company, fewer companies offer them now than in the past. Some companies have switched to offering 401(k) accounts instead.

401(k) and 403(b) Accounts

Some employees have the option to enroll in a 401(k) or 403(b) retirement account. A 401(k) account is for employees of private companies. A 403(b) account is for employees of non-profit organizations. Teachers, nurses, and ministers are examples of employees who might have a 403(b) account.

For both types of accounts, the employee puts in money each month through a payroll deduction. Often the employer matches the amount put in by the employee, up to a certain amount. Both accounts are tax deferred. This means that the employee does not pay tax on the money before it is contributed to the account. Instead, tax is paid on the money when it is drawn

Focus on BUSINESS

IRAs

Many companies and other organizations provide pension plans or other retirement accounts for employees. However, some people want to save money for retirement in addition to having an employer-sponsored plan. For this reason, banks, investment firms, and other financial institutions offer IRAs.

An IRA (individual retirement arrangement) account is a personal savings plan. It allows you to set aside money for retirement and has certain tax advantages. This is why you might want to have an IRA rather than simply keeping money in a savings account or buying stocks or bonds. Money placed in a traditional IRA and the money earned on the investment are generally not taxed until you draw out the money during retirement. To have a traditional IRA, you must be under age 70 1/2 and have taxable income, such as wages or salary.

A Roth IRA is another type of personal retirement plan. You can open a Roth IRA at any age. You cannot deduct money placed in a Roth IRA on your tax return. However, if you meet certain rules, the earnings on your investment are not subject to federal taxes. This means that generally you will not have to pay taxes on the money you withdraw during retirement.

Certain rules affect the amount that can be contributed to both a traditional IRA and a Roth IRA. There are also rules regarding withdrawing money and the type of investments that can be made. Details about IRAs can be found on the IRS website.

> What is an advantage of a traditional IRA? What is an advantage of a Roth IRA?

out during retirement. Employees choose investments for the money in the account that they think will help the account grow. Specific rules state how much employees and employers can contribute each year. There are also rules about the type of investments that can be made and how the money can be withdrawn. You can find more information about these accounts on the IRS website.

Other Benefits

You have read about some of the most common employee benefits. Other benefits that some employers offer are listed below.

- Paid training programs or seminars on topics related to the employee's work
- Tuition reimbursement programs for college courses
- Profit-sharing plans that pay employees based on company profits
- Employee discounts for purchases of goods or services from the company
- Childcare options at the workplace
- Exercise programs or rooms available for employees
- Cafeteria with reduced food prices
- Uniforms to wear during work

 CHECK POINT What type of retirement account is typically for employees of non-profit organizations?

Payroll Records

payroll a list of the amount of salary, wages, or other payments for work due to employees

A **payroll** is a list of the amount of salary, wages, or other payments for work due to employees. Payroll information must be accurate and should be kept confidential. The procedures used to handle the payroll vary depending on the size of the workforce. Common tasks related to handling a payroll include:

- Keeping employee payroll records up to date
- Calculating deductions and changes in salary, commissions, or overtime
- Updating attendance, vacation, and sick leave data
- Processing payments
- Creating tax reports related to payroll that must be submitted to local, state, and federal agencies

Some companies use time and attendance recording systems. Employees register their attendance at a computer terminal. Attendance data go directly into the company's payroll system. In other companies, this information is kept manually.

Deductions from Earnings

As you have learned, salaries and wages are quoted at their gross figures, which is before any deductions are considered. The earnings actually received will be less than the gross wages or salaries. Some payroll deductions are required by law. Others are voluntary as requested by the employee.

Deductions Required by Law

Federal income tax deductions are required by law. Each employee must complete an Employee's Withholding Allowance Certificate (Form W-4). An example Form W-4 is shown in Figure 7-2.1. The number of withholding allowances (also called exemptions) claimed affect the tax withheld. This form is kept on file by the company. The employee must

Figure 7-2.1 Employee's Withholding Allowance Certificate

---------- **Cut here and give Form W-4 to your employer. Keep the top part for your records.** ----------

Form **W-4** — Department of the Treasury, Internal Revenue Service

Employee's Withholding Allowance Certificate

▶ **Whether you are entitled to claim a certain number of allowances or exemption from withholding is subject to review by the IRS. Your employer may be required to send a copy of this form to the IRS.**

OMB No. 1545-0074 — **2011**

1 Type or print your first name and middle initial.	Last name	2 **Your social security number**
Jeffrey C.	Hunter	321 22 4697

Home address (number and street or rural route): 45 Elmwood Place

3 ☐ Single ☑ Married ☐ Married, but withhold at higher Single rate.
Note. If married, but legally separated, or spouse is a nonresident alien, check the "Single" box.

City or town, state, and ZIP code: Matawan, NJ 07747-6321

4 **If your last name differs from that shown on your social security card, check here. You must call 1-800-772-1213 for a replacement card.** ▶ ☐

5 Total number of allowances you are claiming (from line **H** above **or** from the applicable worksheet on page 2) . . . **5** 1

6 Additional amount, if any, you want withheld from each paycheck . . . **6** $ --0--

7 I claim exemption from withholding for 2011, and I certify that I meet **both** of the following conditions for exemption.
- Last year I had a right to a refund of **all** federal income tax withheld because I had **no** tax liability **and**
- This year I expect a refund of **all** federal income tax withheld because I expect to have **no** tax liability.

If you meet both conditions, write "Exempt" here . . . ▶ **7**

Under penalties of perjury, I declare that I have examined this certificate and to the best of my knowledge and belief, it is true, correct, and complete.

Employee's signature
(This form is not valid unless you sign it.) ▶ *Jeffrey C. Hunter* **Date** ▶ *July 5, 20- -*

8 Employer's name and address (Employer: Complete lines 8 and 10 only if sending to the IRS.)	9 Office code (optional)	10 Employer identification number (EIN)

For Privacy Act and Paperwork Reduction Act Notice, see page 2. Cat. No. 10220Q Form **W-4** (2011)

Source: U.S. Internal Revenue Service at http://www.irs.gov/pub/irs-pdf/fw4.pdf.

notify the company of any changes in the number of exemptions. The amount withheld also varies depending on the gross wages or salary and the employee's marital status.

Social Security is a social insurance program run by the U.S. government. Social Security benefits are paid when a person retires or becomes disabled. The program may also pay benefits to a surviving spouse or dependent of an insured person in the event of that person's death. The program is funded by payroll taxes.

Deductions for Social Security are a percentage of gross wages or salary, up to a set maximum amount. In 2011 the maximum amount taxed was $106,800. Employers must pay Social Security taxes for employees as well. For wages paid in 2011, employees paid 4.2 percent and employers paid 6.2 percent. The rate and the maximum amount taxed are sometimes changed. Social Security taxes are sometimes called FICA taxes. This is because the law that authorizes the taxes is the Federal Insurance Contributions Act (FICA). You can find the up-to-date percentages for deductions, the amount of earnings subject to Social Security taxes, and answers to questions on the Social Security Online website.

Medicare is a health insurance program run by the U.S. government and is for people age 65 or older. Certain younger people also qualify, such as those who have disabilities. The program pays for part of the cost of health care for those covered. The program is funded primarily by payroll taxes. In 2011, the Medicare tax rate was 1.45 percent for employees. Employers also paid the same rate. Currently, there is no limit on taxable earnings for Medicare taxes.

Most states and many local governments tax the earnings of citizens. These governments issue instructions regarding the taxes to be withheld. The tax rates and rules vary. The company should have this information on file. Deductions for federal income taxes, Social Security, and Medicare are shown on the payroll register in Figure 7-2.2 on page 258.

Arthur Tilley

Disabled persons may qualify for Social Security benefits.

Figure 7-2.2 Earnings Records and Payroll Register

EMPLOYEE EARNINGS RECORD

Employee: Jeffrey Hunter
Employee No.: 3415

SS No.: 321-22-4679
Marital Status: Married
No. Allowances: 1

Year Ending: December 31, 20--
Position: Data Entry Clerk
Yearly Salary: $25,292.00

Pay Period	Ended	Regular Pay	Total Gross Pay	Federal Income Tax	Social Security Tax	Medicare Tax	State Tax	Total Tax	Health Ins.	Net Pay	Gross Acc. Earnings
1	31-Jan	$2,166.00	$2,166.00	$324.90	$90.97	$31.41	$43.32	$490.60	$150.00	$1,525.40	$2,166.00
2	28-Feb	2,166.00	2,166.00	324.90	90.97	31.41	43.32	490.60	150.00	1,525.40	$4,332.00
3	31-Mar	2,166.00	2,166.00	324.90	90.97	31.41	43.32	490.60	150.00	1,525.40	$6,498.00
4	30-Apr	2,166.00	2,166.00	324.90	90.97	31.41	43.32	490.60	150.00	1,525.40	$8,664.00
5	31-May	2,166.00	2,166.00	324.90	90.97	31.41	43.32	490.60	150.00	1,525.40	$10,830.00
6	30-Jun	2,166.00	2,166.00	324.90	90.97	31.41	43.32	490.60	150.00	1,525.40	$12,996.00
7	31-Jul	2,166.00	2,166.00	324.90	90.97	31.41	43.32	490.60	150.00	1,525.40	$15,162.00
8	31-Aug	2,166.00	2,166.00	324.90	90.97	31.41	43.32	490.60	150.00	1,525.40	$17,328.00
9	30-Sep	2,166.00	2,166.00	324.90	90.97	31.41	43.32	490.60	150.00	1,525.40	$19,494.00
10	31-Oct	2,166.00	2,166.00	324.90	90.97	31.41	43.32	490.60	150.00	1,525.40	$21,660.00
11	30-Nov	2,166.00	2,166.00	324.90	90.97	31.41	43.32	490.60	150.00	1,525.40	$23,826.00
12	31-Dec	2,166.00	2,166.00	324.90	90.97	31.41	43.32	490.60	150.00	1,525.40	$25,992.00
		$25,992.00	$25,992.00	$3,898.80	$1,091.66	$376.88	$519.84	$5,887.19	$1,800.00	$18,304.81	

MODERN SOFTWARE INC.
Payroll Register
January 31, 20--

Employee No.	Employee Name	Regular Pay	Overtime Pay	Total Gross Pay	Federal Income Tax	Social Security Tax	Medicare Tax	State Tax	Total Tax	Health Ins.	Net Pay
4568	Acosta, B.	$2,150.00		$2,150.00	$322.50	$90.30	$31.18	$43.00	$486.98	$150.00	$1,513.03
4321	Beres, W.	1,088.00		1,088.00	163.20	45.70	15.78	21.76	246.43	150.00	691.57
3257	Cantrell, T.	2,840.00		2,840.00	426.00	119.28	41.18	56.80	643.26	75.00	2,121.74
3921	Evans, T.	2,010.00		2,010.00	301.50	84.42	29.15	40.20	455.27	75.00	1,479.74
3415	Hunter, J.	2,166.00		2,166.00	324.90	90.97	31.41	43.32	490.60	150.00	1,525.40
3401	Park, J.	3,455.00		3,455.00	518.25	145.11	50.10	69.10	782.56	150.00	2,522.44
4563	Stevens, B.	1,920.00	90.00	2,010.00	301.50	84.42	29.15	40.20	455.27	75.00	1,479.74

Voluntary Deductions

Voluntary deductions are amounts taken from pay at an employee's request. In some companies, employees may choose to have money deducted for health insurance, retirement plans, charitable donations, and other purposes. Employees who prepare the payroll must keep the records up to date for employees' individual deductions.

 CHECK POINT What are three types of deductions from payroll that are required by law?

Payroll Records

Companies maintain careful records of all payments made to employees. Employee earnings records are prepared for each pay period and for the year to date. The earnings records show earnings, deductions, and net pay. Many companies issue payroll checks that have an attached voucher showing similar information. An earnings record report and a payroll register are shown in Figure 7-2.2.

At the end of the year, the company should give each employee a Wage and Tax Statement (commonly called a W-2 form) for the calendar year. The information needed to prepare the W-2 form is found on the payroll register. This register records all the earnings and deductions for the payroll period. The company should make weekly, monthly, or quarterly reports to government agencies of taxes withheld and taxes the employer must pay. At certain times during the year, the company makes deposits of the amounts withheld and the taxes owed.

A company may distribute checks in person or mail them to employees. Other companies use direct deposit. That is, they electronically deposit wage and salary payments to employees' bank accounts. The company provides the employee with a document that details the deposit. In some companies, employees may choose their payment method.

net pay wages or salary after deductions for taxes and other items

 CHECK POINT What information is recorded in a payroll register?

21st Century Skills

Interacting with Others

PARTNERSHIP FOR
21ST CENTURY SKILLS

You work as an administrative assistant in a real estate firm. The company has seven real estate agents and a manager. The agents and the manager often express their appreciation for the good work you do at the firm. They go out to lunch together regularly and usually invite you to come along. Occasionally, they meet after work to have dinner and attend a concert or sports event. You are asked to take part in these activities also. The other employees make a lot more money than you do and do not seem to worry about the expense of eating out or the other activities. You want them to know that you appreciate their friendship, but you are worried about your budget.

1. Should you keep going out with the other employees even if you cannot really afford the cost? Why or why not?
2. What can you say or do in this situation to keep the goodwill of the other employees?

Making Academic Connections

Reinforcing Math Skills

You work for a small business. The company offers employees a 401(k) plan. The company matches employee contributions to the plan up to 3 percent of the employee's gross pay.

1. Find each employee's contribution to a 401(k) account by multiplying the employee's gross pay by the contribution percentage. Find the employer's matching contribution and the total contribution amount for each employee. The employees are listed by employee number.
2. Find the employer's total contribution for all employees.

		401(k) CONTRIBUTIONS			
		Period Ending February 14, 20--			
EMPLOYEE NO.	GROSS PAY	EMPLOYEE %	EMPLOYEE AMOUNT	EMPLOYER AMOUNT	TOTAL AMOUNT
4568	$2,150.00	3%			
4321	1,088.00	2%			
3257	2,840.00	5%			
3921	2,010.00	1%			
3415	2,166.00	2%			
3401	3,455.00	3%			
4563	1,920.00	4%			

7-2 Activity 1

Salary and Wage Plans (Outcome 7-2a)

1. Find the total gross pay for the three workers listed below. Overtime pay is 1.5 times the hourly rate for hours more than 37 per week.

EMPLOYEE NO.	HOURS WORKED	HOURLY RATE
2786	37	$9.50
2704	42	8.00
2954	40	12.50

2. An employee's gross yearly salary is $42,500. If the employee is paid monthly, how much will the gross pay be? If the employee is paid weekly, how much will the gross pay be?

3. An employee has a base salary of $24,000 per year. The employee also receives a 2 percent commission on sales over $10,000 per month. The employee is paid monthly. In March, the employee sold $15,750 in products. What will the employee's gross pay be for March?

4. The employee in question 3 was offered a change in salary plans to a straight salary (with no commission) of $30,000. For the month of March, how much more or less would the employee make under the new straight salary plan?

7-2 Activity 2

Employee Benefits (Outcome 7-2b)

In this activity, you will conduct an interview to learn about employee benefits.

1. Interview someone who is currently working and receives employee benefits. The interview may be conducted in person, by phone, or by e-mail.

2. Ask the employee you interview to describe the employee benefits she or he receives (without giving confidential information). Ask which benefits the employee finds most valuable and why.

3. Write a short report that includes the employee's job title, place of employment, and main job duties. Summarize the information you learned about the person's employee benefits and their importance.

Summary

7-1 Banking Procedures

- Cash is a valuable asset of a business. It must be safeguarded in all its forms. Internal control methods fall into three categories—preventive, detective, and corrective.

- Proving cash involves verifying the amount when a cash drawer is received and verifying that the proper amount of receipts is in the drawer when it is returned.

- Many companies receive checks that must be deposited in the company's bank account.

- An endorsement is a signature on the back of a check that authorizes the bank to cash or deposit the check.

- A check is a written order to a bank to make a payment using funds from the depositor's bank account. Checks may be handwritten, printed on a check form, or computer generated.

- Electronic funds transfer (EFT) is the use of a computer network to transfer funds from one party to another.

- A bank reconciliation is prepared to be sure that receipts and payments shown in the company records are also reflected in the bank's records.

7-2 Payroll and Employee Benefits

- Typical employee payment plans include salary, hourly wages, commission, and combination plans.

- Gross pay is wages or salary before any deductions. Net pay is wages or salary after deductions have been made for taxes and other items.

- Overtime is hours worked beyond the set standard hours per week. Workers are typically paid 1.5 or 2 times the hourly rate for overtime hours.

- Some workers' earnings are based on a percentage of the price of what they sell. This payment is called a commission. The employee may also have a base salary in combination with a commission.

- Typical employee benefits include paid time off, group insurance, and a retirement plan. Some companies also offer other benefits such as tuition reimbursement programs, employee discounts, and profit-sharing plans.

- A payroll is a list of the amount of salary, wages, or other payments for work due to employees.

- Deductions from payroll that are required by law include federal income taxes, Social Security taxes, and Medicare taxes. In some areas, state and/or local income taxes are also required deductions.

- Voluntary deductions are amounts taken from pay at an employee's request. These deductions may be for items such as health insurance, retirement plans, and charitable donations.

Chapter 7 Activity 1

Bank Statement Reconciliation
(Outcome 7-1c)

You work at Harcourt View Company in the Accounting Department. One of your duties is to reconcile the bank statement each month. On October 30, you received a bank statement dated October 25. Follow the steps below to prepare a bank statement reconciliation.

1. Use your spreadsheet software to prepare a bank reconciliation. Format the document and key appropriate headings as shown in Figure 7-1.7. Use *October 31* of the current year as the date.

2. The bank statement dated October 25 shows an ending balance of $4,452.03. The statement also shows a service charge of $15 for checks you ordered and received. Key these amounts in the appropriate places on your spreadsheet.

3. You have checked all the deposits and all the checks shown on the statement. You also have compared the returned canceled checks with your check register. Key the following information from your worksheet in the appropriate places on your spreadsheet:

   ■ The check register balance on October 31, before adjustment, is $3,560.58.

   ■ One deposit dated October 27 for $1,256.50 is in transit (outstanding).

   ■ The following checks are outstanding: #457 for $356.76, #481 for $125.00, #482 for $890.65, and #483 for $790.54.

4. Enter formulas to calculate the adjusted check register balance and the adjusted bank balance. These two amounts should be the same. If they are not, check to see that the numbers and formulas have been entered correctly.

Chapter 7 Activity 2

Payroll Register
(Outcome 7-2c)

You are an office employee in Furniture Galore, a retail store in a suburban mall. You have been given a schedule of salaries to use in preparing a payroll register for the pay period November 1-15. The information you will need appears below.

Pay Period: Employees are paid twice monthly, on the 15th and on the last day of the month. The pay date is two weeks after end of the pay period. This allows time for the sales amount for each salesperson to be finalized.

Commissions: Some of the employees are salespersons. Commissions for these employees are based on their net sales for the two-week period before the current pay date.

Taxes: Use 15 percent as the tax rate for federal income tax. Use 4.2 percent as the tax rate for Social Security. Use 1.45 percent as the tax rate for Medicare. Use 2 percent as the tax rate for state tax. (For purposes of this problem, use the same tax rate for all employees. In reality, the income tax and state tax rates might vary.)

Health Insurance: A deduction for health insurance is made from each paycheck. The deduction for single coverage is $80 per month. The deduction for family coverage is $160 per month. Your payroll register for each pay period should show a deduction for half of the monthly amount. Some employees decide not to participate in the health insurance plan and have no deduction for health insurance.

EMPLOYEE NO.	EMPLOYEE	MONTHLY SALARY	COMMISSION %	NET SALES NOV. 1–15	HEALTH INSURANCE
2782	Chase, Eric	$1,160	6%	$16,000	Single
2794	Hayward, Louise	1,160	6%	21,000	Family
2984	Dallas, Inell	1,625	None		Single
2986	Alvarez, Ricardo	1,500	None		Family
2999	Phillip, Michael	1,500	None		Single
3020	Flynn, Kizzi	2,875	None		Family
3025	Birin, Otto	1,400	None		Single
3148	Myers, James	1,160	6%	12,436	Single
3241	Saha, Eunice	1,300	6%	17,540	None
3249	Majia, Dora	1,200	6%	15,560	Single
3325	Pedro, Silvia	1,200	6%	10,500	Family
3354	Kramer, Elsie	1,200	None		None

1. Use spreadsheet software to create a payroll register similar to the one shown in Figure 7-2.2. The register is being prepared two weeks after the pay period ends and should be dated November 30 of the current year. Use the heading *Bonus Pay* rather than *Overtime Pay*.

2. Enter formulas to calculate:

   ■ The regular pay for the employees for the pay period. The regular pay is the monthly salary divided by two.

   ■ The bonus pay amount for employees who receive a commission.

   ■ The total gross pay.

   ■ The federal income, Social Security, Medicare, and state tax amounts.

   ■ The total tax amount.

3. Enter the health insurance deduction for each person.

4. Enter a formula to calculate the net pay for each person.

Payroll Accounting Event

The purpose of the event is to evaluate skills in processing payroll using manual procedures. You will be evaluated on skills and tasks such as computing gross pay, preparing a payroll register, posting employee records, and completing payroll tax forms.

After a few minutes for orientation, you will have 90 minutes to complete a test. You are allowed to bring a cordless calculator and certain reference materials.

Performance Indicators Evaluated

Participants will demonstrate skills related to the finance career cluster and the financial services pathway. Sample indicators include the ability to:

- Apply appropriate accounting principles to payroll and income taxation
- Complete new employee personnel forms
- Apply various methods used to determine gross earnings
- Explain the purpose of withholdings and other deductions
- Calculate employees' payroll taxes and other payroll deductions to determine net pay
- Create and maintain employee earnings records
- Calculate employer's payroll taxes as well as other employee benefits paid by the employer
- Prepare federal payroll reports
- Identify laws and regulations relating to payroll procedures
- Record in a journal and post transactions associated with payroll activities
- Generate payroll checks, prepare payroll tax deposits, and complete a payroll register

These performance indicators are from the Business Professionals of America guidelines as shown on their website. For more detailed information about this event, go to the BPA website.[1]

http://www.bpa.org

Think Critically

1. What kind of plans might be used to determine gross earnings in this event?
2. Which of the skills listed in the performance indicators do you have? Which ones would you like to learn or improve?

---

[1]"Business Professionals of America, Workplace Skills Assessment Program, Secondary 2011" (Business Professionals of America, 2011), http://www.bpa.org/download.aspx?dl=2011_WSAP_SECONDARY.pdf.

Early Childhood Development

Jobs in early childhood development relate to helping children learn and develop skills. The work setting may be in preschools, daycare centers, private homes, or after-school programs.

Employment Outlook

There are many jobs in early childhood development. The U.S. government provides job projections for 2008-2018. Jobs in this career area are expected to increase faster than the average for all jobs.[2]

Job Titles

- Preschool teacher
- Nanny
- Childcare assistant
- Daycare center director
- Teacher's aide
- Family resources educator

Needed Education/Skills

The education and skills needed in early childhood development jobs vary somewhat. Jobs as a teacher's aide or childcare assistant may require a high school diploma and some specialized training. Preschool teachers and center directors may need a college degree and related work experience. Some jobs require certification by a state agency.

What's it like to work in... Early Childhood Development?

Vicki works as the director of a family resource center. The center provides daycare and after-school programs for young children. It also offers classes for new or expecting parents and for childcare providers in the area. Vicki's degree in elementary education and several years' teaching experience in primary school helped prepare her for this position. She attends seminars to keep abreast of current information and regulations related to caring for young children.

Vicki's duties are varied. As director of the center, she plans the programs and activities for the center. She meets regularly with members of the center's advisory board to get input and feedback on issues related to the center. Vicki schedules work hours and supervises the teachers and aides who work at the center. She sometimes meets with parents to discuss a child's progress or other issues. Reporting on the center's activities and applying for grants are important parts of Vicki's job. Money received from grants allows the center to provide more services for the children. The center is open at least 10 hours per day, so Vicki's work hours vary. She typically works eight hours or more per day. Sometimes she works in the evening, conducting classes for new parents or helping with programs for the children. The part of her job that Vicki enjoys most is the time she spends with children. She finds helping the children learn new skills and watching them grow during the months or years they attend the center very rewarding.

What About You?

Does a job in early childhood development sound appealing to you? Would you rather work in a childcare center or as a nanny in a private home? Why?

[2]*Occupational Outlook Handbook*, 2010-11 Edition, Bureau of Labor Statistics, U.S. Department of Labor, http://www.bls.gov/oco/ocos317.htm.

Financial Reports and Procedures

8-1 Financial Reports

8-2 Financial Procedures

Jose Luis Pelaez Inc/Blend Images

Business owners and managers want to make more money than is spent in operating the business. The amount of money made in a given time and other important data are shown in financial statements. Nonprofit organizations also use these statements. You should understand the importance of financial statements to company employees, investors, and others.

Billing customers and making payments are routine tasks for company employees. However, it is very important that these tasks be done correctly and on time. You will learn about procedures for billing customers and making payments in this chapter.

Wire_man/Shutterstock.com

OUTCOMES

8-1a Describe procedures for preparing and monitoring a budget.
8-1b Apply procedures for creating and formatting financial reports.

fiscal year a period of 12 months used for accounting purposes

budget a detailed plan of expected income and expenses for a period of time

expense financial cost, fee, or charge

Budgets

Many companies develop plans to outline the direction in which the company wants to move. Strategic plans are long term in nature (from three to five years). These plans are usually developed by top managers. The plan may include decisions such as whether to introduce new products or expand into new markets.

Short-term plans are also needed. The success of a business rests largely on how well the resources of the business are managed. A plan is developed that shows how the business intends to use its resources, such as money, equipment, and personnel. The short-term plan is typically prepared for a fiscal year, which is a period of 12 months used for accounting purposes. Some companies prepare a plan for each quarter (three-month period).

A budget is a detailed plan or estimate of expected income and expenses for a period of time. Budgets are created to help ensure that the company is moving in the direction outlined in its strategic plan. In a small business, much of the budget planning and control is handled by the owner or manager. In a large business, many people may provide information for a budget. Preparing a budget for the coming months or year is a critical task. All employees are affected by the budget whether or not they actively take part in the budget process.

Preparing a Budget

To begin preparing a budget, workers review expenses from the past year. Financial reports also provide valuable information for creating a new budget. Procedures for preparing a budget will depend upon the size and nature of the business. In large businesses, many employees may help create a budget. Department managers and members may keep notes to help prepare a budget for the coming quarter or year.

Separate budgets may be created for completing specific projects. A particular type of expense, such as

Several people may be involved in preparing a budget for a department or company.

Konstantin Chagin/Shutterstock.com

supplies or travel, may also have a separate budget. In addition to a travel budget for a quarter or a year, you may be asked to prepare a budget for each business trip you will take. A sample business trip budget form is shown in Figure 8-1.1.

Figure 8-1.1 Microsoft Excel was used to create this budget for a business trip.

TRIP BUDGET						
Dates: October 4-7, 20--						
Destination: Columbus, Ohio						
Airfare	Total cost of tickets	$325.00	for	1	Round-trip ticket	$325.00
Hotel	Cost per night	125.00	for	3	nights	375.00
Food	Cost per day	50.00	for	4	days	200.00
Car rental	Cost per day	52.00	for	4	days	208.00
Gas	Cost per gallon	3.56	for	20	gallons	71.20
Parking	Cost per day	15.00	for	4	days	60.00
Entertainment	Amount	0.00				0.00
Meeting registration	Amount	250.00				250.00
Miscellaneous	Amount	25.00				25.00
					Total	$1,514.20

© Cengage Learning 2013

If you take part in planning budgets, these suggestions will be helpful to you:

- Learn all you can about the company's budget process. Study the forms used. Find out what data are needed and the deadlines for submitting data.

- Prepare a first draft of the budget as soon as the budget information and instructions are received. You will often receive some guidelines. For example, you might be told that every department budget must have a 10 percent decrease in expenses from the previous year. Use your financial records to help you determine what effect such guidelines will have on your department.

- Consider needs in relation to the company's priorities for the coming year. What new projects will your department handle that may require additional expenses? What improvements have been made that may lower expenses?

- Collect data to support your requests. This data might be costs for new equipment or a recommended salary for a new employee who is to be hired for the department.

- Be prepared to answer questions related to the data you helped prepare.

The company's overall goals and limited resources are considered in making a final budget for the company. Highlight or prepare a summary of the parts of the company budget that relate to your department or job. Be aware that the budget may be revised at some point during the budget period.

The budget provides a plan for how resources will be used. You or your department may have approval to spend for certain expenses up to the budgeted amount. In many companies, however, some expenses must be approved in advance even if they are included in a budget.

CHECK POINT What is the purpose of a budget?

Monitoring a Budget

A budget is generally a plan for a particular period of time, such as a fiscal year or one quarter of a year. Budgets for shorter periods are developed from the annual budget. As the budget period progresses, budget reports are prepared. These reports compare the money spent in each category to the budgeted amount. Budget reports are typically prepared monthly or quarterly.

If expenses in any category are too high, steps are usually taken to limit spending. In some cases, however, the budget amount might be increased. Circumstances may have changed in a way that makes the original budget amount unrealistic. For example, a delivery company may budget a certain amount for fuel costs for the delivery trucks. If fuel prices increase a great deal, the budget amount may not be enough to buy the fuel needed to keep the trucks running and the company operating. Cuts might be made in other areas to offset the increase needed for fuel expenses.

✳ WORKPLACE CONNECTIONS ✳

Johnson Company's budget included $15,000 for staff training for the year. More training than expected was needed to train employees to use the new order entry software. By August 1, $12,650 of the $15,000 budgeted amount had been spent. As a result, the manager, Anna Lui, changed the procedure for approving training. She issued a memo stating that all staff training for the remainder of the year must receive her prior approval as well as the usual approval from the department head.

Suppose you work for Johnson Company and want to attend a training seminar that is held each year in October. You know the company's training budget is often spent by August each year. What might you do in this situation?

A monthly or quarterly budget report is often combined with a year-to-date budget report. The year-to-date report shows the amount spent in each category from the beginning date for the budget to the date the report was prepared. An example of a budget report for Dan's Bakery is shown in Figure 8-1.2.

Combining both a monthly and a year-to-date report provides a better view of expenses as they relate to the entire budget time period. Some expenses, such as insurance or taxes, for example, may be paid quarterly. When the payment is made, the amount of the payment may be larger than the quarterly budgeted amount. Yet the payment may be within the total amount allotted annually.

Figure 8-1.2 **This report shows budgeted amounts and actual expenses.**

DAN'S BAKERY
OPERATING EXPENSES BUDGET REPORT
For the Month Ending June 30, 20--

June Actual	June Budget	Variance	Variance Percent	Item	Year-to-Date Actual	Year-to-Date Budget	Year-to-Date Variance	Variance Percent
$4,500	$4,500	0	0.0%	Salaries	$27,000	$27,000	0	0.0%
1,125	375	-750	-200.0%	Payroll Taxes	2,250	2,250	0	0.0%
45	42	-3	-7.1%	Advertising	245	250	5	2.0%
210	42	-168	-400.0%	Delivery	610	250	-360	-144.0%
60	67	7	10.4%	Office Supplies	395	400	5	1.3%
280	333	53	15.9%	Utilities	1,400	2,000	600	30.0%
350	350	0	0.0%	Depreciation	2,100	2,100	0	0.0%
35	42	7	16.7%	Miscellaneous	255	250	-5	-2.0%
$6,605	$5,751	-$854	-14.8%	Total Expenses	$34,255	$34,500	$245	0.7%

CHECK POINT What is the purpose of a monthly or quarterly budget report?

Financial Reports

Financial progress is reported using documents such as an income statement, a balance sheet, and a cash flow statement. Financial reports give information about a company's financial status. Investors and lenders use these reports to make judgments about the business. These reports can also show the results of operations. Some reports, such as budgets, are typically for internal use only. Others are provided to those outside the company. For example, corporations typically provide statements to shareholders for each quarter and the fiscal year.

Income Statements

An income statement is a report that shows the results of operations for a period of time. Revenues, expenses, and the net income or loss for the reporting period are shown. A projected income statement is often created as part of a company's plans. It lists the revenues (also called income) and expenses the company expects for the reporting period. A net income (profit) results if revenues are greater than expenses. A net loss results if expenses are greater than revenues. An income statement for Dan's Bakery is shown in Figure 8-1.3 on page 271.

Most businesses cannot continue to operate in the long term if they do not make a profit. Nonprofit organizations often seek to break even. They want to have enough income to pay expenses, but not a significant amount more than expenses.

Notice in Figure 8-1.3 that certain numbers are also shown as a percent of sales. Net income after taxes is 15 percent. (The calculation is $36,900 divided

revenue income, money, or other gain received

Figure 8-1.3 This income statement shows a net profit of 15 percent.

DAN'S BAKERY
INCOME STATEMENT
For the Year Ended December 31, 20--

			% of Sales
Sales		$250,000	
Cost of Goods Sold	125,000		
Gross Profit on Sales		$125,000	50%
Operating Expenses			
Advertising Expense	1,000		
Delivery Expense	1,500		
Office Supplies Expense	1,000		
Payroll Taxes Expense	4,100		
Salaries Expense	54,600		
Utilities Expense	3,800		
Depreciation Expense	4,000		
Miscellaneous Expense	500		
Total Operating Expense		70,500	
Net Income from Operations		$54,500	22%
Other Income and Expenses			
Interest Expense		3,000	
Net Income before Income Tax		$51,500	21%
Less Income Tax		14,600	
Net Income after Tax		$36,900	15%

by $250,000.) This means that 15 cents of every dollar in sales is what the business makes as profit. This figure is called the profit margin. Profit margins are one figure that investors often look at when comparing companies to select an investment. In general, the higher the profit margin, the more successful the business is. The business owner or manager can compare the company's profit margin for the current year to that of previous years. This shows whether the company is improving through growing sales or decreased expenses.

CHECK POINT What condition results in a net profit? a net loss?

Miguel is an office assistant to Dan Burts, the owner of Dan's Bakery. The company's cookies and baked goods are sold in several local supermarkets. Mr. Burts is planning to expand soon and sell his baked goods in nearby towns. One of Miguel's duties is to prepare both actual and projected financial statements. These statements will be used to present Mr. Burts' plan to the bank when he applies for a loan. The money received from the loan will be used to expand the business.

What are some additional expenses that the business may have if it expands to sell goods in nearby towns?

Balance Sheets

A balance sheet is a report that shows the condition of a company as of a specific date. It shows the assets, liabilities, and owner's equity on a certain date. A projected balance sheet is often created as part of a company's plans. This report shows the assets, liabilities, and owner's equity projected for the end of the plan period. The assets of a company include money and all the goods and property owned by the firm. Amounts due to the company from others, such as accounts receivable, are also assets. Liabilities are the debts the company owes, such as accounts payable. The owner's equity (also called capital) is the owner's share of the worth of the firm. This amount is the difference between assets and liabilities. On every balance sheet, the total assets must equal the total liabilities plus the owner's equity. A balance sheet for Dan's Bakery is shown in Figure 8-1.4 on page 274.

balance sheet a report that shows the financial condition of a company as of a specific date

assets money and goods or property owned

liabilities debts owed to others

owner's equity the owner's share of the worth of a firm

 CHECK POINT What three categories of data are shown on a balance sheet?

Cash Flow Statements

A cash flow statement is a document that shows incoming and outgoing cash for a given period. Keeping track of cash is important. The company needs to have enough cash on hand to pay employees and pay bills. However, company managers typically do not want to have more cash than is currently needed in an account that pays no interest. Businesses often have funds in a money market account with a bank. The bank pays the business interest on these funds. So the business owner or manager wants to keep just enough money in a checking account and the rest in a money market account or other short-term investment that will earn money for the business.

interest money earned on an investment or paid on money that is borrowed

Cash flow statements are typically created monthly or on an as-needed basis. A sample cash flow statement is shown in Figure 8-1.5 on page 275. Notice that the ending cash balance is the same as the cash balance on the balance sheet with the same date. The cash outflow items and amounts can vary by month. For example, some expenses, such as insurance, may not be paid every month.

 CHECK POINT Why is it important for a company to keep track of its cash balance?

Figure 8-1.4 **The balance sheet shows assets of $160,000.**

DAN'S BAKERY
BALANCE SHEET
December 31, 20--

Assets

Current Assets		
Cash	$43,500	
Accounts Receivable	5,000	
Baking Supplies Inventory	4,000	
Office Supplies	500	
Total Current Assets		$53,000
Fixed Assets		
Delivery Van	14,000	
Baking Equipment	8,000	
Building and Land	105,000	
Less Accumulated Depreciation	-20,000	
Total Fixed Assets		107,000
Total Assets		$160,000

Liabilities

Current Liabilities		
Notes Payable	$5,000	
Accounts Payable	1,500	
Salary and Wages Payable	500	
Total Current Liabilities		$7,000
Long-term Liabilities		
Long-term Note Payable	7,000	
Mortgage Payable	32,000	
Total Long-term Liabilities		39,000
Total Liabilities		$46,000

Owner's Equity

Dan Burts, Capital Beginning Balance		$82,100
Net Income for 20--	$36,900	
Less Withdrawal	5,000	
		$31,900
Dan Burts, Capital Ending Balance		$114,000
Total Liabilities and Owner's Equity		$160,000

Figure 8-1.5 A cash flow statement helps companies manage their cash accounts.

DAN'S BAKERY
CASH FLOW STATEMENT
For the Month Ended December 31, 20--

Cash Inflows		
Cash Collections	$17,000	
Credit Collections	3,500	
Investment Income	500	
Total Cash Inflows	$21,000	
Cash Outflows		
Advertising Expense	$300	
Delivery Expense	400	
Office Supplies Expense	150	
Payroll Taxes Expense	372	
Salaries Expense	4,850	
Utilities Expense	320	
Total Cash Outflows	$6,392	
Net Cash Flow		$14,608
Beginning Cash Balance		28,892
Ending Cash Balance		$43,500

© Cengage Learning 2013

Formatting Financial Documents

When you are asked to key financial documents, study earlier copies of these documents. If possible, use the same formats as in the previous documents. Continuing to use the same formats allows easier comparison of data from year to year. Guidelines for income statements and balance sheets may be included in a company's procedures manual.

Formats for financial statements and reports may vary. Follow the format guidelines below if no company standards are given.

- Leave at least a one-inch margin at the top and bottom and on both sides.
- Center the lines in the statement heading—company name, statement name, and the date(s) covered by the statement.
- Use a single line (bottom border) underneath the last figure to indicate addition or subtraction.
- Use double lines (double bottom border) underneath a final column total.
- Use the dollar sign with the first figure of each new column of figures to be added or subtracted or with every sum or difference if the figure is keyed directly underneath a single line.

Proofread the documents carefully, even if you have used a computer to prepare the statements. Give attention to detail. If another worker is available to help you, proofreading can be easier. One person can read aloud from the original document while the other person proofreads the prepared copy. In addition to the words and figures, the person reading aloud should indicate details such as punctuation, underscores, and dollar signs. Watch for transposed figures (for example, 1,245 for 1,254). As a final proof, check all totals. If you are using spreadsheet software to prepare the statement, check the accuracy of any formulas used in the statement.

 CHECK POINT When creating financial documents, what is the advantage of using the same formats as in the previous documents?

Working with a coworker makes proofreading financial documents easier.

peepo/iStockphoto

Focus on BUSINESS

E-commerce and Planning Strategies

"They can have any color they want, as long as it's black."
Attributed to pioneer automaker Henry Ford

E-commerce is changing the way businesses operate. It is creating a need for new planning strategies. Before e-commerce became established, most manufacturers used one of two basic business models. The models were either mass production or customized production. Strategies for both these business models have been well known and practiced for many years.

At the height of the Industrial Revolution, mass production allowed companies to lower costs by making large numbers of products that were exactly the same. For example, the early cars sold by Henry Ford were standard models. Customers were not able to choose many options for a car as car buyers can today. The lower costs were passed on to customers in the form of lower prices.

Using a customized product business model, a product is made according to a particular customer's needs or wishes. For example, a bridal gown might be designed and made in accordance with the bride's wishes. In the past, customized products were often expensive to make. Few people could afford customized products of good quality.

With the advent of e-commerce, many companies sell directly to customers via the Internet. E-commerce has made a third business model, mass customization, more widely used. In this model, many products are made to meet specific customers' needs. Customers enter their product order on the company's website. For example, a youth group leader orders 15 shirts printed with the youth group's name and logo. Although the company makes thousands of products each year, each one can be customized for a particular customer.

Companies can now offer the best of both worlds—customized products at reasonable prices. This business model requires creative strategies for planning and budgeting. Customers may have several choices when ordering products. Companies who use this business model often rely on market research to help them create forecasts for future sales and supply needs.

> Have you ordered a customized product from a retail store or using the Internet? Were you pleased with the product? Describe your experience.

REVIEW 8-1

21st Century Skills

PARTNERSHIP FOR
21ST CENTURY SKILLS

Thinking Critically

Financial statements provide valuable information to company managers and potential investors. Apply your understanding of financial statements to answer the following questions.

1. On Company A's income statement, the net income after tax is $150,000. This figure is 10 percent of sales. On Company B's income statement, the net income after tax is $75,000. This figure is 25 percent of sales. If you were considering buying stock in one of these two companies, which company would you choose? Why?

2. On Company C's balance sheet, the total liabilities are $250,000. The owner's equity is $500,000. On Company D's balance sheet, the total

liabilities are \$350,000. The owner's equity is \$250,000. Judging by these numbers alone, which company is more financially sound? Why?

3. During July, Company E decreased accounts receivable by \$10,000 and increased accounts payable by \$5,000. During July, Company F increased accounts receivable by \$4,000 and decreased accounts payable by \$5,000. For which company did receivables and payables have a positive effect on cash flow?

Making Academic Connections

Reinforcing Math Skills

You work as an employee in the Accounting Department at Mica Associates. You have been preparing an office supplies budget for the company. Complete the budget calculations as directed below.

1. Open the file 8-1 Math Skills found in the data files. This file contains a list of the office supplies items used by the company last year and the prices of the items last year.
2. Enter formulas to find the total amount for each item.
3. Enter a formula to find the sum of the Total Amount column.
4. You assume that you will purchase the same supplies this year and that the prices will be 5 percent higher than last year. Enter a formula to find the yearly budget total.
5. Enter a formula to find the quarterly budget amount (the yearly budget amount divided by four). Save this file for use in a later activity.

8-1 Activity 1

Monitoring a Budget (Outcome 8-1a)

In this activity, you will continue your work at Mica Associates. Assume this is the end of the second quarter of the year for which you prepared a supplies budget. You need to compare the amount you have spent for office supplies to the budgeted amounts for the first and second quarters.

1. In quarter 1, you spent \$766.28 for office supplies. In quarter 2, you spent \$902.45. Compare these amounts to the amounts budgeted for quarters 1 and 2 on the office supplies budget you created earlier. (Refer to the 8-1 Math Skills file that you edited earlier.)
2. For each quarter, are you over or under budget and by how much? For each quarter, what percent of the budgeted amount is the actual amount spent?
3. Report your findings in a memo:
   - Create a memo form with the appropriate headings.
   - Write the memo to the Accounting Department head, Freda Amosa.
   - Use the date *July 6, 20--* and an appropriate subject line.
4. In the memo, tell Freda whether or not the office supplies expenses for quarters 1 and 2 are with the budgeted amounts. Discuss the following:
   - The amount you had budgeted for office supplies for quarters 1 and 2 and the amounts you have actually spent
   - The amount you are over or under budget for each quarter
   - What percent of the budgeted amount the actual amount is for each quarter
   - Whether you are over or under budget for the two quarters combined

5. Create a bar graph to compare budgeted and actual amounts for office supplies for quarters 1 and 2. Copy the graph into your memo to illustrate the data.

6. Proofread carefully and correct all errors before printing the memo.

8-1 Activity 2

Projected Income Statements (Outcome 8-1b)

You are an office worker for Duncan's Auto Detailing. The owner, Mr. Leon Duncan, has asked you to create two projected income statements for next year based on two different levels of potential business.

1. Open the file 8-1 Activity 2 from the data files. This file contains last year's income statement for Duncan's Auto Detailing.

2. Make two copies of the last year income statement sheet in the workbook. Name the copies *Best Case* and *Worst Case*. Change the second line of the title of the Best Case and Worst Case sheets to *Projected Income Statement*. On the Best Case and Worst Case sheets, insert a row above the date and add the heading *Best Case* or *Worst Case*.

3. Make the changes Mr. Duncan projects for the best case as listed below:
   - Sales will increase 25 percent compared to last year.
   - Detailing labor will increase $20,000.
   - Supplies will increase 25 percent.
   - Advertising will increase $400.
   - Payroll taxes will increase $1,500.
   - Utilities will increase 25 percent.
   - Miscellaneous expense will stay the same.
   - Income tax expense will be at the same rate as last year. To find last year's rate, divide the income tax by the net income before tax on last year's sheet.

4. Make the changes Mr. Duncan projects for the worst case as listed below:
   - Sales will decrease 20 percent compared to last year.
   - Detailing labor will decrease $20,000.
   - Supplies will decrease 20 percent.
   - Payroll taxes will decrease $1,500.
   - Utilities will decrease 20 percent.
   - Miscellaneous expense will stay the same.
   - Income tax expense will be at the same rate as last year.

5. Format the Best Case and Worst Case sheets to print attractively on the page. Print copies of the sheets for the best-case and worst-case projections. What were the gross profit on sales percentages for the two alternatives? How much profit or loss after taxes will Mr. Duncan have under each alternative?

OUTCOMES

8-2a Describe procedures for billing customers.
8-2b Describe procedures for making payments.
8-2c Describe procedures for handling petty cash.

KEY TERMS

credit p. 280
sales invoice p. 280
discount p. 281
accounts payable p. 282
purchase order p. 282
credit memo p. 282
voucher p. 283
petty cash p. 286

credit permission to pay later for goods or services

sales invoice a document showing charges for goods or services provided to a customer

Billing Customers

Customers may pay for goods or services at the time the goods are received, or they may establish credit with the seller. The seller then bills the customer periodically for the goods or services. The request for payment is commonly in the form of a sales invoice or a statement of account.

Sales Invoices

Sales invoices are usually created at the time a company ships products or performs services for a customer. An invoice can be sent with the products. It can be left with the customer after a service is performed or mailed (electronically or in paper form) to the customer. Although some invoices are handwritten, many companies use invoices generated from computer records. A sample invoice is shown in Figure 8-2.1.

Figure 8-2.1 This sales invoice was prepared using computer software.

Invoice

Shred-Rite Shredder Company
2200 New Prussia Road
Delray Beach, FL 33445-5688
(561) 555-0124

Date	July 17, 20--
Invoice #:	SR 107206
Terms:	2/10, net 30
Ship Via:	UPS Ground

Bill To:
Levitz Office Supply
108 Wabashaw Court
Ferguson, KY 42502-4644

Ship To:
Same

Qty.	Stock #	Description	Unit Price	Total
10	SR100	Personal shredder with waste receptacle	$ 89.00	$ 890.00
10	SR200	Medium duty console shredder	399.00	3,990.00

Subtotal	$ 4,880.00
Shipping	130.00
Subtotal	$ 5,010.00
Sales tax	
Total	5,010.00
Payment Recd.	
Amount Due	**$ 5,010.00**

© Cengage Learning 2013

A sales invoice includes information such as the invoice date, quantities and prices of items purchased, and the invoice total. The invoice in Figure 8-2.1 shows payment terms of 2/10, net 30. This means that the customer may take a 2 percent discount from the invoice total if payment is made within 10 calendar days of the invoice date. If the discount is not taken, full payment is due within 30 days of the invoice date.

Verifying that the data on an invoice are correct is very important. A sales invoice documents a customer's legal obligation to pay for products or services received. In some cases, the information on an invoice may not agree with what a customer ordered or expected to receive. In this case, the customer has the right to delay payment until any questions are settled.

discount reduction in an amount paid or owed

> **CHECK POINT** What do the payment terms "2/10, net 30" mean?

Statement of Account

A statement of account is a listing of unpaid invoices as of a certain date, usually the end of a month. A sample statement of account is shown in Figure 8-2.2. Many businesses mail statements of account as a courtesy to their customers. The statement provides a routine reminder of the amounts owed. Customers can report errors if payments have not been recorded correctly. A business may prepare separate checks to pay for each invoice or one check to pay for several invoices from the same seller.

Figure 8-2.2 A statement of account lists invoice amounts for a period of time.

Statement of Account

Shred-Rite Shredder Company
2200 New Prussia Road
Delray Beach, FL 33445-5688
(561) 555-0124

Date: July 31, 20--
Customer No.: 5690
Terms: 2/10, net 30

Customer:
Levitz Office Supply
108 Wabashaw Court
Ferguson, KY 42502-4644

Invoice No.	Invoice Date	Invoice Total
SR 107005	July 2, 20--	$ 849.32
SR 107006	July 2, 20--	1,150.00
SR 107150	July 6, 20--	3,090.49
SR 107206	July 17, 20--	5,010.00
	Total Due	**$ 10,099.81**

© Cengage Learning 2013

A statement of account includes information such as the statement date and the seller's name and address. The customer's name and address, invoices, and the total amount due are also shown. The statement of account in Figure 8-2.2 shows four invoice amounts.

✓**CHECK POINT**   What is the purpose of a statement of account?

✳ WORKPLACE CONNECTIONS ✳

Paducah Builders, a company that builds houses, has several workers who pick up materials at a building supply store. When a worker picks up items at the store, he or she signs a form to show who picked up the items. The worker also receives an invoice for the items. This invoice is forwarded to the company's business office. The store sends a statement of account at the end of the month listing all the invoices. Paducah Builders pays all the invoices for the month with one check, which is more convenient than paying the invoices separately.

Why is it important that the worker who picks up items at the building supply store signs his or her name rather than just the company name?

Making Payments

accounts payable   short-term debts owed to others

In many firms, employees in accounts payable positions process payments. Accounts payable are the short-term debts the company owes to others. In a small business, one person may handle all the financial transactions, including receiving goods and making payments. If you make payments for your company, you will be involved in several related tasks. You will review purchase-related documents, prepare vouchers, and prepare checks.

Review Documents

Companies want to be sure that payments are only made for goods or services purchased and received. Employees should review all the documents related to each purchase. Several related documents may be generated with each purchase. The documents and their usefulness in making payments are as follows:

purchase order   a document that shows items ordered and to what address they should be shipped

- A purchase requisition shows the items requested and an approval to make the purchase. Note the signature on the form in Figure 8-2.3.
- A purchase order shows items ordered and to what address they should be shipped.
- A receiving report shows the goods that were actually received by the company.
- An invoice from a vendor shows what is owed for the purchases.

credit memo   a document that shows a reduction in the amount owed, such as for returned goods

- A credit memo shows a reduction in the amount owed. This reduction could be for returned goods, goods not received, or damaged goods.

Employees should check to see if all the appropriate documents are present for each purchase. The details on all of the documents should be the same. Payment should not be made until all documents are accounted for and agree with each other. If the forms do not agree but there is a reasonable explanation for the differences, payment can be made.

 CHECK POINT Why is it important that employees review all the documents related to each purchase before making payments?

Figure 8-2.3 A purchase requisition shows items requested for purchase.

Purchase Requisition

The Lampshade Store
426 Monroe Street
Cedar Falls, IA 50613-3467

Date: October 17, 20--

Vendor	Description	Qty.	Unit Price	Total
Shred-Rite Shredder Company 2200 New Prussia Road Delray Beach, FL 33445-5688	SR200 Medium duty console shredder	1	$ 399.00	$ 399.00

Project No.: _____

Account No.: _____

Purchase Approved
Harold Norton

Date
10/20/- -

© Cengage Learning 2013

Prepare Vouchers and Payments

In many offices a voucher system is used for payments. This system requires the preparation of a voucher before a check is written. A **voucher** is a document that shows the vendor name, invoice date, terms, and amount owed. The approved voucher serves as the approval to make the payment. Figure 8-2.4 on page 284 is an example of a voucher. If you have the responsibility for preparing vouchers, you should follow these general steps:

1. Check that all the documents related to the purchase are present. The documents may in paper or electronic form.
2. Prepare the voucher, checking every detail required on the form.
3. Obtain the authorized approval. This approval is often a handwritten or an electronic signature.
4. File the vouchers appropriately.

voucher a document that shows the vendor name, payment information, and an approval to make the payment

Tickler File

Vouchers typically are filed by the dates on which they must be processed in order to meet the payment due dates. Filing vouchers in this way creates a tickler file. This file is reviewed daily for the purpose of taking action to clear the items from the file. In companies where the policy is to take all discounts allowed, the voucher is filed in the tickler file by the discount date.

The terms on the voucher in Figure 8-2.4 are 2/10, net 30. If the invoice is paid within 10 days of the invoice date, a 2 percent discount can be taken from the invoice amount. If the invoice is paid after the 10th day and before the 30th day, the full amount of the invoice is paid. If payment is made after the 30th day, a late fee may be charged. Therefore, many businesses plan to pay their bills in time to take advantage of the discount and avoid being charged late fees.

Figure 8-2.4 **A voucher authorizes payment of an invoice.**

Checks

If you prepare checks to pay invoices, you should check the tickler file or other reminder system daily. Retrieve all vouchers for which checks are to be prepared. If you are creating a check in time to take advantage of a discount, compute the discount. The check should show the current date and the name of the company or individual to whom payment is to be made. The amount should appear correctly in words and numbers. The purpose of the payment may be shown on the memo line. If you are using accounting software or check writing software, verify that any information entered automatically is correct. Enter the data in the check register or verify data if it is entered automatically.

Some companies use voucher checks. Voucher checks are ordinary checks with an additional portion that gives a description of the payment. Figure 8-2.5

shows an example. The two parts are perforated so they can be separated easily. The voucher is detached before the check is deposited. The procedures for preparing voucher checks are the same as those for ordinary checks, except that you complete the voucher portion rather than merely indicating the purpose of the check on the memo line.

Figure 8-2.5 Voucher checks include a description of the payment.

The Lampshade Store				2267
Payee: Just Shades				

Check Date	Description	Gross Amount	Discount or Adjustment	Net Amount
10/25/--	Payment for Invoice No. 5479	$4,469.68	-0-	$4,469.68

The Lampshade Store   2267
426 Monroe Street   69-439
Cedar Falls, IA·50613-3467   October 25, 20 --   515

Pay to the
order of   Just Shades-- $ 4,469.68

Four thousand, four hundred sixty-nine and 68/100 ------------------------ **Dollars**

Memo Invoice No. 5479

⑆051504393⑆   3   8953   4⑈   0226

Voucher Check   **Authorized signature here**

© Cengage Learning 2013

Electronic Funds Transfer

As discussed in Chapter 7, payments can be made electronically rather than using paper checks. For example, electronic funds transfer (EFT) can be used to pay vendor invoices. Just as consumers can set up automatic payments from a bank account, so can businesses. If a company frequently buys supplies, parts, or other goods from a vendor, the company can authorize the bank to make electronic payments to the vendor. The payments can be set up to be paid by the discount date on an invoice or by the regular due date of the invoice. Companies must be careful to keep enough cash in the bank account to pay for these withdrawals. Many companies also use EFT for wage and salary payments to employees.

Whether paying with a paper check or using EFT, an employee should verify that all the documents related to the payment are in order and agree with the invoice. If using EFT, an employee should verify that the proper amount was paid to the vendor and that any applicable discounts were taken.

 CHECK POINT   How are payment vouchers typically filed?

Petty Cash

In many offices cash is needed occasionally to pay for small expenses, such as delivery services, postage due, and taxi fares. To handle such payments, departments are given a small sum of money called a petty cash fund. Amounts in such funds can range from $20 to as much as $1,000.

✶ WORKPLACE CONNECTIONS ✶

The sales office of a women's clothing manufacturing company has a petty cash fund of $500. The fund is used to provide money for lunch ordered at a local coffee shop for visiting buyers. Funds are also used for late dinners when staff members must work or to entertain buyers who come to view the new clothing samples. The fund is often used to pay for taxis and special delivery services. Kim Yao, the petty cashier, keeps careful records. She requires sales receipts and signed petty cash receipts for all payments made from the fund.

> Why is it important to ask the person who will receive the cash to sign the petty cash receipt?

Payment Records

Company managers decide how much money will be kept in the petty cash fund. Once this amount is approved by the manager responsible for payments, a check is written payable to the petty cashier, the person in charge of the petty cash fund. The petty cashier will cash the check and keep the cash in a locked cash box. Only the petty cashier has access to the key. In some organizations, petty cash funds are kept in a separate checking account. In others, a company credit card rather than cash is used to pay for various small expenses. However, the discussion here will be limited to a cash box system only.

Making Payments

The petty cashier should keep complete and accurate records for every payment made from the petty cash fund. Petty cash receipt forms are filled out each time cash is given out. A sample form is shown in Figure 8-2.6.

Figure 8-2.6 A petty cash receipt is issued with each payment.

	Petty Cash Receipt
Hardesty Security Systems	
892 Elm Grove Avenue	No: *48*
Somerset, KY 42503-0045	
Date: *November 17, 20- -*	
Amount: *$8.75*	
Eight and 75/100	
For: *Postage*	
	Received by
	Wanda Davis

© Cengage Learning 2013

The following procedure is commonly followed in offices:

1. Ask each person who seeks payment from the petty cash fund to submit a sales receipt that shows the item purchased and the price paid. Generally, payment should not be made without some kind of receipt. Occasionally, cash payments are made even though no sales receipt is provided. On such occasions, the employee should present a brief memo giving the amount spent and describing the item or service purchased.

2. Prepare a petty cash receipt for each payment. Ask the person who will receive the cash to sign the receipt. The receipt indicates the amount paid, to whom payment is made, and the purpose of the payment.

3. Attach the sales receipt or other document to the petty cash receipt and place these papers in the cash box.

Keeping a Record

In offices where many transactions require petty cash, a petty cash record may be kept for receipts and payments. Such a record is shown in Figure 8-2.7. Note the headings of the columns under which the payments are recorded. The column headings for your office may be different from the ones shown here. By recording payments as they are made, the task of preparing a report at the end of the month or when you need to add money to the fund will be simplified.

Petty cash records can be kept manually. Spreadsheet software can also be used to record petty cash transactions. In either case, attention to detail and entering all data accurately are critical when keeping petty cash records.

 CHECK POINT What information is typically shown on a petty cash record?

Figure 8-2.7 A petty cash record shows details of the money paid from the fund.

Petty Cash Record

Hardesty Security Systems
892 Elm Grove Avenue
Somerset, KY 42503-0045

Date: November 20, 20--

Date	Receipt No.	Balance	Books	Taxi	Office Supplies	Postage	Art Supplies	Misc.
1-Nov Beg. Bal.		$250.00						
6-Nov	39	237.05	12.95					
8-Nov	40	228.55		8.50				
8-Nov	41	220.85			7.70			
11-Nov	42	210.10				10.75		
17-Nov	43	203.65						6.45
19-Nov	44	184.90	18.75					
21-Nov	45	161.90		23.00				
22-Nov	46	150.40		11.50				
24-Nov	47	120.25					30.15	
25-Nov	48	108.80				11.45		
26-Nov	49	90.30			18.50			
29-Nov	50	78.20						12.10
30-Nov End. Bal.		78.20						
Item Totals			$31.70	$43.00	$26.20	$22.20	$30.15	$18.55

Money for a petty cash fund is kept in a lock box and used to reimburse employees for small expenses.

Replenishing the Fund

From time to time, money must be added to a petty cash fund. In some offices, the fund is replenished when a certain balance is reached. In others, the fund is restored to its original amount at the end of each month regardless of the level of funds. This procedure is commonly used in offices:

1. Count the money in the cash box and total the receipts in the petty cash box.

2. Compare the petty cash box total to the petty cash receipts total. They should be the same. If they are not, determine why there is a difference. Did you fail to include a receipt in your total? Did someone fail to turn in a receipt?

3. Add the amount of the petty cash receipts to the amount of petty cash remaining in the cash box. The total should equal the amount of petty cash you had when you last balanced and/or replenished the petty cash fund.

4. Investigate any differences. Careful attention to managing the petty cash fund will result in few, if any, errors. If, after your investigation, you find that you are over or short by a few pennies, note this difference on your petty cash record. For example, if in step 2 you found only $78.00 in cash and you should have $78.20, you would indicate on your petty cash record that the fund is short $0.20.

5. Prepare a voucher for a check for the amount needed to replenish the fund. Submit your petty cash record report, the receipts, and your check voucher for approval to your department head or other designated person.

6. Once approved, follow up by sending a copy of the report to the Accounting Department and by sending the voucher to the proper office.

7. Cash the check and immediately place the cash in the cash box.

 CHECK POINT When is a petty cash fund typically replenished?

REVIEW 8-2

21st Century Skills

Making Decisions

Assume that you are the cashier for the petty cash fund in your department. The fund is maintained at $1,000 because of the many small payments that must be made during the month. One Wednesday shortly after the fund had been replenished, Juan, one of your friends in the department, said to you: "I certainly didn't budget my money very well this week; I'm down to my last $5. You know that I'm dependable. Would you let me borrow $25 from the petty cash fund? You have almost $1,000 just lying there! If I had only $25, I'd be able to take care of my expenses until Friday, which is payday."

1. Would you lend your friend money from the petty cash fund? Why or why not?

2. What might be the consequences of making an unauthorized payment from the fund?

Making Academic Connections

Reinforcing English Skills

Reports and letters prepared by office workers often contain numbers. Write or key the sentences expressing the numbers in correct form.

1. 15 people attended the meeting.
2. The report identifies 5 departments that are over budget.
3. The package weighs two pounds 11 ounces.
4. The sales forecast for next year is 3,000,000 dollars.
5. Of the 15 companies, 7 sent executives to the training session.
6. 4 managers reported expenses totaling one thousand dollars.
7. You have been asked to purchase eighty reams of paper for use by three departments.
8. The new printer is ten inches tall and 17 inches wide.
9. The pens with red ink cost fifty cents each.
10. Last year we sold five hundred and twenty-five different types of products.

8-2 Activity 1

Sales Invoice (Outcomes 8-2a)

You work for Lemon Aides, a company that provides cleaning services for offices. Prepare an invoice for a customer using the information below.

1. Open the file 8-2 Activity 1 from the data files. This file contains an invoice form.

2. Complete the invoice using this information:
   - Customer: Dallas Associates, 4042 Cedar Springs Road, Dallas, TX 75219-7812
   - Invoice number: 2374
   - Date: June 2 of the current year
   - Terms: 2/10, net 30
   - Quantity: 2

- Plan: Office A
- Description: Regular office cleaning
- Unit price: $150.00

8-2 Activity 2

Petty Cash Record (Outcome 8-2c)

You work at Lawrence Industries, a small manufacturing company. You are responsible for handling the petty cash fund, along with other duties. The fund is replenished each month to the amount of $250. This is May 1 and you are ready to complete your petty cash report.

1. Use a spreadsheet program to prepare a petty cash record similar to the one shown in Figure 8-2.7. Use column heads appropriate for your company. The company address is 125 Fourth Street, Middlefield, OH 44062-1250.

2. The fund beginning balance on April 1 was $250. Key the data from the petty cash receipts in your cash box as shown below. Enter formulas to keep a running balance of the money remaining in the fund.

RECEIPT NO.	DATE	AMOUNT	ITEM
Beg. Bal.	April 1	$250.00	
156	April 2	14.90	Office Supplies
157	April 5	25.00	Food
158	April 5	13.00	Taxi
159	April 15	18.50	Office Supplies
160	April 18	42.67	Food
161	April 20	3.45	Miscellaneous
162	April 22	33.68	Food
163	April 25	11.30	Postage
164	April 26	7.42	Miscellaneous
165	April 28	12.98	Postage

3. Total the items columns of your petty cash record. Using the ending balance on your petty cash record, determine the amount needed to bring the fund to $250.

Summary

8-1 Financial Reports

- Many companies develop long-term strategic plans for their operation. Short-term plans are also created. A budget is a detailed plan or estimate of expected income and expenses for a period of time.
- As the budget period progresses, budget reports are prepared. These reports compare the money spent in each category to the budgeted amount.
- Financial progress is reported using documents such as an income statement, a balance sheet, and a cash flow statement.
- An income statement is a report that shows revenues, expenses, and net income or loss for the reporting period.
- A balance sheet is a report that shows the condition of a company. It shows the assets, liabilities, and owner's equity on a certain date.
- A cash flow statement is a document that shows incoming and outgoing cash for a given period.
- When you are asked to key financial documents, use the same formats as in the previous documents to aid in comparing statements.

8-2 Financial Procedures

- When customers establish credit with a seller, the seller bills the customer periodically for the goods or services purchased.
- A sales invoice shows charges for goods or services provided to a customer. An invoice may be sent to the customer in paper or electronic form.
- Discounts on the amount owed are often given to customers who pay invoices within a certain number of days.
- A statement of account is a listing of unpaid invoices as of a certain date, usually the end of a month.
- Employees should review all the documents related to each purchase before making a payment.
- In some companies, an approved voucher is required before a payment is made. Vouchers are often filed by date and paid in time to take advantage of discounts.
- Checks are prepared for payments on the appropriate dates or payment is made by electronic funds transfer.
- In some companies, a petty cash fund is used to make payments for small expenses. The payments must be authorized and tracked. The fund must be replenished as needed.

Chapter 8 Activity 1

Balance Sheet
(Outcome 8-1a)

You are the assistant to Catrina Cooper, the owner of Catrina's Crafts. The company sells hand-crafted items and craft supplies. Catrina also hosts craft parties at the company location or in customer's homes. Catrina has asked you to create a balance sheet for the company.

1. Open the file 8 Activity 1 found in the data files. The data is in rough format. Format the balance sheet similar to the one shown in Figure 8-1.4. Use appropriate headings, number formats, and rules under numbers as shown in the figure.

2. Enter the appropriate headings and date the balance sheet December 31 of the current year.

3. Enter formulas to find the total current assets, the total fixed assets, and the total assets.

4. Enter formulas to find the total current liabilities, long-term liabilities, and the total liabilities.

5. Enter a formula to subtract Catrina Cooper's withdrawals from the net income. Enter a formula to add the remaining income to the capital beginning balance.

6. Enter a formula to add the total liabilities and the capital ending balance to find total liabilities and owner's equity. This number should equal the total assets.

Chapter 8 Activity 2

Voucher and Check
(Outcome 8-2b)

In this activity, you will continue your work for Lawrence Industries. You need to prepare a voucher for approval and a check to replenish the petty cash fund.

1. Refer to Figure 8-2.4 for an example voucher form. Create a similar voucher form for Lawrence Industries.

2. Prepare voucher no. 4926. Use *May 1, 20--* as the date. Key *Petty Cashier* after Pay to. Key *5/1/--* in the Invoice Date column. Key *Petty Cash Fund* in the Invoice No. column. Key the amount for the check in the Gross Amount and Net Payable columns. Leave the Terms and Discount columns blank. Attach the petty cash record to the voucher as a supporting document.

3. Assume you submitted the voucher and petty cash record to the person authorized to approve payments. The voucher has been signed to approve payment, and the records have been returned to you.

4. Prepare a check for payment of the voucher. Open and print the file 8 Activity 2 from the data files. This file contains a blank check form and a check register. Write the check using *May 1, 20--* as the check date. Make the check payable to *Petty Cashier* for the amount shown on the voucher.

Write *Voucher 4926* on the memo line. Leave the signature line blank to be signed by an authorized person.

5. Go to the sheet named Check Register in the data file. This file contains a section of the company's check register. Post the check information to the check register. Copy down the formula in the last column to update the balance forward amount. Print the updated check register page. Once the check is signed, you would cash the check and place the money in the cash box.

Automotive Services Marketing Event

In this competitive event, you will be judged on your skills and knowledge in the area of automotive services marketing. You will evaluate business situations related to service stations, auto parts stores, or related businesses. You will identify possible problems and recommend courses of action.

The event includes a written test and two role-playing situations. Finalists in the events will have a third role-playing situation. No reference materials are allowed. You may make notes to use during the role-play during the time when you read the role-play description and prepare for the event.

Performance Indicators Evaluated

Participants will demonstrate skills related to the marketing cluster and marketing management pathway. Sample performance indicators include:

- Develop a project plan
- Identify routine activities for maintaining business facilities and equipment
- Investigate the use of visual merchandising
- Explain the relationship between customer service and distribution
- Explain the selling process

The following indicators are in addition to the specific ones listed above

- Communication (writing, speaking, reading, or listening)
- Analyzing data to form conclusions and recommendations
- Critical thinking and problem solving
- Setting priorities and managing time

For more detailed information about this event, go to the DECA website.[1]

http://www.deca.org

Think Critically

1. What does the term *visual merchandising* mean?
2. What are some other businesses that are considered part of the automotive services group?

---

[1]1DECA, "High School Competitive Events Guidelines" (DECA, 2011), http://www.deca.org/competitions/highschool.

Businesses and other organizations keep financial records to measure the success of the organization and for tax purposes. They also need to share information with stockholders and potential investors. Employees who work in accounting create and manage these records. They also analyze financial data and offer advice on investments, tax strategies, and other issues. Jobs in accounting are found in private companies or organizations and in government agencies. Some accountants have their own small businesses and do accounting for individuals or other companies.

Employment Outlook

There are many jobs in accounting. The U.S. government provides job projections for 2008-2018. Some jobs in this career area are expected to increase as fast as the average for all jobs. Others are expected to increase faster than average for all jobs.[2]

Job Titles

- Accounts payable associate
- Accounts receivable associate
- Auditor
- Budget analyst
- Certified public accountant
- Controller
- Cost accountant
- Forensic accountant
- Payroll clerk
- Tax accountant

Needed Education/Skills

Jobs in accounting require strong math skills and the ability to pay careful attention to details. Computer skills are also important. Some jobs, such as accounts payable associate, may require training at a technical or community college for a certificate or associate's degree. Many jobs in accounting require a bachelor's degree in accounting or other business area. Some jobs, such as certified public accountant, require licensing by a state board. Candidates must pass a rigorous exam, and work experience may be required in some states.

What's it like to work in . . . Accounting?

Paul works as an accounts payable associate at a manufacturing company. He has an associate's degree in accounting. His work experience as an intern while completing school also helped prepare Paul for this position.

Paul's duties are related to processing payments for the company and keeping the related records. He sorts and matches invoices and check requests. He prepares accounts payable checks and processes electronic payments. Using automated accounting software, Paul enters or updates vendor information and posts payment transactions. He monitors accounts to see that payments are made on time and answers inquiries from vendors regarding payments. He also prepares monthly reports related to payments.

Paul appreciates working in a quiet office environment and seldom having to work overtime. He understands the importance of keeping financial data confidential. He enjoys keeping all the paper and electronic records in order and following up on the details that lead to success in his job position.

What About You?

Does a job that requires working with computers and being very detail-oriented appeal to you? What skills other than the ones mentioned here would be helpful to a person in this career?

---

[2]*Occupational Outlook Handbook*, 2010-11 Edition, Bureau of Labor Statistics, U.S. Department of Labor, http://www.bls.gov/oco/ocos001.htm.

Managing Your Work Life

Vadym Andrushchenko/Shutterstock.com

As an office worker, you need to use effectively the resources that support your work activities. These resources include time, reference sources, office supplies and equipment, and paper and electronic records. You need to take part in meetings with coworkers, make travel arrangements for yourself and others, and process mail. You also need to be aware of the critical concerns for office health, safety, and security that affect all office workers. You will build skills in these important areas as you study this part.

Dmitriy Shironosov/Shutterstock.com

Time and Workstation Management

9-1 Managing Your Time

9-2 Workstation Management and Office Safety

Colin Young-Wolff/PhotoEdit

H ow you manage your actions in relation to time is important. The term *time management* refers to this process. Managing the resources used in your work is as important as managing your time wisely. Arranging furniture and equipment in your work area properly can increase your productivity. It can also make your workplace safer.

In this chapter, you will learn to use your time in a productive way. You will learn about safety and security concerns that affect office workers. You also will learn about how factors such as lighting, office equipment, and furniture affect how you feel in the office environment.

Wire_man/Shutterstock.com

9-1 Managing Your Time

OUTCOMES

9-1a Apply procedures for managing your time.
9-1b Apply procedures for managing your work.
9-1c Describe reminder systems.

KEY TERMS

time management p. 298
interruption p. 298
procrastinate p. 299
analyze p. 299
PIM program p. 302
prioritize p. 302
chronologically p. 306
recurring p. 309

time management managing your actions in relation to time

Manage Your Time

Time management is the process of planning your activities to gain better control over how you spend your time. Managing your time effectively is critical to your success on the job. You will want to learn how to eliminate time-wasters and handle tasks efficiently. Analyzing how you spend your time will increase your effectiveness in managing your work. One of the first steps in learning how to use your time is to recognize how it can be wasted.

Common Time-Wasters

Not all time spent at work is productive. You can waste time without realizing it. Some common time-wasters, along with suggestions for overcoming them, are discussed in the following paragraphs.

Unnecessary Telephone Conversations

The telephone can be either a time-saver or a time-waster, depending on how you use it. Often, a telephone call that could save time wastes time instead. For example, suppose an office worker takes 10 minutes to verify price information by telephone. In the same call, the worker takes five minutes to discuss the latest episode of a favorite television program. A conversation that began productively ends by wasting time. If this happens two or three times a day, the time wasted can add up rapidly.

Frequent Interruptions

interruption a person, sound, or event that distracts you or stops you from doing an activity

An **interruption** is a person, sound, or event that stops you from completing work. Interruptions to your work can come from many sources. Unplanned visits or questions from coworkers or customers, phone calls, and delays in receiving work or material from others are common ones. On the surface, each of these events may appear to be a time-waster. Remember, however, that working with coworkers and customers is an important part of most jobs. Questions from coworkers and customers that relate to your work are not time-wasters.

Excessive Socializing

Some socializing will help you keep good working relations with your coworkers. Too much socializing, however, is a misuse of company time. Some workers may socialize excessively. You will be wise to avoid engaging in long conversations with them. When a coworker tries to involve you in idle conversation, offer a simple response such as: "I really must get back to work. Maybe we could discuss this at lunch." You will maintain good working relations while excusing yourself to continue your work. If you are consistent in your responses, the coworker will soon learn that you are not easily distracted from your work. Be careful also to limit your lunch and breaks to the planned or approved times.

Socialize with coworkers at appropriate times, such as at lunch or during breaks.

Ineffective Communication

As an office worker, you will receive information in both written and oral form from customers and coworkers. You also will give information in written and oral form to others. If the information that is given or received by you is inaccurate or incomplete, lost time and money can be the result of the poor communication. Be certain the information you give others is specific and accurate. Ask for feedback from those to whom you give information to be sure your message is clear and complete. Likewise, be sure that you understand any instructions or information you receive. Ask questions to verify data and gain all the needed information.

Disorganization

Being disorganized can be a major time-waster. Searching for the paper you just had in your hands, forgetting important deadlines, and shifting unnecessarily from one project to another are all signs of a disorganized person. Take the time to organize your work area and prepare a daily plan for your work. Think through and plan complicated jobs before starting them. Group similar tasks together. Avoid jumping from one project to another before finishing the first one. Do not procrastinate. If unpleasant or difficult tasks are needlessly delayed, they can become problems later.

procrastinate   put off, delay intentionally

 CHECK POINT   What are some common time-wasters for office workers?

Time Analysis Procedures

Time is a valuable resource that should be used wisely; it cannot be replaced. You have learned about common ways time can be wasted. One of the smartest things you can do is to analyze how you spend your time on the job. Time analysis aids in determining how effectively your time is used. By keeping a written account of what you do, you can determine whether you are using your time effectively. With this information, you can then develop a plan of action to correct or redirect the use of your time.

analyze   study to determine parts, qualities, operations, or relationships

Keep a Time Log

Start a time analysis by keeping a written record of what you do and how much time is used. Record all activities in a time-use log. Note tasks accepted and completed. Record telephone calls, meetings, discussions, receiving and responding to e-mail messages or other correspondence, and so forth.

You may choose to keep a time-use log for a day, for several days, or even a week. The longer you keep the log, the more representative it will be of how your time is spent. A partial time-use log is shown in Figure 9-1.1.

Figure 9-1.1 A time-use log will help you see how effectively you spend your time.

Time-Use Log

Name __Michele Fitch__

Time	Monday	Tuesday	Wednesday	Thursday	Friday
8:45 a.m.	Arrived early Opened office	Arrived early Opened office	Arrived early Opened office	Arrived early Opened office	Arrived early Opened office
9:00 a.m.	Checked calendar and task list	Checked calendar and task list	Checked calendar and task list	Checked calendar and task list	Checked calendar and task list
9:15 a.m.	Met with supervisor	Met with supervisor	Keyed report	Met with supervisor	Met with supervisor
9:30 a.m.	Wrote report	Composed letter		Organized trip folder	Wrote e-mail to staff
9:45 a.m.		Took notes at meeting		Keyed new expense report form	Made copies
10:00 a.m.					
10:15 a.m.			Coffee break	Phone calls	Coffee break
10:30 a.m.	Coffee break		Keyed supplies requisition form	Coffee break	Meeting with Nancy
10:45 a.m.	Phone calls	Sorted and opened mail	Sorted and opened mail	Sorted and opened mail	Filing

Analyze How You Spend Your Time

When you have completed your time-use log, you are ready to analyze the results. By studying your time-use patterns, you will be able to spot problem areas quickly. Be alert to the following points as you review the log:

■ During what time of the day was I most productive? Least productive? Why?

- How did I lose (or waste) my time? Was it because of unnecessary interruptions, visitors/socializing, crises, telephone calls? Who and what was involved in each case?

- Does a pattern emerge that might show the times when most interruptions occur? Does a pattern indicate that more time is needed to handle crises or emergency tasks that may arise? Do I need more time to complete specific tasks?

- Do I think I have used my time wisely?

Develop a Plan of Action

After you have analyzed how you spend your time, determine how well the tasks you complete contribute to meeting your work goals. Look at each activity you have listed in your time-use log. Ask yourself whether that activity helped you complete your work. If not, develop a different approach to your work that will increase the effective use of your time.

✓ CHECK POINT What is the purpose of keeping a time-use log?

Manage Your Work

Using time efficiently requires developing an organized approach to your work. Calendars and time-management systems can help you identify busy and slow work periods. Once you know when to expect such periods, you can plan your work to allow for more productive use of your time and a more even workload. To accommodate a busy or peak period, think ahead to identify jobs that could be completed in advance. Then the peak period will not place undue pressure on you. Planning for the slow periods is equally important. During these times, you can catch up on those tasks that do not have deadlines, but nevertheless must be done.

Plan Your Work Activities

Planning your daily work activities will help you avoid forgetting tasks that need to be completed. Take 5 or 10 minutes either at the beginning or the

Take time to plan your tasks at the beginning of the day.

Elena Elisseeva/Shutterstock

close of the workday to plan the coming day's work. Prepare a tasks list or update an ongoing list and complete the tasks according to their order of importance or to meet deadlines. Keep the list at hand as you work. Check it frequently. This list should guide you through your daily activities. When a task is completed, indicate this on the list. Tasks not completed can be carried over to the next day's list. Be alert, however, to any item that seems to be carried over too many times. Perhaps it should be broken down into smaller segments. Perhaps you are procrastinating in completing the task.

Your task list can be a simple handwritten or keyed list. If you have the software available, your list may be created using a calendar program or PIM program. These programs allow you to manage appointments and schedule tasks as well as other functions. Figure 9-1.2 shows a tasks list from Microsoft Outlook.

PIM program personal information management software for managing appointments, contacts, and tasks

Figure 9-1.2 **This tasks list shows work to be completed by category.**

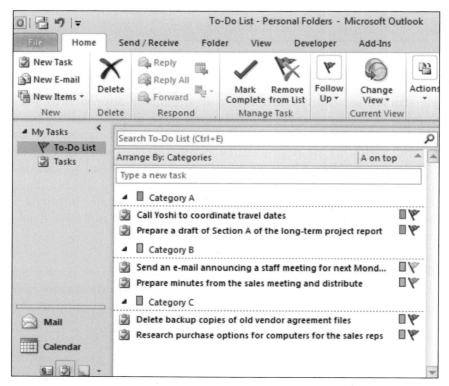

Setting Priorities

prioritize rank in order of importance or urgency

Once you have identified tasks for the day, prioritize them. Rank the tasks on your tasks list and complete the most important ones first. To determine the priority of the tasks, ask yourself these questions:

- How much time will the task require?
- By what date (time) should the task be completed?
- Are others involved in completing the task?
- What will happen if this task is not completed on time?
- Do I have all the information (or materials) I need to complete the task?

At times you may need to discuss your priorities with coworkers or a supervisor. You need to be certain that you agree on the order for doing tasks. Once you set your priorities, finish the tasks in their priority order. Remain flexible, however, about revising your priorities as circumstances change.

A tasks list is shown in Figure 9-1.2. Notice that the tasks are identified as Category A, B, or C. The A-level tasks need immediate attention or completion. B-level tasks can be done once the A-level tasks have been completed. C-level tasks have no specific deadline but can be done when the A and B tasks have been completed. If the item is a long-term project, the portion of the task that should be finished that day is listed.

Completing Large Projects

Sometimes, getting started on a large project is difficult even though it may be very important. Smaller tasks can be checked off your task list with ease; a large task may seem overwhelming. Do not let the size of a project keep you from getting organized and moving toward completion of the task. Follow these suggestions for handling a large project:

- Break the large project into smaller tasks.
- Determine the steps to be taken in each of the smaller tasks.
- Establish deadlines for each section or smaller task and meet those deadlines.
- Look for ways to improve your procedures and simplify the completion of the project.
- If the large project is one that will be repeated periodically, record your procedures for later use. Note suggestions you want to follow in the future for improvements.

Project management programs are available to help users schedule and manage large projects. These programs may be accessed in the cloud (Internet) or reside on your computer. Some of the programs are very detailed. They offer features for scheduling personnel and other resources and assigning project costs. However, you can also use a simple program, such as Microsoft Outlook, to schedule tasks for a project. Figure 9-1.3 shows a schedule for conducting research and analyzing data for a presentation. Time for writing the presentation and creating visual aids is also included.

Figure 9-1.3 **The calendar feature of Microsoft Outlook can be used to schedule tasks for a project.**

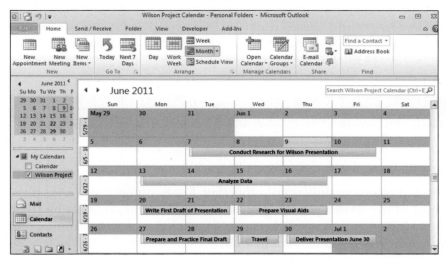

Simplify Your Work

Work simplification is the process of improving the procedures for getting work done. The process often involves simplifying some steps and eliminating others. Your goal is to use the most efficient procedure for completing a task. As you complete a task, be aware of the steps you are completing. Eliminate any unnecessary steps and/or details. Consider alternative methods for completing the task. Are those methods more efficient than those you are using? Look at the task and your procedures objectively to find ways to improve your productivity.

Analyze the Workflow

Consider the information and work assignments you receive and those you forward to others. Ask yourself these questions to help you analyze the workflow:

- Does the flow of work to my desk make good use of my time and effort? Of everyone's time and effort?
- Does the flow of work provide the right information to customers or others outside the company in a timely fashion?
- Are the materials and equipment needed to complete my work readily at hand or nearby?
- Am I using the features of my office equipment and software to their fullest extent?

Your answers to these questions should provide clues to simplifying your work.

✳ WORKPLACE CONNECTIONS ✳

Juan uses the address book feature of his personal information management software to store names, addresses, and work, fax, and cell telephone numbers. He also stores e-mail addresses and specific notes about the clients and coworkers he contacts on a regular basis. Juan's e-mail, word processing, and database programs can access information from the address book. This process reduces the time needed to create letters because he does not have to rekey the information. For example, when Juan wants to send a letter to all his clients, he can use his address book as the data source for names and addresses for a form letter.

What feature of Microsoft Word might Juan use to create personalized letters for names from an address book?

Incorporate these suggestions into your workflow analysis:

- Group and complete similar tasks together. For example, if you need photocopies of the letters you are preparing, make them all at once rather than making several trips to the copier. If you have several related phone calls to make, try to make them in sequence.

- Combine tasks if doing so will increase your efficiency. For example, suppose you plan to leave a request at the records center for a series of files you need to complete a report. If the records center is near the company cafeteria, stop by the records center on your way to lunch.

- Determine how to best organize and arrange the equipment and supplies you use to complete a task. For example, do you cross a room every few minutes to retrieve pages from a printer? If yes, perhaps you can change the placement of the equipment to provide a smoother flow of work.

- Enlist the help of others when you have an important deadline to meet and the workload is overwhelming. Be sure to help other workers when the roles are reversed.

Martin Novak/Shutterstock

Arrange printers and other equipment to promote a smooth workflow.

Handle Information Overload

When the amount of information you receive on a daily basis becomes overwhelming, you are experiencing information overload. You need to provide and receive information in a timely manner. You will save time (for you and others) by trying to handle each message, file, or paper just once. Take any needed action immediately if that is appropriate. Otherwise, add the task to your tasks list for completion at the proper time. In this way, the amount of information you receive will not become overwhelming. A good rule of thumb is to make a decision about how to handle every message, piece of paper, or file the first time you view it.

 CHECK POINT What is work simplification? Why should you practice work simplification?

Reminder Systems

As an office worker, you must keep track of appointments, meetings, travel dates, and deadlines. Perhaps the most widely used device for keeping track of such items is a calendar. A reminder file, arranged chronologically, also can be helpful. This file can provide a convenient place to keep notes about tasks to be performed on specific dates.

Manual Systems

A well-maintained desk calendar can assist you in keeping track of the many tasks and deadlines in your job. It can also be helpful to others who may have access to it. It can be used to record appointments, deadlines, meetings, or other important data.

Personal planners, also called day planners or organizers, are popular with many people. These small notebooks contain a calendar and space for recording appointments. Tasks lists, notes, and contacts can also be recorded. Many businesspeople find these manual aids very helpful in organizing tasks and schedules.

Wall calendars also are useful when large projects or those involving a number of people are broken into various small tasks with many deadlines. By displaying the wall calendar, you and others can keep track of deadlines.

 CHECK POINT Why do you think some people prefer to use manual reminder systems rather than electronic systems?

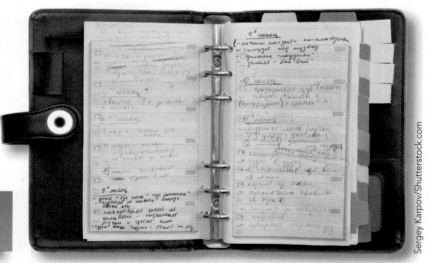

Manual information systems can help users plan and organize tasks.

Sergey Karpov/Shutterstock.com

Electronic Systems

Calendar and personal information management (PIM) programs have various features. They can be used to keep track of project deadlines, appointments, and work schedules. These programs often include task lists. For each task, related notes, deadlines, and completion dates can be entered. PIM programs usually include an address book where you can record contact information for coworkers, clients, and other people or companies. Reminders

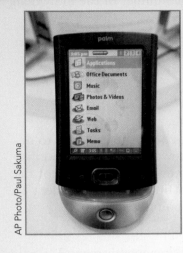

AP Photo/Paul Sakuma

For people who want an electronic reminder system that is portable, a PDA is good tool. A PDA (personal digital assistant) is a handheld computer. Programs can be loaded onto a PDA to do a variety of tasks. PDAs usually come with programs for storing contact data, scheduling appointments, and creating task lists. Other typical tasks a user can do with a PDA include:

- Use handwritten input
- Access and send e-mail messages
- Work with programs such as word processors or spreadsheets
- Do calculations such as currency conversions
- Upload data to or download data from desktop or laptop computers
- Record notes of telephone calls
- Recognize schedule conflicts
- Sound alarms as reminders of meetings or deadlines
- Search the Internet

Some PDAs can share data with calendar or PIM programs on a desktop computer. Sharing data allows the user to coordinate schedules easily. Some devices, called smartphones, combine the features of a PDA and a mobile phone. You can review the information you learned about smartphones in Chapter 6.

Why might be an advantage of having a PDA that allows handwritten input?

(similar to those used in a paper tickler file) can be recorded on a computer using a PIM or database program. Some programs sound an alarm to remind users of specific tasks or deadlines.

As soon as you become aware of a deadline or a detail that needs to be checked in the future, place a reminder under the relevant day. For example, assume your employer says to you, "Please call the Morgan Company on Monday. Make an appointment for us to discuss our purchasing contract with them." You would prepare a reminder to make the phone call and record it under next Monday's date.

 CHECK POINT What are some typical features of a PIM program?

Scheduling Appointments

Typically, you will have your own calendar to maintain. You also may make appointments and schedule meetings for coworkers. People request appointments in different ways. The request may be made in person, by telephone, by letter or memo, by e-mail, or via an automated calendar program. Although the manner in which you respond to these requests may vary, the basic categories of information you need will be the same:

- **Who:** Name, e-mail address, and telephone number of the individual requesting the appointment
- **When:** Date, time, and approximate length of appointment
- **Where:** Location of the appointment
- **Why:** Purpose of the meeting

Responding to Appointment Requests

When you receive a request for an appointment, check the calendar to determine whether the date and time requested are available. If not, you may suggest other appointment dates and times. By knowing the purpose of the meeting, you can determine and provide all supporting materials needed. To maintain a calendar properly, clarify the following points:

- To what extent do you have authority to make appointments for others?
- When should you check with others before making appointments?
- At what regular times are appointments not to be made, such as the first half-hour of the day?
- To what extent will the manager or coworkers make appointments without checking with you?
- Does the person for whom the appointment is made want to know the purpose of each appointment you schedule?

The authority you have to make appointments will depend in great part on the nature of your job. For example, if you work in a doctor's office, most of the appointment requests would be from patients. You would be expected to schedule appointments without having to verify each one with the doctor. On the other hand, you may work in a general office where both you and your coworkers make appointments. You must agree on procedures that will allow you to operate effectively.

You may use a calendar program for your individual schedule or to set up group activities. An electronic calendar on a computer network often can be updated by everyone using the calendar. Changes made are shown instantly and may be viewed by anyone using the calendar.

✳ WORKPLACE CONNECTIONS ✳

Dewanda needs to schedule a meeting with six other people. She can access a program on the company's computer network to check the schedules of the six people for times available for the meeting. She can either check all of the schedules herself or enter the names of the people she wants to attend the meeting and a general time frame. The program then will look at everyone's schedule and find a meeting time. Depending on the program available to her, she also might be able to schedule a meeting room.

What could Dewanda do if the program indicates that there is no time (in the general timeframe requested) when all six people can attend a meeting?

Follow these guidelines when making appointments:

- Do not schedule overlapping appointments. Try to determine the amount of time needed for each one. Leave some time unscheduled between appointments to allow for meetings that run longer than planned, to return telephone calls, or to prepare for the next appointment. Keep complete information. Record names, telephone numbers, e-mail addresses, and other related data.

- Use clear handwriting to record entries on handwritten calendars. Avoid crossing out and rescheduling over scratched-off entries. To make changes easily, write appointment information in pencil.

- If you make appointments for a manager or coworker, you may need to set a time for the appointment and then confirm that time with the individual. Use some symbol to indicate confirmed appointments. As appointments are confirmed, record the symbol. Commonly used symbols include a check mark, an asterisk, or an underscore of the individual's name.

- If you are responsible for keeping a manual calendar for others, provide a daily listing of appointments and reminders at the beginning of the workday. Show the appointments for the day in chronological order. If an automated calendar is used, this data can probably be accessed easily by the person.

- Keep the previous year's appointment data. You may find it necessary to refer back to the data to find needed information. If you use an electronic calendar, print a copy of the calendar before deleting the data, or save the information in an electronic file.

Entering Recurring Items

Some meetings and tasks are performed weekly, monthly, quarterly, or annually. For example, the members of your department might have a staff meeting every Monday morning. As you set up your calendar at the beginning of the year, enter the **recurring** meetings and tasks. Figure 9-1.4 shows the screen for indicating a recurring meeting using Microsoft Outlook. If you block out the times for recurring events, both you and others will know what time is available for scheduling other appointments.

Figure 9-1.4 Microsoft Outlook users can schedule recurring meetings.

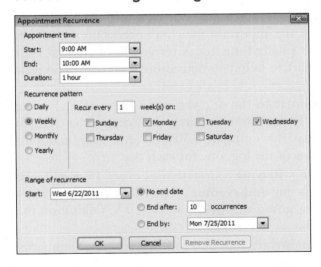

recurring happening again after an interval or periodically

 CHECK POINT What four basic categories of information do you need to respond to an appointment request?

21st Century Skills

Making Decisions

PARTNERSHIP FOR 21ST CENTURY SKILLS

Ana Maria arrived at the office a few minutes early to review the items on her task list for the day. Just as she was about to begin, her supervisor, Mr. Wang, arrived and told Ana Maria he had received a call at home last night. The national sales meeting scheduled for three weeks from today had been moved to one week from today because of an emergency. Ana Maria said, "This definitely changes the priorities for today."

1. Open the file 9-1 Making Decisions from the data files. The items that Ana Maria had on her task list for today are shown in the file. She had not prioritized them.

2. Think about the changes Ana Maria needs to make in her task list. List the items that will be affected by the supervisor's news. Will other items be added to her task list? If yes, list them.

3. Prioritize the items to reflect the change in the date and time of the national sales meeting. Key a revised task list.

Making Academic Connections

Reinforcing English Skills

You work in the Human Resources Department of Raleigh Corporation, which makes modular business furniture. Your supervisor has prepared a punctuation test to be administered to job applicants. She asks you to complete the punctuation test to be sure that the instructions are clear before she has large quantities of the test printed.

1. Open the file 9-1 English Skills from the data files.

2. Follow the instructions to complete the test.

9-1 Activity 1

Analyzing a Time Log (Outcome 9-1a)

As you have learned in this chapter, managing your time and developing an orderly approach to your work are important for your success on the job. In this activity, you will complete a daily time log. After you have charted your activities, you will use your chart to help you determine your most and least productive time periods.

1. Prepare a time-use log similar to the one shown in Figure 9-1.1 using spreadsheet software. Use 15-minute time intervals. Prepare the chart to cover your entire waking day (for example, 6:30 a.m. until 11:00 p.m.) for one week. Print seven copies of the log, one for each day.

2. Complete your time-use log. Record your activities every 15 minutes as you progress through each day and evening. Record all your activities: studying, attending class or going to work, watching TV, talking on the telephone, eating, and so on.

3. Enter the data from your handwritten logs into your spreadsheet. Summarize your time spent by hours into categories; for example, school, work, leisure, sleep, hobbies, and so on. Use an *Other* category to group activities that occurred only once or twice for very short periods. Create a pie chart showing the percentages of time spent in each different category as part of your total time.

4. Analyze your time log. Identify the hours where you used your time most productively as well as those hours where you wasted your time. During what hours do you get the most accomplished? During what hours do you tend to waste your time?

5. Write a short report titled *Time Use Analysis* discussing your time-use log. Include the pie chart in your report. Format the report in unbound report style. Describe what you intend to do differently as a result of your time analysis.

9-1 Activity 2

Prioritize and Schedule Tasks (Outcome 9-1b)

Your manager, Mr. Jorell Jones, has asked you to plan and submit a schedule for advertising a sale of office equipment. The sale will begin two months from today. He hands you a rough draft of the inventory list of the products that will be included in the sale. Items marked with an asterisk (*) will have to be ordered from the suppliers so that they arrive in time for the sale.

1. Create a list of tasks for the sale. Open and print the file 9-1 Activity 2 from the data files. This file contains a partial list.

2. Create a form that includes these columns: *Priority*, *Task*, and *Completed*. Place the items on the form in the Task column. Next, prioritize the items by ranking them in order of importance:

   A Most important

   B Medium importance

   C Least important item

3. Key the rank in the Priority column. If an item is listed as a C item, does it need to be completed at all? If not, delete the item. Are there other items that need to be added to this list? If yes, add these items.

4. Create a schedule for preparing for the office equipment sale. Use spreadsheet software or the calendar of a program such as Microsoft Outlook to create the schedule.

   • List tasks to be completed from your task list in order by date using the dates when a task should begin. Start with your ending deadline and work backward to create your schedule. For example, if a task should be completed one week before the sale and the task takes two weeks to complete, then list the task on the date three weeks prior to the sale.

   • Show the dates when each task should be completed.

   • Include a column to check off tasks and confirm that they have been completed on time.

OUTCOMES

9-2a Describe procedures for managing your workstation.
9-2b Describe procedures for office safety.

KEY TERMS

workstation p. 312
preventive maintenance p. 314
ergonomics p. 315
carpal tunnel syndrome p. 317
wellness program p. 318
surge suppressor p. 321
emergency procedures p. 322
evacuation p. 323

workstation the physical area in which a worker performs a job

Workstation Management

Office workers must be able to manage work effectively to be productive. Lighting and the way materials and the work area are arranged affect your work. Most companies try to provide comfortable and safe work areas for their office employees. Your workstation is a key part of your work environment. A workstation is the physical area in which a worker performs a job. A typical workstation provides a work surface and space for equipment and supplies.

Manage Your Workstation

Arrange your work area to give easy access to the items used frequently. A computer keyboard, telephone, supplies, and reference materials should be within easy reach. Many companies use modular workstations. These workstations are made up of parts that can be put together in various ways. Wall panels, storage areas, and a desktop surface are typical workstation parts. Note the workstation parts shown in Figure 9-2.1.

Figure 9-2.1 Many companies provide workstations that can be arranged to meet specific user needs.

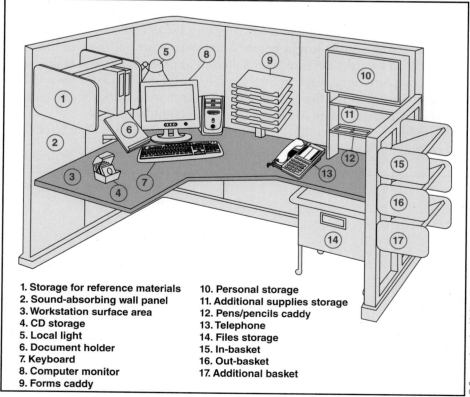

1. Storage for reference materials
2. Sound-absorbing wall panel
3. Workstation surface area
4. CD storage
5. Local light
6. Document holder
7. Keyboard
8. Computer monitor
9. Forms caddy
10. Personal storage
11. Additional supplies storage
12. Pens/pencils caddy
13. Telephone
14. Files storage
15. In-basket
16. Out-basket
17. Additional basket

© Cengage Learning 2013

Desktop Area

Keep your workstation's surface clear. Clutter on the desktop can cause unnecessary delays as you search for papers or objects. Remove materials that do not relate to your current project. Put descriptive labels on file folders, and place documents in the folders when they are not needed. Place the folders in your file drawer.

Arrange your equipment and supplies to allow easy access so that you avoid making unnecessary movements. Keep frequently used supplies, such as pencils and paper clips, in a caddy on the surface of your work area. Reaching for the caddy is more efficient than opening and closing a drawer each time you need an item.

Having an organized desktop area can help you be more productive.

Jason Henry/iStockphoto.com

Drawers

Reserve your center drawer for frequently used supplies, such as a letter opener, scissors, and paper clips, that are not needed on the surface area. Arrange the contents of the center drawer so the most frequently used supplies are closer to the front where you can reach them easily.

The top side drawer may be used to store supplies or file folders containing current work so that they are at hand when you need them. You avoid cluttering the desktop by putting the file folders in a specific location in your desk. In this way, you also can protect any confidential items.

A desk also may contain either a file drawer or additional side drawers. A file drawer can be used to store files that are referred to often but are not in current use. Other drawers can be used to store supplies.

Reference Materials

The nature of your job will determine which references you will use most often. Some items may be in print form. Others may be accessed via your computer. Reference materials that should be at your workstation may include a dictionary, telephone directories, company and office reference manuals, safety handbooks, and equipment and software manuals. Other reference items used less often may include an almanac, atlas, and vendor supply catalogues.

Supplies and Accessories

Office employees use a variety of supplies and accessories to do their jobs. The right resources help you perform your job more efficiently. What you need at

Supplies can be arranged neatly in a desk drawer.

your workstation will depend on your particular job. An adequately stocked workstation is essential to your productivity. If you run out of supplies in the middle of a critical task, you could lose valuable work time by stopping to gather needed supplies. Also, you run the risk of not completing the task on time. Use supplies properly for best results and to save money. Follow these guidelines:

- Select the quality of the supply according to the nature and importance of the task. For example, if you are preparing a rough draft of an important letter, don't use expensive letterhead paper. Use a lower-quality paper for the rough draft and the letterhead paper for the final copy.

- Learn to read product labels for the correct use of a product. For example, paper designed for use in a laser printer may not work well in an inkjet printer.

- Look for ways to conserve supplies. For example, reuse file folders by placing new file folder labels over the old ones. To save paper, preview documents carefully onscreen before printing.

- Do not keep more supplies than you need in your workstation. Check your workstation periodically. If you have not used a supply item in several weeks, perhaps it should be returned to the supply cabinet.

Office Equipment

The condition of your equipment affects the quality of your work. You will want to keep your equipment in top working order. To get dependable service from your equipment, you will need to do **preventive maintenance** and give your equipment routine care. This involves servicing equipment and replacing parts while the equipment is working properly in order to keep the equipment in working order. Fewer repairs are necessary when equipment is cared for properly on a regular basis. By caring for equipment properly, you can extend the life of the equipment. Follow these maintenance guidelines:

- Learn how to use and care for the equipment properly. Read and understand the manufacturer's operating instructions. Follow the care guidelines so that you are able to recognize and correct minor problems.

preventive maintenance
servicing equipment and replacing parts, as needed, to keep equipment in working order

- Inspect and clean equipment regularly. Know the basic care routines your equipment requires. Make repairs as needed.

- Report problems right away to the appropriate person. Many minor problems can be corrected before they become serious and require costly repair.

 CHECK POINT Why is performing routine care and maintenance tasks for equipment important?

Manage Ergonomic Factors

Ergonomics is the study of the effects of the work environment on the health of workers. The way a workstation and its parts are designed can affect your physical well being. Figure 9-2.2 shows a workstation designed to be comfortable and reduce physical stress. This workstation allows the user to adjust the chair, desk, lighting, and computer equipment.

ergonomics the study of the effects of the work environment on the health of workers

Figure 9-2.2 **Ergonomic factors affect productivity.**

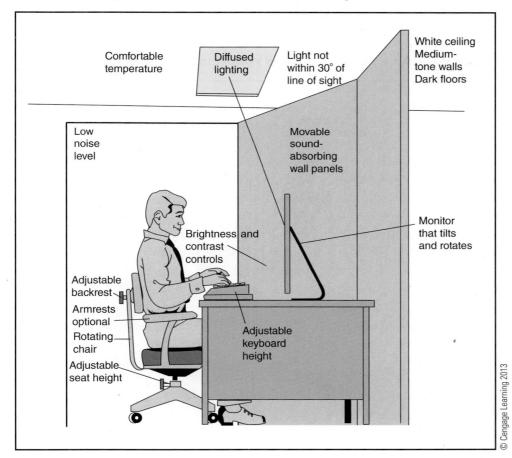

© Cengage Learning 2013

The height of the desktop should allow your elbows to be parallel to the computer keyboard and floor as shown in Figure 9-2.2. This arrangement prevents unnecessary strain on the arms and wrists. Keep the desktop clear of materials not related to the current task.

Two kinds of lighting are often found in workstations: ambient and task. Ambient lighting is provided by overhead light fixtures for the entire work area. Although you may not be able to adjust the overhead lighting, you can adjust the arrangement of your workstation. Task lighting focuses on the immediate work area and should be adjustable for your specific needs. Adjust the task lighting to prevent glare on your computer monitor or the desktop. Eliminate dark or dimly lit areas where you may have to retrieve files or work away from your desktop.

Your computer monitor should be placed at eye level, as shown in Figure 9-2.2, to help reduce eyestrain and neck pain. Glare on the monitor often contributes to eyestrain. Common symptoms of eyestrain are teary or burning eyes, blurred vision, and headaches. Glare from outside light can be prevented by placing the computer monitor so that you do not face a window or have your back to a window. Peripheral input devices, such as the mouse, should be located next to the computer keyboard. The movement of the arm from the keyboard to the input device should be natural and without strain.

A well-designed chair is essential because many office workers spend much of their time sitting. A chair should be adjustable, like the one shown in Figure 9-2.3. Office workers should be able to adjust their chairs to fit individual physical requirements for comfort and good posture.

 CHECK POINT What are two kinds of lighting are often found in workstations and how do they differ?

Figure 9-2.3 **An adjustable chair is important for comfortable seating.**

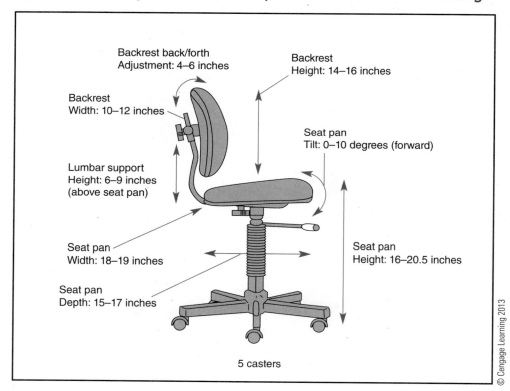

5 casters

© Cengage Learning 2013

Manage Your Office Health

Be aware of the physical responses your body has to your work procedures and habits. Doing so will enhance your job satisfaction, comfort, and productivity. The following guidelines may help you complete your work without feelings of strain, fatigue, or other physical discomforts.

■ Learn to adjust the workstation parts for the best fit to your work habits and procedures. Follow the manufacturer's recommended work postures and practices even if at first they feel unnatural.

- Take rest breaks often—at least 15 minutes every two hours. Do not sit in front of your computer monitor or at your desk for long, uninterrupted periods of time. Arrange your work so that you have to get out of your chair and walk to the copier or to the supply cabinet. If you feel yourself becoming bored, stop working and do simple breathing or relaxation exercises.

- Learn stretching exercises for your hands, wrists, arms, and fingers to relieve pressure on them. Carpal tunnel syndrome is a repetitive strain injury that occurs when stress is placed on the hands, wrists, or arms. It can occur while working at the computer keyboard or using the computer input device for long periods of time.

carpal tunnel syndrome a repetitive strain injury that can occur when stress is placed on the hands, wrists, or arms

- Focus your eyes away from your computer monitor often. Remember to blink your eyes. If possible, face your computer monitor against a wall to avoid looking directly out of a window or into glare from other bright light sources. Place antiglare filters over the monitor screen, if needed. Filters reduce glare, static electricity, and dirt and smudge buildup on the screen.

- Adjust the screen brightness to a contrast level that is comfortable for you. Adjust the screen angle so that it is at eye level or slightly lower. Adjust the screen display properties for comfortable viewing. Resolution and color quality settings for a system with two monitors are shown in Figure 9-2.4.

Figure 9-2.4 **The display settings can be adjusted for comfortable viewing.**

Workplace Wellness

Many Americans spend more hours at work than ever before. The office has become an important place for employees to understand health and wellness. Wellness includes issues such as nutrition and controlling stress. Balancing work and family life activities are also wellness issues.

Wellness in the workplace is now an important focus in business. Employers know that when these lifestyle factors are controlled, everyone benefits. This is why companies are consulting with wellness experts. Many companies have wellness programs that promote a healthy lifestyle. As a result, medical expenses and work time lost due to illness may decrease.

Eating healthy food, getting enough exercise, and managing one's weight are important parts of wellness. Many Americans have busy work schedules. They find it hard to make time for exercise and cooking healthy meals. Employers can take steps to help employees stay healthy. Some of these include:

- Providing purified water or juice as an alternative to soft drinks.
- Posting the calories and fat grams of foods served in the company dining room.

- Encouraging employees to include physical exercise in the workday. For example, workers could use the stairs instead of the elevators. Workers might use an on-site gym for exercise before or after the workday.

Some companies provide incentives or rewards for workers who take part in wellness programs. For example, workers may earn points that can be redeemed for prizes. Other companies offer reduced rates for health insurance to employees who take part in wellness programs.

Wellness programs benefit both employers and employees. If your company has a wellness program, consider taking part in it. You can also develop your own personal plan for a healthy lifestyle. Articles related to wellness issues can be found on the Internet and in magazines and newspapers. This information can help you learn to eat properly, exercise, and manage work-related stress.

> What are some other things a company might do to promote employee wellness?

wellness program activities designed to promote good physical and mental health

- Learn and use good posture. Keep your back straight against the back of your chair and your feet flat on the floor. Adjust your chair so that your feet do not dangle above the floor. Use a footrest if your feet don't reach the floor. Use a back pad, if needed, to keep your back in a straight line, and adjust your computer monitor to the right height and angle for you.

- Arrange your work materials so that you do not have to reach far to a telephone or supplies. Take care when lifting heavy binders or boxes or bending to reach files. Do not strain to use staplers or paper punches. Avoid repetitive motions for long periods of time without taking a break.

- Report any prolonged physical discomfort that affects your work performance to your supervisor.

 CHECK POINT How often should you take rest breaks (at minimum) when working at a computer?

Office Safety

Most of us think of the office as a safe place to work. Office workers are not required to use heavy equipment or power tools. They are seldom exposed to poisonous chemicals or dangerous working conditions. Yet thousands of office workers have disabling accidents each year. Falling, tripping, or slipping account for many office accidents. Common causes of falls include drawers partially open, slippery floors, torn or loose carpeting, objects left on stairs or in walkways, and dangling telephone or electrical cords.

Faulty or poorly maintained equipment can be a cause of accidents in the office. Falling objects and fire and electrical hazards can pose dangers. Human carelessness can also be a cause of accidents in the office. With knowledge of correct safety procedures, however, you can learn how to correct and report safety problems. Reporting problems will help prevent injury to you and your coworkers.

Becoming aware of safety hazards in an office is the first step to preventing accidents. Workers should develop positive safety attitudes. They should try to see potential safety problems and take steps to remove them.

✳ WORKPLACE CONNECTIONS ✳

Marletta came around the corner with her arms full of supplies for the supply cabinet. She could not see where she was going very well because her arms were so full. She should not have been trying to carry so much, but she was trying to save a few steps and not have to make a second trip.

Larry looked up from the phone to see Marletta just a few feet from his open file drawer. When Larry realized that Marletta could not see where she was walking, he called, "Watch out!" Too late—Marletta fell with a loud crash over the bottom file drawer. X-rays showed that Marletta had broken her wrist while trying to catch herself in the fall. She was unable to resume her full duties for eight weeks.

What could Marletta and Larry have done differently to prevent this accident?

Workstation Safety

Most office employees spend the majority of their working time at their workstations. Applying safety practices at your workstation will help prevent accidents and injuries.

Desktop Area

As you work, you will occasionally use scissors and other sharp objects. Place them away from the edge of your workstation so they will not be knocked off easily. Pencils stored on the top of your desk with the sharp points up are dangerous; they are best stored flat or with points down. Use a staple remover, rather than your fingernail, to remove staples. Never examine a jammed stapler by holding it near your eyes or testing it over your finger.

Drawers

Keep your workstation drawers neat. Do not allow papers to collect to the point of clutter. If the drawers are cluttered, your hands could easily be punctured by hidden scissors, pins, or pencils. Sharp objects such as pins and thumbtacks should be placed in closed containers.

Even with these precautions, never reach blindly into a desk drawer or file drawer. Take time to look where you are placing your hands, even if you are rushed or are talking to someone. Close workstation and file drawers by the handle. Do not push a drawer shut by placing your hand at the top or side of the drawer. You may lose a fingernail or suffer a crushed finger or hand.

Chairs/Mats/Static Control

Most office chairs have casters, which are small wheels that provide ease of movement for the worker. This same ease of movement can produce painful injury unless you look at the chair and hold onto its arms or seat as you sit down. When seated, be careful not to lean too far forward or backward to prevent falling out of the chair.

Chair mats allow chairs with casters to roll easily.

Courtesy of American Floor Mats

A chair mat is a vinyl pad placed underneath the chair to eliminate wear on the carpet from rolling the chair. Static control mats are designed for use on floors underneath workstations and computers. The static control mat safeguards valuable computer data and electronic equipment from possible harm from a charge of static electricity. Chair mats and static control mats can cause you to trip, particularly if the edges are beginning to curl. Replace worn mats when they become a hazard.

✓ CHECK POINT What danger might be posed by a chair mat or static control mat?

Work Area Safety

In addition to your workstation, other objects in your immediate work area can add to your comfort and work productivity. They can also become a source of injury.

Office Furnishings

Learn how to use small furnishings, such as a step stool and paper cutter. In using a step stool with casters, step firmly in the middle of the stool. Never step to the side because this can cause the stool to slide out from under you. When using the paper cutter, keep your fingers away from the blade and never leave the blade up. Furniture with rough or sharp edges should be sanded or taped to prevent injury to employees, as well as to prevent clothing from being torn. Report tears in carpets, burned-out lights, broken handles on equipment, and other potential hazards related to office furnishings to the appropriate person.

File drawers should be filled beginning with the bottom drawer of the cabinet and moving to the top drawer. They should be emptied from the top drawer down. When working with file cabinets, pull out only one drawer at a time. You do not want to change the cabinet's center of gravity and cause it to tip over. Avoid placing objects that have the potential to harm you or your coworkers on top of filing cabinets. Coffeemakers or heavy plants can slip off the cabinet and cause serious injuries.

Electrical Equipment

Office workers use many pieces of equipment that require cords and cables. These cords and cables can become a safety hazard. Cables and cords should never extend into traffic areas. Do not overload electrical outlets. If necessary, use a power strip or surge suppressor made for use with multiple appliances. An extension cord should be used only to extend the position of the electrical appliance. It should not be used to increase the power load.

surge suppressor an electrical outlet that controls sharp increases in electricity

Cords, cables, and power strips should be placed behind equipment or within the walls of the workstation. If cords must be placed where people walk, tape them down or cover them with materials made specifically for this purpose.

A surge suppressor can help you protect valuable equipment and organize power cords.

General Office Equipment

Office equipment can be dangerous if it is not operated properly. Keep the following safety procedures in mind when you use office equipment.

- Follow the manufacturer's directions for safe and efficient equipment use.
- Avoid other activities that will distract you from the operation of the equipment.

- If you feel a tingling sensation, notice smoke, or smell something burning while you are operating the equipment, turn it off. Investigate the problem or report it to the appropriate person immediately.

- Know where the power switches are located on the equipment in your general area. In the event of an emergency or power outage, you may need to turn off the equipment.

✔ CHECK POINT   What is the purpose of a surge suppressor?

Emergency Procedures

emergency procedures steps to follow in times of trouble or danger

Emergency procedures are steps to follow in time of trouble or danger. A fire, storm, or robbery in progress are examples of emergencies you might face at work. Learn emergency procedures as soon as you begin a new job. If your office does not have established procedures, do what you can to help initiate practices such as those described in the following paragraphs.

Emergency Telephone Numbers

Telephone numbers to call in times of emergency should be posted beside each telephone. The most important ones are those of the company medical and security personnel. Numbers for the local police, fire department, and paramedics should be included in the list. If your area has a general emergency number, such as 911, include it also. Emergency numbers may also be stored in each telephone's memory. The memory feature saves valuable time. You press only one or two buttons, and the number is automatically dialed.

First Aid Procedures

First aid kits should be located conveniently within the office. They should be inspected frequently and restocked whenever supplies from the kit are used. Some firms will send an employee from each floor or work group for first aid training and/or CPR (cardiopulmonary resuscitation) classes. These courses are given periodically by the American Red Cross and other organizations. Each employee should know who has completed first aid training and who is qualified to help in the critical first minutes of an emergency. First aid posters can be placed where they can easily be seen to further assist employees.

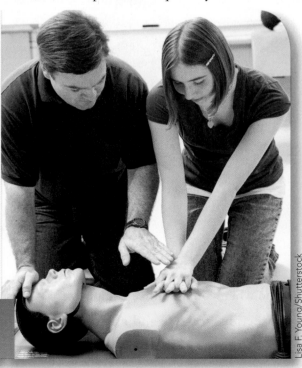

Employees should know which coworkers have had training in first aid or CPR.

Lisa F. Young/Shutterstock

Fires

Some companies prohibit the use of appliances, such as cup warmers and space heaters, because of their potential fire hazard. If appliances are allowed in your office, always unplug them when they are not in use and before leaving the office. Know the location of the nearest fire exit, fire alarm box, and fire extinguisher. Large office buildings generally have the fire alarm boxes and fire extinguishers in the same location patterns on each floor. Learn how to use the fire extinguisher and what type of fire it is intended to put out. Never attempt to fight a fire alone. Always have someone report it to the proper agency.

Building Evacuation Plans

Learn the established escape routes and evacuation procedures for your building. Emergency exit routes should be posted in noticeable places throughout the building. Employees should know their duties during a drill or evacuation. Who, for example, is responsible for checking conference rooms, restrooms, and other areas where the alarm may not be heard?

evacuation departure or flight, the clearing of an area

CHECK POINT What are three things you should know related to a fire emergency at the office?

Employees should know the evacuation routes for fire or other emergencies.

Personal Security on the Job

Protection for yourself and your property requires continuous attention on your part. Most businesses strive to provide a safe and secure work environment for their employees. To support the company's effort in providing for your safety and security on the job, always use good common sense. A purse left at a workstation, a jacket slung over the back of a chair or left in an unoccupied office, cash left out in plain sight—all are invitations to a would-be thief. Keep personal belongings out of sight and locked in a drawer, file cabinet, employee locker, or closet. The key to this drawer or other container should be issued only to the employee who is assigned its use.

Sometimes you may find it necessary to stay late at the office or to come in early. Follow your company's procedures for being in the building during non-working hours. If no after-hours procedures exist, create your own security routine and follow it. Follow these security procedures when you work alone:

- Always work near a phone and keep emergency telephone numbers handy.
- Lock all doors to your work area. Do not open the door to anyone you are not expecting or cannot identify.
- Get to know the cleaning staff and when to expect them.
- If you use the elevator to leave the building, do not enter the elevator if anyone you find suspicious is in it.
- Avoid using a restroom located away from your work area.
- When working late, phone home before leaving the office to let someone know what time to expect you. If you live alone, call a friend before leaving the office and again when you get home to let her or him know you've arrived safely.
- Park your car near the building entrance and/or in a lighted parking lot. Check the parking lot visually before leaving the building. Have your car keys in your hand and ready to use. If security personnel are available, ask to be escorted to your car.

 CHECK POINT What are three steps you can take to promote personal safety at work?

Be cautious in parking areas after normal working hours.

Monalyn Gracia/Fancy (RF)/Jupiter Images

Building and Office Security

Many businesses take a serious approach to fulfilling building and office security needs. Discontented workers, theft, sabotage, and fire are major security concerns of a business.

Many companies have security procedures to guard against actions by employees who have been fired or who are under pressures from work. Sometimes upset workers can pose a hazard to themselves and to other workers. Be alert to changes in your coworkers' behavior. Notice statements they may make that sound like threats against employees or the company. Know the procedures for protecting yourself from these workers:

- Do not get involved in a verbal argument.
- Leave the work area if you feel threatened and go to a safe area.
- Report any unusual behavior to your supervisor and/or company security personnel.

The protection of data is an issue in many companies. Entrance to secure areas where data are kept or can be accessed is carefully controlled. Employees may need access codes or passwords to enter these areas.

✳ WORKPLACE CONNECTIONS ✳

Ornella looked up to see a repairman coming through the doorway. "Hi, I'm Tim Sanyal. I'm here to check your computer. Apparently, you had a large electrical surge last night. Here's the order," he said, as he flashed a copy of a repair order in front of Ornella. "This will take a few minutes—why don't you just take a short break?"

Ornella got up from her desk, but she was puzzled. She hadn't heard that an electrical surge had occurred. "Besides," she thought, "we have surge suppressors for the equipment." Ornella felt she should check this with her supervisor, Ms. Calibre. Ms. Calibre was not aware of an electrical surge occurring either. "Let me check on this before we do anything," she said. Ornella stepped back into her office to see the repairman disconnecting the computer.

Repairman:	"Looks like I'll have to take your computer back to the shop for repairs."
Ornella:	"You'll have to wait until my supervisor authorizes you to take the computer."
Repairman:	"Well, I have several other computers to check. Why don't I come back after I've checked them and pick this one up."

The repairman left hurriedly, and a minute or so later Ornella's supervisor appeared at the door: "No one authorized a computer repair check. We had better report this."

Ms. Calibre called the police immediately to report the incident. She spoke to Sergeant Roberts. He told her that several businesses had recently lost computers and other equipment in this manner. "You're lucky to have an alert employee," the sergeant told Ms. Calibre.

What might have happened if Ornella had not questioned whether the repairman's visit was authorized?

Controlling Outsider Access

Many companies must be open to the public to do business. However, the public does not need access to all parts of most office buildings. Businesses use varied security means to protect employees and assets.

Some companies have security personnel who make sure each visitor signs a log. The log shows the visitor's name, address, and the name of the person or office being visited. Some companies send an employee to the lobby to escort a visitor back to the office. In smaller offices, the receptionist may be present in the front office and may screen visitors.

Controlling Employee Access

At some companies, employees must wear identification (ID) badges. These badges are used to gain entrance to parts of the building. The badge may con-

A scanner can read a person's fingerprint (or eye patterns) for identification purposes.

tain the employee's photo or a fingerprint. The badge may have a magnetic code. The code may be read by a card reader to allow entrance to a room or use of equipment. Fingerprint scanners or eye scanners may also be used to allow access to a secure area.

Some badge codes can be read by proximity readers. The reader automatically identifies the badge when the wearer is in a restricted area. The reader sends data to a computer. This data provides a record of who enters and leaves designated areas, the time of entry, and in some instances, the time of exit—all valuable security information.

Your cooperation in wearing your ID helps assure your personal safety and security on the job. A lost or stolen ID should be reported right away to the appropriate person.

Detection Systems and Alarms

A detection system consists of devices and alarms that sense and signal a change in the condition of an area. Some systems detect entry into an area while others detect movement in an area. An alarm sounds or is displayed on a computer screen when an intruder is detected. Such systems reduce a company's reliance on an on-site security guard. Even if a firm has security officers, they cannot be at all stations at once.

Closed-circuit television can be used to monitor corridors, entrances, or other areas. When used with a videotape recorder, closed-circuit television provides the firm with a record of events for later review.

 CHECK POINT What are some methods companies use to control access to secure areas?

REVIEW 9-2

21st Century Skills
Thinking Critically

At a department meeting, your manager, Ms. Tia Petersen, discusses a memo regarding company security. She shakes her head and says, "This is the second memo the managers have received about security leaks. One of our competitors has just introduced a new product, and it's identical to a product we have been working on. Apparently they discovered our plans. The president wants our thoughts on how to improve our product security. In addition to the main shredder in the copy center, he is suggesting a shredder for each office. Well, I'm just glad everyone in our department can be trusted." As you hear this, you remember several situations you have observed in the office:

- You have seen poor photocopies—even photocopies of confidential material—discarded in the wastebasket.
- Computer printouts with product-testing results are stacked next to the filing cabinets rather than being locked inside them.
- Workers often talk about current projects during their breaks.
- Workers sometimes use the offices of other workers who are out of town.
- Workers too freely give out unnecessary information to callers, such as telling a caller exactly where an individual is.

"Tell me," Ms. Petersen says, "do you think we need a shredder? What other measures can we take to tighten security? Please give this matter some thought and send me your ideas."

1. Prepare a response to Ms. Petersen in an e-mail message. Send the message to your instructor's e-mail address (or save and print the message). Prepare a memo to Ms. Petersen instead if you do not have access to e-mail.

2. In the message, include suggestions for correcting the problems discussed as well as other security measures that you think would be effective.

Making Academic Connections
Reinforcing Math Skills

1. Janna spends 1.25 hours of her 8-hour work day answering e-mail messages. What percentage of the work day is this time?

2. Chin typically spent 2.5 hours per day filing paper records. After a new filing system was implemented, he now spends 1 hour per day filing records. What is the percent of decrease in the filing time?

3. Pablo is a technical writer who works 7.5 hours per day. He spends twice as much time on writing tasks as he does on other work tasks. How much time per day does he spend on writing tasks?

4. A company implemented a new work safety program. Accidents were reduced by 20 percent to 12 accidents per year. How many accidents per year did the company have before the new program was begun?

5. Myra pays 4 cents per minute for long-distance telephone calls with a per call minimum charge of 75 cents. What is the actual cost per minute for a call lasting 15 minutes?

9-2 Activity 1

Ergonomics Evaluation (Outcome 9-2a)

You have learned about various factors related to ergonomics of a work space. In this activity, you evaluate the ergonomics of a work space you use frequently.

1. Select one area in which you often perform tasks using a computer. The area could be a classroom or lab at school, a work station at a library you visit often, or a space in your home.

2. Considering what you have learned about ergonomics, evaluate the elements of the workspace listed below. Rate each element as good, acceptable, or needs improvement.
   - Lighting
   - Seating
   - Work surface
   - Monitor
   - Keyboard and mouse
   - Other

3. Create a table that lists the workstation elements down the left side and the ratings at the top. Place an *X* in the table to indicate the rating for each item.

4. Place a section for comments below the chart. Comment on any item that needs improvement. List the changes that you think would bring the item to an acceptable or good rating.

9-2 Activity 2

Office Safety Guidelines (Outcome 9-2b)

Your supervisor is concerned that each employee takes an active interest in good safety practices. She would like you and a coworker to develop a list of office safety guidelines for employees. The guidelines will be posted on the company intranet to promote office safety during the company's Safety Month. Work with a classmate to complete this activity.

1. Use your textbook, magazine articles, websites, or other resources to research safety as it relates to an office environment.

2. Compose a list of 10 to 15 office safety guidelines. Arrange the items in order of importance. Give the list an appropriate title and include a short introductory paragraph.

3. Since the list will be viewed on the screen, use a background color and add at least one graphic in the document. Save the document as a single file web page. View the page in a browser. Make any changes needed to the format of the file to make it attractive and easy to read in the browser.

Summary

9-1 Managing Your Time

- Time management is the process of planning your activities to gain better control over how you spend your time.
- Common time-wasters include unnecessary telephone conversations, interruptions, socializing, ineffective communication, and disorganization.
- Time analysis aids, such as a time log, can help you determine how effectively your time is used.
- Planning and prioritizing your daily work activities will help you complete tasks on time and in the proper order.
- To control large projects, break the large project into smaller tasks. Establish deadlines for each smaller task, and meet those deadlines.
- Work simplification is the process of improving the procedures for getting work done.
- Manual and electronic reminder systems can be used to schedule tasks and appointments. In some jobs, you may be expected to schedule appointments for coworkers as well as for yourself.

9-2 Workstation Management and Office Safety

- Office workers must be able to manage work effectively to be productive. Your work area should be arranged to give easy access to the items used frequently.
- To get dependable service from office equipment, you will need to do preventive maintenance and give the equipment routine care.
- Ergonomics is the study of the effects of the work environment on the health of workers. The way a workstation and its parts are designed can affect your physical comfort as you work there.
- To enhance comfort and productivity, be aware of the physical responses your body has to work procedures and habits.
- Many companies have wellness programs that promote a healthy lifestyle for their employees.
- Thousands of office workers have disabling accidents each year. Becoming aware of safety hazards in an office is the first step to preventing accidents.
- Emergency procedures are steps to follow in time of trouble or danger. Learn emergency procedures to follow as soon as you begin a new job.
- Employees should take reasonable precautions to help ensure their personal safety while at work.
- Many companies have security procedures to guard against actions by employees, customers, or others that may endanger people or company property.

Wire_man/Shutterstock.com

Chapter 9 Activity 1

Reminder Systems
(Outcome 9-1c)

Using a reminder system can help you manage your time and be more productive. Many software applications are available that allow users to keep track of appointments and other activities. Other programs allow users to plan tasks for a long-term project or schedule meetings for a group of people. Some programs are designed to be used on a personal computer, and some are designed for PDAs or smartphones.

1. Do research on the Internet to learn about at least two reminder, scheduling, or calendar programs.

2. Write a brief description of each program. Include the following information:

   - Program name
   - Device for which the application is designed
   - Main purpose of the application
   - Features of the application

Chapter 9 Activity 2

Long-Term Portfolio Project
(Outcome 9-1b)

As an office worker, you will need to prioritize work to fulfill duties and meet deadlines. Office work often involves planning and completing long-term projects. In this activity, you will plan, schedule, and complete a long-term project: a portfolio to display your work.

The general purpose of a portfolio is to demonstrate your skills and abilities related to work. A portfolio can contain samples of your work, awards or other recognitions, certificates or degrees related to training or education, a description of assignments or projects that have been successfully completed, and letters or recommendations related to your work abilities. A good portfolio can be helpful in getting a job.

1. This project should be completed four to six weeks from now. You and your instructor should agree on the specific timeline for this activity. Consult with your instructor to determine the deadline for completing the project.

2. List the steps to complete the portfolio. For example, define clearly the purpose for your portfolio, research portfolio layouts, schedule time to work on the portfolio, collect materials (classroom and other), and plan initial documents to go into the portfolio.

3. List the materials and resources you will need to complete the portfolio, such as folders, time, money, paper, dividers, notebooks, classroom projects, and so forth. You can create the portfolio in hard copy or scan materials to create an electronic portfolio.

4. List the people you need to contact to complete the project: instructors, administrators, students, parents, businesspeople, etc.

5. Create a long-range schedule. Use spreadsheet software to list the dates and tasks to be completed by specific dates. (Hint: Key your ending date or deadline first.) Key a title and beginning date on your schedule to make it uniquely yours. Print a copy of your schedule to use as you complete your portfolio project.

6. Follow your plan to prepare the portfolio. Make a note of the changes that have to be made to your original schedule as you complete your project. Were your deadlines realistic? Were the people available at the times you listed? Did you find the materials and resources available when you needed them? Did you follow your schedule? If not, why not?

7. Write a short report in unbound style summarizing your experiences as you created the portfolio. Discuss the factors listed above and your own observations. Include in your summary a copy of your beginning and ending schedule for comparison purposes.

8. Display or share your portfolio with other class members. Update your portfolio periodically as you gain new skills, complete training, or produce documents that will demonstrate your skills effectively.

Fundamental Spreadsheet Applications Event

The purpose of the event is to evaluate skills in spreadsheet design and use. During the event, you will create a spreadsheet, enter and format data, create and copy formulas, and print documents or cells.

After a few minutes for orientation, you will have 90 minutes to complete an application test using spreadsheet software. You are allowed to bring reference materials, such as a dictionary.

Performance Indicators Evaluated

The desktop publishing event is in the Financial Services assessment area. The event has performance indicators such as those listed below.

- Create and format cells, worksheets, and workbooks
- Analyze, enter, and edit data on cells, worksheets, and workbooks
- Analyze, create, and modify charts from data
- Display formulas
- Create formulas appropriate for particular tasks
- Modify print options

These performance indicators are from the Business Professionals of America guidelines as shown on their website. For more detailed information about this event, go to the BPA website.[1]

http://www.bpa.org

Think Critically

1. What are some tasks for which office workers might use spreadsheet software?
2. What spreadsheet formulas have you found challenging to create? Where can you get assistance for working with formulas?

---

[1]"Business Professionals of America, Workplace Skills Assessment Program, Secondary 2011" (Business Professionals of America, 2011), http://www.bpa.org/download.aspx?dl=2011_WSAP_SECONDARY.pdf.

The health science career area includes many types of jobs. Are you interested in doing medical research or providing care or counseling for medical patients? Perhaps support services, such as handling medical records, appeal to you. Maybe you would enjoy working as an administrator in a hospital or nursing facility. These are just a few of jobs available in health science. Jobs in health science are found in hospitals, doctor's offices, nursing facilities, businesses, and other organizations.

Employment Outlook

The continued need for health-care providers, new medicines and treatments, and related support services means that jobs in health science are an important career area. The U.S. government provides job projections for 2008-2018. Many jobs in health science are expected to increase faster than average for all jobs.[2]

Job Titles

- Acute care nurse
- Biologist
- Dentist
- Medical transcriptionist
- Nurse practitioner
- Patient representative
- Pharmacist
- Physical therapist
- Physician
- Radiologist
- Surgeon

Needed Education/Skills

The knowledge and skills needed for a career in health science can be obtained in technical schools, colleges/universities, and medical schools. The education and experience needed vary widely depending on the job. For example, a job in medical records may require an associate's degree from a junior college. A job as a hospital administrator may require a degree in business and related experience. A job as a nurse or medical technician typically requires a degree and courses in the specialty area. Physicians and medical researchers need advanced degrees and related experience or internships.

What's it like to work in ... Health Science?

Michele works as a patient representative in a hospital. The hospital serves patients from several counties in a rural area. Patients and their families have to deal with doctors, hospital procedures, insurance, and payment options. Some have to plan for continuing care after the patient leaves the hospital. All these issues can be overwhelming for some people. Michele's job is to help patients and their families understand the patient's care and related issues.

Michele talks with patients or their families to identify problems or issues of concern related to the patient's care. She acts a coordinator between the patient or family and the medical staff and hospital. Her goal is to help patients receive appropriate care and services. She must be very organized to handle records and issues for many patients.

Michele was an emergency room nurse before moving to this position. Her medical training, experience, and ability to empathize with patients helps her do her job well.

What About You?

What professionals have you met who work in health science? What job does each person have? What skills do you think are important for one of those jobs?

[2]*Occupational Outlook Handbook*, 2010-11 Edition, Bureau of Labor Statistics, U.S. Department of Labor, http://www.bls.gov/oco/oco1002.htm.

Meetings and Travel

10-1 Planning and Participating in Meetings

10-2 Arranging Travel

Stockbyte/Jupiter Images

Business meetings are held for many purposes. Workers often meet to share information or solve problems. Formats for meetings can be informal or formal. Meetings can have many participants or only a few. Employees often travel to attend meetings. Travel arrangements must be made. A schedule for the trip and related documents must be prepared.

In this chapter, you will learn about planning and taking part in meetings. You will also learn about making travel arrangements and supporting activities related to business travel.

Wire_man/Shutterstock.com

OUTCOMES

10-1a Plan business meetings and prepare related documents.
10-1b Participate effectively in meetings.
10-1c Apply procedures for planning teleconferences.

OUTCOMES

10-1a Plan business meetings and prepare related documents.
10-1b Participate effectively in meetings.
10-1c Apply procedures for planning teleconferences.

KEY TERMS

agenda p. 338
consensus p. 341
brainstorming p. 341
minutes p. 342
quorum p. 344
motion p. 344
second p. 344
action plan p. 345
teleconference p. 347

Planning Business Meetings

Business meetings bring people together to communicate. Meetings may range from an informal chat in a manager's office to a formal gathering of the board of directors. Although many meetings are held in person, technology allows people in different locations to attend meetings without leaving their offices. Well-organized meetings are necessary for businesses to run smoothly. Your role in assisting with these meetings will vary. It will depend on the degree of formality, purpose, size, and location of the meeting.

Types of Business Meetings

Office workers should understand the differences in the nature of meetings. They should also know their roles in planning and participating in them. The nature of the organization, the duties of the department, and the purpose of the meeting will determine the size and formality of the meeting.

Informal and Small Group Meetings

Many of the meetings in which office workers are involved will be informal discussions and small group meetings. Informal meetings often are set up as committee meetings. These meetings address specific topics or ongoing concerns and issues, such as safety and security.

Informal, small group meetings are held frequently in businesses.

B Busco/Photographer's Choice/Getty Images

This example shows how one office worker carried out her duties for setting up and taking part in a small, informal meeting.

Carmen's manager sent her an e-mail as follows: "Carmen, see if you can get the other four Pikesville project engineers together tomorrow at three o'clock. We need to meet for about an hour to discuss the status of the Pikesville project. See if the conference room is available." As she read through the message, Carmen noted the materials she needed to bring to the meeting. Immediately after reading all the instructions, Carmen checked through the company's electronic calendaring system to see if the engineers would be free. She noted that all four of the other engineers were free at that time. She added the meeting to their calendars.

Next, Carmen checked the conference room schedule. Finding it free at the hour requested, she added her name as the person requesting the meeting and her telephone number as a reference. She sent an e-mail message to each of the engineers about the meeting. She then arranged for the necessary equipment and copied materials for the meeting. To follow up the request, she sent an e-mail message to the manager to confirm the arrangements. She noted the meeting on her own calendar. The next day, Carmen checked the conference room before the meeting to see that everything was in order.

What information should be included in an e-mail message about a meeting such as the one Carmen sent?

Working with customers or clients may also take the form of small group meetings. These meetings may be more formal than small group meetings with coworkers, especially if the meeting is an initial contact with a client. Follow the steps described in the following sections to plan and conduct a meeting.

Formal Business Meetings

A formal meeting follows a definite order of business. It involves a specific audience and requires some preparation. Many organizations set up formal staff meetings at a specific time each week or month. Other formal business meetings, such as conferences or quarterly sales meetings, may be planned for longer periods of time. You may be asked to help plan a meeting. You may need to prepare meeting materials and make sure that follow-up actions are noted and carried through.

Many companies conduct meetings in which all participants do not speak the same language. All the people may not be in the same physical location. Multinational meetings for large groups are likely to be very formal. They may require detailed planning and preparation. Time differences for the different locations must be considered.

Knowledge of international and business etiquette is important for these meetings. Your role as a coordinator who arranges the meeting details will be critical. Your role may include working with hotel personnel if the meeting is held away from company offices. You may need to send the meeting plans to the people who will take part in the meeting. You may also work with equipment providers. You may need to know how to use equipment and the proper person to call for help if the equipment does not work properly.

Seating Arrangements

Interactions among group members will depend on the purpose of the meeting. In almost all meetings, communications will be improved when group members can see one another. Eye contact can be used to help gain attention or control a discussion. When all participants can see the leader and the visual aids, they can understand the discussion better.

A round table or circle may be used when the leader is seeking a true cooperative form of decision making. This format also reduces the appearance of differences in rank between the participants.

A circular seating arrangement may be used when the leader is seeking cooperative decision making from the group.

A U-shaped arrangement can be used for larger meetings—those that include 10 or 12 participants. In this arrangement, the leader may sit in the middle of the U to maintain eye contact with everyone. At the same time, all participants can see each other and are less likely to engage in side conversations.

A rectangular table layout, with the leader at one end of the table, allows the leader to control the discussion. In this arrangement, all communication tends to flow toward the head of the table (where the leader is seated).

CHECK POINT Which seating arrangement reduces the appearance of differences in rank between the participants in a meeting?

Preparing for a Meeting

The following suggestions will be helpful to you in your planning. You may not use all the suggestions for each meeting. However, these guidelines will be helpful as you plan for most business meetings.

- **Establish a meeting folder.** Once you are aware that a meeting will take place, set up a folder for it. Use this folder to collect items related to the meeting, such as the list of attendees, the agenda, notes, and copies of materials to be distributed. Create an electronic folder on your computer to store documents related to the meeting. An example of an electronic folder to store documents is shown in Figure 10-1.1.

Figure 10-1.1 **Store documents related to a meeting in a separate folder.**

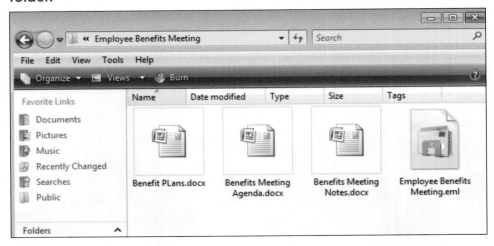

- **Determine a meeting time.** You may be told the time at which a meeting is to take place. In some cases, you may have to schedule a time when all needed participants can attend. Contact each person with a couple of suggested meeting times. Ask if one of the times is convenient. This is especially important when the meeting involves clients or others from outside your company. If the participants are all from within your organization and use calendaring software, you may be able to simply check each person's calendar for a time when he or she is available.
- **Reserve a meeting room.** When you know the date, time, and location of the meeting, check to see if the desired meeting room and time are available.
- **Key an agenda.** An agenda is a document that lists the topics to be discussed at a meeting and other related information. The agenda items are typically decided by the person who calls the meeting. All participants should receive a copy of the agenda prior to the meeting. Topics should be stated concisely and listed in the order they will be discussed. The starting time for each agenda item may be listed, along with breaks in the program. The person who will lead the discussion for each topic may be listed. Other relevant information, such as the meeting rooms or materials required, may also be included. An agenda typically contains many of the items shown in Figure 10-1.2.
- **Arrange for needed equipment.** Many times the purpose of the meeting will determine the kind of equipment that will be needed. Rooms may be equipped with overhead projectors, but electronic projection systems may be required. Special equipment may be needed if the information will be sent to an off-site location.
- **Notify the meeting participants.** Notify people as soon as possible of the time, place, approximate length, and purpose of the meeting. Identify any materials or supporting documents they should bring.

agenda a document that lists the topics to be discussed at a meeting and other related information

Approximately 2" top margin

Default or 1"side margins

Agenda

Pikesville Improvement Council

June 30, 20--

9:30 a.m., Conference Room C

1. Call to Order .... Nancy Wong, Pikesville Improvement Council Chairperson

2. Roll Call .... Roberto Sanchez, Secretary

3. Reading of the Minutes of the Previous Meeting .... Roberto Sanchez, Secretary

4. Treasurer's Report.. Sean Petersen, Treasurer

5. Committee Reports
   Recognitions Committee Report .... Latoya King, Chairperson

6. Unfinished Business
   Telecommunications Improvement Project

7. New Business
   East Pikesville Drive Improvement Project

8. Date of Next Meeting

9. Adjournment

■ **Use reminder systems.** Mark your and others' calendars with the meeting time and place. Use a tickler file or other reminder system to help you schedule the details. For example, if you must prepare 20 copies of a report to present at the meeting, create a reminder to do so. A meeting appointment in Microsoft Outlook is shown in Figure 10-1.3.

Figure 10-1.3 **Enter meetings and other appointments in your calendar.**

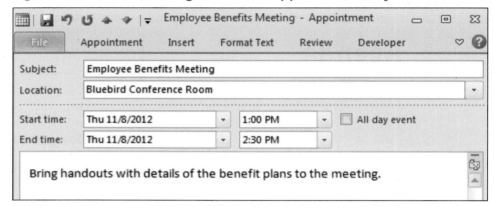

■ **Organize meeting materials.** You may be expected to gather materials. Notepads, pencils, file folders, ID badges, and parking stickers are examples of these items. Also, organize materials and handouts such as reports or letters that will be used at the meeting. Review any material to be presented at the meeting on the equipment that is available in the meeting room.

■ **Prepare the meeting room.** The room temperature should be comfortable, and the seating arranged to fit the meeting style. A room arrangement in which all participants can be seen and heard will make discussion easier. Any presentation aids should be positioned so that they are near the leader and can be seen by everyone in the room. Check to be sure that the requested equipment is present and working properly.

 CHECK POINT What types of information are typically included on an agenda?

Participating in Meetings

Meetings are an important part of business operations. People need to communicate with one another on a daily basis to complete the work of the organization. As an office worker, you should be prepared to lead or take part in meetings you attend.

Leader's Responsibilities

All employees use leadership skills in their jobs. They meet deadlines, improve how tasks are performed, and work with people to get their jobs done. These same leadership skills are important in meetings.

Every meeting should have a clear purpose; without it, there is no need for a meeting. The meeting leader should keep the purpose in mind while planning and conducting the meeting. A good meeting leader conducts the meeting in an assertive way that accomplishes the goals of the meeting. At the same time, he or she also uses a nonaggressive communication style that makes everyone feel comfortable. Follow the guidelines below to develop a nonaggressive, yet assertive communication style when leading a meeting.

- Make the goals of the meeting clear to all participants.
- Be familiar with the background material and have relevant documents at hand.
- Offer suggestions and ask questions during the meeting.
- Always be willing to listen to others' suggestions.
- Manage the time for the meeting. Begin and end the meeting at the appointed times.
- Keep the meeting on topic and moving toward a solution or a consensus.
- Ensure that all participants have an opportunity to take part in the discussion.
- Remain open to new and creative approaches.
- Summarize the decisions or plans that have been made during the meeting.
- Identify clearly the duties or tasks assigned to each group member in following up or completing plans.

consensus common agreement or mutual understanding

Brainstorming

Leaders may have the group take part in brainstorming. Brainstorming is offering ideas or suggestions in an effort to find a solution to a problem or to create a new approach. The objective is to come up with as many ideas as possible.

During the brainstorming process, the following rules are usually observed:

- All ideas are recorded, no matter how unrealistic they may appear.
- Criticism of ideas is not allowed until all ideas have been expressed. Comments such as "that will never work" or "we tried that once already" may block the flow of ideas.
- Explanations and combinations of ideas are encouraged. The value of brainstorming is that one idea may build on another.

brainstorming offering ideas or suggestions in an effort to find a solution to a problem or to create a new approach

Dmitriy Shironosov, 2010/Used under license from Shutterstock.com

Brainstorming in a meeting generates ideas.

To encourage brainstorming, a meeting leader must be willing to give time to the process and encourage everyone to take part.

Evaluating the Meeting

With informal meetings, a formal evaluation is typically not necessary. However, an informal evaluation should be done by the leader. The leader may want to ask two or three individuals who took part in the meeting how they thought the meeting went. The leader may also consider questions such as the following to help evaluate the meeting:

- Did everyone in attendance actively take part in the meeting?
- Did everyone seem interested and involved in the discussion?
- Were the goals of the meeting accomplished?
- Were appropriate decisions made?
- Can I improve the ways I handled the issues or related to the people present?

CHECK POINT What is the purpose of brainstorming in a meeting?

Participants' Responsibilities

The degree to which you participate during a meeting will depend on the purpose of the meeting, where it is held, and the planning that has been done. You may be expected to take part in the discussion or take notes for the .

minutes an official record of the proceedings of a meeting

Participating in a Meeting

Just as a leader has responsibilities, so do the participants. As a participant, you are responsible for reading the meeting notice, the agenda, and any related materials received before the meeting. You should arrive on time to the meeting and contribute thoughtful or well-researched comments. You should listen nonjudgmentally to others, respect the leader's role, and be courteous to others.

Although taking part in this way sounds simple, it is not always so. Your mind may wander, focusing on other work-related tasks or on personal issues. However, your comments might be the ones that help solve a problem or keep the meeting focused. You should always try to contribute in a positive way to the success of the meeting. Give your full attention to the meeting and do not answer text messages, e-mails, or cell phone calls during the meeting. Cell phones and pagers should be turned off or placed on silent alert.

Minutes

You may be asked to record minutes for a meeting. Minutes are an official record of the proceedings of a meeting. Minutes for a council meeting are shown in Figure 10-1.4. Minutes provide the reader with a concise record of what took place at the meeting. The minutes should not be a word-for-word transcript of the meeting. However, the recorder should make note of all important information. The minutes must give a clear, accurate, and complete accounting of the happenings of the meeting.

Figure 10-1.4 **Minutes are the official record of a meeting.**

© Cengage Learning 2013

Approximately 2" top margin

Default or 1" side margins

Minutes

Pikesville Improvement Council
June 30, 20--

1. The regular weekly meeting of the Pikesville Improvement Council was held on June 30, 20--, in Conference Room C at City Hall. The meeting was called to order at 9:30 a.m. by Nancy Wong, Pikesville Improvement Council Chairperson.

2. Present were members Elizabeth Larkin, Rodger Aycock, Douglas Ivey, Laura Johnson, Steven Minnhausen, Latoya King, Sean Petersen, Roberto Sanchez, and Nancy Wong. A guest, John Byrd, was also present. Council member Kelly Pearce was absent.

3. The minutes of the June 23, 20--, meeting were read and approved.

4. The treasurer, Sean Petersen, reported that the Improvement Projects Fund has a balance of $359,450.

5. Latoya King gave the Recognition Committee report, recommending Jane Ann Adamson be submitted for employee of the month. Laura Johnson moved that Jane Ann Adamson be submitted to the city council as employee of the month. Steven Minnhausen seconded the motion, and the motion was approved by the council. President Wong directed the secretary to prepare the resolution for submission (attached to the minutes).

6. The council addressed unfinished business. President Wong reported that the three recorded bids for the Telecommunications Improvement Project have been forwarded to the City Engineering Department for evaluation.

7. The council addressed new business. Douglas Ivey reported that a community meeting will be held on July 6, 20--, to discuss the project with residents.

8. Pre...
9:3...

Pikesville Improvement Council
Minutes for June 30, 20--
Page 2

Approximately 1" top margin

Default or 1" side margins

9. Douglas Ivey moved and Rodger Aycock seconded that the meeting be adjourned. The motion was approved and the meeting was adjourned at 10:30 a.m.

_____   _____
Roberto Sanchez, Secretary   Nancy Wong, President

Attachment: Resolution of Recognition

© Cengage Learning 2013

Although various reporting formats are acceptable for recording minutes, the following information appears in most of them:

- Name of group, committee, organization, or business holding the meeting
- Time, date, place, and type of meeting (for example, weekly, monthly, annual, called, special)
- Name of presiding officer
- Members present and absent (In a large organization, only the number of members present must be recorded to verify that a quorum was present.)
- Reading and approval of the minutes from the previous meeting
- Committee or individual reports (for example, treasurer's report, standing committees, special committees)
- Names of the persons making a motion or giving a second and whether the motion was passed
- Unfinished business (includes discussion and action taken)
- New business (includes discussion and action taken)
- Time, date, and place of next meeting (if known)
- Time of adjournment
- Signature of the individual responsible for the minutes

quorum the minimum number of people who must be present to conduct business at a meeting

motion a proposal formally made in a meeting

second a formal statement of support for a motion

Taking notes for minutes may be one of your duties at a meeting.

StockLite/Shutterstock

If you prepare minutes frequently, use a parliamentary procedures reference source (such as *Robert's Rules of Order Newly Revised*). This resource will help you better understand the meeting proceedings and the correct terms to use when taking and preparing minutes. For example, motions should be recorded word for word.

Sometimes at the following meeting, corrections must be made to the minutes before they can be approved. If only a few words are affected, lines may be drawn through the incorrect words and the proper insertions made above them. An example is shown in Figure 10-1.5. If more than a few words are affected, lines may be drawn through the sentences or paragraphs to be

Pikesville Improvement Council
Minutes for June 30, 20--
Page 2

6. The council addressed unfinished business. President Wong reported that the ~~three~~ *four* recorded bids for the Telecommunications Improvement Project have been forwarded to the City Engineering Department for evaluation.

7. The council addressed new business. Douglas Ivey reported that a community meeting will be held on July 6, 20--, to discuss the project with residents.

© Cengage Learning 2013

corrected and the changes written on a new page. The page number of each correction should be indicated on the original minutes. The minutes should not be rewritten after they have been read and approved at the meeting.

Action Plans

For many meetings, developing an action plan to solve a problem or accomplish tasks is appropriate. A written plan of action can replace the traditional minutes of a meeting. The plan focuses on the actions to be taken after the meeting rather than simply recording the proceedings. An action plan is shown in Figure 10-1.5 on page 346. The basic information about the meeting that should be included in an action plan is listed below.

action plan a description of tasks to do or actions to be taken after a meeting

- Topic of the meeting, meeting date, the chairperson's name, and the recorder's name
- Specific actions to be taken and the person(s) responsible
- Deadlines for the actions and completion dates
- Key issues discussed and the participants
- The meeting length
- Announcement of the next meeting

To arrive at a plan of action, the meeting leader should be sure that all meeting participants have input into plans and decisions. Everyone should have clear assignments to put the plan into action.

Follow-up After the Meeting

Once the meeting is over, you may need to complete follow-up activities. Make calendar or reminder notations for any item from the meeting that will require future attention. Prepare the minutes or action plan as soon as possible if that is one of your duties. Preparing the minutes will be easier when the details of the meeting are fresh in your mind. Use examples of previous minutes for the format or follow the sample shown in Figure 10-1.6. Ask the chairperson of the meeting to review the minutes before they are distributed to be sure there are no omissions or errors.

Approximately 2" top margin

Default or 1" side margins

Action Plan

Pikesville Improvement Council
April 30, 20--

1. The purpose of the Pikesville Improvement Council meeting held on April 30, 20--, was to discuss the downtown improvement project. President Wong called the meeting to order at 7:30 p.m. and declared a quorum present. Ms. Wong called the members' attention to the information that was delivered to them during the week prior to the meeting.

2. Present were members Elizabeth Larkin, Rodger Aycock, Kelly Pearce, Douglas Ivey, Laura Johnson, Steven Minnhausen, Latoya King, Sean Petersen, Roberto Sanchez, and Nancy Wong. Guests, John Byrd and Sharon Young, were also present.

3. The council discussed the plans to acquire an additional piece of property that joins the downtown area. The property will be used for a park with an amphitheater and petting zoo for children. Mr. Byrd and Ms. Young discussed details on each piece of property under consideration.

4. President Wong appointed Kelly Pearce, Elizabeth Larkin, and Rodger Aycock to study each piece of property and make recommendations to the council on which piece of property to purchase. The recommendation should be ready to present at the meeting on May 14, 20--.

5. The next meeting will be held on May 14, 20--. The meeting was adjourned at 8:30 p.m.

_____   _____

Roberto Sanchez, Secretary   Nancy Wong, President

Complete any correspondence related to the meeting. Write thank-you letters to speakers or resource persons. Items to be added to the agenda for the next meeting also should be noted.

CHECK POINT How should corrections to meeting minutes be handled?

Teleconferences

A teleconference is a meeting of three or more people in different locations. Those taking part are connected by a telecommunications system. Teleconferences can be used to deliver training or exchange information. They can allow people to discuss problems and make decisions, just as face-to-face meetings can.

teleconference a meeting of three or more people in different locations using a telecommunications system

Types of Teleconferences

Teleconferences may be thought of as virtual meetings. They may also be called conference calls, video conferences, or web meetings, depending on the technology used. Virtual meetings have both advantages and disadvantages just as face-to-face meetings have. Advantages of virtual meetings include:

- Savings in travel time and costs, including meals and hotel rooms.
- Bringing people together who have expertise in a number of different areas with a minimum of effort.

Disadvantages of virtual meetings include:

- Less chance for effective brainstorming on issues.
- Less spontaneity among individuals because of a structured environment.
- No chance for the interaction before or after the meeting that is often so effective in face-to-face meetings.

Oliver Eltinger/Corbis

Employees may discuss problems or make decisions during a conference call.

Conference Calls

A conference call (also called an audio conference) is a meeting in which a number of people can take part via telephone. A conference call differs from other telephone conversations in that it involves more than two people in at least two locations. The calls may involve using speakerphones or a meeting room with microphones and speakers. Services supplied by telephone companies allow participants in multiple locations to dial a single phone number to talk with each other.

Video Conferences

A video conference is a meeting in which two or more people at different locations see and hear each other. Those taking part use equipment such as computers, video cameras, and microphones. A web camera, a microphone, and speakers may be connected to computers and used to transmit video and audio to other computers. Skype is a popular program used to hold video conferences. On a larger scale, a videoconferencing room may be used to provide equipment for use by several people.

Web Meetings

A web meeting is a meeting in which two or more people at different locations communicate and share information via computers and a network connection, such as the Internet or a local area network. Some web meetings are fully interactive. Participants can see video of one another, talk in real time, and exchange information via computers. For other web meetings, participants may speak with one another via a traditional telephone conference while using meeting software to share information. Windows Meeting Space is a program that allows you to set up a meeting and share documents, programs, or your computer desktop with several other people who have the same program.

 CHECK POINT What are two advantages of having a teleconference rather than a face-to-face meeting?

✴ WORKPLACE CONNECTIONS ✴

Project team leaders of a South Carolina firm need to meet as often as six times a week to refine ideas and reach decisions on project questions. When the executive assistant, Tom Yu, is asked to set up a teleconference meeting, he first checks all team leaders' electronic calendars for an open time. He then notifies the leaders of the meeting date and time, lists a call-in telephone number and password, and provides the web address.

On the day of the meeting, leaders dial the telephone number to be connected to the audio portion of the meeting through their speakerphones. They access a website via their computers to see documents. A small digital camera sits on top of each team leader's computer. The team leaders can see each other as they speak or ask questions. The company's executives feel that being able to meet and share information in this way helps them solve problems quickly and be more responsive to market changes.

> **What type of teleconference is described in this scenario?**

Preparing for a Teleconference

Technology allows flexibility in planning, preparing for, and taking part in meetings. Teleconferencing can be expensive, so the meeting time should be used wisely. Your role in preparing for a teleconference may include the following responsibilities:

- Reserve the conference room and necessary equipment, if a special room is to be used.
- Notify the participants of the date, time, length, and purpose of the meeting. Include a telephone number and the name of a contact to call in the event of technical difficulties.
- Prepare and distribute any related materials well in advance of the meeting. If several documents are to be sent, use descriptive file names to make it easy to identify the documents during the meeting. Verify that the documents are in a format the recipients can use.
- Prepare and distribute an agenda well in advance of the meeting.
- The room may be equipped with computers, an electronic tablet, or other systems for sharing documents during the meeting. Be sure these systems are operating properly.
- If the services of a technician or coordinator are needed, arrange to have that person available during the conference. Learn the less complicated technical details of using the equipment, so that you can expand your skills and knowledge in this area.

 CHECK POINT What file format might be used for documents for a teleconference to help ensure that all those taking part can access the documents?

21st Century Skills

PARTNERSHIP FOR
21ST CENTURY SKILLS

Thinking Critically

Mr. Burris has asked you to take charge of preparations for a meeting with union leaders and company officials on April 2. In addition, he has asked you to sit in during the meeting and take minutes. You know from the agenda that the meeting has been scheduled for his conference room.

1. Key a list of the preparations you may need to make for the conference room.
2. Key a list of questions you have for Mr. Burris regarding the meeting preparations. For example: Will there be breaks for refreshments? If yes, how many and when?
3. What items will you need to take to the meeting with you?
4. Key a list of tasks you may need to do before, during, and after the meeting.

Making Academic Connections

Reinforcing English Skills

Pronouns are words that serve as substitutes for nouns. Pronouns must agree with their antecedents (nouns for which they stand) in person, number, and gender. Write or key the following sentences, selecting the proper pronouns.

1. The executive (that, who) directed the meeting is an effective business leader.
2. Neither Juan nor Jim thinks that (his, their) itinerary should be changed.
3. The executives said that (them, they), along with a group from another company, would attend the seminar in Paris.
4. Office workers who take the minutes of meetings need a parliamentary procedures resource available to (them, they).
5. The committee has promised to have (its, their) findings ready for review at the departmental meeting next week.
6. The executives traveling on business from that office often use (its, their) company's credit cards.
7. The executive and her associate were uncertain how (she, they) should reschedule the trip.
8. The members of the group attending the meeting wanted (its, their) opinions aired before a final vote was taken.
9. The oval table (that, who) was placed in the meeting room will be there only a short time.
10. Mai and Lecia reviewed the meeting agenda before (it, they) was sent to the participants.

10-1 Activity 1

Agenda for a Meeting (Outcome 10-1a)

You work in Atlanta for Ernest Fogg, director of the Marketing Department. Mr. Fogg is making arrangements for a teleconference with marketing vice presidents located in five different regional offices. The teleconference will originate in Atlanta. Mr. Fogg sends you an edited copy of the agenda for the teleconference. He says, "Please complete this agenda in final form. Make the changes I've indicated and list the participants in alphabetic order according to city. Proofread very carefully to ensure that all numbers are correct."

1. Open the file 10-1 Activity 1 found in the data files. This file contains the rough draft agenda and comments from Mr. Fogg.
2. Create the final agenda following Mr. Fogg's oral and written instructions. Use Figure 10-1.2 as an example for format.

10-1 Activity 2

Meeting and Action Plan (Outcome 10-1b)

Work in a group with three or four classmates to apply the meeting and planning skills you learned in this topic.

1. Identify a group chairperson who will lead the meeting and a recorder who will make notes during the meeting.
2. Choose one of the following problem scenarios as the reason for your meeting. Discuss the possible causes of the problem and related factors. Also consider what you have learned in previous chapters.
3. Brainstorm ideas for solving the problem. Your goal is to be an active participant with an assertive, but not aggressive, communication style.
4. Create an action plan detailing the steps your group will take toward solving the problem. Assign one or more people to complete each task and set deadlines for completing the tasks. Key an action plan document using Figure 10-1.6 as a guide.

Scenario 1 You are employed in a small company that has five other office workers. All the office workers need help in handling office tasks such as keying reports, preparing mailings, and responding to inquiries.

Scenario 2 Your company's petty cash fund does not balance with the fund records. Cash is missing. The same situation has occurred for each of the past three months. The petty cash is kept in a small metal box in the secretary's desk. The desk is locked at night, but it is usually not locked during the day. The secretary's duties often take her away from her desk.

Scenario 3 You work for a small company that uses a local area computer network. Users can connect to the Internet via the LAN. Employees are supposed to follow procedures to log on and log off when using the network. Over the past month, computer viruses have been detected frequently on the company's computer network.

OUTCOMES

10-2a Use appropriate procedures for planning business travel.
10-2b Describe the factors involved in travel etiquette.
10-2c Discuss completing work while traveling and travel follow-up activities.

KEY TERMS

itinerary p. 352
electronic ticket p. 353
confirmation number p. 354
passport p. 358
visa p. 359
consulate p. 359
embassy p. 359
etiquette p. 360

Preparing for Business Travel

People travel for various business reasons. They may need to supervise company operations or meet with clients or company associates. They may attend conferences related to work. Many companies, both large and small, do business with others from around the world.

Travel arrangements are made according to company policies. Some large firms may have a travel department for this purpose. Others may rely on the services of a travel agency. In smaller firms, however, an office worker or the traveling employee may make the travel arrangements.

You may have an opportunity to choose the mode of travel for a business trip. The choice of hotels may also be yours. When such choices are available, you will need to know your personal preferences. When you are making the arrangements for another person, you will need to know that person's preferences.

When you travel on business, you will want to complete your duties or tasks effectively. You should arrive at meetings on time and with the needed supporting materials. Carefully made travel plans are important to the success of a business trip.

A travel folder (or trip file) will help you organize the details of an upcoming trip. Use the folder to collect information as it becomes available. Notes on reservations, tickets, hotels, and meeting confirmations may be placed in the file. The information in the travel folder will help you prepare an itinerary and complete company travel documents. It can also serve as a reminder system for tasks related to the trip.

itinerary a document that gives detailed travel plans for a trip

Travel Appointments and Reservations

As you plan the trip, set aside time to schedule meetings to be held during the trip. Shortly before the trip, contact each person with whom you plan to meet to confirm the date, time, and meeting place. Organize the names, titles, company names, addresses, and telephone numbers or e-mail addresses of the individuals with whom meetings are scheduled. Make reservations for transportation and overnight lodging.

Commercial Air Travel

Time is money for the busy business traveler. The popularity of air travel reflects this point. Often, the only way to manage a tight schedule is by air travel. An extensive network of airline routes is provided by national, regional, and commuter airlines. Airline schedules are available free of charge at ticket counters in airports, at airline offices in major cities, at large hotels, and from travel agents. Most airlines have websites that provide travel details and where tickets can be purchased. Tickets can also be purchased by telephone or in person at airports or ticket offices.

If you use several airlines, you will find the Official Airline Guide (OAG) a valuable source of flight information and schedules. The OAG is available online as a subscription service. To find the site, enter the name in a search engine. The OAG Traveler pages provide information for travelers and travel planners. You can indicate the departure and arrival cities and the date of travel. The flight number and airline, times, cities, number of stops, and other related information will be displayed.

You may make flight reservations by calling a travel agent, by calling an airline directly using a toll-free number, or by accessing various websites. When you purchase airline tickets online, you typically receive an **electronic ticket** receipt.

electronic ticket document and receipt that contain ticket information in electronic form

If you use the services of a travel agent, your flight itinerary and an invoice may be received with the airline ticket receipt. Each of these documents serves a specific purpose. The flight itinerary can be checked against your records and used to create a traveler's itinerary. Many travelers attach a copy of the flight itinerary to the overall itinerary for the trip. The invoice is kept to attach to the travel expense report.

Plan to arrive at the airport well ahead of your flight departure time (one to two hours). You will need time for checking in at the airline desk to receive boarding passes, check luggage, and move through security checkpoints. Be sure to have a current photo ID such as a driver's license or passport. When checking bags, verify that the luggage tag attached by the airline attendant has the correct destination code. Wait until you see your bags placed on the conveyor belt before leaving the check-in area. Do not pack money, notebook computers, or other valuable items in checked luggage. Keep these items in a carried bag instead.

Comply with all reasonable requests of security personnel. Be aware that your checked bags or carried bags, as well as your person, may be subject

imagebroker/Alamy

Have a photo ID and ticket information at hand when checking bags for a flight.

to search. Never leave your bags or other possessions unattended or in the care of a stranger. Never agree to carry a bag or other items from a stranger. Check with the airline for a current list of items that are not allowed in checked or carried bags. For example, knives, lighters, and strike-anywhere matches are generally not allowed in carried bags.

Other Forms of Business Travel

Rental cars and trains provide alternative forms of business travel. You may have occasion to make travel arrangements using one of these forms of transportation.

For short trips, particularly in a local area, many people prefer to rent cars. A rental car may also be suitable when you fly to a city and have appointments in outlying areas. Be sure to allow ample time to reach your destination. Rental cars are available at most airports and other convenient locations. Rental fees vary in price according to the size of the car, the length of time the car is needed, and the miles driven. Follow your company's guidelines for renting a car. Many rental car companies have websites where you may choose and reserve a rental car.

✳ WORKPLACE CONNECTIONS ✳

Joe Park rented a car on his arrival at the Kansas City International Airport. He left the car rental agency at 1 p.m. for a meeting near Kansas City scheduled for 2 p.m., giving himself ample travel time for the half-hour trip. Joe arrived at the office where the meeting was scheduled and introduced himself to the receptionist. "Oh, I'm glad you finally made it. We were concerned that something might have happened to you," the receptionist said. "I don't understand," said Joe. "The meeting is scheduled for 2 p.m. It's only 1:40." "Let's see," said the receptionist. "You traveled from Cincinnati, right? Did you remember that Kansas City is in the Central time zone?" Joe was embarrassed about being late for the meeting and promised himself to check carefully all times, including the time zone, in the future.

> In what time zone is Cincinnati, Ohio, located?

Train travel is popular in some sections of the country. Train stations are located in the centers of cities and can provide an alternative to air travel on certain routes. Overnight trains have sleeping and dining rooms on board. Check with a travel agent or look in the yellow pages of your telephone directory for information on the railway lines serving your area.

Amtrak, a company that provides train services in many areas of the United States, provides a website where customers may make reservations online. To find the site, enter the company name in a search engine.

Hotel/Motel Accommodations

Many business travelers must be away from home overnight and stay in a hotel or motel room. In some cases, you may be allowed to request a particular hotel. In other cases, you may rely on a travel agent or coworker to select the lodging.

When you make reservations by telephone, use toll-free telephone numbers whenever possible. Write down the names of the persons who make and confirm reservations. Always make a note of the rates you are told. Record the **confirmation number** and repeat it to the reservation agent to make sure it is correct. The confirmation number should be included in the itinerary. A written confirmation from the hotel is helpful. Many hotels have websites where reservations may be made. A confirmation number is usually provided. The reservation may also be confirmed by e-mail.

Reservations for hotels can also be made online at travel sites that have information about many hotels. At many travel sites, information can be found about

confirmation number a series of letters and/or numbers that identify a reservation

hotels in a specific area. Descriptions, prices, and dates available are shown. Using a travel site may require less time than checking individual hotel sites.

 CHECK POINT How can you use the Internet to research and make travel arrangements?

Itinerary and Supporting Materials

Once the travel plans are set, you should prepare an itinerary. You will need to assemble travel documents and related materials for meetings or appointments. If the plans for the trip change, other arrangements may need to be made. Changes can generally be made at the time you cancel the original plans. Have your confirmation numbers and other details available when you call or go online to change reservations or appointments.

Prepare an Itinerary

An itinerary is a detailed plan of a trip. It serves as a guide for the business traveler. Travel plans, meetings, hotel locations, and reminders or special instructions should be included. A sample itinerary is shown in Figure 10-2.1 on page 356. When planning a trip, allow enough travel time between meetings to avoid having to rush to make the next appointment.

Adrian Weinbrecht/Jupiter Images

Some hotels provide special rates or services for business travelers.

You may need several copies of the itinerary. One hard copy should be carried with you. Another copy can be carried in the baggage. One copy should be left with a contact person at the office. You may want to give one copy to family members. The itinerary should be in an easy-to-read format that gives the day-by-day schedule for the complete trip. An electronic copy can be stored on your notebook computer or PDA and carried with you. If changes in travel plans occur during the trip, the electronic copy can be updated and e-mailed to the office and family members.

Gather Supporting Items

Before the trip, gather the travel documents, supplies, and supporting materials, such as those listed below, that are needed for the trip.

■ Itinerary
■ Travel tickets or receipts

Figure 10-2.1 **Travel Itinerary**

Approximately 2" top margin

Default or 1" side margins

Itinerary for Charlene Stanford

May 17 to May 19, 20—

DATE	TIME	ACTIVITY
Wednesday May 17	9:43 a.m.	Leave Hartsfield International Airport on Delta Flight 1745.
	10:50 a.m.	Arrive Dallas/Ft. Worth International Airport. Pick up rental car key at the Sun Rentals counter, confirmation number 388075.
		Hotel reservations at Fairmont Hotel, 1717 W. Akard Street. Phone: 214-555-0102. Confirmation number 7K4995F.
	2:30 p.m.	Meeting with George Thatcher, Vice President of Marketing, Fabric Wholesalers, 1314 Gaston Avenue (Phone: 214-555-0196) to discuss purchase agreements.
	7:00 p.m.	Dinner with staff at the hotel to review plans for the Apparel Fair.
Thursday May 18	12:32 p.m.	Leave Dallas/Ft. Worth International Airport on Delta Flight 444. Return rental car keys at Sun Rentals and take a shuttle to the airport.
	1:55 p.m.	Arrive at Lindbergh Field International Airport and meet Richard Stanley (Phone: 619-555-0152) at the baggage claim area. Travel to Naples plant with Richard, take a tour, and return to the hotel.
		Hotel reservations at the Seven Seas Lodge, 411 Hotel Circle South (Phone: 619-555-1022). Confirmation number 4478S84.
Friday May 19	7:55 a.m.	Leave Lindbergh Field International Airport on Delta Flight 880. Richard will meet me at my hotel at 5:30 a.m. and drive me to the airport.
	3:52 p.m.	Arrive Hartsfield Atlanta International Airport.

- Travel funds
- Travel and health documents
- Hotel/motel and car rental confirmations
- Maps of cities or states as appropriate
- Directions to offices or other meeting locations
- Speeches, supporting correspondence, reports, or files for each appointment/meeting
- Forms for recording expenses
- Extra notepaper, pens, and business cards
- Equipment, such as a laptop computer, portable phone, or presentation projection system

If the supporting materials, such as a large number of handouts, will be too heavy or bulky to carry with you, arrange to have them shipped to your hotel or meeting location. Arrange for special packaging for equipment, such as computers and projection panels, to prevent damage to these items while en route. Confirm the safe arrival of supporting materials prior to or immediately on arrival and have a backup plan to follow in case items are lost or damaged. For example, you might carry one set of handouts with you so that copies can be made at your destination if necessary.

Jupiter Images

Gather and pack supporting documents and equipment for safe transport.

 CHECK POINT What types of information are typically included on a travel itinerary?

Documents and Currency for Foreign Travel

Two documents are required for foreign travel in most countries: a passport and a visa. Other documents, such as work permits, prescriptions for medicine carried, and health records, may also be needed.

The U.S. government provides a smart traveler service for U.S. citizens who are traveling to a foreign country. The website is shown in Figure 10-2.2. The information you provide may help the Department of State assist you in case of an emergency.

Figure 10-2.2 The U.S. Department of State STEP Page

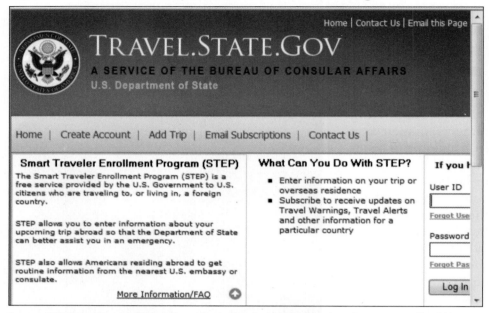

Source: U.S. Department of State, Travel.State.Gov, https://travelregistration.state.gov/ibrs/ui/.

Passport

A passport is an official document granting permission to travel. Issued by the United States Department of State, it states a person's right to protection in the foreign country. A passport is needed for travel in most foreign countries.

To secure a passport, application forms may be obtained from government offices and many travel agencies. Information about how to get a passport is available at the passports page on the U.S. Department of State website. You can also look in the white pages telephone directory (under *Government Agencies*) to find the passport office nearest you.

The requirements to obtain a passport for the first time are listed on the passport application and on the U.S. Department of State website. Processing the application normally takes up to six weeks. You should allow enough lead time to avoid having to delay travel plans. After the passport is received, it should be signed, and the information requested on the inside cover completed. To replace an expired passport, obtain a renewal application. Submit the renewal application well in advance of the expiration date for the current passport to avoid being without a current passport.

A passport should be carried or kept in a hotel security box or safe and never be left in a hotel room. Make a photocopy of the identification page so the passport can be replaced if it is lost. Report the loss of a passport immediately to the nearest passport office or as instructed on the U.S. Department of State website. If traveling abroad, report the loss to the United States Embassy.

Visa

A visa is a permit granted by a foreign government for a person to enter its country. The visa usually appears as a stamped notation in a passport, indicating that the person may enter the country for a certain purpose and for a specific period of time. Be sure to note the effective dates of a visa.

Always check to see whether you need a visa for the country in which travel is planned. Contact the consulate or embassy of the country or a travel agent before leaving the United States. Addresses and telephone numbers of consulates of most foreign countries in the United States can be found online. Search using the term *embassy*. You can also look in the yellow pages of telephone directories in major cities under *Consulates* to find phone numbers. Addresses and telephone numbers for many consulates are provided on the U.S. Department of State website. Again, allow lead time to obtain the visa stamp from the appropriate consulate prior to traveling to that country.

Health Documents

When traveling to some countries, certain vaccinations may be required to protect against a variety of diseases. A country may require people entering the country to have health tests, such as testing for contagious diseases. A travel agency or the consulate of the country to be visited can supply information about required vaccinations or tests. Records of the vaccinations and tests must be signed by a doctor. They must also be validated by the local or state health officer on a specific form. The form may be obtained from a travel agent, the passport office, the local health department, or some doctors. Even if the country to be visited does not require vaccinations, a traveler should carry a written record of childhood vaccinations and booster shots.

Other health factors should be considered for international travel. Taking medicine for air sickness may make travelers more comfortable on long flights. Prescriptions from a doctor for medicines that must be taken by the traveler can be helpful. Permission to carry medicines that might not be available in the country to be visited may be required. Check with a travel agent or the country's consulate to see what arrangements must be made for these medicines.

visa a permit granted by a foreign government for a person to enter its country

consulate a person appointed by a government to serve its interests or citizens in another country

embassy the offices of an ambassador in a foreign country

Bob Pardue - Medical Lifestyle/Alamy

Vaccinations may be required before traveling to some countries.

Currency

Before leaving the United States, you can exchange money for the currency of the country being visited. The rate of exchange for various countries is published in some newspapers and available online. If you prefer, a small amount of money can be exchanged in the United States and more money exchanged upon arrival at your destination. Be aware of the exchange rates before traveling to another country and pay attention to the exchange rates once in the country. Exchange rates are not always the same at different locations. For example, the exchange rate at a bank may be more favorable than the exchange rate at an airport.

✔CHECK POINT   What is the purpose of a passport and of a visa?

Travel Etiquette

U.S. companies of all sizes deal with companies in other countries. This activity is handled differently in each company. Some companies have a special division to deal with their branch offices in other countries. Your behavior as a business traveler reflects on you, your company, and your home area. Proper dress and travel **etiquette** will contribute to a successful business trip.

etiquette standards for proper behavior

Dress

Remember that you represent your organization when you travel. Your dress will contribute to that most important first impression you make on others. Dress appropriately for the type of meeting or function you are attending. Many companies send employees to training sessions in which the attire is less formal than while on the job. If the meeting is to take place at another company's site, the attire may be more formal.

Dress for Travel

Many times, employees need a day to travel to a business destination. Dress in this case will be less formal on the airplane or in a car. When a short plane or car ride is all that is necessary to reach your destination, however, dress more formally to be ready to conduct business on arrival.

✳ WORKPLACE CONNECTIONS ✳

Jagu Patel looked forward to attending a conference at a popular golf resort in Florida. He carefully packed his business suits as well as casual clothes for playing golf and sightseeing. On Monday morning, Jagu ate breakfast early and arrived on time for the first meeting session. As other people began to enter the room, he noticed that he was the only person wearing a business suit. Jagu quietly left the meeting area and went back to his room. Reviewing the conference agenda booklet again, he found that it did, indeed, indicate that business casual or resort wear would be the appropriate dress for the conference. Jagu was glad that he had packed plenty of casual clothes as he changed outfits and returned to the meeting.

What might Jagu have done to be more casually dressed if he had packed only business attire?

Dress to Impress

Consider the persons with whom you will be doing business and the impression you want to leave about your organization. Many companies may permit less formal dress while on the job. However, while on business in another city or country, formal business dress may be expected. Proper dress is especially important when traveling in foreign countries or meeting with persons from a culture different from your own. Be aware of the dress customs for the country in which you will do business and dress accordingly.

 CHECK POINT   How should you dress while traveling on business?

Customs

Proper etiquette plays an important role in conducting business successfully, both in the United States and in foreign countries. Etiquette will vary from country to country. Various print and electronic resources are available to provide in-depth information about business and travel etiquette. For information about a specific country, consult a travel agent or someone who has lived there or done business there. Consider the following customs and protocols related to business travel:

- Be on time for appointments. Arrange your schedule to allow time for unexpected delays in travel.

- Take an ample supply of business cards. Business cards are always presented by a caller and serve the purposes of introducing the person who is visiting and providing an easy future reference. Business cards should include your name, your company's name, your position, and your title. Avoid using abbreviations on the card. For international travel, have the same information printed in the local language on the reverse side of the card.

- If and when appropriate, provide a gift that is company associated, such as a pen or sweatshirt with a company logo. Flowers are generally a safe and appreciated gift in almost every country.

- Paying for meals and tipping for clients is generally accepted as the role of the host—the person who set up the meeting.

A smile is generally appropriate when greeting someone from any culture.

- The universal business greeting in the United States is the handshake. When you offer your hand or reach out to take another's hand, be sure your grasp is firm but not too tight. Make eye contact with the person at the same time.

- Know the body language and gestures that may be offensive or have different meanings in other cultures. The universal form of communication that all people recognize and appreciate is a smile. Use it often to break the ice and ease tense situations that may arise.

- Know how to pronounce the name of the person you are visiting, as well as how to address the person. Use academic or honorary titles when appropriate.
- Taste any food that is offered by the host. Many hosts will proudly present the best delicacy the area has to offer.
- Speak standard English. Avoid using slang terms. This is especially important when meeting with people for whom English is a second language.

Focus on BUSINESS

Travel Safety

Personal safety and the security of luggage, computers, and other items while traveling are concerns for many business travelers. Follow these safety suggestions as you travel or make travel preparations:

- Access the U.S. Department of State website for travel warnings, consular information sheets, and public announcements regarding travel.
- Do not leave your luggage or other items unattended in hotel lobbies or in waiting areas in airports.
- Keep your passport and travel funds in a safe, secure place.
- Do not display cash, expensive jewelry, or other valuable items when traveling.
- Do not agree to carry items in your luggage for another person.
- Use all locking devices on doors and windows in your hotel room.

- Do not leave valuables in your car, and be sure to lock your vehicle.
- Be aware of your surroundings, and look around before entering parking lots late at night. Always return to your hotel through the main entrance after dark.
- Protect your credit or bank card and account passwords or numbers at all times.

Many motels and hotels place safety guidelines on specially printed cards in rooms. Read and follow their guidelines for your personal safety.

Why should you not leave your luggage or other items unattended in hotel lobbies or in waiting areas in airports? What can you do to protect your credit or bank card and account passwords or numbers?

Work Tasks and Travel

Business travelers may need to complete work while traveling. The work may relate to meetings with clients or business partners during the trip. Routine tasks that do not relate to the trip, such as completing monthly reports, may also be completed while traveling. Once the trip is over, the traveler may need to complete follow-up tasks, such as an expense report or thank-you letters.

Business travelers may depend on an office assistant or coworker to handle routine tasks and messages while away from the office. Before the traveler leaves for a business trip, the coworker should understand how to deal with routine matters. Plans for handling crisis situations and out-of-the-ordinary situations should also be made.

Staying in Touch

Technology makes it easy for travelers to stay in touch with the office or clients. Data can be sent and received using computers, networks, and mobile phones. Some hotels provide fully equipped business centers for travelers. Many hotels offer wireless network access in rooms and common areas that allow users to access the Internet. Travelers can often complete tasks such as:

- Send and receive business data by fax
- Access messages (voice or electronic mail)
- Participate in teleconferences
- Access the Internet for travel information
- Record travel expense information
- Check availability of products for clients
- Place orders and receive confirmation of orders placed by clients
- Access a company intranet for policy or procedural changes that occur while the traveler is out of the office

Technology will continue to play an important role in how work is handled while workers are traveling on business.

CHECK POINT How can using technology aid an office professional in completing work while traveling?

moodboard/Jupiter Images

Many hotels offer wireless Internet connections for guests.

Follow-Up Activities

Certain follow-up activities should be completed as soon as possible after a trip. These activities include reporting travel expenses, writing a variety of reports, and writing correspondence.

Expense Reports

Typically, a company will have a form that employees use to report travel expenses. The expenses listed may include charges for items such as hotel rooms, meals, and car rentals. Other expenses, such as those for entertaining clients, may also be approved expenses. Some travelers may receive travel money in advance from the company. These funds are accounted for on the travel expense report. Receipts may be required for travel expenses. Follow company procedures to prepare expense reports. Be sure to obtain the necessary signatures or approvals of the completed forms.

Meeting Reports

Examples of meeting reports include sales summaries, client visit logs, project progress updates, and others that present the results of the business trip. The completed reports may provide a written record of decisions that were made or goals that were set. They may discuss complaints or suggestions from customers or ideas for new products or services. Reports are sent to persons who will be affected by the decisions, goals, complaints, or ideas.

Correspondence

Thank-you letters or messages may be sent to people with whom you meet during the trip. The need for thank-you letters will depend on the purpose of the travel and business etiquette guidelines.

Other follow-up messages may provide a written record of agreements made during the visit. They may give details that were not available during the meeting or discuss tasks related to the meeting. When writing follow-up letters, remember to use the five characteristics (5 Cs) of effective communications to evaluate your documents. You can review the 5 Cs in Chapter 4.

 CHECK POINT What are two examples of reports that might be completed following a trip?

REVIEW 10-2

21st Century Skills

Thinking Critically

You are a department manager for Ellis Tools, Inc. An employee in your department has submitted a travel expense form for your approval. Your company pays employees 30 cents per mile for travel in their personal cars. The maximum amounts allowed per day for meals are: breakfast, $10; lunch, $15; and dinner, $25. Employees must submit a receipt for any expense item greater than $25. The purpose of the business trip should be clearly explained on the form. The form should include the destination, the people with whom the employee met, and the purpose of the meeting.

1. Open and print the file 10-2 Thinking Critically from the data files. This file contains a travel expense form and related receipt.

2. Verify the numbers on the form and note any needed corrections. Circle any other items on the form that are incorrect or require more information.

3. Create a memo form for Ellis Tools, Inc. to include the company name and appropriate memo headings. Write a memo to the employee indicating the changes that should be made to the form and indicate that the form is attached.

Making Academic Connections

Reinforcing Math Skills

Your supervisor, Corine Johnson, has asked you to calculate the estimated cost of an off-site staff meeting. The meeting will take place in a conference room at a local hotel. Forty-three people will attend the meeting.

1. Open the file 10-2 Math Skills from the data files. Using the information you collected in this file, calculate the cost of each expense item for the meeting.

2. Calculate the total estimated cost of the meeting.

3. A salesperson at another hotel that you called said that she would beat any deal you get at a local hotel by 10 percent. Calculate the total estimated cost of the meeting if you use this competing hotel.

10-2 Activity 1

Travel Reservations and Itinerary (Outcome 10-2a)

Your manager, Miss Paulina Walker, has sent you some notes for a conference she plans to attend in Orlando, Florida. She asks you to research and make reservations for the trip. You should also key an itinerary for her trip.

1. Open the file 10-2 Activity 1 from the data files. This file contains an e-mail from your manager with notes about the trip.

2. Using the Internet, research flights for Miss Walker's trip. Miss Walker prefers coach nonstop flights if available. Choose the flights you think are most appropriate, considering the costs and the schedule. Pretend that you have reserved these flights for Miss Walker. Make a note of the flight information for her itinerary or print the information from the website if possible.

3. Miss Walker would like to stay at a hotel near the Orange County Convention Center. Use the Internet to find a hotel near the convention center and to find rooms available and rates. Choose the room and rates you think are most appropriate. Pretend that you have reserved a room for Miss Walker. Make a note of the information for her itinerary or print the information from the website if possible. Use the confirmation number MH2933X2.

4. Miss Walker will need a rental car while she is in Orlando. Use a rental car website to find the costs of a mid-size car. Pretend that you have reserved a car for Miss Walker. Make a note of the information for her itinerary or print the information from the website if possible. Use the confirmation number C835LX1.

5. Create an itinerary for Miss Walker. Use the itinerary in Figure 10-2.1 as an example. Attach any reservation information you have printed from websites for the airline, hotel, or car rental. If you did not print information, key notes about each reservation and attach the notes to the itinerary.

10-2 Activity 2

Travel Etiquette and Safety Brochure (Outcome 10-2b)

Your manager, Antonio Alvarez, has asked your work group to create a brochure about travel etiquette and safety tips for business travelers in your company. Many managers are traveling to U.S. and foreign destinations. The brochure would be helpful to them and their office assistants. Work in a group with two classmates to complete this assignment.

1. Create a list of travel etiquette and safety tips that both domestic and international travelers need to know. Add to the information found in the textbook with information you can find from magazines or from an online search. Use search terms such as *travel etiquette*, *business etiquette*, *travel tips*, or *travel safety tips*.

2. Plan the format for your brochure. The answers to the following questions may be helpful to your group:
   - What is the name of your brochure?
   - What are the most important points you should emphasize?
   - What supporting information can you provide?
   - What kind of clip art will you need and what is available to you?
   - What software is available to you to create your brochure?

3. Use word processing or desktop publishing software to complete your brochure. Your finished brochure should include bulleted items and clip art or other graphics to enhance the brochure.

Summary

10-1 Planning and Participating in Meetings

- Meetings may be informal or formal. A formal meeting follows a definite order of business, involves a specific audience, and requires some preparation.
- The purpose of a meeting should determine the seating arrangement.
- Using a folder to collect items related to the meeting can be helpful.
- An agenda is a document that lists the topics to be discussed at a meeting and other related information.
- The meeting leader should keep the purpose in mind while planning and conducting the meeting.
- Leaders may have the group take part in brainstorming to generate ideas or suggest a new approach to a problem.
- Meeting participants should read the agenda and any related materials received before the meeting. They should arrive on time and contribute thoughtful comments.
- Minutes are an official record of the proceedings of a meeting. An action plan is a description of tasks to do after a meeting and can be used in place of minutes.
- Teleconferences may be thought of as virtual meetings. They may also be called conference calls, video conferences, or web meetings, depending on the technology used.

10-2 Preparing for Business Travel

- Many business travels use commercial air flights. Rental cars and trains provide alternative forms of business travel.
- Reservations for transport and hotels can be made on travel or company websites.
- Once the travel plans are set, you should prepare an itinerary and gather the travel documents, supplies, and supporting materials that are needed for the trip.
- A passport and a visa are required for foreign travel in most countries. Foreign currency and other documents, such as work permits and health records, may also be needed.
- Your behavior as a business traveler reflects on you and your company. Proper dress and travel etiquette will contribute to a successful business trip.
- Personal safety and the security of luggage, computers, and other items while traveling are concerns for many business travelers.
- Business travelers may need to complete work while traveling and complete follow-up activities after a trip.

Wire_man/Shutterstock.com

Chapter 10 Activity 1

Teleconference on Travel Etiquette and Safety
(Outcome 10-1c)

Your manager, Esmeralda Diaz, has asked your work group to plan a teleconference that will focus on international travel etiquette and safety. She indicates that the teleconference should be planned for three weeks from today. It will be held in the company's interactive teleconference room. Those who will attend the teleconference include office workers in various positions. These workers may travel to new company sites abroad. Office assistants who will help make travel arrangements will also attend. Work with two classmates to complete this assignment.

1. Decide on the date and time for the teleconference. Key a paragraph or list describing the procedures and information you would use to prepare before the meeting.

2. Choose a city and country where the company has the new branch office. Obtain the address of the U.S. consulate for the country you have chosen. You can find this information by completing an online search. For example, if the country you have chosen is Japan, you might search using the term *U.S. consulate Japan*. Write a letter to the consulate asking for information about traveling and doing business in the country.

3. Because it may take some time for your request to the consulate to be processed, also search for information from other sources. Complete an online search for customs, business etiquette, and travel safety tips for the country you have chosen. Revise the brochure on travel etiquette and safety that you created earlier to include customs and etiquette guidelines and safety tips for a traveler to that country.

4. Research the travel documents needed to travel in that country. Key a list and description of travel documents a traveler needs for the country. Obtain samples of or applications for the documents if possible.

5. Plan the topics to be discussed during the teleconference based on the information you have collected. Key an agenda for the meeting. Review the contents and format of an agenda in Figure 10-1.2.

6. Submit the following items to your instructor:
   - List describing the meeting preparations
   - Letter you have written to the consulate
   - Revised brochure describing customs, etiquette guidelines, and travel tips
   - Samples or applications for travel documents
   - Teleconference agenda

Chapter 10 Activity 2

Follow-Up Letter
(Outcome 10-2c)

Writing thank-you letters is an important follow-up activity for business travelers. In this exercise, you will edit and key a thank-you letter.

1. Key a thank-you letter from the rough draft shown below.
2. Correct the grammar and punctuation mistakes. Revise the letter as needed to make it clear and concise. Use an appropriate letter style and the current date. Assume the letter will be printed on company letterhead.

Send the letter to: Dr. Debra Huntington at Dearborn Manufacturing, 8888 Highland Avenue, Dearborn Park, IL 45599-8888

Dear Debra

Thanks for inviting the other members and I of our department to visit your new manufacturing process and to learn more about your company. We were very impressed with your training program and hope that we can profit by our visit.

The warm reception and tour your people gave us at the plant was very edifying. You msut have spent a long time getting ready for us. We thought it was great! Everyone said how much they liked it and how much they learned. Especially the demo of the new training program.

Thanks again. I have noted that you and some of the your people are interested in returning the favor. I will be in touch with you to set up a date.

Fred J. Miller
Vice President, Manufacturing

Food Marketing Event

In this competitive event, you will be judged on your skills and knowledge in food marketing and marketing management. Topics relate to marketing and management tasks in retail businesses, wholesale businesses, and manufacturing firms resulting in the sale of food.

The event includes a written test and two role-playing situations. Finalists in the events will have a third role-playing situation. No reference materials are allowed. You may make notes to use during the role-play during the time when you read the role-play description and prepare for the event.

Performance Indicators Evaluated

Participants will demonstrate skills related to the marketing career cluster and marketing management pathway. Performance indicators such as the following will be evaluated.

- Identify product's/service's competitive advantage
- Develop positioning concept for a new product idea
- Describe factors used by marketers to position products/services
- Explain the nature of product/service branding
- Describe factors used by businesses to position corporate brands

The following indicators are in addition to the specific indicators listed above

- Communication (writing, speaking, reading, or listening)
- Analyzing data to form conclusions and recommendations
- Critical thinking and problem solving
- Setting priorities and managing time

For more detailed information about this event, go to the DECA website.[1]

http://www.deca.org

Think Critically

1. Describe an advertisement for food that you think is effective. Why does the advertisement appeal to you?
2. What skills or traits do you think are needed to be successful in an advertising job?

---

[1]DECA, "High School Competitive Events Guidelines" (DECA, 2011), http://www.deca.org/competitions/highschool.

Hospitality and Tourism

The hospitality and tourism career area includes a variety of jobs. Chefs, hotel managers, bell captains, tour guides, event planners, and theme park workers are just a few of the jobs in this category. All relate in some way to restaurants and other food services, lodging, attractions, recreation events, or travel services.

Employment Outlook

The U.S. government provides job projections for 2008–2018. Because there are many types of jobs in hospitality and tourism, job prospects vary. For example, job opportunities are expected to be good for chefs, cooks, and other food services workers. Jobs for travel agents may decline due to a slow economy and reduced travel for pleasure. Jobs in recreation, such as theme parks, are expected to grow. However, many of these jobs are part-time or seasonal. Jobs in the hotel industry are expected to grow at a slower than average rate. However, there will be many job openings due to a high turnover in many of these jobs.[2]

Job Titles

- Caterer
- Club manager
- Concierge
- Cook
- Director of tourism
- Front desk clerk
- Hotel manager
- Meeting planner
- Park director
- Park ride attendant
- Restaurant manager
- Travel agent
- Zoo exhibit developer

Needed Education/Skills

The education and skills needed for jobs in hospitality and tourism vary. High school students may qualify for some part-time or seasonal jobs, such as food servers or park ride attendants. Some workers, such as hotel cleaning staff or desk clerks, may need only a high school education. Other jobs, such as restaurant manager or museum director, may require a college degree with emphasis on the related area.

What's it like to work in . . . Hospitality and Tourism?

Anna is an entrepreneur who runs a small bed and breakfast inn. Many of the guests are tourists who come to hike in the scenic mountains or for fishing or water sports on a nearby lake. The inn, once a large private home, can accommodate up to six guests. It has a spacious living area, kitchen, and dining room on the ground floor. Upstairs there are four suites. When Anna inherited the family home, she did renovations to reconfigure the upstairs and add three baths. Now each suite has a bedroom, a sitting area, and a private bath. Anna occupies one of the suites and rents the other three to guests. Visitors enjoy sitting on the large porch that overlooks a colorful flower and herb garden.

Anna does a variety of tasks to make the inn successful. Making the guests comfortable is important for repeat business. Anna decorates the inn with seasonal themes and tests new recipes for breakfast items to serve the guests. Anna's college degree in business has prepared her to handle all the business details of running the inn, such as accounting and marketing. Her creative talents help her make the inn's website both attractive and informative. Guests can make reservations online or by phone. Anna also helps with the shopping, cooking, and cleaning involved in running the inn. She is fortunate to have a part-time employee to help with these tasks. Anna enjoys meeting people from many areas and walks of life and sharing her home with them for a brief time.

What About You?

Do you know of part-time or seasonal jobs in hospitality or tourism in your area? Describe one of the jobs. Which area of the career group (food service, travel, or recreation) appeals most to you?

---

[2]*Career Guide to Industries*, 2010–11 Edition, Bureau of Labor Statistics, U.S. Department of Labor, http://www.bls.gov/oco/cg/cg1009.htm.

Records Management

11-1 Introduction to Records Management

11-2 Managing Physical Records

11-3 Managing Electronic Records

Heath Korvola/Digital Vision/Jupiter Images

Wire_man/Shutterstock.com

Information is important to the operation of a company. A system is needed for organizing, storing, and retrieving records and for removing outdated records. As an office worker, you will need to follow records management procedures carefully. These procedures include how to organize, store, retrieve, and dispose of records. This series of steps is known as the record life cycle. This chapter will give you the latest information about the various media used for storing records and the skills to use the most common filing systems.

OUTCOMES

11-1a Classify records according to their value to an organization.
11-1b Describe the activities in each phase of the record life cycle.
11-1c Apply procedures of a records management system.

Value of Records

A record is stored information that has continuing value and is made or received by an organization. Records are valuable because they are used for daily operations or provide a history of the organization. Employees use the information contained in records to make decisions, complete tasks, and plan for the future. For example, each time an item is sold by a company, a record is made that shows details of the sale. This record can be referred to later when shipping the item to the customer or sending an invoice for the item. This record, along with others, will provide a sales history for the item. The sales history will help employees predict how many items may be sold in the coming year.

Some records are more valuable to an organization than others. Records are classified according to their usefulness and importance as described below. Examples of each type of record are shown in Figure 11-1.1.

record stored information that has continuing value and is made or received by an organization

- **Vital records** are essential to the company. These records are often not replaceable. They may be stored permanently in a secure location.

- **Important records** are needed for the business to operate smoothly. These records would be expensive to replace. They may be stored for a long term in a secure location.

- **Useful records** are convenient to have but are replaceable. They are stored in a location that is easy to access for as long as they are referenced often.

- **Nonessential records** have one-time or very limited usefulness. They may be kept only for a few days or weeks until they are no longer needed.

Figure 11-1.1 Records Class by Value

CLASS	EXAMPLES
Vital records	Articles of incorporation, deeds, copyrights, reports to shareholders, and mortgages
Important records	Financial statements, tax returns, personnel files, and contracts
Useful records	Business letters, purchase orders, policy manuals, banking records, and customer addresses
Nonessential records	Meeting announcements, routine telephone messages, and advertisements

© Cengage Learning 2013

CHECK POINT Why are records valuable to an organization?

Record Life Cycle

record life cycle the creation, distribution, use, maintenance, and disposition of a record

The usefulness of each record has a beginning and an end. Therefore, each record has a life cycle. The record life cycle consists of the creation, distribution, use, maintenance, and disposition of a record. Different activities occur in the different phases of the life cycle. The phases of the record life cycle are the same regardless of whether the records are kept on paper or microfilm or in computer files.

The phases of the record life cycle are listed here in numerical order. However, the distribution, use, and maintenance phases may occur several times for one record. For example, a record may be sent to a person who requests information, used to complete a task, and then filed. Later the same record may be needed again by someone else, so the process will be repeated.

1. **Creation or collection.** The cycle begins when records are created or collected.

2. **Distribution.** During this phase, records are sent to the persons who will use them.

3. **Use.** Records are commonly used in decision making, for reference, in answering inquiries, or for satisfying legal requirements.

4. **Maintenance.** When records are kept for later use, they must be organized and stored, retrieved as needed, stored again, and protected from damage or loss. The exact procedure you use in this phase will vary depending on the type of record.

5. **Disposition.** Records are disposed of either by destroying the records or by moving them to permanent storage, often at less expensive storage sites.

CHECK POINT What happens to records in the disposition phase of the record life cycle?

Records are stored and retrieved in the maintenance phase of the record life cycle.

James Hardy/Jupiter Images

Records Management Systems

Records management is the control of records from creation or receipt to their final disposal. Because records are valuable, being able to store and retrieve records quickly and easily is very important. Using a records management system makes this possible.

To make wise decisions or complete a task well, workers need accurate, current information. For example, to prepare a monthly sales report, you need to have the sales figures for each salesperson. Before you pay an invoice, you should check your records to be sure the charges are correct. Before you can mail a package, you need to know the recipient's complete address. You must be able to access needed records easily and quickly. An effective records management system will help you be more productive. You will not waste valuable time searching for information that should be easily available. A records management system includes procedures for:

- Selecting storage media and equipment
- Filing and retrieving records
- Retaining and disposing of records

Storage Media and Equipment

Records are stored on a variety of media. The most common storage medium is paper. Although other storage media are becoming more popular, paper records will likely remain a major part of filing systems for years to come. Many records are stored on microfilm, magnetic media, and optical disks. These records require less space to store than paper records.

Data stored on paper and microfilm are called **physical records**. Data stored on magnetic media, such as a computer hard drive, on flash drives, and on optical disks (CDs and DVDs) are called **electronic records**. You will learn more about these storage media later in this chapter.

Storage equipment, such as filing cabinets, should be chosen with specific storage media in mind. For example, if your records are on paper, you might use file folders and a filing cabinet. However, the same cabinet might not be appropriate for filing DVDs that contain records.

Valuable records can be kept in fireproof cabinets or vaults. A good records management system includes policies that help you decide which records require special protection. For example, you may need to protect original copies of contracts by storing them in a fireproof vault.

Vertical file cabinets, lateral file cabinets, and shelf files are the most common types of equipment for storing paper records. These are described below.

- Vertical file cabinets contain one to five drawers. Five-drawer cabinets provide the most filing space for the amount of floor space used. Vertical file cabinets must be arranged so there is space in front of each one to allow drawers to be opened fully.
- Lateral file cabinets are made in a variety of drawer heights, widths, and depths to fit different office needs. Fully opened drawers in such a cabinet do not open as far out into the room as do drawers in a vertical file cabinet.

records management the control of records from the creation or receipt to final disposal

physical records data stored on paper and microfilm

electronic records data stored on magnetic media, flash drives, and optical disks

File cabinets are common storage equipment for paper records.

AbleStock.com/Getty Images/Jupiter Images

■ Shelf files store records on open shelves instead of in drawers. They come in a wide variety of sizes. Records on open shelves can be removed easily. Shelf filing is most appropriate for filing and retrieving entire folders and is ideally suited for numeric filing systems.

Each drawer in a file cabinet or shelf contains two different kinds of filing supplies: file folders and guides. A folder is a container made of strong, durable paper and is used to hold papers. Each folder is larger than the papers it contains so that it will protect the contents. Guides are heavy cardboard sheets that are the same size as or slightly larger than the file folders. The guides divide the drawer into sections and serve as signposts for quick reference. They also provide support for the folders and their contents. Labels are attached to file folders and guides to identify the files. Labels are also placed on the file cabinet drawers to identify the contents.

✓ **CHECK POINT** What media are used for physical records? for electronic records?

Filing Procedures

filing the process of storing records in an orderly manner within an organized system

Filing is the process of storing records in an orderly manner within an organized system. The procedure used to file records varies. It depends on the storage media and the filing system used. Records can be arranged in a filing system by various methods, depending on the needs of the organization.

Alphabetic Filing Systems

alphabetic filing system an arrangement of records according to letters of the alphabet

In an alphabetic filing system, records are arranged according to the letters of the alphabet. Letters and words are used as captions on the guides and folders. These words may be names, subjects, or geographic locations. Both guides and folders are arranged in alphabetic order according to the captions.

In an alphabetic filing system, records may be arranged alphabetically by correspondents' names, by subjects, or by geographic locations. For example, in an alphabetic name filing system, each record is reviewed to determine the name by which it should be filed. The names are marked and the records are placed in order according to standard filing rules. (Rules for alphabetic filing are presented later in this chapter.)

When records are arranged by subject or geographic locations, employees must refer to an index to find the subject title or the location assigned to a person or organization. Then records are filed or retrieved at that location in the files.

Numeric Filing Systems

In a numeric filing system, records are stored by number. The numeric method of filing is often used when records are already assigned numbers. For example, insurance companies may arrange their records according to policy number. Utility companies often identify records by customer account number.

Some companies file records by number even though they are not already numbered. A number would be assigned to the person or organization for which records are kept. Having records labeled with numbers rather than names helps keep information confidential. For example, a visitor to a medical office who sees three file folders placed on a desk would see only numbers— not the names of patients.

Several arrangements can be used for numeric files. Three common types of numeric files are described in the following list.

- In a consecutive numeric file, records are arranged in simple numeric order.
- In a chronologic file, records are arranged by date.
- In a terminal-digit numeric file, groups of digits in a number are read from right to left when placing numbers in order (rather than from left to right as with consecutive numbers).

numeric filing system an arrangement of records according to numbers

---

✳ WORKPLACE CONNECTIONS ✳

Today is Carlos's first day of work. Mimi Yung, Carlos's supervisor, briefed him on the filing system they use:

Carlos, the records in our department are confidential. We use a numeric filing system so that unauthorized people cannot locate specific records easily. To keep these files secure, we have a policy that allows only workers in our department to have access to the name index and the records.

What types of records might a company want to keep confidential?

Charging Out Records

Regardless of the filing system used by the company, employees often remove records from the files for use in their work. Retrieving a record from the files and noting information about the record is called charging out. Company procedures should provide guidelines for charging out records. The following information is usually recorded when a record is removed from the files:

- Name and department of the worker who is taking the record
- Date the record was retrieved
- Date the record will be returned

Charge-out information is kept in case someone else must locate the record while it is out of the files. A retrieval procedure also should indicate whether all workers or only certain staff members have free access to the records.

CHECK POINT   What information is recorded when a record is charged out?

Records Retention

Records that are used often are kept in active storage. When records should be kept but are not used often, they are moved to inactive or permanent storage. This transfer leaves more space for active records. Many businesses, particularly small ones, store inactive records in commercial records centers.

Services may include pickup and delivery of records, initial storage, and destruction at appointed times. Customers are often required to use boxes of a standard size to make the best use of storage space.

Vital records or special records of historical value are often stored apart from other records. An archive is a storage area dedicated to organizing and preserving historical records. These archived records may be in the form of paper, computer files, or microfilm.

archive a storage area dedicated to organizing and preserving vital or historical records

✳ WORKPLACE CONNECTIONS ✳

Carla Nagai works in the Accounts Payable Department. Workers in this department often refer to vendor invoices from the current or the previous year. The company keeps invoices in active storage for two years. A new calendar year has just started. Carla collected the invoices from the year before last for transfer to inactive storage. According to the retention schedule, invoices are kept for a total of seven years. Any invoices in inactive storage that are more than seven years old will be collected and destroyed.

In what phase of the record life cycle does transferring records to inactive storage fall?

retention schedule a document that shows how long particular types of records should be kept

A retention schedule is a document that shows how long particular types of records should be kept. Figure 11-1.2 shows a partial example of a retention schedule. The retention period (how long the record should be kept in each type of storage) is given for each type of record.

Government authority dictates how long certain records, such as tax returns, should be kept. Company managers may set policies for how long to keep other records, such as bank statements, expense reports, budgets, and correspondence. Therefore, retention schedules will vary from company to company.

CHECK POINT What is the purpose of a retention schedule?

Figure 11-1.2 **Retention Schedule**

RECORDS RETENTION SCHEDULE			
Records	**Years Active**	**Years Inactive**	**Total Years**
Accounting			
Accounts payable invoices	3	3	6
Accounts payable ledger	3	3	6
Banking records	3	3	6
Annual audit reports	3	Permanent	Permanent
Administrative			
Correspondence, executive	1	1	2
Policy statements and directives	3	Permanent	Permanent
Advertising			
Contracts, advertising	1	2	3 years after term
Drawings and artwork	10	Permanent	Permanent
Samples, displays, labels	5	Permanent	Permanent
Human Resources			
Applications, job changes, job terminations	1	0	1
Attendance/vacation records	3	4	7
Medical folder, employee	While employed		30 years
Training manuals	3	Permanent	Permanent
Insurance			
Claims, group life/hospital	1	3	4
Claims, workers' compensation	1	9	10
Expired policies: fire, liability, workers' compensation	1	2	3 years after expiration
Operations			
Inventories	1	0	1
Office equipment records	3	3	6
Requisitions for supplies	1	0	1
Records Management			
Records destruction documents	3	Permanent	Permanent
Records inventory	1	0	1
Records management policies	1	Permanent	Permanent

Disaster Recovery Plans

A disaster recovery plan provides procedures to be followed in case of an event that causes serious harm or damage. Every business may not be involved in a major crisis. However, every business needs a disaster recovery plan. A disaster may be caused by a natural event such as a hurricane, tornado, or earthquake. Disasters may be due to fires, computer viruses, bombs, or even human error. Disaster recovery planning can help prepare a business to deal with a crisis situation and to resume normal business operations as soon as possible.

Companies must be concerned about the disaster recovery plans of partners and suppliers. If a partner or supplier cannot operate normally, this situation can have a serious effect on a company. Companies that work closely together may coordinate their plans.

A disaster recovery plan should include phases for prevention, readiness, reaction, and recovery.

- **Prevention** involves taking action to avoid a disaster. For example, antivirus programs can prevent damage to computer data. Buildings can be checked regularly for fire hazards. Important data files can be stored in secure locations to prevent loss. Many companies use off-site records storage to limit data loss.
- **Readiness** is being prepared for a disaster. Companies must try to judge the damage that events may cause and plan to minimize the damage. The plan should be updated and tested regularly. Training for employees on putting the plan into action is an important part of readiness.
- **Reaction** is setting a disaster plan in motion. Companies may move to backup sites when a disaster happens. They may use alternate means of communication, such as home e-mail addresses, pagers, and cell phones. Reaction also involves taking steps to begin recovering from the event and to prevent further damage.
- **Recovery** means getting back to normal operations. In the area of records management, recovery involves replacing data lost in a disaster. Computer data may be restored from backup copies. Computers and other office equipment may be repaired or replaced.

Many organizations and companies promote awareness and education about disaster recovery. The Disaster Recovery Institute International has a professional certification program for business continuity/disaster recovery planners.

> What four phases are covered in a disaster recovery plan? Which phase do you think is the most important? Why?

REVIEW 11-1 _____

21st Century Skills

Interacting with Others

An important folder is missing from the central files. You discover that someone in your department has signed it out. You go to this person, who is above
your level in the company, and he says that he does not have it. The folder is
essential for your work. What should you do?

1. Should you confront the higher-ranking person and insist that he give you
   the file? Why or why not?

2. Should you go to your supervisor and ask her to help resolve the situation? Why or why not?

3. Should you attempt to do your work without the folder and make mistakes because you do not have the information you need? Why or why
   not?

Making Academic Connections

Reinforcing Math Skills

1. A single file drawer contains 75 folders. Documents from 15 of these folders were converted to microfilm. The records were transferred to inactive
   storage. Of the remaining active folders, six had their contents divided
   into two folders each.

   a. How many active folders are now in the file drawer?

   b. What is the percentage of decrease in the number of folders in the
      active file?

2. Eight departments have requested file folders. Folders are ordered from
   the supply company in boxes, each containing 25 folders. The number of
   folders each department needs is shown below.

   a. How many folders are required to meet the needs of all the departments?

   b. How many boxes of folders should be ordered?

   c. How many folders will be left after each department has received the
      number of folders requested?

Accounting	21	Production	175
Finance	48	Public Relations	100
Human Resources	99	Marketing	260
Information Systems	125	Customer Service	32

11-1 Activity 1

Value of Records (Outcome 11-1a)

Classify the records below according to their value to an organization (vital, important, useful, or nonessential).

1. Filing procedures manual
2. Job termination record
3. Contract to supply services to a customer
4. Bank statement
5. Deed to property
6. Routine telephone message
7. Mortgage
8. Advertisement for a sale on office equipment
9. Income statement for the previous year
10. Purchase order

11-1 Activity 2

Record Life Cycle (Outcome 11-1b)

1. Review the activities that occur in each phase of the record life cycle.
2. Create a flow chart that illustrates the record life cycle.
   - Give the chart an appropriate title.
   - Use chart elements to show the order in which the activities occur (for one cycle).
   - Include a brief list of the activities with each phase.
   - Add a footnote to indicate the phases that may be repeated several times for one record.

Physical Records

Wherever you work, whether in a small company or a large one, you will probably work with physical records. Even in offices where computer storage is used for many records, certain physical records are needed. For this reason, you should understand how to maintain physical records.

Media for Physical Records

Two common types of physical records are paper and microfilm. Paper is used for many records for both short-term and long-term storage. Microfilm is typically used for long-term records storage.

Paper

Each time you print a document or write a telephone message form, you are recording information on paper. These paper records are referred to as hard copy. The advantage of keeping paper records is that you can easily read the information they contain. With electronic records, such as a word processing file stored on your computer, you need a display screen or printer to read the information. Two disadvantages of storing records on paper are that paper records take up a great deal of space and they can easily be filed in the wrong location. This makes finding the records difficult.

Fuse/Jupiter Images

Paper is a common records storage medium.

Many records systems use a mixture of paper and other storage media. Paper records should be kept to a minimum and should be easy to find and retrieve. Filing procedures for physical records are discussed later in this chapter.

Microfilm

Microfilm is a storage medium that contains small images of records on a roll or sheet of film. Documents may be stored on a roll of microfilm or on sheets of film called microfiche. The following steps are involved in creating microfilm:

1. Paper records to be stored on microfilm are gathered.
2. A special camera is used to take pictures of the hard copy documents.
3. The film is developed. Each record then appears as a tiny picture—a microimage—on the film.
4. A device called a reader is used to display the microimage for reading. Some readers, referred to as reader/printers, will also print a hard copy of the image.

Microfilm is popular for long-term records storage.

Photo Researchers, Inc.

Microfilm is used when paper or computer files would be less practical. For instance, a car dealer usually will keep parts lists for vehicles from past years on microfiche. Because the list is unchanging, keeping the data in computer files that can be updated is not necessary. Because the fiche is less bulky, it is easier to store and retrieve than paper records. Libraries often keep back issues of magazines and newspapers on microfilm.

Storing records on microfilm has several advantages. Microfilm takes up less space than a record stored on paper. The records are always in the same order regardless of how often they are retrieved and filed. Microfilm records last for many years when stored properly. A disadvantage of storing records on microfilm is that the records cannot be altered or updated. Also, workers must have special training so they can operate the equipment to create microfilm records.

CHECK POINT What are two media on which physical records are stored?

During their break, Mario and Suma began discussing the new imaging system their company had recently begun using.

Mario: "At first, I wasn't sure that placing records on microfilm would be helpful. But now I'm glad we have the system."

Suma: "I was looking forward to having our records on microfilm! Our file cabinets were so crowded that filing and retrieving records was difficult."

Mario: "What I've enjoyed is being able to refer to a record without cluttering my workstation with more paper. But if I need a hard copy, I can make one by using the microfilm reader/printer."

Why will having records on microfilm help solve the problem of overcrowded files?

Preparing Records for Storage

Before filing a record for the first time, you need to prepare it properly for storage. By doing so, you speed up the filing process and increase filing accuracy. Follow these steps to prepare physical records for storage:

1. Collect the records.
2. Inspect the records.
3. Index and code the records.
4. Cross-reference the records, if needed.
5. Sort the records.

Collect Records

Throughout the workday, you will collect records that need to be filed. Place these records in a certain place such as a tray labeled TO BE FILED. Then at scheduled times, such as after lunch or at the end of the day, prepare the records for storage.

Inspect Records

When preparing records for storage, inspect each record by following these procedures:

- When a record is being filed for the first time, look for a release mark. The initials of someone authorized to release the record, written on the record or an attached note, often serve as the release mark.
- Remove all paper clips or rubber bands from the records.
- For paper records, staple all related materials together.
- Repair any torn paper records with transparent tape.
- Attach small paper records to a full sheet of paper so that they will not be lost or crumpled in the file.

Index and Code Records

Indexing is the mental process of deciding how to identify a record for filing purposes. The name, subject, geographic location, or number used to identify a record is called the filing segment. The name or subject most likely to be

indexing   the mental process of deciding how to identify a record for filing purposes

filing segment   the name, subject, geographic location, or number used to identify a record

used in asking for the record is the one to be used for storage. For example, on an outgoing letter, the name of the recipient (company or person if no company is shown) is usually the most important. This name would be used for the filing segment.

Coding is marking or writing the filing segment on a record. Coding is typically done directly on paper records. For microfilm records, coding is done on a label or a container that holds the records. Coding a record allows you to tell quickly how to file a record by glancing at it. You will file the record the same way each time it must be refiled.

To code a paper record indexed by subject, geographic location, or number, write the filing segment in the upper-right corner of the record. When records are coded for a name file, the name typically appears on the record. Underline the filing segment the first place it appears on the record. Identify the indexing units of a name according to standard alphabetic indexing rules (presented later in this chapter). For example, there are four indexing units in the name *Casey and Bird Associates*. Use diagonal marks to divide the filing segment into separate indexing units. Number the units in proper indexing order. The units would be numbered (1) *Casey*, (2) *and*, (3) *Bird*, and (4) *Associates*.

Figure 11-2.1 shows part of document that has been indexed and coded for filing. The name of the company that sent the letter (Casey and Bird Associates) is used for the filing segment. Note that the name is underlined, diagonal marks appear between the indexing units, and numbers appear above the units.

Cross Reference Records

A cross-reference is prepared when a record may be requested by more than one name or subject. A cross-reference is a notation at one place to indicate a record in another place. For example, a letter filed under the name *Casey and*

Figure 11-2.1 **This record has been coded for filing.**

Bird Associates might be requested as *Bird and Casey Associates*. In this case, you would write the cross-reference caption (*Bird and Casey Associates*) on the letter followed by an *X*. You would also code the cross-reference filing segment as shown in Figure 11-2.1. The letter would be filed using the filing segment *Casey and Bird Associates*. A copy of the letter or a cross-reference sheet would be filed using the filing segment *Bird and Casey Associates*. A cross-reference sheet includes:

- The name or subject under which the record was cross-referenced
- The date of the item
- A brief description of the record
- The location of the record in the files
- The name of the authorized person who released the record and the date it was released

If a permanent cross-reference is desired, you would need to prepare a cross-reference guide. A cross-reference guide might be needed when a company changes its name. You would label a fresh folder using the new company name and place in it all materials from the old folder. Then you would replace the old folder with a permanent cross-reference guide that directs users to the new location for the records. The guide remains in the file as long as the name or subject is still active.

TECHNOLOGY CONNECTION

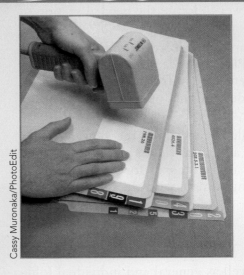

Cassy Muronaka/PhotoEdit

Records may be coded by hand, the conventional method, or by barcoding. A bar code is a pattern of vertical lines of varying widths that contains coded data that can be read by a scanner. The scanner is also called a reader or tracker. A bar code can be printed on a label and attached to an item such as a file folder or box. Bar code labels can be printed on labels as needed, or preprinted labels may be purchased. The advantage of using preprinted labels is that an office worker will not accidentally assign the same bar code to two files.

When bar codes are used, a code on a record is scanned into an electronic tracking system. This process is much the same as how product prices are scanned at a register in a store. The computer will add the date and time the record is filed or retrieved. When an item is refiled, the computer identifies the date and time of the return. Using bar codes allows less chance for human error, and fewer files are lost.

What is an advantage to using preprinted labels for bar codes?

Sort Records

After you have coded the records and created the needed cross-references, you are ready to sort the records. Sorting is the process of arranging the records alphabetically or numerically before placing them in folders or other containers.

Sorting serves two important purposes. First, it saves filing time. Because records are in proper sequence, you are able to move quickly from file drawer to file drawer as you place the records in folders. Second, if records are requested before you file them, you can find them quickly.

 CHECK POINT What is the difference between indexing and coding records?

Alphabetic Name File

Once you have followed the five steps for preparing records for storage, you are ready to file the records. This section discusses filing records in an alphabetic name file. It also presents alphabetic indexing rules used for indexing and coding records.

Filing Procedures

The procedures discussed here are similar for other filing systems. Refer to Figure 11-2.2 as you read the following steps for filing records.

1. Locate the proper file drawer by reading the drawer labels.
2. Search through the guides in the drawer to locate the needed section of the files.
3. If an individual folder has been prepared for records with the filing segment, place the record in the folder. Place records in an individual folder according to date, with the most recent date in front. Place the front of the record facing the front of the folder and the top of the record at the left side.
4. If no individual folder is available, file the record in the general folder for that section. Arrange records in a general folder alphabetically by filing segments. If there are two or more records for the same filing segment, they are arranged according to date with the most recent in front.

Using Special Folders

Some companies use special folders as well as general and individual folders. Special folders are useful when you want to keep together records of the same type that are from different people. For example, you might want to keep all job applications the company receives together. A special guide and a special folder with the caption APPLICATIONS could be used for this purpose. Arrange records alphabetically in a special folder. When there is more than one record with the same filing segment, arrange the records by date.

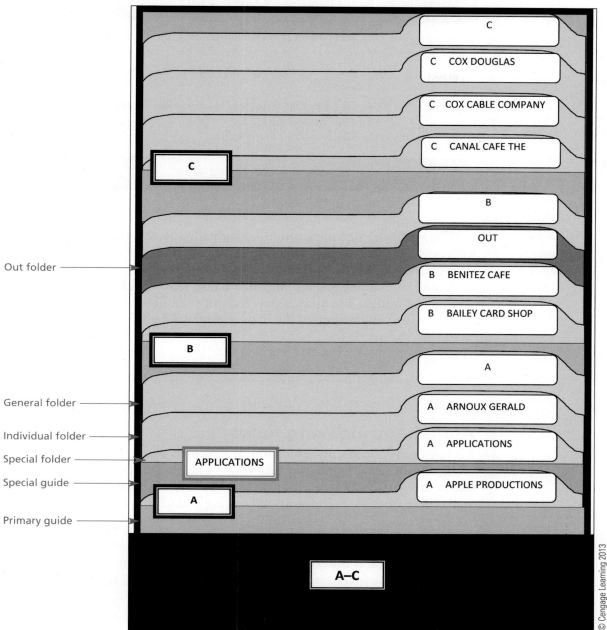

Figure 11-2.2 **Alphabetic Name File**

Out folder

General folder

Individual folder

Special folder

Special guide

Primary guide

© Cengage Learning 2013

Note the out folder shown in Figure 11-2.2. An out folder is used to hold records for an individual or organization when a folder is removed from the files. The out folder may have a space provided to write the name of the folder it is temporarily replacing or a note may be placed inside the folder.

out folder a container used to hold records for an individual or organization when a folder is removed from the files

Avoiding Overcrowded Files

Never allow folders to become overcrowded. Usually, a folder has score lines at the bottom. Creasing the score lines widens the folder and allows it to hold more records. A folder should not contain more than an inch of filed material.

Employees must understand proper filing procedures in order to store records in the correct folders and ensure that the records can be found later.

Carrie: "Roy, there is no folder labeled Carson Real Estate in the file. Where do I file this letter?"

Roy: "If there is no individual folder for Carson Real Estate, file it in the general C folder behind the C guide. Place the letter in alphabetical order with the other records in the folder."

> **When would an individual folder be set up for Carson Real Estate?**

When a folder becomes too full, subdivide the records into two or more folders. The labels of each should reflect the contents of the new folders. For example, they could be labeled by date or subject.

Be sure to examine general folders often so that you can prepare individual and special folders when necessary. Do not fill a file drawer completely. You should have enough room in the drawer to move the folders easily.

 CHECK POINT What is the purpose of an out folder?

Alphabetic Indexing Rules

ARMA International, an association for records management professionals, recommends using standard filing rules. The alphabetic indexing rules that follow are written to agree with the ARMA International standards. You will apply these rules when indexing and coding records for an alphabetic file.

Rule 1: Names

A personal name is indexed in this order: (1) the surname (last name) is the first unit, (2) the given name (first name) or initial is the second unit, and (3) the middle name or initial is the third unit.

Rule 1 Personal Names

NAME	UNIT 1	UNIT 2	UNIT 3
Russ Evans	Evans	Russ	
Ruth T. Evans	Evans	Ruth	T
Sam Thomas Evans	Evans	Sam	Thomas
Alice Kim	Kim	Alice	
Kala Perez	Perez	Kala	

Business names are indexed as written using letterheads or trademarks as guides. There is one exception. When *The* begins a business or organization name, index *The* as the last unit.

Rule 1 Businesses and Organizations

NAME	UNIT 1	UNIT 2	UNIT 3
1st National Bank	1	National	Bank
Avalon Valley Church	Avalon	Valley	Church
Beacon Memorial Hospital	Beacon	Memorial	Hospital
The Cincinnati Enquirer	Cincinnati	Enquirer	The
Juan Juarez Foods	Juan	Juarez	Foods
Kentucky Living Magazine	Kentucky	Living	Magazine
Tallahassee Auto Repair	Tallahassee	Auto	Repair
University of Michigan	University	of	Michigan
Wall Street Cleaners	Wall	Street	Cleaners
The Wayside Inn	Wayside	Inn	The
Western High School	Western	High	School

Rule 2: Minor Words and Symbols

Articles, prepositions, conjunctions, and symbols are considered separate indexing units. Symbols are considered as spelled in full. When the word *The* appears as the first word of a business name, it is considered the last indexing unit.

Rule 2 Minor Words and Symbols

NAME	UNIT 1	UNIT 2	UNIT 3	UNIT 4
A Special Place	A	Special	Place	
The $ Tree	Dollar	Tree	The	
Lawton & Park Shoes	Lawton	and	Park	Shoes
Short but Sweet Candles	Short	but	Sweet	Candles

Rule 3: Punctuation

All punctuation is disregarded when indexing personal and business names.

Rule 3 Punctuation

NAME	UNIT 1	UNIT 2	UNIT 3
A-Z Filing Systems	AZ	Filing	Systems
Iris B. Mason-Peters	MasonPeters	Iris	B
North/South Baseball League	NorthSouth	Baseball	League
Tom's Foods	Toms	Foods	

Rule 4: Single Letters and Abbreviations

Initials in personal names are separate indexing units. Abbreviations of personal names (Wm., Jos., Thos.) and nicknames (Liz, Bill) are indexed as written. Single letters in business and organization names are indexed as written. Radio and television station call letters are indexed as one unit.

Rule 4 Single Letters and Abbreviations

NAME	UNIT 1	UNIT 2	UNIT 3	UNIT 4
E K M Inc.	E	K	M	Inc
EG Environmental	EG	Environmental		
KBER Radio	KBER	Radio		
L & M Enterprises	L	and	M	Enterprises
Liz P. Park	Park	Liz	P	

Rule 5: Titles and Suffixes

In personal names, a title before a name (Dr., Mr., Mrs.), a seniority suffix (II, III, Jr., Sr.) or a professional suffix (Mayor, MD, Senator) after a name is the last indexing unit. Numeric suffixes (II, III) are filed before alphabetic suffixes (Jr., Senator, Sr.). If a name contains a title and a suffix (Ms. Emily Pagel, MD), the title (*Ms*) is the last unit. Royal and religious titles followed by either a given name or a surname *only* (Princess Anne, Father Mark) are indexed and filed as written. (Titles in business names are indexed as written.)

Rule 5 Titles and Suffixes

NAME	UNIT 1	UNIT 2	UNIT 3	UNIT 4
Dr. Joe's Diner	Dr	Joes	Diner	
Gerald J. Estevant, II	Estevant	Gerald	J	II
Gerald J. Estevant, Jr.	Estevant	Gerald	J	Jr
Father Ryan	Father	Ryan		
Mr. Aiken's Bait Shop	Mr	Aikens	Bait	Shop
Tanesha D. Painter, MD	Painter	Tanesha	D	MD
Miss Tanesha D. Painter	Painter	Tanesha	D	Miss

Rule 6: Prefixes, Articles, and Particles

A foreign article or particle in a personal or business name is combined with the part of the name following it to form a single indexing unit. Spaces in the prefix or between a prefix and the rest of the name (Amber De La Cruz) are disregarded.

Rule 6 Prefixes, Articles, and Particles

NAME	UNIT 1	UNIT 2	UNIT 3
Gloria R. De Gabriele	DeGabriele	Gloria	R
LeMay's Fine Foods	LeMays	Fine	Foods
Mark P. O'Connell	OConnell	Mark	P
St. Germain and McDougal	StGermain	and	McDougal
Alex P. Von der Grieff	VonderGrieff	Alex	P

Rule 7: Numbers in Business Names

Follow these guidelines for indexing business names that contain numbers.

- ■ Numbers spelled out (Sixth Street Grocery) are filed alphabetically.
- ■ Numbers written in digits are filed in ascending order before letters or words (*3 Day Cleaners* is filed before *Adams Cleaners*).
- ■ Arabic numerals (2, 3) are filed before Roman numerals (II, III).
- ■ For a range of numbers (33-37 Fence Court), use only the first number in the range (33).
- ■ For names with numbers that contain *st*, *d*, and *th* (1st Mortgage Co.), ignore the letter endings and consider only the digits (1, 2, 3).
- ■ When indexing names with a number (in figures or words) linked by a hyphen to a letter or word (10-Minute Photo, A-1 Laundry), ignore the hyphen and treat it as a single unit (10Minute, A1).
- ■ When indexing names with a number plus a symbol (55+ Social Center), treat it as a single unit (55Plus Social Center).

Rule 7 Numbers in Business Names

NAME	UNIT 1	UNIT 2	UNIT 3	UNIT 4
5 Step Cleaners	5	Step	Cleaners	
65+ Senior Center	65Plus	Senior	Center	
400-700 Rustic Way	400	Rustic	Way	
The 500 Princess Shop	500	Princess	Shop	The
XXI Club	XXI	Club		
Fifth Street News Shoppe	Fifth	Street	News	Shoppe
Finally 21 Club	Finally	21	Club	
I-275 Garage	I275	Garage		
#1 TV Deals	Number1	TV	Deals	
Sixty-Six Highway Deli	SixtySix	Highway	Deli	

Rule 8: Identical Names

When names are identical, filing order is determined by the addresses. Compare the addresses in the following order: city names, state or province names, street names, and house or building numbers.

Rule 8 Identical Names

NAME	UNIT 1	UNIT 2	UNIT 3	UNIT 4	UNIT 5	UNIT 6
Stop-N-Shop 5185 Texas Ave. Abilene, TX	StopNShop	Abilene				
Stop-N-Shop 2600 Teal Rd. Barstow, CA	StopNShop	Barstow				
Stop-N-Shop 1903 Hwy. 192 London, KY	StopNShop	London	KY			
Stop-N-Shop 1692 Apple Ave. London, OH	StopNShop	London	OH	Apple	Ave	
Stop-N-Shop 1522 Birch Ave. London, OH	StopNShop	London	OH	Birch	Ave	
Stop-N-Shop 21500 Birch St. London, OH	StopNShop	London	OH	Birch	St	21500
Stop-N-Shop 32890 Birch St. London, OH	StopNShop	London	OH	Birch	St	32890

Rule 9: Government Names

Government names are indexed first by the name of the governmental unit—country, state, city, or county. Next, the distinctive name of the department, bureau, office, or board is indexed. When indexing foreign government names, use the English translation of the name.

Rule 9 State, Local, and Foreign Government Names

NAME	UNIT 1	UNIT 2	UNIT 3	UNIT 4	UNIT 5
Alabama Department of Education	Alabama	Education	Department	of	
Govern d'Andorra	Andorra	Government			
City of Arlington Public Library	Arlington	City	of	Public	Library
City of Arlington Senior Center	Arlington	City	of	Senior	Center
Barstow Municipal Court	Barstow	Municipal	Court		
Druk Yul	Bhutan	Kingdom	of		
Jamhuri ya Kenya	Kenya	Republic	of		

For United States federal government names, use three indexing "levels" (rather than units). Use *United States Government* as the first level. The second level is the name of a department; for example, *Department of Agriculture*. Level three is the next most distinctive name; for example, *Forest Service*. If necessary, invert the names. (Change *Department of Commerce* to *Commerce Department*.) The words *of* and *of the* are not considered when indexing. They may be placed in parentheses for clarity.

Rule 9 U.S. Federal Government Names

	NAME	LEVEL 1	LEVEL 2	LEVEL 3
1.	National Weather Service, Department of Commerce	United States Government	Commerce Department (of)	National Weather Service
2.	Office of Civil Rights, Department of Education	United States Government	Education Department (of)	Civil Rights Office (of)
3.	Federal Emergency Management Agency Department of Homeland Security	United States Government	Homeland Security Department (of)	Federal Emergency Management Agency

 CHECK POINT Are numbers written in digits filed before or after numbers written as words?

Numeric Filing Systems

In a numeric filing system, records are given numbers that are arranged in order when stored. The numeric method is particularly useful to organizations such as these:

- Insurance companies that keep records according to policy numbers
- Law firms that assign a case number to each client
- Real estate agencies that list properties by code numbers

Filing Procedures

The filing procedures for storing records in a consecutive or terminal-digit numeric filing system are basically the same. Those procedures are listed below.

1. When a document is ready to be filed or retrieved, the alphabetic index is consulted. An alphabetic index is a list of names of individuals, organizations, and companies and the number that has been assigned to each one.

2. The number is placed on the record and the record is placed in the numeric file. The numeric file has guides and folders with numbers on the captions.

3. If the filing name is new and no number has been assigned, the record may be placed in an alphabetic file until there are enough records for this name to open an individual numeric file.

4. If it is necessary to establish a new numeric folder, an accession log is consulted. An accession log is a document or file that shows the numbers that have been assigned to records and the next number to be used.

> **alphabetic index** a list of names in a filing system and the number that has been assigned to each one

> **accession log** a document or file that shows the numbers that have been assigned to records and the next number to be used

A chronologic filing system is typically used only for certain types of records, such as invoices that are to be paid by a set date. In a chronologic file, records are arranged by reverse date order. This arrangement places the oldest records at the back of the file and the newest records at the front. The files may be divided by year or month, depending on the number of records. An accession log and an alphabetic index are not used for this type of file.

✓ CHECK POINT Why do you need an alphabetic index file in a numeric filing system?

Consecutive Numeric File

In the consecutive numeric file, also called a serial or straight-number file, each digit is an indexing unit. The first digits of a number are compared to determine filing order. When the first digits are the same, the second digits are compared, and so on. The numbers used may be part of the record itself, such as a number on an invoice, or the number may be written on the record.

As each new record is added to the system, the number assigned becomes larger. Figure 11-2.3 shows part of a numeric file in which consecutive numbers are used. Primary guides divide the file drawer into sections. Folder labels show individual numbers. Folders can also show the names of the correspondents to the right of the number if privacy or security is not a factor.

Figure 11-2.3 **Numeric File**

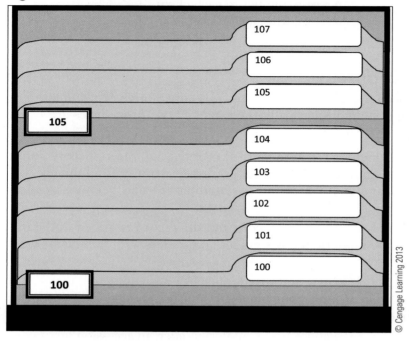

© Cengage Learning 2013

Terminal-Digit Numeric File

In a **terminal-digit file**, numbers are assigned to records. The numbers are divided into three groups of digits. For example, *129845* becomes *12-98-45*. Zeros may be added to the left of a smaller number to make all numbers the same length. For example, the number *68559* becomes *06-85-59*.

The primary (first), secondary, and tertiary (final) groups of numbers indicate the filing location of the record.

06	85	59
Tertiary (Folder number)	Secondary (Guide number)	Primary File (Section, Shelf, or Drawer number)

To locate the record 06-85-59, you would go to the 59 shelf or drawer, look behind the 85 guide, and locate the 06 folder. Note that you read the numbers from right to left in terminal-digit filing. The next number (folder) to be assigned would be 07-85-59. After 99-85-59, a new guide, 86, would be created. The first new number behind the guide 86 would be 01-86-59.

 CHECK POINT   In what direction are the numbers read in a terminal-digit filing system?

REVIEW 11-2

21st Century Skills

Thinking Critically

 **PARTNERSHIP FOR 21ST CENTURY SKILLS**

For three months you have worked in the office of Davis Rider Inc., which is a company with 12 employees. When you began the job, your supervisor, Ms. Johari Davis, told you that you would be generally in charge of the files as well as having other duties. Although everyone has access to the files, she explained that you need to make sure the files are neat and that records to be filed do not pile up.

Although the task seemed simple when Ms. Davis explained it to you, it has become a source of frustration. Some employees remove records and do not return them for several weeks. Other employees open file drawers and place folders on top of the other folders instead of inserting them in their proper places. Needless to say, the files are not being managed well. Because you are generally in charge of the files, you are being held accountable for the situation.

1. What steps could you take regarding your own work habits to help correct this problem?
2. What steps could you ask others to take to help correct this problem?

Making Academic Connections

Reinforcing English Skills

Using *it's* and *its* incorrectly is a common writing mistake. *It's* is a contraction of *it* and *is* or *has*. *Its* is a possessive pronoun. To help you know which term to use, ask yourself: Could I substitute the words *it is* or *it has* in the sentence and have it make sense? If you can, use *it's*; if not, use *its*. Key or write the following sentences, inserting either *it's* or *its*, whichever is appropriate.

1. You need to put the folder back in _____ place.
2. _____ time to remove the inactive files from active storage.
3. He replied, "_____ necessary to charge out each record."
4. This folder has lost _____ label.
5. _____ been returned to the files.
6. Please let me know when _____ ready.
7. The company improved _____ image.
8. _____ on the top shelf of the bookcase.
9. When you finish the job, let me know how long _____ taken.
10. _____ number is keyed on the folder label.

11-2 Activity 1

Alphabetic Filing (Outcomes 11-2a and 11-2b)

Practice filing skills for an alphabetic name filing system in this activity. The names of individuals, companies, organizations, and government agencies below appear on paper records.

- Write or key each name.
- Index and code each name.
- Sort the names in proper order for storing in an alphabetic name file. Indicate the filing order for the names by listing the numbers beside the names.

1.	Javier R. Fernandez	13.	D. A. Schwartz	25.	Gleason Company
2.	J. Gerald O'Neal	14.	David F. MacCormack	26.	Gabriela de la Vega
3.	Albert's Ice Cream Shop	15.	E. Charles Albertz	27.	Mrs. Denelle C. Aaron
4.	Rosa Wong	16.	Edward C. Albert	28.	Henry Elison Bowers, Jr.
5.	Dr. Elizabeth Blackwell	17.	Ethel M. Schwarzkoff	29.	Inman D. Parker, DDS
6.	Allen Parks & Sons	18.	5 Dollar Diner	30.	Maya Angelou
7.	Latasia E. Bonds	19.	Kwon Woo	31.	J. George O'Neal
8.	Betty Geneva Mohr	20.	Frank H. von Hoff	32.	500 Cafeteria
9.	A Stitch in Time	21.	Mr. Joe Park	33.	Mae J. Kim
10.	Carolyn DeBaca, MD	22.	Susie's Diner	34.	B & B Repairs
11.	WFLW Radio	23.	1st Regional Bank	35.	Sister Elena
12.	City of Chicago Grants Administration	24.	United States Department of Agriculture	36.	Druk Yul (Kingdom of Bhutan)

11-2 Activity 2

Numeric Filing (Outcome 11-2c)

Practice filing skills for consecutive and terminal-digital filing systems in this activity.

1. List the 16 numbers below. Arrange the numbers in order for a consecutive numeric filing system. Ignore the spaces in the numbers for this step.
2. List the 16 numbers below again. Arrange the numbers in order for a terminal-digit numeric filing system. Spaces in the numbers indicate the number groups.

786	67	1258	231	55	2187
303	99	2891	189	40	2891
947	28	6314	287	29	6314
502	64	9284	502	64	9485
786	67	1269	287	40	2756
303	89	2977	647	28	6325
502	63	8922	287	29	2341
946	40	2891	303	52	2977

OUTCOMES

11-3a Create and access electronic records.
11-3b Apply procedures for managing electronic records.
11-3c Manage records in a database.

Electronic Records

An electronic record is information on electronic storage media that can be readily accessed or changed. Electronic records are created and accessed using a personal computer or other devices such as a digital camera or phone. A computer can also be used to keep records inventories and store records retention and destruction data.

Types of Electronic Records

Electronic records may be contained in individual files created by office employees. For example, letters, reports, and contracts may be stored as word processing files. Budgets and balance sheets may be stored as spreadsheet files. Technical drawings and photos may be stored as graphic files. Electronic records may also be part of an electronic database, which may or may not be part of an automated system. A database is a collection of records about one topic or related topics. For example, customer names, addresses, and telephone numbers may be recorded in a database table.

database a collection of records about a topic

Individual Records

Creation and receipt of electronic records is a routine process for most office workers. For example, you will key letters and reports and receive many e-mail messages. Not all electronic information that you create or receive should be treated as a record. Only those items that have continuing value should be considered records. An e-mail that you receive from a coworker reminding you about a meeting later that day would not have continuing value and would not be considered a record.

Database Records

Electronic records may be created automatically by a system, such as an order system. For example, when a customer enters an order online, a record of the order is created and stored in a file. The customer's contact and payment information are added to a customer database. (When the customer orders from the company again, that information can be accessed so that the customer does not have to enter it again.) Database records can also be created by employees using a program such as Microsoft Access.

 CHECK POINT What kinds of information might be stored in individual electronic records?

Media for Electronic Records

Electronic records can be stored on the hard drive of a computer. They can also be stored on a variety of external storage media. This is called secondary storage. This section discusses magnetic media, flash drives, and optical disks.

Magnetic Media

magnetic media materials or devices that store computer files by using a disk or tape coated with a magnetic material

Magnetic media are materials or devices that store computer files by using a disk or tape coated with a magnetic material. Computer hard drives and tape drives are examples of magnetic media. Computer hard drives can be housed inside the computer case or they can be separate pieces that connect to a computer using a USB port.

A tape drive stores computer files on magnetic tape. Tape drives are typically used to make copies of hard drives. Records can be retrieved from the tape if the hard drive is damaged or files have been deleted.

Flash Drives and Memory Cards

flash drive a device that stores computer files on a printed circuit board and connects via a USB port

memory card a device that stores computer files on a printed circuit board and connects via a card reader

Flash drives and memory cards are external devices that store computer files. Although the two devices have different shapes, they both store data on a printed circuit board. The records remain on the device when it is not connected to a power source. A large volume of records can be stored on flash drives and memory cards, and these records can be retrieved quickly.

Flash drives connect to a computer using a USB port. They are also called pen drives or memory sticks. Memory cards use a card slot in a card reader, computer, camera, phone, or other device to connect to a computer or other devices.

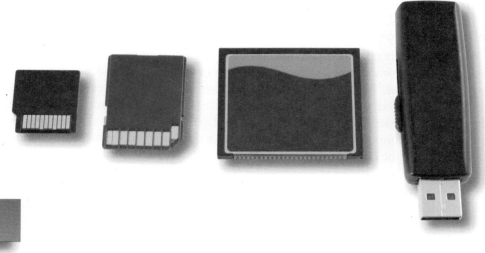

Flash drives and memory cards are external storage devices.

Dim154/Shutterstock

Optical Disks

optical disk a device coated with plastic on which digital data can be stored using a laser

An optical disk is a device coated with plastic on which digital data can be stored using a laser. CDs (compact disks) and DVDs (digital video disks) are optical storage media. Data are stored and read on an optical disk using a special drive in a computer. These disks can hold large amounts of information.

CDs and DVDs should be handled carefully. Keep disks in protective jackets or cases to prevent them from being scratched or getting dirty. Scratches or dirt on the surface and warping, which can be caused by extreme heat, may make a disk unreadable. Disks in plastic cases or pockets are often stored in boxes, cases, or trays.

Optical disks are an important part of a records management system. Optical disks offer large storage capacity and can be stored in a retrieval system called a jukebox. A jukebox contains many disks and allows records to be retrieved quickly. Jukeboxes can be linked together, which further increases storage capacity.

jukebox a device that stores many optical disks and allows records to be retrieved quickly

---

✳ WORKPLACE CONNECTIONS ✳

Kassa is a customer service supervisor at a savings and loan company. All questions from customers about their mortgage accounts are directed to her. The company stores all its customer accounts on optical disks in a jukebox. Kassa is describing the features of the system to Montel, a new employee.

Kassa: "Our electronic records system lets me retrieve documents quickly. When a customer calls with questions about a mortgage payment, I just key the customer's account number at my computer. The system quickly locates the account and displays it on my screen. I can even get a printout if I want."

Montel: "That's certainly efficient."

Kassa: "Right! Before, locating document files took so long that I had to tell customers that I'd call them later after I'd pulled the folder."

How does having optical disks stored in a jukebox speed access to records?

 CHECK POINT What are two types of magnetic media used to store electronic records?

Advantages and Disadvantages

Electronic records are widely used in organizations. Some records are kept in both paper and electronic form. Other are kept only in electronic form. Using electronic records has both advantages and disadvantages. The advantages to storing records in electronic form are:

- Records can be retrieved quickly and easily.
- The storage space required for housing records is much less than that required for physical records.
- Records stay in the same order even after being retrieved several times.
- Records can be organized and updated easily on hard drives, flash drives, and memory cards.

The disadvantages to storing records in electronic form are:

- An output device, such as a monitor or printer, is needed to read the records.
- Electrical power surges and failures can erase or change the data recorded on magnetic media.
- Storage media require protection from extreme heat and cold and should be kept away from magnetic fields.
- Records stored on standard CDs and DVDs cannot be updated. (Rewritable CDs and DVDs do allow records to be changed.)
- Records on tape must be accessed in the order they were recorded, which slows access time.

 CHECK POINT What are some disadvantages to storing records in electronic form?

Procedures for Electronic Records

Electronic records should be managed through the five steps of the record life cycle: creation or receipt, distribution, use, maintenance, and disposition. Special attention is required to keep electronic records secure. Backup copies and security procedures help accomplish this goal.

Creation or Receipt

During the creation or receipt phase, electronic files must be assigned to a folder or directory and given a name so they can be identified and accessed when needed. You should understand the system of drives and folders on your computer or network so you can store and retrieve files efficiently. You should also name files in a logical and consistent way that indicates the information they contain. Doing so will make finding information easy when it is needed.

File Names

Using consistent procedures to name and organize the records is very important. Files can be named and stored using an alphabetic or numeric arrangement. You may wish to organize records into folders on your computer that are the same or similar to the way folders are organized in the company's physical records system.

As with physical records, think about how the record will be requested when selecting a name for the file. In addition to using a consistent naming procedure, many programs allow you to enter metadata for records you create. Metadata are identifying details about a record or document. For example, for a Word document, you can enter details such as a title, author name, subject, and keywords that identify the document's topic or contents. These properties can be used to search for the document in the event that you cannot locate it by name. Document properties for a Word letter are shown in Figure 11-3.1.

metadata identifying details about a record or document

Figure 11-3.1 Document Properties

El Cazador Restaurant 7-20-11.docx Properties

| General | Summary | Statistics | Contents | Custom |

Title: Services Update for El Cazador Restaurant

Subject: Financial Services

Author: William Diamond

Manager:

Company: Diamond Financial Services

Category: Response to client request

Keywords: insurance, retirement

Comments: |

Hyperlink base:

Template: Normal.dotm

☐ Save Thumbnails for All Word Documents

OK   Cancel

Some operating systems limit the length of a filename to eight characters. Other systems allow longer, more descriptive names to be used. Some systems allow you to add an extension (such as "docx" for document) to further identify your file. Many programs add the extension for you. Filenames should reflect the type of data stored in the file. For example, the name assigned to a mailing list file could be Maillist or Austin TX Mailing List. Guidelines for storing electronic files are shown in Figure 11-3.2.

Figure 11-3.2 Storing Electronic Files

GUIDELINES FOR STORING ELECTRONIC FILES

- Create folders to group related files. When a large number of files accumulate in the folder, move files into two or more new folders.
- Give each file a unique name even if it is stored in a different folder than a file with a similar name.
- Use abbreviations that are commonly recognized; for example, *Dept* for department or *Proj* for project.
- If your system allows the use of long file names, use as many characters as needed to make identifying the file easy.
- Use numbers or dates to label versions of a file. For example, your fourth letter to the Accounting Department might be labeled *AcctDpt4* or *Acct Dept Letter 4-2-11*.
- Use the default file extension or allow the program to assign the extension.

© Cengage Learning 2013

File Paths

The filename alone may not be enough information to retrieve a file quickly. You need to know the drive and folder name where the file is stored. This information is called the file path. Figure 11-3.3 on page 404 shows a list of files and folders in the Abbott Project folder on the C: drive (hard drive) of a computer. The Abbott Project folder contains several subfolders. Individual

file path the complete location (drive, folders, and name) for a file

files are shown for a schedule, a project summary, and a press release. File extensions are shown in this figure. You may or may not see file extensions on your system depending on the options set in the software. The complete path for the Excel file that contains the project schedule is:

C:\Abbott Project\Abbott Proj Schedule.xlsx.

Figure 11-3.3 **The drive and folder name are needed to locate a file.**

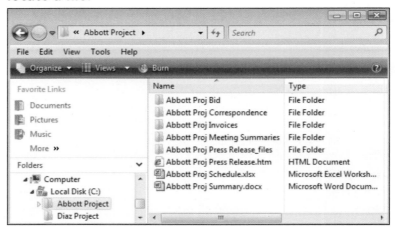

 CHECK POINT What information does a file path include?

Distribution and Use

Distribution of electronic records may be done in several ways. For example, the record could be sent as an e-mail attachment. It could be saved on a network where it is accessible to those who need it. The record could be posted on a website, shared in a web meeting, or saved on a CD and mailed or given to the recipients.

Use of electronic records is as varied as use of physical records. The record may be used to answer questions, make decisions, or complete other activities. Because a copy of the record is sent, the file can be deleted after its use. The original file remains in storage.

 CHECK POINT Why do office workers typically not need to return electronic records requested from the files?

Maintenance

Maintenance for electronic records involves accessing records, making backup copies, and keeping files secure. As with paper records, locating electronic records should be easy if the proper procedures were followed for storing the records.

Accessing Records

Accessing individual electronic records involves entering the file path to indicate the record location. Files typically are retrieved using the program with which they were created. Some files can be accessed by more than one program. For example, graphics files that contain photos or clipart can be accessed by several photo editing and drawing programs.

Once you have opened an electronic file, you can read it on the screen or print it. You can also send an electronic or hard copy of the file to authorized persons who need the information.

Making Backup Copies

Data files can be expensive to create again or replace if they become damaged and are no longer usable. For this reason, backup copies are made. A **backup copy** is a duplicate of data that can be used if the original data is lost or destroyed. A backup copy should be made if loss of the data would have serious consequences. Backing up a hard drive or disk means making a copy of all the data onto another storage medium. Backing up a file means making a copy of an individual file onto a different disk or drive.

Most computer operating systems provide easy-to-follow procedures for making backup copies. Figure 11-3.4 shows a dialog box with options for making a copy of a disk using the Windows operating system. You should research and practice the backup or copy commands for your particular system if you are not familiar with them. Backup disks should be labeled in the same manner as their original, perhaps with the word Backup added to the label. Backup copies should be stored in a separate, safe location.

Figure 11-3.4 **Select appropriate options when creating backup disks.**

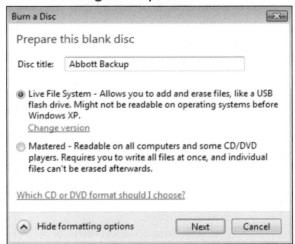

In many companies, computers are linked together in a local area network. They may also be linked to a wide area network of computers. In some cases, files may be backed up automatically to a network location. In other cases, each employee is responsible for backing up files regularly.

Some companies store backup copies of records on a cloud file server. A cloud file server is a computer at a distant location that is accessed via the Internet. Egnyte Cloud File Server is one company that provides this online service. Using a cloud file server has several advantages:

- You can have access to your files from any computer with an Internet connection.
- Files stored online can serve as backup in case your computer is damaged or files are deleted by mistake.

- You can control who has access to the stored files. For example, you could give access to your files to a coworker.

- A company can use only the services needed and pay for only those services.

Controlling File Security

The security of electronic files should be a concern to all office workers. You would not want a competitor to have access to a customer mailing list or a sales report that you keyed. Some companies use security measures such as access logs and passwords. A **password** is a series of characters used to gain access to a system, program, or file. These measures allow only authorized employees to access certain files. In some companies, employees are required to change passwords frequently.

Choose passwords carefully so others cannot easily guess your password. For example, do not use variations of family members' names or birthdates or a favorite sport or hobby as a password. Choose a series of meaningless letters and numbers instead. Do not leave your password in a location where others can access it easily, such as taped to your monitor or under your keyboard. Store your password in a safe place.

Take steps to safeguard files when in use. For example, clear a document from the computer screen when you take a break or leave your computer for other reasons. Log off the computer network before leaving your computer so others cannot use your computer to access files. Do not send files containing confidential information as e-mail attachments. Store disks in a concealed location rather than on top of your desk. Store disks with highly confidential information in a locked cabinet or drawer.

password a series of characters used to gain access to a system, program, or file

CHECK POINT What are two tips for creating an effective password?

Disposition

You may not be involved in disposing of records you use that are created by an automated system. However, someone in the company will be responsible for moving the records to offline storage at the correct time. The records will eventually be destroyed or placed in permanent storage.

Follow your company's records retention schedule to determine how long to keep individual electronic records you create or receive. The schedule may indicate times for active and inactive storage of files. Active files would be stored on your computer hard drive or readily accessible storage devices. Inactive storage would be on secondary devices, such as flash drives or optical disks. These devices may be stored in a location for files that are not used often.

Transfer electronic records to a DVD for inactive storage.

Jaimie Duplass/Shutterstock

As with paper records, it is important to store electronic records promptly and not let them pile up. For example, when you read an e-mail, determine whether it has continuing value. If it does, it is a record and should be filed in the proper folder and using an appropriate name. If it does not, it is not a record and should be moved to the Delete folder. For some e-mail systems, messages remain in the Delete folder until you indicate that they should be permanently deleted. Remove messages from the Delete folder regularly.

Handle other electronic documents, such as those you receive as e-mail attachments, in a similar manner. Determine whether they should be kept. If yes, file then in the appropriate folder. If not, delete them.

 CHECK POINT How should you determine how long to keep electronic records you create?

Using Database Records

A database is any collection of related records. An electronic database is a collection of records stored and retrieved by computer. These databases are useful because thousands of records can be searched in only a few seconds. Searching the same number of records stored on paper would take a long time. In many companies, workers can get data from a database by using a computer network. This prevents the need to have the same data stored in each department or work group.

Database Management Systems

A database management system (DBMS) organizes large numbers of records in a database. A major advantage of a DBMS is that data can be compared and shared among the tables in the database. For example, an employee at the Internal Revenue Service might use a DBMS to compare data on a person's current income tax return with data on past tax returns. Another advantage of a DBMS is data security. Access to parts of the database can be limited to authorized employees who have been issued passwords.

✳ WORKPLACE CONNECTIONS ✳

Lao Ji works for The Supply Closet, which sells office supplies. The company's DBMS contains a master record for each customer. When Lao Ji inputs data for a customer order, he simply enters the customer name in the customer order form screen. Other data, such as the customer number and address, are displayed by the system. This data is stored in the customer master record. Lao Ji can create the customer order quickly and accurately because he does not need to key the customer number, name, and address.

What other information about the customer might display when the account is accessed?

A DBMS helps users keep database records up to date. Suppose you work in a company that uses a DBMS to manage its personnel and payroll records. If an employee's last name changes, you need to make the change only in the personnel record. The system will automatically update the payroll record.

CHECK POINT What is a major advantage of a database management system?

Individual Databases

Not all information in databases needs to be available to many users via a network. A database can also be stored on a single computer for use by a few employees or one person. Microsoft Access is an example of a popular database program used by many office employees.

Creating a Database

When creating a database, group data into tables of related information. For example, suppose you work in a car dealership. You might place customer contact information (name, address, e-mail address, and telephone number) in one database table. The brand, model, year, and date of purchase of vehicles bought by each customer might be placed in another table. The tables can be related using a common field in each table, such as a customer number. You can create reports that show data from several related tables at once.

When deciding which fields to use in a database table, consider the smallest unit of information you might to use separately from the other information. For example, when creating personalized letters using mail merge, you might want to include a person's last name in the salutation of a letter. This field will not be available if you created only one field in the database for the customer name. If you created separate fields for the customer title, customer first name, and customer last name, you can easily create personalized salutations that include the customer's title and last name. Figure 11-3.5 shows the fields in the Clients database table.

Figure 11-3.5 **Use a different field for each unit of data in a database table.**

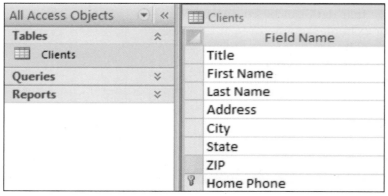

Indexes for Physical Records

A database is often used to create an index or an accession log for a physical records system. If you want records in the database and the physical system to be sorted in the same way, experiment or read the program help information to see how text and numbers are sorted in the program. You might need to make adjustments to the way you enter data or file records so that both systems work in the same way. For example, some programs require the use of leading zeros to make all numbers to be sorted the same length.

CHECK POINT How can tables in a database be related?

REVIEW 11-3

21st Century Skills

Interacting with Others

You and two of your coworkers, Neema and Paula, are working late one evening. All the other employees have gone for the day. During a brief break, Paula says to you: "I hear the company is about to close some pretty big real estate deals. You know the access code for the financial database. Let's look and see what's going on." Neema agrees, saying, "Sure! No one else is here. What difference will it make? We won't tell anyone you let us see the information."

1. How would you react in this situation? What would you say to your coworkers?
2. What might be the consequences of accessing and sharing this confidential information with coworkers?

Making Academic Connections

Reinforcing Math Skills

1. Your company estimates that it takes you 20 minutes less each day to complete your filing tasks using folders with color-coded file labels than using folders without them.
   a. How many hours will the use of color-coded file labels save you each week (5 working days)?
   b. How many hours will the use of color-coded file labels save you each month (4 weeks)?
   c. How many hours will the use of color-coded file labels save you each year (50 weeks)?
2. Eight file folders have captions with *Randolph* as the first indexing unit, six folders have *Reynolds* as the first unit, and two folders have *Rogers* as the first unit. One hundred and thirty folders are filed under the letter *R*.
   a. Of the total *R* folders, what percentage are *Randolph* folders?
   b. What percentage are *Reynolds* folders?
   c. What percentage are *Rogers* folders?
   Round your answers to the nearest whole percentages.

11-3 Activity 1

Organizing Electronic Files (Outcomes 11-3a and 11-3b)

You have recently begun a new job working with three executives in the accounting firm Carson Associates. Several files that were created by the person who previously had this job are stored on your computer. However, no clear organization or consistent file names have been used.

1. You have quickly scanned the contents of the files on your computer and made notes about what each file contains. Open and print the file 11-3 Records from the data files. This file contains the information you noted about the files.
2. Review the guidelines for naming electronic files found in this chapter. Then create a plan that includes folders and subfolders that will let you

quickly find files about a particular topic for any of the three executives. Outline your plan showing the structure and names of main folders and subfolders so that it would be easy for someone else to understand.

3. Create a plan for naming files that will be consistent and simple. For each file (as listed on the printout), key the current file name. Then key the file path (main folder and any subfolders in which the file will be stored and the new name you will give the file). Assume that the computer is set to show file extensions.

Example:

Star bid 1.docx   C:\Stone\Bids\Stardust Bid 6-23.docx

---

4. Show the structure of your new file system. Arrange the folder names and new file names in groups to show each main folder, each subfolder within each main folder, and each new file name within a main folder or subfolder.

11-3 Activity 2

Accession Log and Alphabetic Index (Outcome 11-3c)

You work for Philips Associates, a company in Miami, Florida. To help keep the records confidential, a numeric filing system is used. You have been asked to use a database file to create an accession log and an alphabetic index for physical records. Work with a classmate to complete this activity.

1. Open the Access file 11-3 Files Index from the data files. This file contains information for the numeric file.

2. Open the Names List table. The personal and company names, along with addresses and telephone numbers, have already been entered in the table. In the Indexed Name field, key the name as it would be indexed for filing on a paper record. Review the alphabetic indexing rules, if needed, until you and your classmate agree on how the name should be indexed.

3. Create a query using the Names List table. Include the Number and Indexed Name fields. Sort the data by the Number field in descending order. In the Criteria row for the Number field, key *Not G*. Save the query using the name Accession Log and print the query results table.

4. Create a report named Alphabetic Index using the Names List table. Include the Indexed Name and Number fields. Sort the data in ascending order by the Indexed Name field. Adjust the format as needed for an attractive report and print the report.

Summary

11-1 Introduction to Records Management

- A record is stored information that has continuing value and is made or received by an organization.
- The record life cycle consists of the creation, distribution, use, maintenance, and disposition of a record.
- A records management system includes procedures for selecting storage media and equipment, filing and retrieving records, and retaining and disposing of records.
- Records in a filing system are arranged alphabetically or numerically.
- A retention schedule shows how long particular types of records should be kept.

11-2 Managing Physical Records

- Two common types of physical records are paper and microfilm. Microfilm contains small images of records on a roll or sheet of film.
- To prepare physical records for storage, collect, inspect, index, and code the records. Prepare cross-references, if needed, and then sort the records.
- In an alphabetic name file, folders are arranged behind guides with captions that identify the sections of the file. Records are stored in individual, special, or general folders.
- Using standard alphabetic indexing rules helps prevents errors in storing and problems in retrieving records.
- In a numeric filing system, records are given numbers that are arranged in order when stored. An alphabetic index and an accession log are used with numeric filing systems.

11-3 Managing Electronic Records

- An electronic record is information on electronic storage media that can be readily accessed or changed.
- Electronic records may be contained in individual files created by office employees or part of an electronic database or an automated system.
- Magnetic media, flash drives, and optical disks are commonly used to store electronic records.
- Electronic records should be managed through the five steps of the record life cycle: creation or receipt, distribution, use, maintenance, and disposition.
- Special attention is required to keep electronic records secure. Backup copies and security procedures help accomplish this goal.
- An electronic database is a collection of records stored and retrieved by computer. These databases are useful because thousands of records can be searched in only a few seconds.

Chapter 11 Activity 1

Code and Cross-Reference Records
(Outcomes 11-1c, 11-2a, and 11-2b)

Paper records, such as letters, must be indexed and coded properly before filing. A cross-reference should be prepared when a record may be requested under a different name than the one it is filed under. Practice coding letters and preparing cross-reference sheets in this activity.

1. Open and print the file 11 Letters from the data files. This file contains six letters to be coded and two blank cross-reference sheets.

2. Index and code each letter for filing in an alphabetic name file. You work at Star Satellite Systems, so the letters with this company name in the letterhead are outgoing letters. The other letters are incoming letters. See Figure 11-2.1 for an example of a coded letter.

3. The letter to Anne Ashby and the letter from William Abbott require cross-references. Code cross-reference captions on the letters and prepare cross-reference sheets for these letters. Which of these letters might require a permanent cross-reference guide?

Chapter 11 Activity 2

Records Retention
(Outcomes 11-1c, 11-3b, and 11-3c)

In this activity, you will continue your work at Carson Associates. You created a file organization and naming plan in an earlier activity. Now you will create a computer index to track the electronic records and their retention dates.

1. Create a new database named Records Index. Create a table named Files Index. Include the following text fields in the table: Filename, File Path, Date, Originator, Key Content, Category, Active Storage, and Inactive Storage. Make the Filename field the primary key.

2. Use the list of new filenames and paths you created earlier. Create a record in your database for each file.

   - Enter the filename in the Filename field; for example, Stardust Bid 6-23.docx.

   - Enter the drive and folder location for the file in the File Path field; for example, C:\Stone\Bids.

   - Enter the date of the file in the Date field.

   - Enter the name of the executive for whom the file was created in the Originator field.

   - Enter a few words that indicate what the record relates to in the Key Content field, for example, cover letter for bid.

   - Enter the type of record, such as letter, report, spreadsheet, presentation, or database, in the Category field.

   - Enter the retention period for which the document will be kept in active online storage on your computer in the Active Storage field. See the table on the next page to determine retention periods.

■ Enter the retention period for which the document will be kept in inactive storage (on a disk or flash drive) in the Inactive Storage field.

Retention Periods

CATEGORY	ACTIVE STORAGE	INACTIVE STORAGE
Bank reconciliations	3 years	Permanent
Bids and related correspondence	1 year	4 years
Client database	Permanent	
Correspondence	1 year	4 years
Financial statements (balance sheets and income statements)	3 years	Permanent
Invoices	2 years	7 years
Presentations	1 year	2 years

3. Having an index of files for each executive will be helpful in locating records.

   ■ Create a query named Files by Originator based on the Files Index table.

   ■ Show the Originator, Filename, File Path, Date, and Key Content fields in the query results table.

   ■ Sort the records in ascending order, first by the Originator field, then by the File Name field.

   ■ Print the query results table.

4. Assume you created your records index on August 10 of the current year. Now assume that 13 months have gone by since the date when the index was created. You need to find all records that have been in active storage longer than the time shown on the retention schedule. In this situation, records with 1 year in the Active Storage field would be ready for transfer to inactive storage.

   ■ Create a query based on the Files Index table.

   ■ Name the query Files to Transfer.

   ■ Show the Originator, Filename, File Path, Category, Active Storage, and Inactive Storage fields in the query results.

   ■ Sort the query results by the Filename field. Key *1 year* in the Criteria row for the Active Storage field.

   ■ Run the query and print the query results table.

Database Design and Applications Event

In this event, you will be asked to design a database for a small business. The database will contain multiple tables with relationships to one another. Various field types will be used in the tables. You will enter data into the tables and create forms and reports using the data. Query statements will be required to find data in single and multiple tables.

You will have one hour for the production portion of this event. No reference materials are allowed. The second part of the event includes a one-hour written objective test to determine your knowledge of database design and applications. The score received on the test will equal 15 percent of the final event score.

Performance Indicators Evaluated

Participants will demonstrate skills related to the information technology career cluster. Sample performance indicators include the ability to:

- Demonstrate knowledge of definitions and terms related to databases
- Demonstrate knowledge of table relationships and normalization of data
- Demonstrate knowledge of database design and SQL queries
- Apply design principles to create a database with multiple related tables
- Apply skills to enter data into tables and to create database forms and reports
- Apply skills to create SQL statements to find data from single and multiple tables

For more detailed information about this event, go to the FBLA website.[1]

http://www.fbla-pbl.org

Think Critically

1. Why should data be placed in two or more related tables rather than placing all the data in one table?
2. Why is it important to set a primary key for each table in the database?
3. Why is referential integrity important for table relationships?

---

[1]FBLA-PBL, "FBLA Competitive Events, Database Design & Applications," 2010, http://www.fbla-pbl.org/docs/ct/gdlrs/FBLA/database%20design%20and%20application.pdf.

Human Resources Management

Do you enjoy working with other people? Are you good at planning, organizing, and directing activities for yourself and others? If the answer to these questions is *yes*, a career in human resources management might be right for you. Workers in this field interview, hire, and train other workers. Some workers in this field manage employee benefits. Others see that the organization follows laws regarding labor, discrimination, and health and safety issues.

Jobs in human resources management are found in businesses, hospitals, schools, and other organizations. Any organization or group that hires several employees must find suitable employees and manage their training and benefits.

Employment Outlook

There are many jobs in human resources management. Many individuals are employees of a company or other organization. Others in the field work as consultants. The U.S. government provides job projections for 2008–2018. Jobs in this career area are expected to increase from new openings and the need to replace retiring workers.[2]

Job Titles

- Director of human resources
- Compensation and benefits specialist
- Recruitment specialist
- Human resources consultant
- Training and development specialist
- Labor and personnel relations specialist
- EEO compliance officer
- Human resources assistant

[2]*Occupational Outlook Handbook*, 2010-11 Edition, Bureau of Labor Statistics, U.S. Department of Labor, http://www.bls.gov/oco/ocos021.htm.

Needed Education/Skills

The human relations and technical skills needed for a career in human resources management can be obtained in high schools, technical schools, and colleges/universities. Visiting job sites, job shadowing, and internships are valuable for gaining the experience needed for success in this career area. Work experience and passing an exam to earn a title such as Professional in Human Resources or Certified Employee Benefits Specialist are helpful in getting some jobs.

What's it like to work in... Human Resources Management?

Shauna works as a human resources assistant in a manufacturing company with 150 employees. She assists the human resources manager, Mr. Aaron, by answering routine correspondence and preparing monthly reports on personnel issues. Today Shauna prepared three letters to acknowledge receiving applications for jobs. She also answered a letter from the local Chamber of Commerce requesting information about the company's personnel needs.

Shauna's boss, Mr. Aaron, is scheduled to give a presentation on a new employee benefits package next week. Shauna gathered the information that Mr. Aaron requested be included and prepared electronic slides for the presentation. Several times during the day, Shauna answered phone calls or e-mails from employees regarding training programs, benefits, drug testing, and other issues. Shauna enjoys her varied job duties and appreciates the confidence Mr. Aaron shows in her. She plans to continue her education to become a Certified Employee Benefits Specialist.

What About You?

Does a job in human resources management sound appealing to you? Which of the jobs in this career area would you like best? What skills would you need to gain or improve for this job?

CHAPTER 12

Processing Mail

12-1 Incoming Mail Processes

12-2 Outgoing Mail Processes

Thomas Michael Corcoran/PhotoEdit

Wire_man/Shutterstock.com

Workers frequently send written messages to coworkers as well as to people outside the company. Mail must be processed efficiently so that these messages are not delayed. The size of a company and the type of equipment available affect the procedures used for processing incoming and outgoing mail. In a small company, one worker may handle incoming and outgoing mail. In a large company, a full-time mailroom staff often uses specialized equipment to process mail. Even in large companies, workers outside the mailroom may have certain mail-handling duties.

In this chapter, you will learn procedures for processing incoming and outgoing mail in both small and large companies. You also will learn about the equipment available to process mail.

OUTCOMES

12-1a Describe procedures for sorting and distributing mail.
12-1b Describe procedures for processing incoming mail.

Sorting and Distributing Mail

Office workers often need to act promptly in response to items received in the mail. They may need to deposit checks, fill orders, or pay invoices. They may read literature, review reports, and answer correspondence. Mail must be accurately sorted and promptly distributed to the appropriate people. This prompt delivery is necessary so actions can be taken without delay.

You may be responsible for sorting and distributing incoming mail for coworkers or just for handling your own mail. You may help your coworkers process their mail after another worker has distributed it. Your role in processing incoming mail will depend on the size of the company, the volume of incoming mail, and your job duties.

Mail for various people and departments is delivered to a company. Most companies want all mail sorted quickly and delivered promptly. Express mail, registered mail, and insured mail may be delivered immediately on receipt. The delivery of such letters usually takes priority over the processing of other mail. The method used for sorting mail will vary depending on the size of the company and how it is organized.

In Small Companies

In a small company, you can easily sort the mail at your workstation. Making a stack of mail for each employee or department makes delivery quicker. In a small company, one person may process incoming mail as well as perform other office tasks.

To distribute the mail, you may place mail in mailboxes located in a central area where other workers will collect their mail. In other companies, mail is hand delivered to the appropriate person or department. If you have several stacks or bundles of mail to deliver, you may need to carry them in a pouch, alphabetized expanding folder,

David Young-Wolff/PhotoEdit

In some organizations, workers collect their mail from a mailbox.

lightweight mail basket, or mail cart as you make your rounds through the office. You could arrange the bundles according to the route you will take.

 CHECK POINT How should you arrange stacks of mail that you will deliver to others?

In Large Companies

Many large companies have mailrooms. A mailroom is an area where large volumes of incoming mail are processed. Mailrooms are easily accessible to postal workers who deliver the mail to the company. Companies often have specialized equipment to aid mailroom workers in handling the mail.

Opening Envelopes and Packages

In some companies, mailroom workers open all the mail (except envelopes marked *Personal* or *Confidential*) before delivering it. An electric envelope opener often is used for opening envelopes. An electric envelope opener trims a narrow strip off one edge of each envelope. The amount trimmed off is very small so there is little risk that the contents of the envelope will be damaged. To reduce the chances of cutting the contents, tap each envelope on the table before placing it in the opener. Doing so makes contents fall away from the edge that you are trimming. Take care when opening packages and boxes not to damage the contents.

Safety Precautions

Office workers (in small and large companies) should take care to protect themselves against dangerous substances that might be present in envelopes or packages received via mail. Wearing gloves and a face mask can provide some protection from airborne substances that might be dangerous. When handling mail, avoid touching your face and mouth to help prevent the transfer of germs. Wash your hands with disinfectant soap after handling mail. The United States Postal Service recommends that you do not handle a piece of mail that you suspect is dangerous.

According to the Centers for Disease Control and Prevention (CDC), characteristics of suspicious packages and letters include inappropriate or unusual labeling, a strange return address or no return address, postmarks from a city or state different from the return address, excessive packaging material, and others. If a package appears suspicious, it should not be opened. The package should be handled as little as possible. The room should be vacated and secured promptly, and appropriate security or law enforcement agencies should be notified. For more information, access the CDC website.[1]

Sorting Mail

A wide variety of sorting units are used to sort the mail. Each compartment is labeled with the name of an individual or department within the organization. To sort the mail, you place each piece of mail in the appropriate compartment.

Companies with a huge amount of incoming mail have found that they can save time and effort by using a rotary sorting unit. The unit turns easily, and the worker can remain in one place as he or she sorts the mail.

Distributing Mail

Once the mail has been sorted, it is ready for distribution. Procedures for delivering mail within organizations vary. For example:

- A worker from each department comes to the mailroom to pick up the department's mail.
- A mailroom employee carries the mail in a basket or cart from the mailroom to the departments.
- In large companies, an automated delivery system transports mail to the various departments. This robot-like cart follows a path on the floor and is programmed to stop at certain locations throughout the building. Employees can then pick up incoming mail and deposit outgoing mail.

CHECK POINT What should you do if you receive a package or letter that appears suspicious?

A mailroom employee may deliver mail to various departments in a company.

Processing Incoming Mail

Some office workers are asked to process the mail before giving it to their coworkers. Some workers may simply separate and open the mail. Other workers may be expected to annotate, route, or prioritize correspondence.

[1]"How to Recognize and Handle a Suspicious Package or Envelope," Centers for Disease Control and Prevention, 2011, http://emergency.cdc.gov/agent/anthrax/mail/suspiciouspackages.asp.

In handling your own mail or mail for others, you may have access to confidential information. This information may be related to business plans or products, employee records, or customer profiles. You will be expected to take steps to protect this confidential information. You may be asked to sign a confidentiality agreement.

Opening Mail

If the mail is not opened when it reaches you, use a letter opener to open all envelopes. (See the Safety Precautions section earlier in this chapter.) When you are opening mail for coworkers, do not open envelopes marked *Personal* or *Confidential*. If you mistakenly open such an envelope, write on it, "Sorry, opened by mistake," and add your initials. Check the outside of each envelope carefully before you open it to avoid making that error.

As you remove the contents from the envelopes, be sure to verify that all **enclosures** referred to in the letter are present. If an enclosure is missing, you should note in the margin of the letter that it is missing. Notify the sender of the missing enclosure right away, especially if it is a check, money order, cash, or stamps.

Check each letter for the signature and the address of the sender before you discard the envelope. If either is missing on the letter, attach the envelope to the back of the letter. The envelope usually has a return address on it. Sometimes the envelope is stapled to a document because the mailing date may be important.

Record the current date on each item received. In some cases, recording the time the item was received may also be helpful. This can be done with a pen or pencil, a rubber stamp, or a time-stamp machine.

As you inspect the mail, put the letters that you will answer or handle yourself in one stack and those that will be handled by a supervisor or coworkers in another stack. You may be able to handle communications that could be answered by a form letter, circular, or advertisement. Requests for catalogs or price lists can also be handled this way. However, your supervisor may wish to see all inquiries that are received.

To help with answering mail, you may want to underline or **annotate** the correspondence. Using good judgment is necessary here, however, because too many marks on a letter can be distracting. An annotated letter is shown in Figure 12-1.1.

enclosure an item included in a package or envelope

annotate write comments related to the content of a message

Ace Lumber Company

3000 Winchester Avenue
Ashland, KY 41101-0077

December 5, 20--

Dec 8, 20-- 11:30 a.m.

Ms. Shauna Carrel
Ashland Computerland, Inc.
405 Laurel Avenue
Ashland, KY 41101-0800

Dear Ms. Carrel

Our new computer system was installed on November 26, and we were impressed with
the efficiency of your installation team. The hardware and software are installed and
working well. Feedback from the end-users has been positive.

Ed Ortiz, your installation team director, advises that we need to add one more workstation to maximize the use of the computer network. Please add another PC2-2020
workstation to our order.

Mr. Ortiz also reminded us to make plans for our unit director, Mary Ann Park, to attend
your end-user workshop on January 6 and 7. Ms. Park is eager to attend, and we know
that this additional education will allow her to help us use our network more effectively.
Please send Ms. Park a registration form for the workshop.

Sincerely

Registration form sent.

Ivan Petrov

Ivan Petrov, Manager

dc

© Cengage Learning 2013

First, underline the key words and phrases in the correspondence that will aid in understanding the content quickly. Note the key phrases underlined in Figure 12-1.1. Then determine the answers to questions in the message. Where appropriate, make related comments on the document. Write the clearly worded answers and/or comments in legible handwriting in the margin, on a note (paper or electronic) placed on the correspondence, or on a photocopy of the correspondence. Note the annotations on the letter shown in Figure 12-1.1.

 CHECK POINT What are some examples of correspondence you may be able to handle for a coworker or supervisor?

Documenting and Routing Mail

You should keep a record of items you expect to receive under separate cover (in another envelope or package) to be sure that you receive them. You might create a spreadsheet or database table to record the current date, the item expected, the date you expect to receive the item, and the person or company who will send the item. A field or column might be included to record the date the item is received. If you handle mail for several people, you would include the name of the person expecting the item. Check the table at least twice a week to see which items have not been received. Then take follow-up action on delayed mail. If you handle mail only for yourself, you might simply enter a reminder in your reminder software, such as Microsoft Outlook, to alert you on the date the mail is expected. Figure 12-1.2 shows such as reminder.

Figure 12-1.2 **Create a reminder of incoming mail you expect to receive.**

📭 1 Reminder		🗕 🗖 ✖
📝 **Wilson report should arrive by 7/22.**		
Due: Friday, July 22, 2011 2:10 PM		

Subject		Due in	
📝 Wilson report should arrive by 7/22.		Now	

| Dismiss All | | Open Item | Dismiss |

Click Snooze to be reminded again in:

| 5 minutes | ▼ | Snooze |

Protecting Confidential Information

Confidential information is data that is private or secret. Release of such data could cause harm to the business or its employees, clients, or customers. Businesses may have several types of confidential data. Inside information is data about the company that has not yet been released to the public. Examples are plans to open a new plant or merge with another company. Proprietary information is data about the company's products or services. An example is the formula or design for a product. Private information about employees and customers, such as salaries or credit card numbers, is often stored in company files. Usually, only those employees who need the data to do their jobs are allowed to see confidential information.

As an office worker, you may come in contact with confidential information as you process the mail, prepare documents, or handle records. The following guidelines will help you keep business information confidential:

- **Know your supervisor's preferences.** Know what information you should and should not give to visitors or callers. When your supervisor is not in the office, know who is to be allowed in your supervisor's office or who can use your supervisor's computer.
- **Follow your company's mail procedures.** Place confidential mail in a folder or in a secure location where it will be seen only by the intended recipient. Do not send confidential information by fax or e-mail. Use overnight mail services if speed is a consideration.
- **Secure your workstation.** Take precautions to keep others from reading confidential information on your computer screen. Turn over confidential mail or papers or place them in a drawer when you leave your desk even for a few moments. At the end of the day, secure papers in a locked desk or file cabinet. Shred confidential documents rather than placing them in your wastebasket.
- **Protect written documents.** Use a folder or an envelope to conceal documents if you carry documents to another office. If you transport confidential documents outside the office, lock them in a briefcase or in the trunk of your car. If you use a briefcase, always keep it in your possession.
- **Reduce electronic information loss.** Use password sign-on and sign-off procedures and change your password frequently. Be alert to remove printouts from the printer when you finish the print job, particularly if the printer is shared with others. Make backup copies of confidential files and place them in a secure location.

> What should you do if you open a confidential letter by mistake? Should confidential information be sent by e-mail? Why or why not?

Copies of previous correspondence, reports, and other related documents might help in responding to the mail. For example, you may attach the file copy of a letter written to Ms. Park to the reply you receive from her. Or you might retrieve a folder related to an inquiry from the files and place it with the incoming letter.

Whether you process incoming mail in a small company or in the mailroom of a large company, you should keep track of the receipt of mail sent by special Postal Services or private mail services. For example, you should record the receipt of certified, insured, registered, or express mail. You might use a printed form or record information in a table as shown in Figure 12-1.3 on page 424.

proprietary information
sensitive data that is not public knowledge and is viewed as owned by the holder

Figure 12-1.3 A mail register can be used to document receipt of special mail.

	Item	For	From	City	State	Date	Time
2	Insured package	Carlos Vargas	Lee Kim	St. Louis	MO	4/5/--	3.20 p.m.
3	Special delivery package	Jelan Nowell	Bates Mfg. Co.	Memphis	TN	4/6/--	9:15 a.m.
4	Registered letter	Jean Patel	Ken Stewart	Des Moines	IA	4/9/--	10:45 a.m.
5	Express mail package	Carmen Castro	Erie Associates	Erie	PA	4/12/--	3:15 p.m.

Mail Register

Referring or Routing Mail

You or your supervisor may decide to refer certain items to an assistant or associate to handle. To help with this process, a **referral slip** is attached to the item. The sample referral slip shown in Figure 12-1.4 lists a series of instructions from which to choose. A check mark is used to indicate the specific instruction to be followed.

referral slip a document that accompanies items sent to another person and indicates a requested action

Figure 12-1.4 Mail is often forwarded to an associate for action.

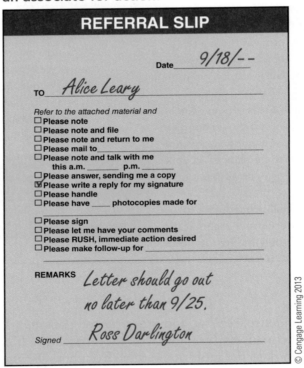

When action is requested of another individual, you should keep a record of the referral. You should note the date the item was referred, the name of the person to whom it was referred, the subject, the action to be taken, and a follow-up date if one is necessary.

Often more than one person in the company should read items, such as correspondence and important magazine articles. You may be asked to make a copy for each person who should read the item, or you may be asked to route the item through the office. To do so, attach a **routing slip**, which is similar to a referral slip, to the item. Indicate with check marks the individuals who should read the item. A sample routing slip is shown in Figure 12-1.5.

routing slip a document attached to an item that shows the names of the individuals to whom the item should be sent

Figure 12-1.5 A routing slip is attached to mail to be distributed to others.

ROUTING SLIP

FROM: _Ryan Talbert_

_____ **Information Services Department**

DATE: _3/25_

TO:	Date Forwarded
___Everyone	
___R. Bernardin	
✓ R. Carlson	_3/25_
___M. Carrell	
___J. Garcia	
✓ J. Hensen	_3/25_
___C. Hickman	
___H. Iwuki	
✓ S. Lansing	_3/26_
___M. Rivera	
___C. Tesch	
✓ R. Wong	_3/27_

Please:

___Read and keep in your files

___Read and pass on

___Read and return to me

✓ Read, route, and return to me

© Cengage Learning 2013

Prioritizing Mail

Incoming mail should be prioritized for further processing. As a general rule, mail is categorized in the order of its importance. The following arrangement is usually satisfactory, moving from the top to the bottom of the stack:

1. Urgent messages, such as documents received by fax or overnight delivery, that require prompt attention
2. Personal and confidential letters
3. Business letters, memos, or other correspondence of special importance
4. Letters containing checks or money orders
5. Other business letters
6. Letters containing orders
7. Letters containing bills, invoices, or other requests for payment
8. Advertisements
9. Newspapers and magazines
10. Packages

Handling Mail While Away from the Office

Technology makes it possible to receive and forward important mail and messages for immediate action while away from the office. In this way, business matters are not delayed, and deadlines are not missed. You will need to decide which mail should be forwarded and which mail should be held for action after returning to the office. The following guidelines may be helpful in keeping track of incoming mail for your supervisors or coworkers who are away from the office:

- Maintain a mail register as described earlier in this chapter.
- Communicate with the traveler immediately if important or unexpected action seems required.
- Refer routine mail to others who can respond.
- Answer mail yourself if it is within your area of responsibility.
- Send a synopsis of received mail (or a copy of the mail log) if the traveler is on an extended business trip.
- After the mail has been prioritized, store it in an appropriate place.

synopsis   overview or summary

Effective processing of the incoming mail helps keep the office running smoothly while the traveler is away and saves time for the traveler upon returning to the office.

 CHECK POINT Give an example of when you might need to contact a traveler immediately regarding his or her incoming mail.

Sorting and prioritizing mail allows employees to handle important or urgent messages before routine mail.

Tim Hall/Digital Vision/Jupiter Images

REVIEW 12-1

21st Century Skills

PARTNERSHIP FOR
21ST CENTURY SKILLS

Interacting with Others

You work as an administrative assistant at Halbrook, Inc. One of your duties is to sort, open, and annotate mail for three executives. Letters that are not marked *Confidential* are normally opened by the staff in the central mailroom. Mr. Santiago, one of the executives you assist, often receives correspondence that contains confidential information regarding acquiring and developing new products. He has requested that his letters not be opened in the mailroom. You have discussed this issue with the mailroom supervisor on two occasions. However, letters continue to arrive at your department opened. You suspect that some of the letters have been removed from the envelopes and replaced in them.

1. What can you say to the mailroom supervisor to indicate the seriousness of this issue?
2. What are some possible reasons your request has not been honored?
3. What steps should you take if talking with the mailroom supervisor again does not result in the letters arriving unopened?

Making Academic Connections

Reinforcing Math Skills

1. Based on records kept by the mailroom supervisor, about 3,000 pieces of incoming mail are sorted and distributed each month in your company. Additionally, the volume of mail is expected to increase by 6 percent next year. How many pieces of mail will be processed this year? How many more pieces of mail will be processed next year than will be processed this year?

2. An envelope has been prepared for each address on a mailing list of 18,000 names. The mailing machine can feed, seal, meter stamp, count, and stack 200 envelopes a minute. Of the 18,000 envelopes being processed, 20 percent are being sent to Minnesota, 30 percent to Wyoming, 15 percent to Wisconsin, and 35 percent to Nebraska. How long it will take to process all the envelopes using the mailing machine? How many envelopes will be sent to each state?

12-1 Activity 1

Sort Incoming Mail (Outcome 12-1a)

You work in the general office of Sperling Enterprises. Because your supervisor receives a large amount of mail of different types, she has asked you to prioritize it prior to delivering it to her.

1. Key a list of the mail items shown below.
2. Arrange the list of mail items in order of priority. (Begin the list with the most important and continue to the least important.)
   - Personal letter from Michelle Jackson
   - Overnight package from Hancock Associates
   - Letter containing an order from Jackie Yung
   - Advertisement for office furniture
   - Newspaper

- Interoffice memo from coworker Paula Flores
- Fax from Karl Shelton, at Shelton Brothers
- Business letter of special importance from Kareen Steel
- *PC Magazine*
- Letter containing a bill from Office Depot
- Letter containing a check from Howard Supply Company
- Fax from David Foster of Foster Insurance
- Business letter from Maria Lopez of Quality Leasing
- Package from Anderson Office Supplies
- Advertisement from Media Plus
- *Business Week* magazine
- Letter containing a bill from Jackson Electric Company
- Letter containing a check from Jerome Patrick
- Letter containing an order from Dan Chin
- Business letter from Creative Calendars, Inc.

12-1 Activity 2

Annotate Letter and Compose Reply (Outcome 12-1b)

You work for Shred-Rite Shredder Company, a retailer for office and personal paper shredders. Your supervisor, Ms. Wanda Albertson, is the customer service manager. You often annotate mail and compose replies for her signature.

1. Open and print the file 12-1 Activity 2 from the data files. This file contains a letter from a customer. Read the letter and underline the important points.
2. The data file also contains the customer invoice. Review the invoice and then annotate the customer's letter with appropriate comments.
3. Compose a reply to the customer for your supervisor's signature. Assume the letter will be printed on company letterhead. Tell the customer how the problem will be corrected and express regret for the customer's inconvenience. Examine your letter for the five Cs of effective writing.
4. Submit the customer's letter with your annotations, the invoice, and your reply to your supervisor (instructor).

OUTCOMES

12-2a Apply procedures for preparing outgoing mail.
12-2b Describe classes of mail and mail services.

KEY TERMS

ZIP Codes p. 430
delivery address p. 430
postage meter p. 433
optical character reader
   (OCR) p. 435
mail merge p. 436
customs p. 439
courier service p. 440

Preparing Outgoing Mail

A company may send several types of mail to those outside the company. For example, you may be asked to send product information to customers. Letters may be sent to businesses. Advertisements may be sent to potential customers. Preparing outgoing mail properly is important for prompt delivery.

The way outgoing mail is processed will depend on the size of your company and the procedures adopted by the company. In a small company, an office worker may process all the outgoing mail, as well as handle other office tasks. In a large company, however, mail tasks may be divided between mailroom workers and workers in other areas. In a large company, the extent of mail-handling duties will be determined by company policy and the worker's specific job.

The United States Postal Service (Postal Service) picks up and delivers mail to some organizations twice a day. In other organizations, a postal carrier may come to the office in the morning, and an office worker may take outgoing mail to a post office or a Postal Service mailbox in the afternoon. You need to know the scheduled times for pickup so you can have the mail ready on time. The Postal Service recommends mailing as early in the day as possible for the fastest service.

✳ WORKPLACE CONNECTIONS ✳

Selena is the receptionist in a small real estate office. On her workstation is an out basket where all the workers place their outgoing mail. A postal carrier usually picks up and delivers the mail at about 10:30 a.m. Selena prepares an envelope for each item in the out basket. Then she stuffs the envelopes, seals them, weighs them, and applies the postage. By 10:30 a.m., the mail is ready to be picked up by the postal carrier.

Brenner Industries is a large corporation with many departments. Office workers in each department address the envelopes and insert letters into the envelopes. Each department has a central location for collecting outgoing mail. A mailroom worker picks up the mail and takes it to the company mailroom. The mailroom workers then seal, weigh, and place postage on the mail in time for scheduled pickups from the post office.

▸ Sometimes employees prefer to give Selena mail with the envelopes already addressed. Why might this be the case?

Addressing Mail

Addressing mail correctly helps ensure that it will reach the correct recipient in a timely manner. Always use ZIP Codes and the correct address elements as discussed in the following paragraphs.

ZIP Codes

In 1963 the Postal Service began using the ZIP Code system. ZIP stands for *Zone Improvement Plan*. This plan assigns numbers to areas of the country to speed mail delivery. The first three digits of the ZIP Code indicate a major geographic area or post office. The next two digits designate a local post office. In a ZIP+4 Code, a hyphen and four digits follow the five-digit ZIP Code. These numbers help the post office sort the mail more specifically. For example, they may indicate part of a street or an office building. To ensure prompt delivery of your mail, always use the five-digit ZIP Code or the ZIP+4 Code.

You can look up ZIP Codes on the Postal Service website. Enter the street, city, and state to find the ZIP Code for that address. You can also find a list of ZIP Codes for a city or find the city/areas to which a ZIP Code is assigned.

Address Format

The delivery address is the location to which the Postal Service will deliver an item. The address should be printed clearly on the envelope or label for each item that is mailed. The characters should be dark, even, and clear. The address should include:

- The recipient's name or other identification.
- A company name and/or title, if applicable.
- The number and street name or the post office box number.
- A secondary location, such as an apartment number, if applicable.
- The city and state.
- The ZIP Code (five-digit or ZIP + 4).

The return address shows where the mail piece should be returned if it cannot be delivered. The return address should include the same parts as the delivery address.

For international addresses, place the foreign postal code on the same line as the city or town name. Place the name of the foreign country in capital letters on the last line of the address. These are general guidelines; address formats vary by country. Address formats for mail to many countries can be found on the Internet by searching for *address format* and the country name. Sample addresses are shown in Figure 12-2.1.

Figure 12-2.1 **Use a proper address format for mail items.**

Mr. Antonio Diaz
993 North Carpenter Lane
Shreveport, LA 71106-0993

Office of Tourism
2 Rue Grande
06570 St. Paul
FRANCE

© Cengage Learning 2013

The Postal Service has an approved list of abbreviations for states, cities, and other words commonly used in addresses. Always use the two-letter state abbreviations with the ZIP Code in domestic addresses. Use other approved abbreviations if the address is too long to fit on a label. State and territory abbreviations are shown in Figure 12-2.2.

Figure 12-2.2 The United States Postal Service provides two-letter abbreviations for states and territories.

State and Territory Abbreviations

Alabama	AL	Illinois	IL	Nebraska	NE	South Carolina	SC
Alaska	AK	Indiana	IN	Nevada	NV	South Dakota	SD
Arizona	AZ	Iowa	IA	New Hampshire	NH	Tennessee	TN
Arkansas	AR	Kansas	KS	New Jersey	NJ	Texas	TX
California	CA	Kentucky	KY	New Mexico	NM	Utah	UT
Colorado	CO	Louisiana	LA	New York	NY	Vermont	VT
Connecticut	CT	Maine	ME	North Carolina	NC	Virgin Islands	VI
Delaware	DE	Maryland	MD	North Dakota	ND	Virginia	VA
District of Columbia	DC	Massachusetts	MA	Ohio	OH	Washington	WA
Florida	FL	Michigan	MI	Oklahoma	OK	West Virginia	WV
Georgia	GA	Minnesota	MN	Oregon	OR	Wisconsin	WI
Guam	GU	Mississippi	MS	Pennsylvania	PA	Wyoming	WY
Hawaii	HI	Missouri	MO	Puerto Rico	PR		
Idaho	ID	Montana	MT	Rhode Island	RI		

© Cengage Learning 2013

Interoffice Mail

Interoffice mail consists of items routed to others within the company. It does not involve transfer by the Postal Service or a private mail company. Thus the recipient's name and department or building location are typically all that is needed for an address. In a small company, processing interoffice mail may involve hand delivering a memo from one worker to another. In a large company, however, interoffice mail is collected from the departments. The mail is sorted in the mailroom and then sent to employees. Interoffice mail envelopes usually differ in color and size from envelopes used for mail going outside the company. That way, interoffice mail will not be sent to the post office accidentally. Many interoffice messages are sent by e-mail. E-mail is discussed in Chapter 4.

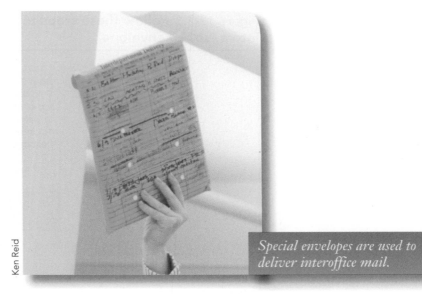

Ken Reid

Special envelopes are used to deliver interoffice mail.

 CHECK POINT What information should be included in the delivery address for a mail item?

Folding and Inserting Mail

Once a document is ready to mail, it is a good idea to give it a final check before inserting it in the envelope. Be sure that:

- Copies have been made, if necessary.
- Letters have been signed.
- Your initials appear below the signature on any letter you have signed for a supervisor or coworker.

- All enclosures noted at the bottom of a letter have been placed in the envelope.
- The address on the envelope agrees with the address on the letter.
- The ZIP Code appears on the last line of both the delivery address and the return address.

You usually will insert documents into standard or window envelopes. Folding business documents correctly to fit into envelopes is a simple but important task. You should take care that the creases are straight and neat. A document should be inserted in an envelope so that it will be in a normal reading position when it is removed from the envelope and unfolded.

Standard Envelopes

The size for a standard envelope used for business letters is 9½" × 4⅛" (No. 10). Figure 12-2.3 shows how to fold a letter and insert it into a No. 10 envelope. The enclosures that accompany a document should be folded with the document and inserted so that they will come out of the envelope when the document is removed.

Figure 12-2.3 **Follow these steps to fold an 8½" × 11" sheet to insert into a No. 10 envelope.**

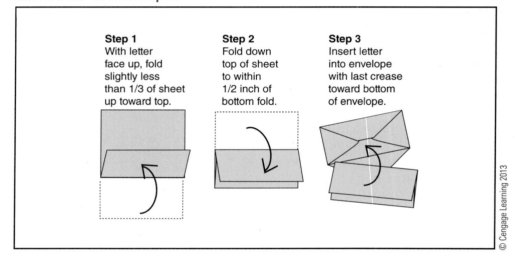

Step 1
With letter face up, fold slightly less than 1/3 of sheet up toward top.

Step 2
Fold down top of sheet to within 1/2 inch of bottom fold.

Step 3
Insert letter into envelope with last crease toward bottom of envelope.

© Cengage Learning 2013

Window Envelopes

A window envelope has a see-through panel on the front of the envelope. A window envelope eliminates the need to address an envelope because the address on the letter or form is visible through the window. The address on the letter or form must be positioned so that it can be seen through the window after the letter is folded and inserted into the envelope. Figure 12-2.4 shows how to fold a letter and insert it into a No. 10 window envelope.

Sealing and Weighing Envelopes

Envelopes must be sealed before they are mailed. When you need to seal more than one or two envelopes, you probably will want to use a moist sponge or moistener. Mail processing equipment that can insert letters into envelopes and seal the envelopes is available. If your office processes large mailings frequently, this equipment can save valuable time.

Each piece of outgoing mail must be weighed accurately so you can apply the proper amount of postage. Electronic scales are available that automatically calculate the correct amount of postage for each piece of mail. You simply

Figure 12-2.4 Follow these steps to fold an 8½" × 11" sheet to insert into a No. 10 window envelope.

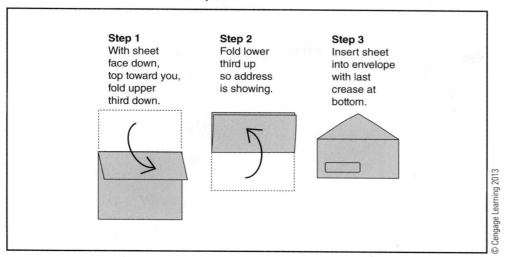

Step 1
With sheet face down, top toward you, fold upper third down.

Step 2
Fold lower third up so address is showing.

Step 3
Insert sheet into envelope with last crease at bottom.

© Cengage Learning 2013

place the item to be mailed on the scale and indicate which postal class you wish to use. The amount of the postage is displayed on a small screen. When postal rates change, you update the scale with the new rates.

CHECK POINT What steps should you include in your final check before placing a mail item in the envelope?

Applying Postage

Postage must be paid for all mail before it is delivered by the Postal Service. You may purchase postage stamps in sheet, booklet, or rolled form. Rolled stamps often are used in business because they can be placed quickly on envelopes and packages. Also, they are less likely than individual stamps to be lost or damaged.

Pre-Stamped Items

The post office sells envelopes and stamped cards (postcard size) that already have the correct postage printed on them. You can buy them one at a time or in quantity. Stamped cards may be purchased in single or double form. The double form is used when a reply is requested on the attached card. Stamped stationery sheets that have space for writing a message on one side and the delivery address on the other side are also available.

Postage Meters

A **postage meter** is a machine that prints postage in the amount needed. The meter prints the postage either directly onto the card or envelope or onto a label that you apply to the mail item. You can set the meter to print postage for a letter weighing one ounce and easily reset it to print postage for a letter weighing three ounces. The postage meter prints the date as well as the postage amount. Always be sure the correct date is set on the meter. Some meters can also print a business slogan or advertisement next to the postmark. Because metered mail is already dated and postmarked, it can be processed faster than stamped mail.

Some postage meters include a scale to weigh the item. Others will also seal envelopes. Some meters allow you to track postage by assigning the cost to two or more accounts, such as for departments in a company.

postage meter a machine that prints postage on a label or envelope

A postage meter prints a postmark and the postage.

age fotostock/SuperStock

Typically, you can purchase postage to be printed by the meter online. The meter is updated using a USB connection to a computer or a modem and a standard phone line.

Printing Labels with Postage

Users can access a service called Click-N-Ship on the Postal Service website. This service allows you to print labels with postage for packages. First, you must register, selecting an account type and giving your contact information. You may also be required to download software, such as Adobe Reader, for printing labels. Once your account has been created, you can enter a delivery address and select a class of service, such as Priority Mail. Other information about the package, such as the weight, must also be entered. An option to purchase insurance for a package is provided. Payment is made by entering your credit card information. You can store delivery addresses in an online address book for later use.

 CHECK POINT What is the main purpose of a postage meter? What other tasks might a meter be able to perform?

TECHNOLOGY CONNECTION

The United States Postal Service authorizes several companies to sell postage on the Internet. You can access the website for one of these companies and subscribe to a postage service plan. The plan typically involves paying a set monthly fee in addition to the postage used. The user receives computer software and, with some plans, a postage scale. The software allows the user to print the appropriate amount of postage on an envelope or label using any computer printer. A graphic, such as the company logo, or text can be also be printed on the envelope or label. Some companies offer a free trial of the service.

Why might a company subscribe to a postage service plan rather than using Click-N-Ship from the Postal Service?

Handling Volume Mailings

A volume mailing involves sending the same items to many people at the same time. For example, a marketing research company may send a questionnaire to all residents in a city asking about products, such as televisions or breakfast cereals. Companies doing volume mailings may qualify for reduced postage rates. To qualify for reduced postage rates, mailings must be prepared according to current Postal Service mailing rules and standards. Address labels may be used for volume mail items or the items may be addressed individually.

Automated Handling

The Postal Service uses high-speed electronic mail-handling equipment in many of its postal centers. This equipment includes optical character readers and bar code sorters. An **optical character reader (OCR)** is an electronic device that quickly scans or "reads" the address on an envelope. A bar code that relates to the scanned address is printed at the bottom of the envelope.

optical character reader (OCR) an electronic device that quickly scans or "reads" the address on an envelope

During the sorting process, the bar codes are "read" by a bar code sorter, and the mail is quickly routed to its proper destination. Not all postal centers are equipped with OCR equipment and bar code sorters. Therefore, not all mail you receive will have a printed bar code on the envelope.

If the OCR device is unable to read an address, the envelope is routed to a manual letter-sorting machine. This, of course, increases the processing time. Some of the reasons an OCR device may be unable to read an address are listed below. Use care when preparing mail to avoid these problems that may slow delivery of the mail.

- The address is handwritten.
- The address is not printed in the proper format.
- The envelope is too small or too large for the OCR equipment to handle. (To avoid this problem, use standard size envelopes.)
- The address is not within the OCR read area, as shown in Figure 12-2.5.
- The complete address is not visible through the panel of a window envelope.

Figure 12-2.5 **The delivery address should be placed on an envelope within the OCR read area.**

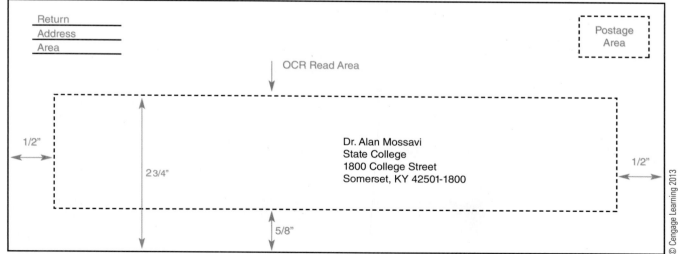

Mailing Lists

Many companies use computer-generated mailing lists. Mailing lists for volume mail may contain addresses for customers, subscribers, or those who live in certain geographic areas. Mailing lists should always be current. Delete, correct, and add addresses as soon as you learn about changes. Some of the advantages of using computer-generated mailing lists include the ability to:

- Quickly retrieve, change, or delete addresses
- Easily avoid duplicate addresses
- Select addresses from a master list to create a smaller list for a special mailing
- Print letter addresses and salutations on form letters as well as address labels

Mail Merge

mail merge a feature of word processing programs that allows you to insert addresses or other data from a list automatically to create personalized items

Mail merge is a feature of word processing programs. This feature allows you to print or insert addresses or other data from a list automatically to create personalized letters, envelopes, or labels. The list of names and addresses is stored in a data file. The list could be in a word processing table, a spreadsheet table, or a database table. You can select all or some of the addresses to be printed. In a word processing file, codes are placed in the label or envelope form where the addresses should appear. The codes match the names of columns or fields in the data file. The mail merge operation creates a new file that contains addresses formatted on the labels or envelopes. Using mail merge is an efficient way to create labels or envelopes for large mailings.

CHECK POINT What are some reasons an OCR device might not be able to read an address?

✳ WORKPLACE CONNECTIONS ✳

Joanne Flag works in the Human Resources Department of a small company. She prepares volume mailings to employees, such as salespeople, who are not located at the company's home office. Benefits information, policy changes, and new procedures must be sent to these employees. Until recently, Joanne keyed the address and printed an envelope for each employee each time a mailing was prepared. She soon realized that she was repeating work needlessly.

Joanne decided to create a database to include the name, address, and other relevant data for each employee. She also created an envelope document and a mailing label document. She can merge data from the database with these documents. Now when Joanne needs to prepare a mailing, she simply enters any updates in the database and completes the merge. Envelopes and labels are printed quickly and correctly.

> What kinds of data (other than addresses) might be included in an employee database?

Mail Classes and Services

The Postal Service processes millions of pieces of mail each day. Businesses all across the country use the varied services of the Postal Service. In some cases, the items are destined for delivery in the same city. In other cases, the items are delivered to an individual in a city halfway around the world. Local, national, and worldwide private mail delivery companies also deliver envelopes and packages.

Chris Smith/PhotoEdit

The United States Postal Service processes millions of pieces of mail each day.

Domestic and International Mail

Domestic mail is distributed by the Postal Service within the United States and its territories (such as Puerto Rico, the United States Virgin Islands, and Guam). Domestic mail is divided into various classes. Some of these classes are described in the following paragraphs.

First-Class

First-Class Mail is commonly used for items such as letters, bills, postcards, checks, money orders, and business reply mail. A minimum amount is charged for all First-Class Mail weighing up to one ounce. An additional charge is made for each additional ounce or fraction of an ounce. If you are sending material in an oversized envelope that does not bear a preprinted First Class notation, print or stamp *First Class* on the envelope. Mail that weighs over 13 ounces must be sent as priority mail to receive handling comparable to First-Class Mail.

Express Mail

Express Mail is the fastest service offered by the Postal Service, with delivery in one or two days to most domestic addresses. No extra fee is charged for Saturday delivery. Delivery on a Sunday or holiday is available in some places for an extra charge. The rate includes signature proof of delivery and $100 in insurance. Additional insurance may be purchased.

Express Mail envelopes, boxes, and labels are available at no charge at post offices. Flat rate envelopes in two sizes are available for Express Mail. For other envelopes and packages, the amount of postage for Express Mail is based on weight and destination.

Priority Mail

Priority Mail offers delivery service to most domestic addresses within two or three days. The maximum weight for Priority Mail is 70 pounds. Priority Mail

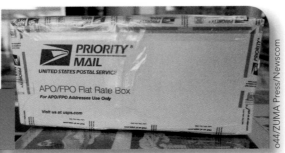

Using Priority Mail flat rate packages can be an economical way to mail items.

o44/ZUMA Press/Newscom

flat rate boxes and envelopes are a convenient way to mail items. As long as the item fits in the box or envelope, it ships for the associated rate. Priority Mail envelopes, boxes, and labels are available at no charge at post offices. Priority Mail items that do not use flat rate boxes or envelopes are priced based on the weight and destination of the package. Some size restrictions also apply. Refer to the Postal Service website for current rules.

Periodicals

Approved publishers and registered news agents may mail items such as newspapers and magazines at the Periodicals postage rates. To do so, you need authorization from the Postal Service, must pay a special fee, and must mail in bulk lots (volume mailings). Other rates, such as First-Class Mail or Standard Mail, must be used when periodicals are mailed by the general public.

Standard Mail

Standard Mail is a bulk mailing service for printed material such as bulletins, brochures, and catalogs. Businesses often use standard mail to advertise products to consumers. Mailings must contain at least 200 pieces or weigh 50 pounds to qualify for standard mail rates. Each item must weigh less than 16 ounces and be marked with a correct ZIP Code. Sorting and postage restrictions apply.

Parcel Post

Parcel Post may be used for small and large packages, thick envelopes, and tubes. The rates are based on the weight of the item and the distance it must travel to be delivered. Packages may weigh 1 to 70 pounds and measure up to 130 inches in combined length and girth.

Follow these guidelines when preparing packages for mailing.

- Select a box that is strong enough to protect the contents.
- Leave space for cushioning inside the carton. Cushion package contents with shredded or rolled newspaper, bubble wrap, or other packing material. Pack tightly to avoid having the item shift.
- Always use tape that is designed for shipping, such as pressure-sensitive or reinforced tape. Do not use wrapping paper, string, masking tape, or cellophane tape.
- Put the delivery and return addresses on one side only of the package. Place a return address label inside the package.

International Mail

Many companies send mail to other countries. A company may have branch offices or customers in countries throughout the world. Postage rates for letters and postal cards mailed to other countries are higher than for domestic mail, and the mail weights are limited. For current rates and weight limitations, contact your local post office or access the Postal Service website.

Delivery for letters and packages is available to many countries from specified post offices. Services include First-Class Mail International, Express Mail International, Global Express Guaranteed, Priority Mail International, and others. Rates vary by weight and destination country. Overseas packages must be packed very carefully to ensure safe delivery.

Customs forms are required when you send letter packages, small packets, and parcels that are subject to taxes to international destinations. The specific customs form is governed by the type of mail, the weight of the item, and the regulations of the country to which the mail is sent. Individual countries may restrict or prohibit certain articles. Specific information about restrictions for individual countries and about the forms required for mailing is listed in the *International Mail Manual.* This publication is available online at the Postal Service website. This website also provides help in choosing the right form for your shipment and allows users to print a form or complete it online.

customs government taxes or duties on imported items

 CHECK POINT What class of U.S. Mail is commonly used for items such as letters, bills, and checks sent to domestic addresses?

Special Postal Services

The Postal Service offers several special services related to mail delivery. Some of these services are described in the following list. You must pay a fee for each of these special services.

- A Certificate of Mailing is a receipt that provides proof of the date when an item was mailed.

- Certified Mail service provides a receipt stamped with the date of mailing and access to online delivery information.

- Delivery Confirmation service provides access to the date and time an item was delivered via an online tracking system or by telephone.

- Insured Mail and Registered Mail services provide insurance for items that are mailed. Items can be insured for their actual value up to $25,000.

- Return Receipt service provides proof of delivery in the form of a card that shows the signature or stamp of the receiver and the delivery address. The card may be delivered to your mailbox or as an e-mail attachment.

- Signature Confirmation service provides the date, time, and location of the delivery of an item and a copy of the signature of the recipient. If you want to require that a specific person sign for mail, use Restricted Delivery service.

You may want to combine services for a mailing. For example, purchasing Return Receipt service along with Certified Mail service provides proof of mailing and proof of delivery for an item. Fees vary by service.

 CHECK POINT Which U.S. Mail service provides a receipt stamped with the date of mailing and access to online delivery information?

Private Courier/Delivery Service

courier service a private mail delivery company

Many companies sometimes use a private courier service rather than the Postal Service. A private service is often used when a guaranteed delivery time is required. Most cities are served by several private mail delivery companies. Check under *Delivery Service* in the yellow pages of the telephone directory for a listing of companies in your area. You will want to ask about services and fees to identify the delivery company that best meets your needs. Private mail services do not deliver to a post office box. Many delivery companies have websites that allow you to track packages that have been sent using the delivery company.

You must prepare a form for the package that includes contact information for you and the recipient. The class of delivery service, weight of the package, payment method or account number, and other data may also be required. Completing the form accurately is essential for prompt delivery.

CHECK POINT For what reason (other than guaranteed delivery time) might a company use a private courier for mail delivery rather than using the Postal Service?

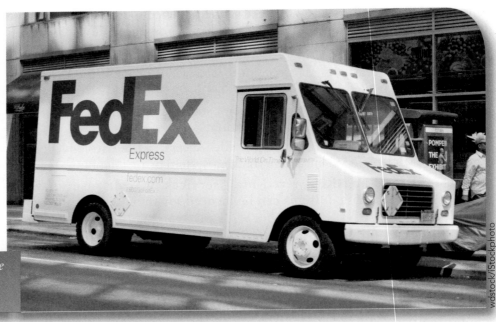

Many organizations use private couriers for mail and package delivery.

widstock/iStockphoto

REVIEW 12-2

21st Century Skills

Interacting with Others

PARTNERSHIP FOR
21ST CENTURY SKILLS

You work in an office where the mail is picked up by postal workers twice a day at 10:30 a.m. and 2:45 p.m. On Monday afternoon you receive a call from the regional vice president in a branch office. He needs six copies of the company's annual report by Wednesday. If the reports are in the 2:45 p.m. mail today, they will be delivered on Wednesday. You gather the annual reports, place them in a large envelope, and take them to the mailroom. You explain to Glenna, a mailroom worker, that the envelope must go with the 2:45 p.m. mail pickup. Glenna says she understands.

Later in the day, you call Glenna to verify that the annual reports were sent. Glenna sheepishly replies that she was on break at 2:45. When she returned, she noticed that the postal carrier had overlooked the envelope. The annual reports were not mailed.

1. You are very annoyed that the envelope was not mailed. Should you tell Glenna how you feel? If so, what should you tell her? Should you report this incident to Glenna's supervisor? How can you and Glenna work together to solve this problem?

2. The reports still need to be sent. How would you suggest that Glenna mail the reports so that they reach the vice president by Wednesday?

Making Academic Connections

Reinforcing English Skills

The following sentences have errors in the use of apostrophes and colons. Key or write the sentences, correcting the errors.

1. Its time for the cat to have it's dinner.
2. Bring these items to the sewing class fabric, thread, scissors, and patterns.
3. A single students' paper was submitted in the writing contest.
4. Our's is the team dressed in blue jerseys.
5. The meeting will begin at 215 p.m.
6. Janets mother asked her to buy the following items milk, bread, and eggs.
7. Only one thing is needed to win the contest talent.
8. Darnell wont need to attend summer school classes.
9. Both Lans and Sues ideas were used in the project solution.
10. My mother-in-laws cookies won first place at the county fair.

13-1 An Effective Job Search

OUTCOMES

13-1a Describe procedures for planning a job search.
13-1b Prepare documents related to a job search.
13-1c Apply strategies for an effective job interview.

KEY TERMS

career goals p. 450
career strategy p. 450
resume p. 451
letter of application p. 451
interview p. 451
job board p. 452
reference p. 455
job scout p. 460

career goals desired
achievements related to work

career strategy plans to meet
career goals

Planning a Job Search

Whatever your present plans for employment or further education, you should
consider your long-term career goals. You might wonder why someone who is
considering a first job should be thinking beyond that job. Thinking ahead may
help you choose a first job that is closely related to your long-term interests.
Thinking ahead to what you see as career goals and planning realistic steps to
meet those goals is known as developing a career strategy. With career goals
in mind, you can evaluate beginning job offers in relation to those goals.

Career Goals

Career planning is not a once-in-a-lifetime task. As you gain experience, you
will become better acquainted with jobs that match your interests and talents.
As you learn more about various jobs and professions, your career goals may
change.

Planning with a Career Goal Established

Perhaps you have clear ideas for your future work goals. If so, you may have
thought about what you can do well, what the opportunities are for your chosen field, and what will be required to achieve your career goals in general.
When thinking about careers, consider the following questions:

- What specific kinds of jobs are available to a person who has chosen the
  career goals I have?
- What job opportunities in this career field are projected for the next 5 to
  10 years?
- What are the educational qualifications for entry-level jobs in this career?
- What education and/or experience is needed to advance in this career?

Planning Without a Career Goal

Even if you do not yet know what career you wish to choose, you can still
enter the workplace and perform successfully. When seeking a job, you can
highlight a willingness to:

- Perform every task assigned according to instructions
- Strive always to improve performance
- Learn more about the company and make a valuable contribution to
  achieving its goals

When you begin working, you will learn about a wide variety of positions
through your dealings with other workers. Such knowledge will be helpful in
exploring career options.

Getting a college degree may help prepare you to achieve your career goals.

Whether you have specific career goals or not, you can effectively plan your search for a full-time job. Your success in meeting job requirements need not be related to whether or not you have a career goal. Common steps in a job search include the following:

1. Become acquainted with the types of jobs you wish to consider.
2. Explore job opportunities related to these jobs.
3. Prepare a resume.
4. Prepare a letter of application when you find a job for which you are qualified.
5. Send resumes and letters of application to companies considering candidates for jobs.
6. Accept interviews with companies that wish to talk with you about available jobs.
7. Complete follow-up activities for all job interviews.
8. Accept a job.

> **resume** document that presents a person's qualifications for a job

> **letter of application** document that expresses interest in a job and requests an interview

> **interview** meeting to question or evaluate, as for a job applicant

CHECK POINT When thinking about jobs with a career goal in mind, what questions should you consider?

Exploring Job Opportunities

A number of sources are available to help you locate specific jobs in which you may be interested and for which you are qualified. Friends, relatives, and former employers often know about good job opportunities for you. Other sources are discussed briefly in the following paragraphs.

School Placement and Counseling Services

Become familiar with the placement and counseling services available in your school. In schools without a placement counselor, employers often inform school guidance counselors or business teachers about jobs in their companies. Let your business teachers and your counselors know about your plans and your job interests. This will help them identify you as a candidate when they learn about a job that may be right for you.

The Internet

job board website that provides job listings and allows users to post resumes

Many sites on the Internet contain job listings. These sites are sometimes called job boards. Job boards allow job seekers to post a resume and to view job listings from many organizations. Job boards allow employers to post job descriptions and review resumes posted by job seekers. Most job boards are free to job seekers. Employers may be required to pay a fee to search for job candidates. Job boards may offer information on a wide variety of jobs, or they may be related to a particular career area or a particular geographic region.

USAJobs is the official federal government job website. This site, shown in Figure 13-1.1, offers listings for entry-level professional, clerical, trade, labor, and summer jobs, among others. Many states and some cities have websites with information about their government jobs.

Figure 13-1.1 **This job board provides information about U.S. government jobs.**

Source: USAJOBS "Working for America," http://www.usajobs.opm.gov/.

Many companies allow applicants to complete a job application online. Job seekers may also be able to post a resume at the company's website. Other company websites provide information about jobs available at the company for which applicants may apply using a hard copy letter and resume.

Newspapers

The classified advertisement sections of newspapers list many job openings. An example is shown in Figure 13-1.2. Some employers advertise directly, asking you to call or to fax your resume to them. Other employers use blind ads that do not identify the employer. Instead, the ads request that applications be sent to a post office box. Magazines, newsletters, and periodicals related to a particular industry also often have job listings.

Figure 13-1.2 **This job ad is typical of those found in newspapers.**

ADMINISTRATIVE ASSISTANT

Entry-level position to assist financial dept., perform data entry, and do various office duties. Requires good computer and math skills. Send resume w/cover letter to P.O. Box 274, New York, NY 10003.

© Cengage Learning 2013

Employment Agencies

Some employers submit job openings to employment agencies. Counselors at the agencies help match applicants' qualifications and goals with jobs available. Private employment agencies charge a fee for their services. Sometimes the person seeking a job pays a fee. At other times, the employer pays a fee. This fee is usually a percentage of the first year's salary. Government employment agencies provide services to citizens and employers free of charge.

Temporary employment agencies hire people to fill temporary jobs. The jobs may last from a single day to many months. Many businesses use temporary workers on a regular basis. By taking temporary jobs, young workers can gain a variety of experiences and understand better what full-time jobs will be most appealing to them. In some instances, temporary workers are asked to accept permanent positions.

✳ WORKPLACE CONNECTIONS ✳

Jerome registered with a temporary employment agency when he graduated from college. Because having a temporary job provided Jerome with an income, he felt less pressure to find a permanent job right away. Jerome worked at three different companies during a four-month period after graduation. At each job, Jerome's manager and coworkers learned about his talents and job skills, and Jerome learned more about the business world. When an opening for a management trainee became available at the first company where Jerome had worked, a former coworker called Jerome about the position. Jerome applied and was hired for the job.

Why might a manager where Jerome had a temporary job be more likely to hire Jerome than another candidate who seems to have similar skills?

Government Announcements

Many different types of employees are required in government agencies. You will be able to get information from your state employment office about state and federal job opportunities. As mentioned earlier, websites that list job openings are available. Candidates for state and federal jobs usually must complete job-related tests. These tests are given periodically with the dates announced in advance.

Personal Inquiry

If you want to work for a particular company, you may want to write a carefully worded letter asking about job possibilities. In your letter, you should explain the reason for your interest in being an employee. Describe the kind of job you want and briefly outline your qualifications. You need not include a resume with your letter of inquiry, but you may want to state that you will be happy to forward a detailed resume.

✔CHECK POINT What are some sources of information where you can learn about job openings?

Documenting Your Job Search

You may find a job in a relatively short time if there are many job openings in your field of interest in the community where you seek employment. Job searches sometimes require a considerable amount of time, however. You may have to make changes in your strategy and in your job expectations before you find a job.

Maintain a job search diary of your activity. Indicate clearly the date, time, company name, and complete names of all persons with whom you talked. Make notes about the communication after each meeting, phone call, or message with someone related to getting a job. This information will be helpful if you are called for a second interview or if you interview for another job with the same company at a later time. A sample job search diary is shown in Figure 13-1.3.

Figure 13-1.3 A job search diary is used to record details related to a job search.

Job Search Diary

Job Title: Order Entry Clerk
Company Name: MBA Manufacturing
Address: P.O. Box 235
Somerset, KY 42501
Phone: 606-555-0127
Contact Person: Robin McCrae, Office Manager

Date	Contact	Comments
6/2	Mailed letter and resume	See attached job ad and copies of resume and letter
6/15	Phone message from Robin McCrae	
6/16	Returned phone call	Interview scheduled for 6/20 at 9 a.m. at the company offices
6/20	Interview	Interview went well. Training is provided for order entry system. Flexible hours. Expect to hear from Ms. McCrae within two weeks.
6/21	Sent follow-up letter	Thanked Ms. McCrae and expressed continued interest. See attached copy of letter.

© Cengage Learning 2013

Documents Related to a Job Search

You will need to prepare some documents as you conduct your job search. A carefully prepared resume and letter of application will improve your chances of being invited to a job interview. A follow-up letter sent after an interview allows you to thank the interviewer and express continued interest in a job. You should be prepared to provide complete information on a job application form when you visit a potential employer.

Preparing a Resume

A resume, also called a data sheet or vita, is a concise, well-organized presentation of your qualifications for a job. The employer usually will see your resume before interviewing you. Your resume should make a positive impression on the reader. A resume should be accurate in every detail.

Hard Copy Resumes

A resume usually has several categories: personal information, job interest, education, work experience, and a statement about availability of **references**.

You may want to include additional categories when appropriate. As a general rule, list the most important information first. Refer to Figure 13-1.4 on page 456 as you read about common resume categories.

■ **Personal Information.** List your contact information clearly at the beginning of your resume. This information should include your name, mailing address, and telephone number. If you have an e-mail address, it can be listed also. Do not provide information such as age, date of birth, or marital status.

reference a person who knows your abilities, skills, and work habits and is willing to recommend you to employers

Wavebreakmedia Ltd/Shutterstock

Ask permission when you want someone to serve as a job reference for you.

Figure 13-1.4 A resume presents an applicant's job qualifications.

Valerie Gomez

3467 Mandelin Drive
Albuquerque, NM 87112-0341
(505) 555-0130

Job Interest

An administrative assistant position in an historical museum or college

Education

Will graduate from Southwest High School, May 20, 20--
Grade Point Average: 3.57
Class Standing: 34th in a class of 329

Related Courses:

American History
Keyboarding
Computer Applications
Office Procedures

Special Skills:

Keyboarding: 65 words per minute
Proficient in Microsoft Office: Word, Excel, and Access
Historical research experience in local libraries

School Activities:

Vice President of the American Historical Club
Member of Student Council

Work Experience

Assistant to the librarian of the historical archives in the Albuquerque Public Library
(Part-time during the school year; full-time during the past two summers)

Student assistant to the school librarian during my first two years in high school

References

References will be provided upon request.

- **Job Interest.** Briefly state the title of the job for which you are applying. An employer will then be able to see how your qualifications relate to specific job openings.
- **Education.** List the name and address of your high school and the graduation date or anticipated date. List the courses you completed that prepared you for the job. You may also include any scholastic honors or awards you have earned. You may want to show any extracurricular activities in which you participated, such as membership in special interest clubs.
- **Work Experience.** List in chronological order the jobs you have had, beginning with the most recent one. For each job, include the name and address of the organization, your job title, a brief description of the tasks performed, and the beginning and ending dates of your employment. If your job experience is limited, include part-time positions as well as any volunteer work you performed. Be sure to indicate clearly the work you did as a volunteer.
- **References.** References are persons who know your academic ability and/or work skills and habits and are willing to recommend you to employers. List references on a separate page. Include a note stating that references will be provided on request on the resume. When you list references, include a complete name, job title, address, and telephone number for each one. Generally, three references are considered sufficient. Ask permission before using a person as a reference on an application or in an interview with an employer.

Because there is no standard resume format, an employer may consider your resume to be an example of your ability to organize data in a useful and meaningful form. The form in which you submit your resume will influence the content and format of the data. You should first create a traditional hard copy resume. You may decide to prepare several versions of your resume. For example, when submitting a resume for a particular job, you can use the title of that job in the job interest section of your resume.

A hard copy resume for traditional use should be attractive and easy to read. Generally, limit a hard copy resume to one page. Use a second page only if needed to list your complete work history. Do not crowd text on the page. Use headings or bold to emphasize categories of information and a leave extra blank space between categories. Print your resume on a laser printer or have it photocopied on high-quality paper. Whichever method you use, be sure the copies are clean with clear, sharp print.

Scanned Resumes

Many companies and employment agencies receive hundreds or thousands of resumes each year. These resumes are often scanned and converted to electronic files. When a company has a job opening, the resume database is searched for key words or terms that relate to the qualifications for that job.

If you do not know whether your resume will be scanned, call the company to which you are sending the resume and ask for this information. If you know that your resume will be scanned, keep the format simple. Do not use

Focus on *BUSINESS*

Online Resumes

Just as job seekers search online for jobs, employers search online for prospective employees. Employers may search resumes that have been posted at job boards or submitted via e-mail or a company website. They use search terms that reflect the skills and qualifications they seek in job applicants.

Preparing your electronic resume in a format that can be easily searched for key terms will increase your chances of being selected as a job candidate by an employer. Follow these guidelines when preparing electronic resumes:

- Use default fonts and font sizes. Save the resume as a plain ASCII text file (also called Text Only by some programs). This file format contains words without any special formatting and can be read by many programs. Keeping the format simple will increase the chances that your online resume will be readable at the many different sites where you may choose to post or send it.
- When submitting an electronic resume via e-mail, send the resume as an attachment.
- Keep the resume fairly short, although you do not need to limit it to a single printed page as is

recommended for hard copy resumes. The computer can search two pages almost as quickly as one page.
- Include contact information and identify the type of job you seek as you would on a hard copy resume.
- Use concise, specific terms that describe your work experience, skills, and education or training. For example, say "Proficient with Microsoft Word" instead of "I have had training and work experience using word processing software."
- When posting a resume for a specific job, use the same terms for a particular skill or other requirement in your resume as are used in the job description or announcement. (Do not misrepresent your skills or experience, however.)
- Use a professional, positive tone for the resume. Be sure all information is current and accurate.

Where might you send/use an electronic resume? How should your electronic resume be similar to your hard copy resume? How should it be different?

---

fancy fonts, bold type, bullets, rule lines, or a complicated layout with tables or columns of text. Begin all lines at the left margin. Describe your skills in specific terms using action words. Avoid vague language. Check the spelling and grammar on the resume carefully. If you use an e-mail address, it should be a professional address—not one with cute or slang names.

 CHECK POINT How should you format a resume that will be scanned?

Writing a Letter of Application

A letter of application introduces you to a prospective employer and requests an interview. A letter of application that accompanies a resume should be an original, not a photocopy. The tone of the letter should appeal to the reader. Its content should be concise and informative. Remember, the reader is interested in you only in terms of your qualifications for a job in the company. An example letter of application is shown in Figure 13-1.5.

Valerie Gomez

3467 Mandelin Drive
Albuquerque, NM 87112-0341
(505) 555-0130

May 10, 20--

Ms. Gretchen T. Wellington, Director
Hansen Historical Center
356 Front Street
Albuquerque, NM 87102-0356

Dear Ms. Wellington

Your job opening for a library assistant came to my attention through my school librarian, Ms. Eva Chi. Please consider me as an applicant for this position. I am very interested in working in an organization that is involved in historical research.

I am currently completing my senior year at Southwest High School. I also work about ten hours each week at the Albuquerque Public Library. A copy of my resume is enclosed to give you more details about my education and experience.

Please consider granting me an interview to discuss employment opportunities with your center. You may telephone me at 555-0130. Because I am at school or work most of the day, please leave a message. I will return your call as soon as possible.

Sincerely

Valerie Gomez

Valerie Gomez

Enclosure: Resume

These guidelines will aid you in writing a letter of application:

- When submitting a hard copy letter, address the letter to a person, not to a department or position. If you do not have the name of the person to whom your letter should be addressed, call the company to ask for the name and title. When submitting a letter of application online, you may not be able to address the letter to a specific person. Follow the directions on the website.

- Explain in the first paragraph the reason for the letter. State specifically the position in which you are interested.

- Briefly indicate why you believe you are qualified for the position. Refer to specific classes, work experience, and/or interests you have that you believe are related to the position. Indicate that a resume is enclosed or also being transmitted to provide more details about your qualifications.

- In a final paragraph, request an interview.

- Limit your letter to a single printed page (or about the equivalent of a printed page for online letters of application).

 CHECK POINT What is the main purpose of a letter of application?

 **TECHNOLOGY CONNECTION**

When you conduct a job search online, you may choose to search only one or two job boards or many job boards and company websites. The wider your search, the better your chances are of finding the job you want. Because new jobs may be posted daily, you should search for jobs frequently. Many job

Source: USAJOBS "Working for America," https://my.usajobs.gov /Agents/ModifyJobAgent.aspx.

job scout computer program that finds and delivers job information based on the set criteria

boards provide intelligent agents, often called **job scouts** or saved searches, that can aid in this process. Simply indicate your search criteria for jobs, such as job titles and geographic locations, and the search frequency you desire (daily, weekly). The job scout will search for jobs that meet your criteria.

When jobs are located by your job scout, you will receive an e-mail containing links to the job postings. You can review these job postings and apply for the jobs that interest you. For some jobs, you can apply online by posting your resume and completing a job application form. For other jobs, you can apply by sending a hard copy resume and letter of application.

What is an advantage to using a job scout?

Effective Interviews

Companies may interview several candidates before hiring someone for a position. Successful interviewing is a critical step in securing a job. There are strategies you can use to prepare for an interview and to take part in an interview effectively.

Prepare for an Interview

Prepare carefully for each interview you accept. Consider how you will present your qualifications and interests to the interviewer. Anticipate questions and think about how you will respond to them. Learn about the company. What are the company's primary products or services? Does the company have branch offices? Is the company owned publicly or privately? What do your family and friends know about the firm? If the company has a website, review the site to learn about the company. If you prepare well, you will approach the interview with confidence, increasing your chances of making a favorable impression on the interviewer.

Anticipate Questions

You will be asked a number of questions during the interview. Some are likely to be ones that are commonly asked in such a situation. Others may be unique to the job. Some common questions and requests are listed below.

- Why does this job interest you?
- What courses did you study that you found most interesting? Why?
- What do you believe are your strongest qualifications for this job?
- What school activities or previous work experience required you to work in groups? On your own?
- How do you evaluate your participation in group activities?
- Why do you think you would enjoy working in our company?
- What are your career goals at this time?
- What new skills or knowledge do you want to acquire?

In the United States, laws have been passed to safeguard a person's right to equal opportunity for employment. Questions regarding age, marital status, ethnic background, religious beliefs, and physical and emotional disabilities (unless job related) are not considered appropriate and may be illegal for many jobs. You can learn more about employment rights on the U.S. Equal Employment Opportunity Commission website, as shown in Figure 13-1.6. If

Figure 13-1.6 The U.S. Equal Employment Opportunity Commission website provides valuable information.

Source: U.S. Equal Employment Opportunity Commission, http://www.eeoc.gov/eeoc/.

you are asked questions on these matters, you may wish to respond simply: "I prefer not to answer that question." You can, of course, answer such a question if you wish.

Prepare Questions

Interviewers sometimes ask: "Do you have any questions about the company or the position?" While you are preparing for the interview, you may want to list any questions that come to mind. Some would naturally pertain to the job for which you are applying: "How much orientation is provided for the job?" "How often are employees evaluated?" "Are there promotional opportunities for which employees may apply?" "Has the company established standards for the tasks related to the job in which I am interested?"

Other questions cover a broad range of subjects, such as the company's mission statement, product lines, and employee benefits. Do not make salary and benefits the main focus of your questions. Ask questions that will help the interviewer focus on the contributions you can make to the company.

Plan your Attire

At an interview, you usually do not know the person who will interview you. Your appearance and manner will influence the interviewer's first impression of you. A day or two before the interview, plan what you will wear. Consider dressing in clothes that are appropriate and at the same time comfortable. Generally, you should choose conservative, businesslike attire. Even though you may know that employees in the organization dress casually at most times, dress in business attire for an interview.

 CHECK POINT What is an example of a question you might ask when being interviewed for a job (other than those given in this chapter)?

※ WORKPLACE CONNECTIONS ※

Joe Chin was excited about his interview at a local garden design and landscape company. He arrived for the interview on time, answered all the questions clearly, and expressed his interest in working for the company. When a letter arrived thanking Joe for his interest and telling him that another candidate had been hired, he was very disappointed. A few days later Joe had lunch with Roberto, a friend who works at the company. "Do you know why someone else was chosen for the job instead of me?" he asked. "If I did something wrong in the interview, I would really like to know so I can improve before my next interview." "Well," said Roberto, "I did hear the manager comment once that he thinks everyone should dress in professional business attire for an interview." "Oh," said Joe. "Then I definitely made a poor decision when I showed up in khakis and a polo shirt. I thought I should dress like the workers I have seen at the company." Joe learned the hard way that appearance can influence an interviewer's impression of a candidate.

What are some examples of professional business attire that would be appropriate for you to wear to a job interview?

Take Part in the Interview

Arrive at the interview shortly before the scheduled time. You will want to be calm and collected when you are called into the interviewer's office. If you are not familiar with the location of the interview, you may want to visit the site in advance. Note how much time you should allow to arrive on schedule. Consider the traffic conditions or possible delays that are likely during the time of day you will be traveling to the interview.

Once you arrive, use a visitor parking space in the company parking lot if available. You may need to give your name and the purpose of your visit to a security guard to be admitted to the parking lot or building. Your manner should be polite and professional. Be friendly, but not overly familiar with people you meet at the company. Parking lots and garages in downtown or other business areas are often crowded during business hours. Allow ample time to find a parking space and walk to the company location if necessary.

Complete an Application Form

A receptionist may greet you and ask you to fill out an employment application form. Complete the form carefully in neat, legible handwriting. Glance over the entire application to see what information is requested in each section before you begin writing. Read each question carefully and completely before answering.

Note every item included and do not leave blanks on an application. You should indicate with an N/A (not applicable) any item that does not apply to you, such as military service, for example. The interviewer then knows that you have read the question. Take a copy of your resume with you as a source for details as you complete the application. Often the interviewer will read the application form before turning to your resume.

Participate Attentively

A common procedure is for the receptionist to introduce you to the interviewer. You should extend your hand for a firm handshake and look directly at the interviewer in a friendly, calm manner.

Being a little nervous at a job interview is natural, especially at your first interview. Instead of dwelling on your uneasiness, concentrate on what the interviewer asks and tells you. Remember that the interview is a two-way communication process. The interviewer is learning about you, and you are learning about the job and the company.

Zsolt Nyulaszi, 2009/Used under license from Shutterstock.com

Greet the interviewer in a friendly manner and shake hands.

When you attend an interview, do the following:

- Dress appropriately.
- Greet the interviewer with a smile and a firm handshake.
- Remain standing until you are asked to have a seat.
- Use good posture when sitting or standing.

- Listen attentively and answer questions honestly and clearly.
- Use correct grammar.
- Exhibit a positive attitude.
- Ask questions about the company and its products or services.
- Make eye contact with the interviewer frequently.

When you attend an interview, do not bring a friend or relative with you. Try not to display nervousness by tapping a pencil, twirling your hair, or using other distracting habits. Never give or imply false information about your strengths or accomplishments. Avoid criticizing past employers or teachers.

The interviewer may write an evaluation of the interview in which judgments are recorded about key factors. Comments may be about your appearance, knowledge and skills, attitude, self-confidence, and other issues.

 CHECK POINT What might be the consequences of giving false information on your resume or during an interview?

Follow Up

After the interview, review it in your mind and jot down notes to yourself about its good points and its weak points. Think of questions that you do not believe you answered well or that you failed to understand. Review this information later before your next interview.

Think about what you did well during an interview and what you can improve the next time.

Andresr/Shutterstock

Write a brief follow-up letter to thank the interviewer for talking with you. Indicate again your interest in the job and how you believe you are qualified for the position. A follow-up letter shows your willingness to follow through after a meeting. If the interviewer does not communicate with you within the time period mentioned at the interview, call and express your continued interest in the position.

If you receive a job offer and decide to take the job, you should accept in writing. If you have determined that you are not interested in the job, you should write a brief letter stating your decision and expressing thanks for the offer.

 CHECK POINT What are the main points you should make in a follow-up letter after an interview?

REVIEW 13-1

21st Century Skills
Thinking Critically

PARTNERSHIP FOR
21ST CENTURY SKILLS

1. Assume that you are ready to begin full-time employment. Identify the type of job you will seek. Choose a job you are qualified for. Describe these factors related to the job:
   - Typical titles for this job
   - Typical tasks or activities associated with this job
   - Typical wages or salary for this job in your area
   - Education, skills, and experience required for the job

2. Describe how your education, skills, or experience qualify you for this job.

3. Assume you have been invited to a job interview for the job you have selected. Prepare written responses for the sample interview questions below:
   - What skills or experience do you have that best qualify you for this job?
   - Where you do want to be in your career five years from now?
   - Why should I hire you rather than another applicant with comparable skills?
   - How would your current employer or teachers describe your work and attitude?

Making Academic Connections
Reinforcing Math Skills

You have been offered two jobs—one as an appliance salesperson and one as an office assistant. Use your math skills to help you evaluate the jobs and make a decision about which one to accept.

1. Read the information about each job below. What you can expect your gross pay less the deduction for health insurance coverage to be per year for each job?

2. Which job would you choose and why? Consider your job interests and the locations of the jobs in addition to salary and health insurance costs.

Sales Position in an Appliance Store

Your base salary will be $960 per pay period (1 month). You will also receive a 5 percent commission on the price of items you sell during the pay period. The store manager says you can expect to sell around $4,000 in merchandise in an average month. This amount can vary widely, however, and will depend on your selling skills. The deduction from your paycheck for health insurance will be $125 per pay period. The job is close to your home, and you can ride the public bus to work.

Office Assistant

As an office assistant, you will work 80 hours per pay period (two weeks) and receive $8 per hour. Your deduction for health insurance will be $50 per pay period. The company is located 20 miles from your home and is not accessible by bus.

13-1 Activity 1

Prepare a Letter of Application (Outcomes 13-1a and 13-1b)

In this activity, you will identify a job opening and prepare a letter of application for a job.

1. Identify a job opening for which you are qualified. Use information from sources such as placement offices, newspapers, the Internet, or personal contacts to identify the job opening.
2. Prepare a letter of application to the organization where the job you seek exists. Express your interest in working for the company in the position you have chosen. Ask to be granted a job interview. See Figure 13-1.5 for an example letter.

13-1 Activity 2

Prepare a Resume and References (Outcome 13-1b)

1. Prepare a hard copy resume to include with the application letter you prepared for 13-1 Activity 1. See Figure 13-1.4 for an example resume.
2. Change the format of your resume to make it appropriate to submit on-line. Save this copy as a separate file.
3. Prepare a references page. Include complete information for three references.

Introduction to a New Job

When you begin a new job, you will have a great deal to learn about the company and how it operates. As you think ahead about your first full-time job, you may have questions such as the following:

- What will they expect me to be able to do immediately?
- Will I be able to learn everything I should know about this job?
- Will my coworkers be willing to help me?

Employers expect to provide new employees with an introduction to the company and to new jobs. Employees who understand their jobs and the total company are more likely to be successful in their work and contribute to achieving company goals.

In some instances, a job introduction or orientation is done informally by the employee's supervisor or manager. In other instances, the job introduction is provided in a formal, organized manner. Formal orientation programs are scheduled for a particular time and include a series of presentations or meetings. These programs are common in large organizations, where a number of new employees may begin their jobs at the same time.

Informal orientation programs are common in smaller organizations where fewer employees are likely to begin their new jobs at the same time. Generally, an informal program is directed by the new employee's immediate supervisor or by an experienced coworker. This person often has a checklist to guide the explanations during the orientation. Some of these topics and activities are likely to be included:

- Goals and policies of the organization
- The company's organization chart and key personnel
- Employment forms (such as the Form W-4 shown in Figure 13-2.1 on page 468)
- Employee benefits provided
- Completion of forms related to benefits such as health-care or retirement plans
- Company policies related to ethics, safety, and security

Goodluz/Shutterstock

In small organizations, a manager may provide an informal orientation for a new employee.

Figure 13-2.1 **Form W-4 documents tax withholding information.**

------------------------------- Cut here and give Form W-4 to your employer. Keep the top part for your records. -------------------------------

Form **W-4** Department of the Treasury Internal Revenue Service	**Employee's Withholding Allowance Certificate** ► Whether you are entitled to claim a certain number of allowances or exemption from withholding is subject to review by the IRS. Your employer may be required to send a copy of this form to the IRS.	OMB No. 1545-0074 **2011**

1 Type or print your first name and middle initial.	Last name	2 **Your social security number**

Home address (number and street or rural route)	3 ☐ Single ☐ Married ☐ Married, but withhold at higher Single rate. **Note.** If married, but legally separated, or spouse is a nonresident alien, check the "Single" box.

City or town, state, and ZIP code	4 **If your last name differs from that shown on your social security card, check here. You must call 1-800-772-1213 for a replacement card.** ► ☐

5	Total number of allowances you are claiming (from line **H** above **or** from the applicable worksheet on page 2)	5
6	Additional amount, if any, you want withheld from each paycheck	6 $
7	I claim exemption from withholding for 2011, and I certify that I meet **both** of the following conditions for exemption.	
	• Last year I had a right to a refund of **all** federal income tax withheld because I had **no** tax liability **and**	
	• This year I expect a refund of **all** federal income tax withheld because I expect to have **no** tax liability.	
	If you meet both conditions, write "Exempt" here . . . . ► 7	

Under penalties of perjury, I declare that I have examined this certificate and to the best of my knowledge and belief, it is true, correct, and complete.

Employee's signature
(This form is not valid unless you sign it.) ►   Date ►

8 Employer's name and address (Employer: Complete lines 8 and 10 only if sending to the IRS.)	9 Office code (optional)	10 Employer identification number (EIN)

Source: Internal Revenue Service, Form W-4 (2011), http://www.irs.gov/pub/irs-pdf/fw4_11.pdf.

■ Personnel policies, including performance evaluations
■ Policies and procedures that guide the new employee's responsibilities

Orientation does not always end with the program offered on the first day of work. Sometimes additional meetings are scheduled after employees have had several weeks of experience in their new positions.

 CHECK POINT Why is orientation provided for new employees?

Learning on the Job

As a new employee, realize that your supervisor is aware that you do not know everything that the job may require. Learning on the job is expected and is considered a part of your job. Some of the learning is guided by an experienced person, and some is done on your own.

As a new worker, you can expect to be given specific information about the tasks you will complete. The company may have a clearly stated job description of what you are to do, or you may be in a newly created position. In the latter case, just a general description of your duties may exist. An employee's actual work duties and tasks may differ from the job description because the job has changed but the description has not yet been updated.

✷ WORKPLACE CONNECTIONS ✷

Vanessa was hired as an assistant to the director of a new laboratory in a growing company. Her background in sciences and her work as a lab assistant while in college were considered appropriate background for a person filling a position not yet fully defined. Vanessa likes having an unstructured job. As she said, "I have to be alert to see where I can be helpful; that's a challenge I'll enjoy."

Would you want to accept a job that does not have a fully defined job description? Why or why not?

A new employee will often find that coworkers are generous in providing help related to job tasks. They understand that a knowledgeable coworker is going to be a valuable asset to the unit or department. You will quickly realize which of your coworkers are most likely to want to answer questions you might have.

 CHECK POINT Why might an employee's duties differ from his or her job description?

References and Resources

When you begin a new job, make a point to become acquainted with basic references available to you. Some of these references may be accessed using your computer, while some may be in print. Some of the references you may have are listed below.

- A company manual or employee handbook of policies and procedures
- A complete organization chart
- A calendar of events and a company newsletter
- An annual report if the company is publicly owned
- A directory of all personnel with phone numbers and possibly e-mail addresses

Companies have developed a wide range of materials to aid employees. You will want to learn what company databases and network or intranet resources are available for your use. An example of an online employee handbook is shown in Figure 13-2.2. If your company has a library or resource center, spend some time getting acquainted with the range of information that you can access. Your department may subscribe to magazines, newspapers, or databases that are useful to you in your job.

 CHECK POINT What types of reference materials might help a new employee learn about the company or its policies?

Figure 13-2.2 **Some companies provide an employee handbook on the company intranet.**

Employee Handbook

This employee handbook is an outline of your privileges and obligations as an employee. It should be your primary reference. When you have questions about policies or procedures outlined in this manual, refer them to your manager or contact the Human Resources Department.

- Attendance
- At-Will Employment
- Company Overview and Mission
- Compensation and Employee Benefits
- Confidentiality Policy
- Drug and Alcohol Policy

© Cengage Learning 2013

Employee Performance

performance review evaluation of an employee's work

Many companies have a plan for evaluating employee performance at least once a year. A company may have several reasons for doing evaluations, also called performance reviews or appraisals. Information from the reviews may be used in giving pay increases or promotions. Disciplinary actions or dismissals may occur if reviews show poor performance. Evaluations help identify what employees do well. They may also identify areas for improvement. Setting goals for the employee to accomplish is often a part of the process.

Formal evaluations may be completed only once a year. However, effective managers provide feedback about an employee's work on an ongoing basis. Companies expect workers to be competent and perform their jobs satisfactorily. Some factors commonly considered in employee evaluations are listed below.

- Job knowledge and skills
- Quality of work
- Quantity of work completed
- Initiative and judgment
- Cooperation and teamwork
- Flexibility and adaptability
- Adherence to schedules and deadlines
- Completion of goals set previously

New workers are given a period of time for learning their jobs. The trial period typically lasts three to six months. The length of the trial period is determined by the complexity of the job and the level of skills needed by the employee. Employees often receive their first formal evaluation at the end of the trial period. Future evaluations follow the company's normal schedule.

New employees may be expected to learn their job duties during a trial period.

Abel Mitja Varela/iStockphoto

Ways of Evaluating Employees

Companies use varying methods to evaluate workers. In some companies, evaluation practices may be informal. Little, if any, information may be recorded in the personnel file of the employee. In such companies, the manager may write an appraisal of each employee at designated times. Generally, the employee will sign the appraisal to indicate that it was read and may add comments to the document.

Other companies use more formal evaluation procedures. Appraisal forms may be completed by an employee and his or her manager. In some cases, coworkers may also provide comments about the employee's work. This approach is sometimes called a 360-degree evaluation. Feedback is sought from several people in different positions (the employee's circle of contacts). This approach may give a better picture of an employee's overall performance.

Performance reviews are often rated or scored in some way. Using a checklist, where skills and traits are listed and points awarded for each area, is a popular method. Using this method, the employee's performance is compared to reasonable standards. Ideally, all employees in a unit or department could receive high scores using this method. In some cases, employees are rated for each item using a simple category system. For example, a worker might be rated *excellent*, *good*, *acceptable*, or *needs improvement* on a particular skill.

Employee performance is often compared to standards for acceptable work. For example, standards based on keystrokes, lines, or pages may be used for an employee doing word processing. Often, standards are given per hour or per day. These measures can be used for workers in factories and in offices where there are repetitive tasks. Standards for some items, such as teamwork or responsibility, may be more subjective. Manager or coworker observations of employee behavior may be used to judge performance for these categories.

 CHECK POINT What is one example of how an employee may be scored or rated in a performance review?

✳ WORKPLACE CONNECTIONS ✳

A manufacturing company wishes to increase productivity of all employees. The company began a study of key tasks. As a part of this project, the work of employees in the largest departments was measured so that performance standards could be set. With the standards in place, the company introduced training courses to aid employees in achieving the new standards, called **benchmarks**.

▶ **What might happen if an employee has been trained but cannot match the benchmarks set for her or his job?**

benchmarks standards used for comparison, such as for job performance

Evaluating Your Own Performance

To progress in your job, you will want to ask yourself: "How well am I doing my job?" Such an evaluation might be scheduled to be completed about a month before the evaluation by your manager. The following steps should be helpful in your evaluation:

1. List the skills, tasks, and goals that relate to your position. For this step, a copy of the performance appraisal form used or your job description will be useful.

2. Think carefully about your work behavior, either daily for one week or one day each week for four or five weeks.

3. Record any instances of very effective or poor performance, indicating the date of each entry.

4. Assess what you have written at the end of your review period. Note especially instances of poor performance. Consider what you might change to improve your performance.

5. Compare your own evaluation with the one given you by your manager or supervisor. Reconsider your own evaluation in relation to that given by your manager or supervisor and make appropriate changes in how you assess yourself.

CHECK POINT Which of the steps listed for self-evaluation do you think is the most important? Why?

Changing Jobs

A typical worker changes jobs several times during his or her career. A job change may be the worker's choice, or it may be caused by events beyond the worker's control. Companies sometimes change their structures as they strive to grow and accomplish their goals. Companies are bought and sold, merged with other companies, relocated to other geographic areas, or downsized. A company may also fail or go out of business. These changes may mean that workers are promoted or transferred to different jobs, asked to move to another city, laid off temporarily, or dismissed from their jobs.

downsize reduce, as in decreasing the number of workers in an organization

Workers may lose their jobs because a company goes out of business.

Kristoffer Tripplaar/Alamy

Job Termination

Being dismissed from a job can be an emotionally upsetting and stressful experience. This is true even when you are dismissed through no fault of your own. You may have some prior warning that the dismissal may happen, or you may have no warning at all. Try to remain calm and professional when faced with a job loss.

Dismissal Procedures

Depending on the size and policies of the company, dismissal procedures may vary widely. Typically, you will be given a written notice or letter stating that you are dismissed from the company's employ. The letter may state the reason for the dismissal. You should receive a final paycheck on or shortly after your dismissal. You may also be paid for items such as unused vacation or sick days.

Companies typically provide **severance pay** to workers who lose their jobs through no fault of the employees. One or two weeks' pay for each year a worker has been at the company is a typical payment. Sometimes workers are dismissed because of poor job performance. Others workers may lose their jobs because of a serious violation of company policies, such as theft or harming or threatening a coworker. Usually these workers do not receive severance pay.

You will be expected to return items such as company keys, credit cards, security badges, or access cards. Your manager or a coworker may escort you to your desk or work area to collect personal items and then out of the building. If the company's dismissal procedures are less formal, you may be allowed to leave on your own, taking time to say goodbye to coworkers.

When employees lose their jobs for reasons such as downsizing or a move to a new location, the company may provide assistance in helping workers find other jobs. Some companies use outplacement services. These services are organizations that provide counseling and other services to help workers find new jobs.

severance pay payment made to an employee being dismissed from a job

Exit Interview

When leaving a company, you may be asked to attend a meeting, sometimes called an **exit interview**. The meeting may be with your supervisor or someone from the Human Resources Department. In this meeting, the reasons you are leaving the company (if not by your choice) and the status of any continuing benefits may be discussed. You may be asked questions about how you think the company could improve operations. Company procedures that you think are effective may also be discussed. Show a cooperative attitude in an exit interview, even if you have been unhappy with your job or company policies. Try to keep the goodwill of the company personnel. You may want to work for this company at some future date. You may need to deal with company personnel for job references or continuing benefits issues.

exit interview meeting with company personnel when leaving a job

kevin nicholson / Alamy

Maintain a cooperative attitude during an exit interview.

References

Remember that while one company may no longer need your services, others are likely to need them. You may wish to ask your supervisor to give you a letter of recommendation or allow you to list him or her as a reference when you look for a new job.

Voluntary Job Changes

You may decide to leave your job for a variety of reasons. You might move to a different city. You might complete training or education that qualifies you for

You may decide to change jobs after you complete a college degree.

a higher-level job. You might find better pay or more opportunity for advancement at a different company. You will want to take advantage of good job opportunities. Be aware, however, that a record of changing jobs too often (sometimes called *job hopping*) may make a poor impression on prospective employers. As a general rule, plan to stay in any full-time job you accept for at least one year. If you have changed jobs frequently, have an explanation for the frequent changes prepared to discuss in interviews.

Resignation Letter

When possible, give the company at least two weeks' notice when leaving a job. Always submit a formal **resignation letter**. The letter should be written to your immediate supervisor and should use a polite, professional tone. Keep the letter short and simple.

In the first paragraph, ask your manager to accept your resignation from your job (state the job title) as of a particular date. In the second paragraph, indicate that you are willing to do whatever you can to organize material or document procedures to help another worker assume your duties. You could offer to train or assist another person during your last few days at work. In the third paragraph, thank the manager for the opportunity to work for the company and wish the company success in the future. You need not give a reason for your resignation.

resignation letter a document stating the intention to end employment on a certain date

Promotions

Although you may be content with your present job, remember to consider opportunities for **promotions**. Your company may post job openings in company bulletins, in local newspapers, or on the company website. An example of a company website where job openings may be accessed is shown in Figure 13-2.3. These job postings may provide information about higher-level jobs. You may deal with people at varying levels of the company. You may be able to learn, in informal ways, about qualifications required for various jobs. Learning about higher-level positions in your

promotion advancement in rank, grade, or position

Figure 13-2.3 **Some companies post job openings on their intranets.**

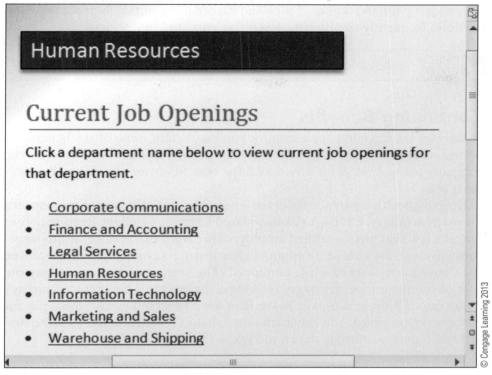

company can help you decide whether you would want to work in one of these positions.

You may find that there are no opportunities for promotions with a current employer when you think you are ready for a more challenging job. In such a case, you may want to consider looking for a job with another company.

Job Portfolio

A job portfolio is a file containing documents, work samples, and information related to employment. A job portfolio can be very helpful when applying for a new job or being interviewed. Keep items such as the following in your job portfolio:

job portfolio information related to talents and skills, such as documents, degrees, awards, and work samples

- Copies of your resume in hard copy and electronic formats
- Sample letters of application and thank-you letters
- Your job search diary that includes job search activities and contact persons
- Copies of any awards or honors you have received
- Letters, notes, and other items related to your work
- Programs and newsletters that report your participation in school or community activities
- School transcripts of courses completed
- Diplomas and certificates of completion of courses
- A detailed work history (job descriptions, evaluations, and related information about earlier full-time positions and about your current position)
- Samples of your work or pictures and descriptions of projects or work completed

As you begin full-time employment or continue your education, continue to broaden your awareness of jobs and career possibilities. Update your job portfolio frequently to reflect new skills, talents, and experiences.

 CHECK POINT What information should be included in a resignation letter?

Continuing Benefits

When you leave a company's employ, you may retain some of the benefits of having worked for the company. For example, if you were employed by the company for several years, you may draw benefits from a pension or retirement plan.

Keeping health insurance coverage when changing jobs is a serious concern for many workers. COBRA (Consolidated Omnibus Budget Reconciliation Act) is a law that gives qualified employees the right to continue health insurance coverage for at least 18 months after leaving a company. The employee must have been covered while employed. The worker typically must pay the cost of the insurance coverage. However, the cost will be at the company's group rate. This cost is usually lower than the cost an individual would pay for purchasing insurance. You can learn more about COBRA on the U.S. Department of Labor website, as shown in Figure 13-2.4.

CHECK POINT What is the main purpose of COBRA?

Figure 13-2.4 **The U.S. Department of Labor website provides information about COBRA.**

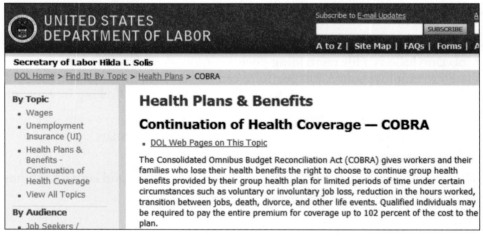

Source: U.S. Department of Labor, "Health Plans & Benefits," http://www.dol.gov/dol/topic/health-plans/cobra.htm.

21st Century Skills

Making Decisions

PARTNERSHIP FOR 21ST CENTURY SKILLS

Bill and Yoshi both accepted full-time jobs in a local company where they had worked during the summers for the last two years. They received information about when they should report for their first day of work and about the first day's schedule of orientation meetings. Bill called Yoshi and said, "Yoshi, did you see the schedule for orientation on Monday, our first day at work? Don't you think we can skip most of the day? I'd say we should plan to arrive at three o'clock when we will learn from our managers what exactly they want us to do on our jobs. Why should we waste our time hearing about things we already know? What do you think?"

1. What types of important information are likely to be presented at the orientation meeting?
2. What impression will the employer have of Bill and Yoshi if they do not attend the orientation meeting?
3. The orientation meeting is being held during regular working hours. Is it appropriate for Bill and Yoshi to decide not to attend this work activity? What might be the result of not reporting for work?

Making Academic Connections

Reinforcing English Skills

The following sentences have errors in the use of quotation marks and question marks. Key or write the sentences, correcting the errors.

1. She wondered who won the award?
2. The teacher said, Read one current article about interview skills."
3. He said, "This job application is not complete.
4. Jamaal replied, "I thought the interviewer asked challenging questions".
5. Do you know how to use word processing software.
6. Janie asked her friend, "What time does the class begin?
7. Did you read the article "Writing Effective Resumes
8. "I will talk with Mr. Hawkins," he said, and let you know what I learn."
9. Maria asked, "What time does the seminar begin;" Mai answered, "It begins at noon."
10. "Levon, did you enjoy the show?"

13-2 Activity 1

Job Orientation and Evaluation (Outcomes 13-2a and 13-2b)

Interview a person who is currently working in a career field that interests you to learn about job orientation and evaluations.

1. Conduct an interview in person or by phone or e-mail with a person who is currently employed.
2. Ask questions such as the following:
   - What is your job title?
   - What are your main job duties?

- What type of orientation does your company provide new employees in this or other jobs?
- How often do you receive a performance review?
- In general terms, how is the review conducted and what kind of rating system is used?

3. Write a short report to give the name and title of the person you interviewed. Include a summary of the information you learned.

13-2 Activity 2

Resignation Letter (Outcome 13-2c)

You have worked for Hinkle Trucking as an administrative assistant for four years. You have accepted a new job, and you must resign from your current position.

1. Write a letter of resignation to your manager, Mr. Juan Alverez. Use the current date for your letter and make the date of your resignation two weeks from today. The company address is 24 Motor Way, Ferguson, KY 42502-0024.

2. Because this is a personal business letter, print the letter on plain paper. Include your return address on the two lines above the letter date or in a letterhead design that you create. Assume your address is 34 Apple Street, Ferguson, KY 42502-8834. Format the letter in block style with open punctuation.

3. Review your letter for the five Cs of effective correspondence. Remember to use the *you* approach. Proofread carefully and correct all errors. Print the letter.

Summary

13-1 An Effective Job Search

- You should consider your long-term career goals and develop a career strategy to meet your goals. Keep your career goals in mind as you evaluate job offers.

- Sources available to help you locate job openings include placement services, the Internet, newspapers, employment agencies, government announcements, and personal contacts.

- Job searches sometimes require a considerable amount of time. You should maintain a job search diary of your activity.

- A carefully prepared resume and letter of application will improve your chances of being invited to a job interview.

- You may need both a hard copy resume and one in plain format for scanning or submitting electronically.

- Prepare carefully for each interview you accept. Consider how you will present your qualifications and anticipate questions you may be asked.

- Send a follow-up letter after an interview to thank the interviewer and express continued interest in a job.

13-2 The First Job and Beyond

- Employers typically provide some type of job orientation for new employees.

- Learning on the job is expected and is considered a part of your job. Plan to make use of references available to you as you learn and complete your work.

- Many companies have a plan for evaluating employee performance at least once a year. Pay increases, promotions, or disciplinary actions may be affected by the reviews.

- Employees should evaluate their own work on an ongoing basis.

- A typical worker changes jobs several times during his or her career for a variety of reasons.

- When leaving a company, you may be asked to attend an exit interview.

- Always submit a formal resignation letter when you decide to leave a job.

- Although you may be content with your present job, remember to consider opportunities for promotions.

- When you leave a company's employ, you may retain some of the benefits of having worked for the company, such as health insurance coverage, for some time.

Wire_man/Shutterstock.com

Chapter 13 Activity 1

Prepare for a Job Interview
(Outcome 13-1c)

1. In 13-1 Activity 1, you identified a job opening and prepared a letter of application for a job. Assume that you have been granted an interview for that job.
2. Write a list of at least ten questions that you might be asked during the interview. Some of the questions should be general ones about your background and your career goals. Some of the questions should relate to the specific job you have selected.
3. Write answers to the interview questions.
4. Write three questions that you might ask about the company or the job if you are given the opportunity.

Chapter 13 Activity 2

Update a Job Portfolio
(Outcome 13-2c)

The purpose of a job portfolio is to demonstrate your skills and abilities related to work. A portfolio can contain samples of your work, awards or other recognitions, certificates or degrees related to training or education, a description of assignments or projects that have been successfully completed, and letters or recommendations related to your work abilities. A good portfolio can be helpful in getting a job.

1. In Chapter 9 Activity 2, Long-Term Portfolio Project, page 330, you were instructed to create a portfolio. Review the portfolio you created and think about what you have learned or accomplished since you completed it.
2. Update the portfolio by adding items such as the following:
   - Samples of your work
   - Awards or other recognitions related to your school work or community service
   - A sample resume
   - A sample letter of application
   - A list of references
3. If you have access to a scanner, scan the documents so you will have the portfolio in electronic form as well as in printed form.

Business Services Marketing Event

In this competitive event, you will be judged on your skills and knowledge of business marketing. Topics covered include providing services to businesses on a fee or contract basis, or providing services to consumers.

The event includes a written test and two role-playing situations. Finalists in the events will have a third role-playing situation. No reference materials are allowed. You may make notes to use during the role-play during the time when you read the role-play description and prepare for the event.

Performance Indicators Evaluated

Participants will demonstrate skills related to the marketing career cluster and marketing management pathway. Performance indicators such as the following will be evaluated.

- Explain the nature and scope of the product/service management function
- Describe the use of technology in the product/service management function
- Identify product opportunities
- Explain the concept of market and market identification
- Explain the nature of corporate branding

The following indicators are in addition to the specific indicators listed above.

- Communication (writing, speaking, reading, or listening)
- Analyzing data to form conclusions and recommendations
- Critical thinking and problem solving
- Setting priorities and managing time

For more detailed information about this event, go to the DECA website.[1]

http://www.deca.org

Think Critically

1. Name two products that are well-known brands. Why do you think these brands are so well known?
2. Do you think a product can be successful without effective marketing? Why or why not?

---

[1]DECA, "High School Competitive Events Guidelines" (DECA, 2011), http://www.deca.org/competitions/highschool.

Education and Training

Are you a "people person"? Are you patient and creative? Do like teaching others new knowledge or skills? If the answer to these questions is *yes*, a job in education and training may be right for you. This career area includes a variety of jobs. All relate in some way to planning, managing, and providing education and training or related learning support services.

Employment Outlook

There are many jobs in education and training. The U.S. government provides job projections for 2008-2018. Good job prospects are expected in this area. Many jobs in education are expected to increase as fast as the average for all jobs. Some jobs are expected to grow faster than the average.[2]

Job Titles

- Coach
- Distance learning coordinator
- Librarian
- Preschool teacher
- Principal
- Professor
- School psychologist
- Teacher
- Teacher assistant

Needed Education/Skills

Jobs in education and training require strong communications and human relations skills. Expert knowledge in the subject being taught is also required for jobs such as teacher, coach, and professor. Technology skills are important due to the growth of electronic learning tools and distance learning. Many jobs in education

[2]*Occupational Outlook Handbook*, 2010–11 Edition, Bureau of Labor Statistics, U.S. Department of Labor, http://www.bls.gov/oco/ocos318.htm.

and training require a college degree. Some jobs, such as teacher assistant, may require only a high school diploma.

What's it like to work in . . . Education?

Donna works as a preschool teacher for a county school system in a rural area. The school has eight preschool classes. Four classes attend in the morning and four attend in the afternoon. So Donna has two classes of about twenty students. The students come to school Monday through Thursday. On Fridays, Donna uses her work time for planning activities, completing reports, and making home visits. Home visits let Donna get to know the child's parents or other caregivers and learn about any special needs the child has.

For many children, preschool is their first experience in a structured environment. Donna helps students learn to follow instructions, focus on a task, and interact with other children in appropriate ways. She teaches students basic skills, such as color, shape, and number recognition. Games, stories, crafts, and field trips help the students build physical, mental, and social skills. Snack time and rest time are important parts of the day for preschoolers. Donna oversees all these activities.

Donna prepared for her job by taking college courses in early childhood education. She also trained on the job under an experienced teacher. She is working toward completing a bachelor's degree in education. While not required for her job, Donna will receive a higher salary once she completes the degree. Donna must be organized, creative, and, most of all, patient. She enjoys working with the children and helping them prepare for kindergarten.

What About You?

What age group would you want to work with if you had a job in education? What one skill or trait do you think is most important for a job in education or training?

Ongoing Professional Development

14-1 Leadership Skills

14-2 Lifelong Learning

Jack Hollingsworth/Jupiter Images

Professional development involves increasing skills or knowledge to succeed on the job. Developing leadership skills is an important aspect of professional development. Employees in many positions need leadership skills. As you study this chapter, you will learn about leadership roles, traits, styles, and strategies.

Lifelong learning is also an important aspect of professional development. As business products, services, and procedures change, you will need to learn new skills and knowledge to be an effective employee. In this chapter, you will learn about the need for ongoing learning as well as formal and informal learning environments.

Wire_man/Shutterstock.com

KEY TERMS

leadership p. 484
management p. 485
trait p. 486
humility p. 486
vision p. 486
autocrat p. 488
democratic p. 488
delegate p. 488
motivate p. 491
altruism p. 491

leadership the act of guiding or directing others

Leadership Roles and Traits

Leadership is the act of guiding or directing others. Having effective leadership helps a company or organization accomplish its goals. In the case of a business, a primary goal is to make a profit and stay in business. In the case of other types of organizations, the primary goal may be to provide services to individuals or groups. Understanding leadership roles and developing leadership traits can help you be more effective on the job.

Leadership Roles

Company managers are in the primary leadership roles. They provide direction for the entire company. Department managers provide direction for major units in the company. Team leaders provide direction for smaller groups. Other employees may lead a committee or group project. All these individuals need effective leadership skills.

Company Managers

Company managers include those in positions such as owner, president, vice president, and general manager. A company may have several vice presidents. These employees may be in charge of different areas of the business, such as manufacturing or marketing. Company managers provide direction for how the company will operate. They create plans for achieving the company's goals. In addition to financial data, the plans may include issues such as:

■ New products or services the company will offer
■ Products or services the company will no longer offer

The ability to lead a meeting effectively is an important leadership skill.

Avava, 2010/Used under license from Shutterstock.com

- New markets in which the company will sell products
- New or remodeled factories or stores
- New equipment for making products
- Increases or decreases in the number of employees
- Campaigns for marketing products or services
- Strategies for decreasing the cost of making or marketing products

Department Managers and Team Leaders

Departments in a company are typically centered on a group of tasks. For example, an accounting department keeps track of the company's financial data. The employees pay the company's bills, send invoices to customers, and prepare the employee payroll. Financial reports, such as income statements and balance sheets, are also prepared by employees in this department. A marketing department handles tasks related to promoting and selling products or services. A manufacturing department handles tasks related to making products. Department managers need skills and knowledge related to the department's tasks as well as leadership skills. They direct employees in completing the department's tasks effectively. A department manager may also conduct performance reviews for employees in the department.

Team leaders or group leaders typically direct a smaller group of employees within a department. For example, an advertising team may be part of a marketing department. The team may focus on advertising the company's products on TV or the Internet. Some teams are made up of employees from various departments. For example, suppose a company is considering making a new product. A team may be created with employees from several departments to evaluate the idea. Team leaders often work closely with the other team members. They need strong interpersonal skills as well as skills related to the specific tasks done by the team.

Yuri Arcurs/Shutterstock.com

A team may have people from one department or several departments.

Other Employees

Although an employee may not be in a management position, she or he may be asked to lead a committee or project. For example, suppose hard copy files seem to be missing from the file drawers too often. A committee may be formed to investigate the problem and offer possible solutions. The committee may

management the act of directing people and using resources to accomplish goals

include an employee from each group that uses the files. Employees must often work together to complete a project. A project leader may be charged with seeing that the project is completed on time. This person may break the project into smaller tasks and assign the tasks to other employees. The leader may also monitor the progress of the work and help solve any problems that arise.

 CHECK POINT What are some positions in a company where the employee needs leadership skills?

Leadership Traits

Have you heard someone described as a "natural born leader"? Some people do seem to show leadership **traits** more than others. However, leadership traits and skills, as described below, can be developed.

Character

Character is the basic values and principles reflected in a person's behavior. Honesty and integrity are generally considered to be important elements of a good character. Good leaders follow ethical standards and treat others fairly. They use tact and show consideration for others. This builds trust in leaders and helps others have confidence in them. **Humility** is another important leadership trait related to character. Having humility means that you are respectful and do not consider yourself superior to others. Showing respect for the ideas and talents of others helps leaders gain respect.

Vision

An effective leader has a **vision** for what an organization or group will accomplish or become. Employees believe that he or she "knows where we're going." The company or group may have a mission statement as shown in Figure 14-1.1. This statement typically includes the company's purpose and the objectives the company plans to achieve. A clear vision is essential for setting goals and making plans for the organization or group.

Figure 14-1.1 Company leaders often state their objectives in a mission statement.

> ## Mission Statement
>
> Corporate Home: About Us : **Mission Statement**
>
> Our mission is to be a respected and innovative provider of consumer home products, achieving profitable growth through effective business management. We are committed to
>
> - Providing quality products and excellent customer service
> - Operating according to high ethical standards
> - Using practices that are friendly to the environment
> - Promoting human rights
> - Being a responsible corporate citizen
> - Providing a safe and healthy working environment
> - Providing professional development opportunities for our employees

Margin glossary:

trait a distinguishing characteristic or quality

humility the state of being modest and respectful of others

vision a mental image of what something will or could be in the future

© Cengage Learning 2013

An effective leader sets goals that are focused and realistic to work toward realizing the vision. A goal that states "We will increase sales" is vague. A goal that states "We will increase sales by 10 percent within one year" is both focused and measurable. Such a goal is probably also realistic—one that can possibly be achieved. Leaders often must be creative in finding ways to reach goals. Exhibiting a positive, enthusiastic attitude is important for inspiring employees. Believing that you can accomplish a goal also is an important step toward doing so.

Organization

A leader might be responsible for a committee of four, an entire company, or any size group in between. In each case, the leader must organize the resources available to accomplish the goals of the group. Leaders must make decisions about how employees and money, equipment, or other resources will be used to get the job done. Sometimes a creative approach is required as companies strive to cut expenses and increase profits. Doing more with less often requires having an open mind and being willing to try new things.

Maturity

Maturity is reflected in the way a person deals with circumstances and other people. A mature leader acts in a reasonable and professional manner. He or she is not ruled by emotions or fears. A mature person can

- Accept criticism without being offended and learn from it
- Admit when he or she makes a mistake
- Consider others' ideas with an open mind
- Share credit for work with others
- Both win and lose gracefully
- Be flexible, adapting to new conditions or situations

Mature leaders show confidence in their ideas and their ability to get things done. This self-confidence inspires others to have confidence in them. However, good leaders realize that they do not know everything. They often rely on the expertise of others. They also accept that they will need to keep learning new information and developing new skills throughout their careers.

 CHECK POINT What is one trait that you think a good leader typically has (in addition to the ones discussed above)?

Leadership Styles and Strategies

Leaders have different leadership styles and use various strategies to achieve their goals. Some leadership styles or strategies work better in certain situations or for certain people than others. Learning about leadership styles and strategies can help you be a more effective leader. It can also help you relate to leaders in your organization.

Leadership Styles

A leadership style is a way of giving direction, putting plans into effect, and motivating people. Leadership styles typically differ from one another regarding the amount of control exercised by the leader and the amount given to the followers. Three traditional styles of leadership, as described by Kurt Lewin in 1939, are still relevant today.[1] These styles are described in the following paragraphs. Variations of these styles may be called by other names.

Autocratic Leadership

autocrat someone who holds complete authority in a situation

An autocrat is someone who holds complete authority. In the autocratic leadership style, all decisions are made by the leader. The leader decides what should be done and how it should be done. The followers (employees) have little or no input or influence. This style works best when the leader has the expert knowledge or skills needed to make decisions and the followers do not. This style might also be used when a decision must be made quickly, allowing no time to consult with others. Followers may have fewer opportunities to be creative in their work when this leadership style is used. Employees who are skilled and experienced in their jobs may resent a leader who uses this style often.

Democratic Leadership

democratic affording equal rights to all

When a democratic leadership style is used, both the leader and the followers (employees) take part in the decision-making process. While the leader may have the final say, followers can offer ideas and suggestions about what should be done and how it should be done. The leader gives serious consideration to the input offered by followers. This style encourages followers to be creative and innovative. Employees may work harder to achieve goals when they help set the goals. This style works best when the leader and the other employees have the knowledge or skills needed to make decisions and there is enough time to request and consider the input.

delegate authorize another person to speak or act for you

Delegative Leadership

To delegate means to authorize another person to speak or act for you. In the delegative leadership style, the leader tells followers (employees) what needs to be accomplished and provides the resources needed. The followers make the decisions about how to accomplish the goals. Some leaders using this style give little guidance to

A delegative leadership style may be effective for leaders who supervise creative artists.

Hill Street Studios/Jupiter Images

[1]Kendra Cherry, "Lewin's Leadership Styles," 2011, About.com Psychology, http://psychology.about .com/od/leadership/a/leadstyles.htm.

employees. Others may be available to consult and offer advice about issues or problems. For this leadership style to work well, the employees must have the expert skill and knowledge needed to complete the tasks. They must also be good at setting and meeting deadlines. This leadership style is sometimes used when the work requires creativity or innovation.

CHECK POINT Which leadership style allows followers to have little or no input into making decisions? Would you want to work for a leader who uses this approach? Why or why not?

Leadership Strategies

A strategy is a plan of action designed to accomplish a goal. Setting a good example, communicating clearly, and motivating others are effective leadership strategies. Delegating work when appropriate is also a helpful strategy.

Leading by Example

Leading by example can be a very effective leadership strategy. Do you want your employees to come to work on time and meet deadlines? Then you, as leader, should do the same. Do you appreciate having others exhibit a positive attitude? As leader, you should model this behavior. A quote attributed to John Quincy Adams, the sixth president of the United States, says, "A leader leads by example, whether he intends to or not."[2] Hold yourself accountable for following the same high standards that you set for employees. This lets employees know that you truly value such behavior.

✳ WORKPLACE CONNECTIONS ✳

Ms. Alice Wong is the vice president of marketing in a manufacturing company. She supervises several employees who plan and carry out marketing tactics and programs. The employees also analyze market research and evaluate marketing campaigns. As the company has grown, so has the workload for these employees. They find it increasingly difficult to complete all the work assigned to them during regular office hours. Many employees work late several days a week. Some say they simply cannot use their vacation time without falling behind on their work. Ms. Wong encourages her employees to leave work at a reasonable time and take all their vacation days. However, employees note that Ms. Wong works late almost every evening and seldom takes vacation time.

What message does Ms. Wong's behavior send to her employees?

Communicating Effectively

Communicating effectively is one of the most important jobs for a leader. A leader can have great ideas or plans for the group. However, these plans are not likely to succeed unless they are shared effectively with others. Managers need to discuss goals with employees in broad terms, giving them "the big picture." Then the discussion can move to how the employees' work contributes to achieving the goals. Detailed plans and instructions may be given for some tasks. Effective

[2]John Quincy Adams, Famous Leadership Quotes, 2011, http://www.self-improvement-mentor.com /famous-leadership-quotes.html.

leaders remember that communication is a two-way process. They encourage employees to ask questions and offer suggestions, and they listen actively.

Giving employees feedback on their work or progress is another important task for leaders. Some feedback will be informal and ongoing. For example, a leader may notice that a project is behind schedule. Discussing the project with the employee provides feedback and an opportunity to learn what may be causing the delay. More formal feedback about the employee's work typically takes place during a performance review.

In Chapter 4 you learned that effective communications are clear, concise, complete, correct, and courteous. These characteristics are important for both spoken and written messages. Consider them in terms of exchanges among a manager and employees.

- A clear message is effective because it eliminates the need for requests for additional comment. Employees do not have to spend time asking questions or wondering how to proceed. Managers are not disappointed because the job is done differently than the way they intended.

- A concise message is effective because it states the message directly (without being abrupt). No time is wasted for managers or employees with words and thoughts that add nothing to understanding the message. A concise message does not include lengthy personal comments or discussions of work issues that do not relate to the matter at hand.

- A complete message provides all the information needed. Messages that are not complete may require employees to spend time seeking more information. Errors may be made or opportunities missed because of incomplete information.

- A correct message is accurate and up-to-date. Careful managers verify details before sharing them with employees. Employees will likely be frustrated if they have to redo work because the information they are given is not correct.

- A courteous message conforms to the expected polite, considerate behavior of the business world. Using a person's name and expressions such as "thank you" and "please" show respect for others. Making eye

Using positive nonverbal behavior can help leaders communicate in a courteous way.

Wavebreakmedia Ltd/Shutterstock.com

contact and using other positive nonverbal behavior is also important. This helps build goodwill among managers and employees. Courteous managers discuss sensitive or confidential issues with employees in private. They use tact when delivering criticism. They are careful to criticize the employee's work or behavior rather than the employee.

Even when a spoken message is effective, employees may not remember the entire message if it is lengthy. Leaders should consider following up lengthy or detailed spoken messages with a written message. Managers should consider sending reminders of important deadlines for projects and having employees submit status reports at set times.

Motivating Others

To **motivate** means to provide an incentive or inspire others to take some action. Effective leaders try to motivate employees to do good work. Employees are motivated by many different things. Some employees value the tangible rewards of work most of all. Examples of these rewards include salary or wages, paid time off (holidays and vacation time), and other employee benefits, such as health insurance or sick days. Motivating these employees may require periodic salary raises or increases in other benefits.

Some employees are motivated by the intangible rewards of work. Examples of these rewards include recognition for a job done well, personal satisfaction for achieving a goal, artistic expression, or **altruism**. Leaders can try to create working conditions that allow employees to experience these rewards. Good leaders get to know the people with whom they work. They spend time learning what is important to them. This knowledge helps them find ways to motivate the employees.

motivate provide an incentive or inspire others to take action

altruism unselfish concern or work for the benefit of others

✳ WORKPLACE CONNECTIONS ✳

Julia is employed as a counselor in a home for abused or neglected children. Children come to the facility when conditions are too unsafe or unstable for them to remain at home. Julia works hard to gain the trust of the children assigned to her. She helps them get settled in their small group living space, called a cabin. Being away from home and enrolled in a new school can be a bit scary for the students. Julia helps them with homework and social issues. She helps carry out the program a psychologist outlines for each child. Julia thinks that her salary is fine, and the job provides good benefits. Her manager is supportive and easy to work for. However, Julia values most the satisfaction that she gets from helping the children.

Do you think Julia's manager finds motivating her to be a challenge? Why or why not?

Delegating

As you learned earlier, delegating is authorizing another person to speak or act for you. Delegating tasks can give a manager more free time to do other things. It can also show an employee that the manager has confidence in his or her abilities. Employees can be challenged to do new tasks while having someone to provide guidance and review the work.

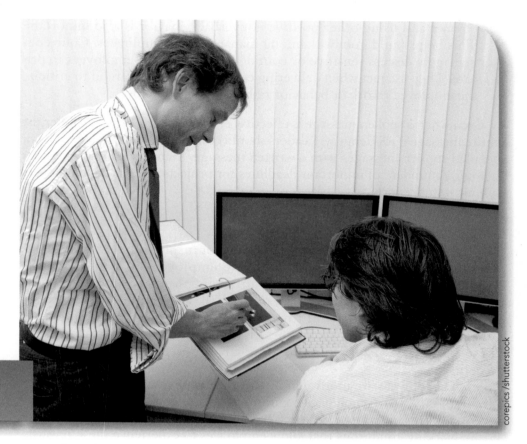

Giving clear directions or guidelines is important when delegating a task.

corepics /shutterstock

When you consider delegating a task, first make sure that the task is one that can be done effectively by someone else. For example, suppose a manager, Ms. Glenworth, has been asked to write a report giving her impressions of a proposed marketing plan. Can another person know Ms. Glenworth's thoughts and write the report for her? The answer is "probably not" unless she has discussed her thoughts at length. So this is probably not a task that should be delegated. Remember that even though you delegate a task to someone, you are still accountable for the task. "I had someone else help with this," is never an acceptable excuse for poorly done or incomplete work.

To be effective in delegating tasks, follow these guidelines:

■ Delegate to a person who has the skills and knowledge to do the task.

■ Give clear directions or guidelines for the task as appropriate. Be sure the person knows what you expect. Be available for follow-up questions or discussion during the project.

■ Provide the resources needed for the task.

■ Give the person to whom you delegate the needed authority to see that the task is done.

■ Do not try to oversee every detail of work you have delegated. Delegate to someone you trust with the job. Establish checkpoints when you will review progress on the task together.

■ Give credit to the person to whom you delegate for completing the work.

 CHECK POINT What are some tangible rewards of work that may motivate employees? What are some intangible rewards of work that may motivate employees?

REVIEW 14-1

21st Century Skills

Interacting with Others

Alisa is an administrative assistant in a small company. She has worked in her job for about six months. During the first month of Alisa's job, she tactfully made suggestions related to her work when her manager, Mr. Jones, gave her work assignments. At first, Mr. Jones seemed to listen to her ideas patiently; but he always found a reason to reject them. One day, Mr. Jones said in a cross manner, "Alisa, I'm in a hurry today. I have no time for your suggestions." Alisa felt discouraged and stopped offering her ideas. Today, Mr. Jones has given Alisa instructions for creating some advertising materials. She knows a way to produce the materials that would cost about half as much as the way Mr. Jones told her to use. Alisa wonders what she should do.

1. What might be the consequences for Alisa of bringing up the cost issue with her manager? What might be the consequences if she does not bring it up?
2. What would you do if you were Alisa? Give reasons for your decision.

Making Academic Connections

Reinforcing Math Skills

1. A survey was conducted in a company with 200 employees. Each employee was given descriptions of three leadership styles: autocratic, democratic, and delegative. Each employee was asked to identify the leadership style that most closely matches the one used by her or his manager. Autocratic leadership style was selected by 20 employees. Delegative leadership style was selected by 5 percent of the employees. What percentage of the employees selected democratic leadership style?

2. When the employee survey (from question 1) was repeated six months later, 150 employees selected democratic leadership style. What is the increase or decrease in the number of people who selected this leadership style? What percent of increase or decrease does this change represent?

3. Employees were asked to rate the effectiveness of their managers on a scale of one to five. The number of responses for each rating score is shown below. What percentage of the total responses did each rating score receive?

RATING SCORE	NUMBER OF EMPLOYEES
1	15
2	10
3	85
4	105
5	21

14-1 Activity 1

Leadership Traits and Skills (Outcome 14-1a)

In this chapter, you learned that leadership traits and skills can be developed. Consider the leadership traits and skills you currently have. Think about the traits and skills you would like to develop. Give yourself a rating of 1 to 5 on each trait or skill listed below. For each trait or skill on which you have a low rating, describe activities you can do to help improve this trait or skill.

LEADERSHIP TRAIT OR SKILL	RATING (1 TO 5)
1. Good character	
2. Flexible	
3. Humble	
4. Mature	
5. Open-minded	
6. Organized	
7. Willing to share credit	
8. Can communicate effectively	
9. Can make decisions	
10. Can set goals	

14-1 Activity 2

Leadership Styles (Outcome 14-1b)

You have learned about three basic leadership styles: autocratic, democratic, and delegative. Read the leadership style descriptions listed below. For each one, tell which leadership style is being described. Some may apply to more than one style.

1. Both the leader and the followers take part in the decision-making process
2. The leader tells the followers what needs to be accomplished and provides the resources needed
3. All decisions are made by the leader
4. The leader has the final say in decisions but listens to input from followers
5. Followers make the decisions about how to accomplish goals
6. Followers have little or no influence in the decision process
7. Works best when followers have expert skill and knowledge and are good at setting and meeting deadlines
8. Works best when the leader and the other employees have the knowledge or skills needed to make decisions
9. Works best when the leader has the expert knowledge or skills needed to make decisions and the followers do not
10. Works best when there is enough time to request and consider input from followers

OUTCOMES

14-2a Describe the need for lifelong learning.
14-2b Explore formal and informal learning as they relate to professional development.

The Need for Lifelong Learning

Learning is acquiring new knowledge or developing skills or behaviors. Lifelong learning is a term used to convey the idea that people continue to learn throughout life. This learning can be on a personal and a professional level.

Personal Ongoing Learning

Many changes occur in an individual's personal life over months and years. As a young person, you have learned new information and skills as you have attended school and taken part in other activities. Perhaps you learned to play a new sport or a musical instrument. Maybe using your new cell phone required you to learn procedures for calling, texting, or playing games. Learning to drive a car may be a skill you have recently acquired. Maybe a family member moved away to take a job or go to college. If so, perhaps you had to learn how to do some of the tasks this family member used to do. Circumstances in one's personal life are always changing in small or large ways and creating the need to learn.

learning acquiring new knowledge or developing skills or behaviors

gchutka/iStockphoto

Learning new skills can be important for doing everyday activities—such as driving a car.

✓ **CHECK POINT** What are some reasons you might need to learn new skills or knowledge related to your personal life?

Professional Ongoing Learning

Learning is an important part of ongoing professional development for all workers. This is true because the business world is constantly changing. New products join or take the place of existing products. Faster computers and new software change the way information is processed and shared. New processes are developed for creating products. New procedures are developed to increase productivity or make the business effective in the global market-place. These changes make it necessary to learn or improve your technical skills and knowledge.

Some skills that you need to learn may relate to your particular job. For example, employees in an accounting department may need to learn how to use new accounting software. Other skills or knowledge may relate to business practices in general. For example, doing business in several countries, as many companies do, requires understanding the needs and wants of people from many cultures. You may need to learn to about the customs and business practices of customers, suppliers, or business partners from cultures different from your own. Other learning may relate to improving your effectiveness as an employee. There is always room to improve in areas such as communication, teamwork, leadership, and interpersonal skills. Lifelong learning is just as important in these "soft skill" areas as it is in specific business or technical areas.

 CHECK POINT What is an example of new knowledge or skills that relate to a particular job that an employee might need?

✳ WORKPLACE CONNECTIONS ✳

Cassandra is a customer service associate for a company that sells products for the home. She works in a call center and helps customers with their concerns: How does the knife sharpener feature of my can opener work? To what address do I send a defective toaster for a refund? Is this product still under warranty? These are examples of the questions Cassandra handles. About a year ago, Cassandra noticed a large increase in the number of Spanish-speaking customers who called with questions. She had to refer these callers to another associate. Cassandra decided to enroll in a Spanish language course at a local community college. She learned conversational Spanish and now feels comfortable helping Spanish-speaking callers. Last week the company announced that the number of employees in the customer service call center will be cut in half to save money. Employees that speak both English and Spanish will be given preference when deciding which employees will keep their jobs. Cassandra is glad she decided to improve her language skills.

> Other than learning to speak Spanish, what else could Cassandra do that might make her better able to help Spanish-speaking customers?

Learning Environments

Learning can take place in a formal learning environment or an informal environment. The class in which you are using this textbook is an example of formal learning. Learning information about your favorite hobby from articles you read on the Internet is an example of informal learning. Both types of learning can be important to your ongoing professional development.

Formal Learning

The term formal learning is used to describe acquiring new skills or knowledge in a structured setting. An instructor typically directs the learning activities rather than the student. Specific goals or objectives for the learning are stated for the student. Learning materials and other resources are identified by the instructor or the organization that offers the instruction. Completion of a formal learning program is often recognized with a grade, diploma, or certificate. Formal learning programs for professional development are available from several sources. Some options are discussed in the following paragraphs.

Colleges and Universities

Colleges and universities offer instruction in many areas related to business. You might want to complete your first degree program or get an advanced degree. In some careers, getting an advanced degree will help you qualify for higher-level jobs in your field. In other cases, you may keep the same job title but receive a higher salary because you have an advanced degree. Rather than working toward a degree, you may simply want to take a few classes as part of your ongoing professional development.

If you are working full-time, you may be able to take college courses in the evenings. Online courses that allow flexible learning times may also be an option. You may have to pay the total cost of your college courses. However, some employers have a tuition reimbursement program. Employees are repaid for the cost of courses that meet the employer's requirements and are completed successfully. For example, your employer might require that the classes be related to your current job or prepare you for other jobs in the company.

Nick White/Getty Images

College courses can be an important part of professional development.

seminar formal presentation by a speaker followed by activities or discussion among the listeners

Some colleges offer special programs designed for industry training. These programs are sometimes called *business institutes*. Standard classes are offered as well as those designed to meet the needs of a particular company or group. Shorter events, such as one-day seminars, are often offered on a variety of topics. Typically, an employer arranges and pays for these types of learning programs for employees.

Technical Schools

Technical schools offer training programs that focus on practical workplace skills. Electronics, web development, computer programming, and drafting are examples of the courses they offer. In addition to lectures, technical schools emphasize hands-on training. They typically have students use the same type of equipment currently used in businesses. For example, students may apply their new learning using the latest computers and software programs. Classes are often offered year-round with flexible starting times and schedules. This flexibility may make it easier for people who are employed to take classes. As with college classes, employers may reimburse tuition for employees who complete classes or programs successfully.

Government Agencies

Some government offices or agencies provide training classes. For example, the U.S. Small Business Administration (SBA) provides several online courses and podcasts. A screen from the SBA website is shown in Figure 14-2.1. The courses relate to starting or managing a business. Suppose you need help writing a business plan. Maybe you are interested in having your company contract to work with government agencies. Perhaps you need information about disaster planning. These topics and many others are covered in the available courses and podcasts. The courses are self-paced, and both the courses and podcasts are free. To find other courses offered, search the Internet using the name of the topic and the word *training*, such as *disaster recovery training*.

Figure 14-2.1 Some government agencies provide training helpful to business employees.

Source: U.S. Small Business Administration, SBA.Gov, http://www.sba.gov/.

Employers

Some companies have training staff members. These employees may be responsible for determining some of the training needs for the company. Other needs may be identified by managers, team leaders, or other employees. Once a training need is identified, the staff determines the best way for the training to be delivered. In some cases, company employees may be qualified to deliver the training. In other cases, instructors who have the needed knowledge and skills may be hired to conduct the training.

Short seminars or longer classes that may have several sessions are conducted to deliver the training. The training may take place during the normal working hours for employees or after hours. Employees may be required to take some training. For example, the company managers might decide that all employees must attend a seminar about sexual harassment. Other classes, such as one about developing leadership skills, may be optional.

Focus on *BUSINESS*

Corporate Training

U.S. organizations spend billions of dollars each year on formal training. Some of this training is done by company employees. However, many businesses pay other organizations to provide training for their workers. Training is the primary business for many companies. Other companies, such as the Disney Institute, also offer training. They seek to share practices that have been successful in their main business (for Disney, entertainment) and that can be adapted to other businesses. Some colleges also provide training services for businesses.

Training services are offered for individuals or groups of employees. The training may take place at the company or at other locations. For example, meeting rooms in hotels are often used for seminars. Webinars are popular and can be accessed from any location with a computer and Internet access. Conference centers, hotels, and resorts are popular locations for training retreats. At a retreat, employees typically spend two or three days away from work focusing on the skills or knowledge they want to develop. For example, several managers from a company may attend a management or leadership retreat.

Corporate training is done on a variety of topics. Leadership, communication, customer service, and team building are popular seminar topics. Software applications, sales strategies, and web marketing are examples of topics for longer classes. Some training companies will customize programs for the needs of a particular business. A training consultant will help assess the company's training needs and recommend a training plan.

> Think about a business with which you are familiar. What types of training do you think would be helpful for the employees? What format would be appropriate for this training?

Professional Associations

A professional association is an organization that seeks to promote a particular profession and provides support for workers in that profession. For example, ARMA International is a not-for-profit association for records management professionals. The American Institute of CPAs serves the accounting profession. The World Organization of Webmasters is a non-profit association for those who create, manage, or market websites. Whatever career area you choose, chances are it has a professional association.

webinar a web-based seminar conducted over the Internet

Professional associations provide valuable services for their members. Many of them publish newsletters, magazines, or articles, either in print or online. Seminars and webinars allow members to keep up to date on current issues or regulations. Longer classes provide in-depth study of topics. Some associations hold yearly conferences. Conferences are typically two- or three-day events that have featured speakers and small-group sessions on relevant subjects. Attending a conference can be a good way to learn about several topics in a short period and network with others in your profession.

TECHNOLOGY CONNECTION

distance learning a type of instructional program in which the students are not physically present in a traditional classroom

Distance learning is a term used to describe instructional programs in which the students are not physically present in a traditional classroom. Some colleges and other organizations offer distance learning courses on a variety of subjects. As with other formal learning, an instructor directs the learning activities. Instruction may be delivered in various ways. For some classes, students are required to "meet" at set times for web conferences or video conferences. For other classes, students decide when to access written materials, videos, or discussion groups online. Assignments are submitted to the instructor, often online, and feedback is given to the students. As with other college classes, students receive grades and earn course credits. If you decide to take a distance learning course, check to make sure that the credits will transfer if you are in a degree program at a different college.

What might be an advantage to taking a distance learning course? What might be a disadvantage to taking this type of class?

Certifications

Some professional associations and other organizations confer certifications or other credentials. Such a recognition shows that a person is qualified to perform a job or tasks. Certifications typically require passing an exam. Some certifications require completing a college degree and having related work experience. For example, the Institute of Management Accountants administers the certified management accountant (CMA) credential. Other certifications are more specific and may require completing training courses. For example, Microsoft offers certifications related to its products, such as the Microsoft Office Specialist certification.

To keep certifications that have been earned, professionals may need to earn continuing education units (CEUs). These units are typically earned by taking classes for a certain number of hours with a qualified instructor or organization. Some jobs that require the professional to be licensed also require CEUs. Engineers, educators, and nurses are examples of professionals who may need to earn CEUs.

 CHECK POINT What are three options for formal learning that you might choose for professional development?

Informal Learning

The term informal learning is used to describe acquiring new skills or knowledge in a setting that is not structured. The student typically directs the learning activities rather than an instructor. Learning materials and other resources are also identified by the student. Goals or objectives for the learning are decided by the student, but may not be formally stated. For example, an employee might read business magazines regularly without consciously stating a goal to learn about current topics in business. Informal learning is typically not recognized with a grade, diploma, or certificate.

Individuals may choose informal learning for a variety of reasons. They may wish to learn at their own pace rather than according to a schedule set by an instructor. They might need new knowledge or skills right away when no formal class is available. They may not have the time or money for a formal learning course. They may want to gain general knowledge that is best acquired through informal learning. Whatever the reason for selecting informal learning, information is available from several sources. Some options are discussed in the following paragraphs.

informal learning acquiring new skills or knowledge in a setting that is not structured

Written, Visual, and Audio Materials

Reading written materials is a common method for informal learning. Books, newspapers, magazines, newsletters, journals, and articles are available in paper and electronic form. Many trade or professional groups publish newsletters or magazines related to their profession or industry. Books are available on many topics related to business and various professions. Books or articles that cover specific skills, such as how to use a particular software program, are plentiful. E-readers, small, light devices that allow users to read electronic books and magazines, are popular. Some books can be purchased online; others can be downloaded for free. Some libraries allow members to check out electronic books to an e-reader.

Courses of varying lengths and about many topics can be found online. These courses may contain written explanations, animations, videos, or activities. Other online resources, such as wikis, blogs, discussion groups, and webinars, can also provide valuable information. Be careful to take into account

Jeffrey Blackler/Alamy

E-readers are light, portable, and able to hold hundreds of books.

the source of any information you find on the Internet. Consider whether the person who is writing or instructing has expert knowledge or experience that can be trusted.

Videos are good sources of information and are available on many topics. They can be purchased for viewing on a TV or computer monitor, or they can be viewed online. Videos that are made available online are sometimes called *podcasts*. Videos are a good choice for visual learners. "A picture is worth a thousand words" is a familiar saying and often a true one. Operating equipment or completing complex steps can sometimes be demonstrated on a video more effectively than they can be described with words.

Television and radio shows can be an important source for informal learning. For example, "The Nightly Business Report" is a popular TV program that covers business news. National Public Radio provides news on business and the economy. Such shows often provide related websites where you can go for more information.

Learning from Others

Learning from others may occur with on-the-job training, through cross training, or with mentors. On-the-job training involves having another person show you how to do a task or complete a procedure. The trainer is typically someone who has in-depth knowledge about the skill or task. On-the-job training may be done as part of an orientation or learning period for new employees. It may also be done when a new procedure or process that employees must learn is adopted by a company. Having a coworker help you with a task or procedure that you find confusing or difficult is another way workers learn on the job. If another worker is assigned to help you on a regular basis, this person may be called a coach.

Cross training is teaching employees how to do other jobs for a company. This can be valuable for both the company and the employees. When employees know how to do more than one job, managers have more flexibility in assigning work. If one employee is out sick or on vacation, another employee can do his or her work. Cross training is good for employees because it makes them more valuable to the company. Cross training may also help prepare employees to move to higher level positions.

✳ WORKPLACE CONNECTIONS ✳

Teresa, Kim, and Jerome work in the accounting department for a small company. Teresa, the department manager, has been working at the company for three months. She is starting to feel settled in her job and confident of her knowledge of the company's operations. In addition to supervising Kim and Jerome, Teresa does financial analysis, prepares reports, and performs other management activities. Kim handles accounts payable and related issues. Jerome takes care of accounts receivable.

Teresa has found that both Kim and Jerome are efficient, hard-working employees. However, their knowledge of accounting tasks and procedures is limited to their own jobs. Teresa has decided to begin an extensive cross-training program. Kim and Jerome will each learn to do the other's job. They will also learn to do some of the tasks that Teresa normally handles.

> **How will the cross training Teresa has planned improve the way the department functions?**

A **mentor** is someone who gives advice and shares knowledge and experience to help another person, sometimes called a protégé. Some professional associations and other organizations have mentoring programs. These programs help individuals find mentors and offer suggestions or guidelines for effective interaction. For example, the Small Business Administration sponsors SCORE, a mentoring program for small business owners. Mentoring is often not done through a formal mentoring program. You can ask someone whose abilities and accomplishments you respect to act as your mentor. You might meet with your mentor once or twice a month to discuss questions or issues of concern. The meeting could be in person or by phone or computer. Do not expect your mentor to spend too much time with you, and remember to express your thanks. Consider the advice of your mentor; but use good judgment in making your own decisions.

mentor someone who gives advice and shares knowledge and experience to help another person

A mentor can provide valuable information and advice.

Learning by Experience

Often the best ways to learn is by experience. Experience involves doing a task or taking part in an activity rather than just reading about it or watching others. Consider the task of keying a letter. You could read about proper keying techniques and watch someone key by touch for days or weeks. Yet you still would not be able to do it yourself. You would have to practice the techniques to learn.

In addition to learning *by* experience you can learn *from* experience. You can consider things you have done in the past that may relate to something you want to do now. For example, you may have talked with many upset customers as part of your customer service job. You have come to realize that when you are patient, the customer usually calms down. You can apply what you have learned from previous experiences when you must deal with an upset coworker.

Sometimes experimenting with different ways of doing something will help you learn. Suppose you are given a new task to do. You follow the steps that you think will be most efficient. However, once you complete the task you realize that completing the steps in a different order would have saved time. You learned from your experience. This is an example of work simplification, which was discussed in an earlier chapter.

 CHECK POINT What are some sources of information for informal learning?

21st Century Skills

Making Decisions

PARTNERSHIP FOR
21ST CENTURY SKILLS

Amanda Coronado works for a company that sells printers and copiers to businesses. She writes product advertising brochures and answers questions for customers who call the company. Some people want to know about technical aspects of the equipment. Others need help with practical issues related to operating or servicing the machines. Still others want to know about sales promotions or lease plans that are available. Amanda's manager has noted how friendly and patient Amanda is in dealing with customers and how well she knows the information about products. He thinks Amanda should consider applying for a sales position that has opened up with the company.

Amanda discussed taking the sales position with her mentor, Leo Gagarin. Leo encouraged Amanda to take the job since it has the potential for higher pay and better possibilities for promotions. Amanda is not sure what she should do. She likes the idea of working with people in a sales job and making more money. However, the sales job involves travel. Amanda would have to be away from home two or three nights a week to visit customers in other cities or attend product training classes. She has two small children and does not know how she can provide for their care while she travels for work.

1. Should Amanda follow her mentor's advice and ignore her own concerns? Why or why not?
2. What would you do if you were Amanda? Give reasons to support your decision.

Making Academic Connections

Reinforcing English Skills

The following sentences have errors in the use of pronouns. Key or write the sentences, correcting the errors.

1. To who did you give the report?
2. The secretary keyed the letters and mailed them to he.
3. We watched they demonstrate the program.
4. Julieta and Roberto gave his books to the librarian.
5. Tell whoever calls that I will be back later this afternoon.
6. Whom will present the award to the winner?
7. The student called their parents.
8. The young girl spoke his lines quietly.
9. Mr. Lee ordered dinner for her family.
10. She brushed the vine lightly, cleaning her leaves.

14-2 Activity 1

Learning Needs (Outcome 14-2a)

You have read some general descriptions of the need for continued learning on the job. In this activity, you will learn about specific learning needs for a particular job.

1. Identify a person you know who is employed in a career that interests you.
2. Interview this person to ask about the ongoing learning needs for his or her career. The interview can be done in person, by phone, or by e-mail. Then write a brief summary of the information you learned. The summary should include the items listed below and any other information you learned from the interview.

   - Person's name, place of employment, and job title
   - Number of years the person has worked in this job
   - Education and training typically required for an entry-level job in this career
   - Specific needs for ongoing learning this person has identified or that are required by the employer
   - Ongoing training required for a license or certification to remain valid

14-2 Activity 2

Formal Learning Opportunities (Outcome 14-2b)

In this activity, you will explore some options for formal learning situations for professional development.

1. Select a skill or topic that workers may need to acquire or improve. For example, workers might need to learn a new software program or improve communication skills.
2. Do research to find at least three sources of training for this skill or topic that are offered in a formal learning environment. For each source, give the following information:

   - The name and type of organization that is offering the training
   - How the instruction is delivered, such as in a traditional class, a seminar, or an online course
   - The length (time) of the training
   - The cost of the training
   - What the student receives upon successful completion, such as a grade or certificate

Summary

14-1 Leadership Skills

- Professional development involves increasing skills or knowledge to succeed on the job.
- Having effective leadership helps a company or organization accomplish its goals. Developing leadership skills is an important aspect of professional development.
- Company managers are in the primary leadership roles. Leadership skills are also needed by department managers, team leaders, and other employees who may be asked to lead a committee or project.
- Leadership traits and skills, such as character, vision, organization, and maturity, can be developed.
- Leaders have different leadership styles and use various strategies to achieve their goals. Three traditional styles of leadership include autocratic, democratic, and delegative styles.
- Leadership strategies include leading by example, communicating effectively, motivating others, and delegating.

14-2 Lifelong Learning

- Lifelong learning is important for both personal and professional development.
- The business world is constantly changing. New products, faster computers, new processes, and changing procedures make it necessary for workers to acquire or improve skills and knowledge.
- Both formal and informal learning can be important in the process of ongoing professional development.
- Formal learning is acquiring new skills or knowledge in a structured setting. Colleges, technical schools, government agencies, employers, and certification programs are some sources of formal learning.
- Informal learning is acquiring new skills or knowledge in a setting that is not structured. This type of learning is directed by the student.
- Sources of information for informal learning include written materials, online materials and courses, videos, and TV and radio programs. Informal learning can also occur through experience or interaction with other people.

Chapter 14 Activity 1

Handling a Delegated Task
(Outcome 14-1b)

In this chapter you learned some guidelines to follow when delegating tasks. These same points can be helpful to consider when someone delegates a task to you. Suppose you have been asked to organize a picnic for a school club to which you belong.

1. Make a list of the information you need to plan the picnic. For example, you need to know the date of the picnic.
2. What guidelines or special instructions might you need from the person delegating this task to you?
3. What resources (money, equipment, or help from other people) will you need to complete this task?
4. What authority do you need to complete this task?
5. Assume that the picnic will be held six weeks from today. What checkpoints will you suggest for reporting on your progress or issues that must be handled?

Chapter 14 Activity 2

Informal Learning Opportunities
(Outcome 14-2b)

In this activity, you will explore some options for informal learning for professional development.

1. Select a skill or topic that workers may need to acquire or improve. For example, workers might need to learn how to operate a piece of equipment or improve teamwork skills.
2. Do research to find at least three sources of informal training for this skill or topic. For each source, give the following information:
   - The name and type of source for the information (book, online article, person, etc.)
   - How the information is acquired (reading, watching a video, consulting with another person, etc.)
   - The length of the information or training (short article, online course that lasts 30 minutes, etc.)
   - The cost of the information or training

Entrepreneurship Event

The purpose of this event is to evaluate skills needed for owning and operating a business. This is a team event, with the team having two or three members. Contestants will also demonstrate their ability to make decisions, work in a team, and speak confidently giving an oral presentation.

During this event, teams members will take one objective test working as a group. The test lasts one hour. A case study activity is also part of the event. The case study will be about a decision-making situation in an area such as business planning, human relations, finance, or marketing. The team will give an oral presentation and address questions related to the case study.

Performance Indicators Evaluated

The entrepreneurship event is related to the business management and marketing career cluster. The event has performance indicators such as those listed below.

- Demonstrate knowledge of business plans, legal issues, credit, personnel management, finance, marketing, taxes, and government regulations
- Present topics in a logical order
- Communicate effectively through voice projection and diction
- Demonstrate critical-thinking and problem-solving abilities
- Present positive and negative aspects of possible courses of action
- Answer questions effectively

These performance indicators are from the Future Business Leaders of America event guidelines as shown on their website. For more detailed information about this event, go to the FBLA-PBL website.[3]

http://www.fbla-pbl.org.

Think Critically

1. What classes have you taken or can you take that will help prepare you to be an entrepreneur?
2. What might be some advantages to participating in a team competitive event rather than an individual event?

---

[3]FBLA-PBL, "FBLA Competitive Events, Entrepreneurship," 2010, http://www.fbla-pbl.org/docs/ct/gdlrs/FBLA /entrepreneurship1.pdf.

Transportation, Distribution, and Logistics

Do you like driving or repairing cars and trucks? Does flying a plane or piloting a ship appeal to you? Are you good at organizing activities and co-ordinating schedules? If the answer to any of these questions is *yes*, a job in transportation, distribution, and logistics may be right for you. This career area includes a variety of jobs. All relate in some way to moving people or goods or related support services.

Employment Outlook

There are many jobs in transportation, distribution, and logistics. The U.S. government provides job projections for 2008-2018. Good job prospects are expected in this career group. For example, jobs for airline pilots, bus drivers, and rail transportation workers are expected to grow about as fast as average. Some jobs, such as those for taxi drivers and water transportation workers, are expected to increase faster than the average for all jobs.[4]

Job Titles

- Auto mechanic
- Aircraft pilot
- Bus driver
- Shipping clerk
- Truck driver
- Flight attendant
- Logistics manager
- Navigation officer
- Marine manager
- Subway operator

Needed Education/Skills

The education and skills needed for jobs in transportation, distribution, and logistics vary widely depending on the job. Some jobs require a college degree and extensive practical training. For example, an airline pilot typically needs a college degree, flight experience, and certification by the Federal Aviation Administration. Other jobs, such as bus driver, may require a high school education, a commercial driver's license, and on-the-job training. Railroad workers typically need a high school education and must complete extensive formal and on-the-job training provided by the company. Requirements for many water transportation jobs are set by the U.S. Coast Guard. Deck officers and engineers must complete training in a merchant marine academy, have many hours of experience, and pass a written exam.

What's it like to work in ... Transportation?

Jamal is a taxi driver in a small city. Each workday morning he reports to a garage where he picks up a vehicle for the day from the cab company. Jamal makes sure the vehicle is in good order, checking items such as the gas, oil, and brakes. He receives calls in the car on a two-way radio from a dispatcher who tells him where to pick up a customer, called a fare. Jamal communicates often with the dispatcher, reporting when a fare has been picked up, the destination, and progress reports along the way for long trips. He also reports accidents or other traffic issues that may be helpful to the other drivers the dispatcher handles. When Jamal does not have a fare, he waits at pickup areas in places such as the airport, the city convention center, and major hotels where taxis are often requested. Jamal usually works an eight-hour shift, five days a week. Because the cab company operates 24 hours a day, the time for his shift varies. He sometimes works longer hours during holidays or weekends when the city has special events and more taxis are requested.

Jamal started working as a taxi driver soon after he completed high school. He got a special taxi driving license as required by the laws in his state. He also completed on-the-job training where he learned to complete paperwork and operate the meter, two-way radio, and GPS device.

Jamal loves to drive and enjoys talking with people. He is patient and helpful with his passengers. He has a way of making fares feel comfortable that often leads to good tips. Jamal likes his work and thinks this job is right for him for now. He is saving money to take college courses but is not sure yet what his major will be. He wants to prepare for a job that will have better pay and employee benefits.

What About You?

What area of the transportation, distribution, and logistics career group appeals most to you? What skills or interests do you have that would help you be successful in this career area?

[4]*Occupational Outlook Handbook*, 2010-11 Edition, Bureau of Labor Statistics, U.S. Department of Labor, http://www.bls.gov/oco/oco1011.htm.

Glossary

A

accession log A document or file that shows the numbers that have been assigned to records and the next number to be used

accounts payable Short-term debts owed to others

action plan A description of tasks to do or actions to be taken after a meeting

agenda A document that lists the topics to be discussed at a meeting and other related information

alphabetic filing system An arrangement of records according to letters of the alphabet

alphabetic index A list of names in a filing system and the number that has been assigned to each one

altruism Unselfish concern or work for the benefit of others

analytical Involving detailed study

analyze Study to determine parts, qualities, operations, or relationships

animation Moving pictures or graphics

annotate Write comments related to the content of a message

anticipate Predict or think about in advance

archive A storage area dedicated to organizing and preserving vital or historical records

asset Money and goods or property owned

audience The recipient(s) for whom a message is intended

audit To verify or check facts or procedures

autocrat Someone who holds complete authority in a situation

automated attendant A computerized system for handling telephone calls

B

backup copy A duplicate of data that can be used if the original data is lost or destroyed

balance sheet A report that shows the financial condition of a company as of a specific date

bank reconciliation A report used to compare bank and company account records

barrier An obstacle or obstruction

benchmarks Standards used for comparison, such as for job performance

bias Preconceived notion or prejudice

blog A web-based journal, also called a weblog

body language Facial expressions, gestures, eye movements, and postures used to communicate without words

bonding Insurance for financial loss due to employee theft or fraud

bookmark A link to a website stored for quick access

brainstorming Offering ideas or suggestions in an effort to find a solution to a problem or to create a new approach

budget A detailed plan of expected income and expenses for a period of time

bullets Small graphics, such as circles or diamonds, used to draw attention to a line of text

career goals Desired achievements related to work

career strategy Plans to meet career goals

carpal tunnel syndrome A repetitive strain injury that can occur when stress is placed on the hands, wrists, or arms

character Basic values and principles that are reflected in a person's behavior

check A written order to a bank to make a payment using funds from the depositor's bank account

chronologically Arranged by date

coding Marking or writing the filing segment on a record

colloquialism Informal word or phrase used among a particular group

commission Payment based on an amount of items sold or produced

compensation Pay or benefits given for a service or a loss

comprehension The ability to understand what you have read, seen, or heard

computer network A group of computers and related devices that are linked and can share information

computer virus A destructive program loaded onto a computer and run without the user's knowledge

concise Brief while including all needed information

confidential Private or secret

confirmation number A series of letters and/or numbers that identify a reservation

consensus Common agreement or mutual understanding

consulate A person appointed by a government to serve its interests or citizens in another country

context The parts of a sentence or paragraph around a word that can help you determine its meaning

continuous improvement Being alert at all times to ways of working more productively

controller A person who supervises company accounting and financial reporting activities

cooperative Willing to agree or take part in what needs to be done to achieve a goal

corporation A business organized under the laws of a state for which a charter is secured

courier service A private mail delivery company

credible Believable, reliable

credit Permission to pay later for goods or services

credit memo A document that shows a reduction in the amount owed, such as for returned goods

cross-reference A notation at one place to indicate a record in another place

customer Someone who buys or uses an organization's products or services

customer focus Paying attention to fulfilling the needs and wants of customers

customs Government taxes or duties on imported items

D

data processing Collecting, organizing, analyzing, and summarizing data

database A collection of records about a topic

debit card A kind of bank card used to make payments from a depositor's bank account

delegate Authorize another person to speak or act for you

delivery address The location to which the United States Postal Service will deliver a mail item

democratic Affording equal rights to all

demographic data Statistics that describe a population, such as age or income level

desktop publishing Producing high-quality documents that include both text and graphics

dialect Speech patterns or vocabulary used by people from a specific area or group

direct approach A style of writing in which the main point is stated early in the message

directory A list of items, such as names and corresponding telephone numbers

discount Reduction in an amount paid or owed

discussion group An online public forum for articles and messages related to a certain topic

distance learning A type of instructional program in which the students are not physically present in a traditional classroom

diversity The quality or state of having differences or variety

documentation Information about the sources of data used in a report

downsize Reduce, as in decreasing the number of workers in an organization

draft A rough or preliminary version of a written message

E

e-commerce Business conducted electronically, as in buying and selling on the World Wide Web

editor A person who reviews written messages to suggest changes in wording, organization, and content

electronic funds transfer Using a computer network to send money from one party to another

electronic imaging Converting paper documents to pictures that are stored and displayed by computer

electronic records Data stored on magnetic media, flash drives, and optical disks

electronic ticket Document and receipt that contain ticket information in electronic form

electronic whiteboard A device that allows users to write text or draw images and print or save them

embassy The offices of an ambassador in a foreign country

emergency procedures Steps to follow in times of trouble or danger

empathy Understanding or concern for someone's feelings or position

empowerment Being able to make decisions or changes without seeking approval

enclosure An item included in a package or envelope

endorsement A name placed on the back of a check that authorizes a bank to cash or deposit the check

enunciation Pronouncing words clearly and correctly

ergonomics The study of the effects of the work environment on the health of workers

ethics Standards or values reflected in behavior

etiquette Standards for proper behavior

evacuation Departure or flight, the clearing of an area

exit interview Meeting with company personnel when leaving a job

expense Financial cost, fee, or charge

extranet An information network like an intranet but partially available to some outside users

F

facsimile Technology used to send images (text, photographs, drawings) using telephone channels, also called fax

feedback Reactions, opinions, or comments

file path The complete location (drive, folders, and name) for a file

filing The process of storing records in an orderly manner within an organized system

filing segment The name, subject, geographic location, or number used to identify a record

firewalls Software and equipment used to prevent un-authorized access to computers and networks

fiscal year A period of 12 months used for accounting purposes

flash drive A device that stores computer files on a printed circuit board and connects via a USB port

font A style or design for a set of type characters

footer Information that appears below the body text on pages of a document

forge Imitate or counterfeit for illegal purposes

formal learning Acquiring new skills or knowledge in a structured setting

freelancer An independent contractor who works for others for a project fee or hourly fee

FTP (file transfer protocol) A tool that allows files to be uploaded to or downloaded from a remote computer

G

goodwill A friendly or kindly attitude

graph A picture that represents data

gross pay Salary or wages earned before deductions are made

H

hardware The physical parts of a computer or related equipment

header Information that appears above the body text on pages of a document

hold A feature that allows a telephone caller to remain connected but waiting for the other person to come back on the line

hoteling Using workspace that is assigned as needed

hotspot A public location that offers network access through a wireless connection

humility The state of being modest and respectful of others

hypertext Information in electronic documents that is organized with links to information at other locations

I

income statement A document that shows profit or loss for a business for a certain period of time

indexing The mental process of deciding how to identify a record for filing purposes

indirect approach A style of writing that give reasons or details to support a main point that comes later in the message

informal learning Acquiring new skills or knowledge in a setting that is not structured

information Data or facts that have been organized in a meaningful form

information management Organizing, maintaining, and accessing records or data

information processing Putting facts or numbers into a meaningful and useful form

insurance A process in which a company agrees to pay compensation for loss in return for payments by the insured

integrity Honesty and trustworthiness

interactive voice response A recorded message accessed and directed by the user to get or record information

interest Money earned on an investment or paid on money that is borrowed

Internet A public, worldwide computer network that spans the globe

interruption A person, sound, or event that distracts you or stops you from doing an activity

interview Meeting to question or evaluate, as for a job applicant

intonation The rise and fall in voice pitch

intranet A private computer network that looks and operates like web pages

itinerary A document that gives detailed travel plans for a trip

J

job board Website that provides job listings and allows users to post resumes

job portfolio Information related to talents and skills, such as documents, degrees, awards, and work samples

job scout Computer program that finds and delivers job information based on the set criteria

jukebox A device that stores many optical disks and allows records to be retrieved quickly

L

leadership The act of guiding or directing others

learning Acquiring new knowledge or developing skills or behaviors

letter of application Document that expresses interest in a job and requests an interview

liabilities Debts owed to others

listening Hearing and focusing attention to understand sounds

M

magnetic media Materials or devices that store computer files by using a disk or tape coated with a magnetic material

mail merge A feature of word processing programs that allows you to insert addresses or other data from a list automatically to create personalized items

management The act of directing people and using resources to accomplish goals

media Materials or means used to communicate

memory card A device that stores computer files on a printed circuit board and connects via a card reader

mentor Someone who gives advice and shares knowledge and experience to help another person

metadata Identifying details about a record or document

microfilm A storage medium that contains small images of records on a roll or sheet of film

minutes An official record of the proceedings of a meeting

modem A conversion device for digital and analog data

modulated Adjusted to a proper level

motion A proposal formally made in a meeting

motivate Provide an incentive or inspire others to take action

N

net pay Wages or salary after deductions for taxes and other items

non-words Spoken sounds with no meaning, such as "ah"

numeric filing system An arrangement of records according to numbers

O

objection Reason to disapprove or reject an idea

office A place in which the affairs of an individual, a business, or an organization are carried out

optical character reader (OCR) An electronic device that quickly scans or "reads" the address on an envelope

optical character recognition (OCR) Scanning text printed on paper and translating the images into words

optical disk A device coated with plastic on which digital data can be stored using a laser

out folder A container used to hold records for an individual or organization when a folder is removed from the files

overhead Business costs not directly related to a product or service

overtime Hours worked beyond the set standard hours per week

owner's equity The owner's share of the worth of a firm

P

pagination The process of dividing a document into individual pages for printing

partnership A business that is not incorporated and has two or more owners

passive voice A style of writing in which the subject is acted upon rather than performing the action

passport Official U.S. government document that grants permission for the holder to travel outside the United States

password A series of characters used to gain access to a system, program, or file

payroll A list of the amount of salary, wages, or other payments for work due to employees

performance review Evaluation of an employee's work

personality The combination of traits that distinguishes one person from another

petty cash Money used for paying small expenses

physical records Data stored on paper and microfilm

PIM program Personal information management software for managing appointments, contacts, and tasks

postage meter A machine that prints postage on a label or envelope

premium The payment for an insurance plan

preventive maintenance Servicing equipment and replacing parts, as needed, to keep equipment in working order

prioritize Rank in order of importance or urgency

procrastinate Put off, delay intentionally

productivity A measure of the amount of quality work done in a certain amount of time

professional Someone who conforms to expected ethical and quality standards and behaviors

proficiency Ability to perform at a satisfactory level

profile Description or picture or to create a description

profit Monetary gain, advantage

projections Estimates or guesses about the future based on known data

promotion Advancement in rank, grade, or position

proofreading Checking a document carefully for errors and mechanical issues

proprietary information Sensitive data that is not public knowledge and is viewed as owned by the holder

protocol Generally accepted customs or rules

purchase order A document that shows items ordered and to what address they should be shipped

Q

quorum The minimum number of people who must be present to conduct business at a meeting

R

record Stored information that has continuing value and is made or received by an organization

record life cycle The creation, distribution, use, maintenance, and disposition of a record

records management The control of records from the creation or receipt to final disposal

recurring Happening again after an interval or periodically

reference A person who knows your abilities, skills, and work habits and is willing to recommend you to employers

referral slip A document that accompanies items sent to another person and indicates a requested action

relational database A program that allows the user to link data from two or more tables to create reports

resignation letter A document stating the intention to end employment on a certain date

resolution The number of dots per inch (dpi) in a printed document

resume Document that presents a person's qualifications for a job

retention schedule A document that shows how long particular types of records should be kept

revenue Income, money, or other gain received

revising Making changes, as in to refine a written message

routing slip A document attached to an item that shows the names of the individuals to whom the item should be sent

S

sales channels Methods of marketing products, such as through retail stores or online

sales invoice A document showing charges for goods or services provided to a customer

screen calls Determine who is calling and the purpose for the call

second A formal statement of support for a motion

seminar Formal presentation by a speaker followed by activities or discussion among the listeners

severance pay Payment made to an employee being dismissed from a job

slang Informal language used in casual conversation

smartphone A device that combines the features of a handheld computer and a mobile phone

software A program that gives instructions to a computer

sole proprietorship A business owned by one individual

sorting The process of arranging records alphabetically or numerically before storing them

spam Electronic junk mail, advertisements, or other unrequested information

speech recognition software Programs that allow voice input, also called voice recognition

storyboard Recorded and organized ideas, as for a presentation

surge suppressor An electrical outlet that controls sharp increases in electricity

synopsis Overview or summary

T

table Data arranged in a format of rows and columns

telecommunications The electronic transfer of data over a distance

telecommuting The practice of working and communicating with others from a home office or other remote location

teleconference A meeting of three or more people in different locations using a telecommunications system

telephony The integration of computer and telephone technologies

terminal-digit file A numeric filing system in which numbers are divided into groups and read right to left when arranging records in order

time management Managing your actions in relation to time

time zone A geographical region that has the same standard time

toll-free Requiring no payment

tone Style, manner of writing or speaking that shows a certain attitude

total quality management Establishing and maintaining high standards in how work is done

trait A distinguishing characteristic or quality

V

vendor A seller of goods or services

videoconferencing Communicating with people at two or more locations using two-way voice and video data

virtual office A setting that allows you to perform work activities as you would in a traditional office

visa A permit granted by a foreign government for a person to enter its country

vision A mental image of what something will or could be in the future

visual aid An object or image that illustrates a point or concept, such as photos, posters, or slides

vocabulary Words you know and understand how to use

voice mail A messaging system that uses computers and telephones to record, send, store, and retrieve voice messages

VoIP (Voice over Internet protocol) A service that allows users to make telephone calls using a high-speed Internet connection

voucher A document that shows the vendor name, payment information, and an approval to make the payment

W

webcam A video capture device connected to a computer

webinar A web-based seminar conducted over the Internet

wellness program Activities designed to promote good physical and mental health

white pages Part of a telephone directory with an alphabetical list of names and related telephone numbers

white space The area on a printed page that is empty, having no text or images

wiki A website to which anyone can add, edit, or delete content

wizard A software feature that gives the user dialog boxes with instructions for completing a task

word processing Creating written documents, such as reports or letters, by using a computer and software

work ethic A value system that places importance on work or other purposeful activity

workstation The physical area in which a worker performs a job

World Wide Web Resources on the Internet that support hyperlinks, text, graphics, and multimedia

Y

yellow pages Part of a telephone directory with names and related telephone numbers arranged by subject headings

Z

ZIP Codes A system of numerical codes assigned to geographic areas and used to route U.S. Mail

Index